Gothic dreams and nightmares

Manchester University Press

Gothic dreams and nightmares

Edited by Carol Margaret Davison

MANCHESTER UNIVERSITY PRESS

Published by Manchester University Press
Oxford Road, Manchester M13 9PL

www.manchesteruniversitypress.co.uk

British Library Cataloguing-in-Publication Data
A catalogue record for this book is available from the British Library

ISBN 978 1 5261 6062 1 hardback

First published 2024

The publisher has no responsibility for the persistence or accuracy of URLs for any external or third-party internet websites referred to in this book, and does not guarantee that any content on such websites is, or will remain, accurate or appropriate.

Typeset
by Deanta Global Publishing Services, Chennai, India

For Marie Mulvey-Roberts, beloved friend, esteemed mentor, formidable red witch

Contents

Contents

Part IV: Twentieth- and twenty-first-century Gothic dreams and nightmares: weird fiction, horror film, television, and video games

Figures

Contributors

Jayson Althofer is an independent scholar who lives in Toowoomba, Australia, on Country of the Giabal and Jarowair peoples. His recent publications include contributions to *The Graveyard in Literature: Liminality and Social Critique* (Cambridge Scholars Publishing, 2022), *TEXTile Manifestoes* (Academy of Arts, Architecture and Design in Prague, 2022) and the special issues of *Ethnologies*, 'Nocturnal Ethnographies: Aesthetics and Imaginaries of the Night' (2022). He also co-writes with Brian Musgrove. Their most recent collaboration appears in *Atrocity and the Literature of Childhood* (SUNY Press, 2022).

Nicola Bowring is a Lecturer in English Literature at Nottingham Trent University. Her work focuses on Gothic literature from the eighteenth century to the present day, with a focus on spatiality. Most recently, she has been exploring materiality and space in Gothic short stories, particularly those of Algernon Blackwood. She has published work on Gothic literary histories and adaptation, and is currently working on a monograph on language and communication in the Gothic. She is a member of the Centre for Travel Writing Studies at Nottingham Trent University, where she works on projects around the relationship between non-fictional travel writing and Gothic fiction.

Carol Margaret Davison is a Professor of Women's and Gender Studies at the University of Windsor. The Series Editor of Anthem Studies in Gothic Literature, she is the author of dozens of chapters and journal articles devoted to the Gothic, *History of the Gothic: Gothic Literature, 1764–1824* (University of Wales Press, 2009), and *Anti-Semitism and British Gothic Literature* (Palgrave, 2004). She is co-editor, with Marie Mulvey-Roberts, of *Global Frankenstein* (Palgrave, 2017), and co-editor, with Monica Germanà, of *Scottish Gothic: An Edinburgh Companion* (University of Edinburgh Press, 2017). Her edited collection, *The Gothic and Death* (Manchester University Press, 2017), was the winner of the Allan Lloyd Smith Memorial Prize for Gothic Criticism in 2019. Her first novel, *Bodysnatcher*, which recounts the untold story of the Burke and Hare serial murders of 1828, was published by Ringwood Publishing (Glasgow) in 2023.

Maria Giakaniki is an independent scholar and co-owner/editor-in-chief of Ars Nocturna, a small publishing house in Athens, Greece, that focuses on Gothic fiction. She has co-edited the short story anthology, *Bending to Earth: Strange Stories by Irish Women* (Swan River Press, 2019), and contributed a chapter to *The Streaming of Hill House: Essays on The Haunting Netflix Adaptation*, edited by Kevin Wetmore (McFarland, 2020), and two chapters to *The Palgrave Handbook of Steam Age Gothic* (Palgrave, 2021), edited by Clive Bloom. Her publications include a chapter in *The Palgrave Handbook of Gothic Origins* (Palgrave, 2021), edited by Clive Bloom.

James Aaron Green is an APART-GSK Fellow (ÖAW) at the University of Vienna, specialising in the intersections of nineteenth-century popular fiction and science, with further interests in game studies. His work is published in the *Journal of Victorian Culture*, *Gothic Studies*, and *Victorian Network*, and his first book, *Sensation Fiction and Modernity*, is due to be published by Palgrave Macmillan in 2024.

Sam Hirst is a Research Fellow at Nottingham University. Their monograph, *The Theology of the Early British and Irish Gothic 1764–1832*, was published with Anthem Press in 2023. Their interdisciplinary research focuses on the intersections of literature and theology. They have previously published on the theology of Radcliffe's dreams, Byron's poetry of place, the Gothic Fairy-Tale, and the Gothic work of Georgette Heyer. They also run the free-to-access online education project 'Romancing the Gothic'.

Murray Leeder is an Adjunct Professor in the Department of English, Film, Theatre, and Media at the University of Manitoba. He is the author of *Horror Film: A Critical Introduction* (Bloomsbury, 2018), and *The Modern Supernatural and the Beginnings of Cinema* (Palgrave Macmillan, 2017), and *Halloween* (Auteur, 2014). He is also the editor of *Cinematic Ghosts: Haunting and Spectrality from Silent Cinema to the Digital Era* (Bloomsbury, 2015) and *ReFocus: The Films of William Castle* (Edinburgh University Press, 2018). He has published in numerous journals, including *Horror Studies*, *The Canadian Journal of Film Studies*, *The Journal of Popular Culture*, and *The Journal of Popular Film and Television*.

Elisabete Lopes is an Adjunct Professor at the Polytechnic Institute of Setúbal and a Researcher at the ULICES (Centre for English Studies) at the University of Lisbon. Her focal areas of research and publication are the

Gothic genre, horror cinema/literature, women's studies in relation to the Gothic and horror, and weird fiction. Her most recent publications include 'Edgar Allan Poe's Gothic Revisited in André Øvredal's *The Autopsy of Jane Doe*' (2016), 'Stranger Than Fiction: Thomas Ligotti's Deceptive Realities in Horror Fiction' (2019), and 'Suburban Gothic Revisited in Jeffrey Eugenides's *The Virgin Suicides*' (2018). She is currently at work on a chapter devoted to cosmic horror in James Wan's *Insidious*.

Kirstin A. Mills is a Senior Lecturer and Director of the Master of Research in the Faculty of Arts at Macquarie University, Sydney, Australia. Her research specialises in Gothic and fantastic literature of the long nineteenth century and its twenty-first-century digital adaptations, with a particular focus on the intersections between space, the sciences of the mind, and scientific and folkloric understandings of the supernatural. She has published on representations of these ideas in the writings of a wide range of authors, including Samuel Taylor Coleridge, Horace Walpole, Washington Irving, Mary Shelley, Edgar Allan Poe, George MacDonald, Lewis Carroll, and Lucas Malet.

Richard W. Moore Jr received his PhD in English from Fordham University in May 2018, and is currently teaching in the English Department of the College of Mount Saint Vincent in the Bronx, New York. His monograph entitled *Revolution, Empire, and the Gothic Dream*, examining dreams, history, revolution, and empire in eighteenth- and nineteenth-century British Gothic literature and twentieth-century Caribbean fiction, is forthcoming from Anthem Press in 2024. He is also writing a collection of short stories entitled *American Silence*.

Brian Musgrove has a PhD from the University of Cambridge, where he taught before moving to Australia and becoming Head of the Department of Humanities and Social Sciences at the University of Southern Queensland. He has published several articles on drug literature, aspects of drug cultures, and their relation to capital. He co-writes with Jayson Althofer, and their most recent contribution in the field of drug writing, Gothicism, and Capital is '"A Ghost in Daylight": Drugs and the Horror of Modernity' in *Palgrave Communications* 4 (2018). He is currently an independent scholar.

Lorna Piatti-Farnell is a Professor of Film and Popular Culture at Auckland University of Technology, where she is also the Director of the Popular Culture Research Centre. She is the President of the Gothic Association of New Zealand and Australia (GANZA). Her research interests lie at the intersection of popular media and cultural history, with a focus on Gothic Studies. She has published widely in these areas, including *Consuming Gothic:*

Food and Horror in Film (Palgrave, 2017), *The Vampire in Contemporary Popular Literature* (Routledge, 2014), and *Gothic Afterlives: Reincarnations of Horror in Film and Popular Media* (editor, Lexington, 2019).

Alice Vernon teaches Creative Writing at Aberystwyth University. Her research examines presentations of sleep disorders in science and culture. Her PhD thesis explored depictions of insomnia, and she is currently being represented by Watson, Little literary agency for her narrative non-fiction book about parasomnias. She is particularly interested in the delusions of REM-state sleep, from lucid dreams to hypnopompic hallucinations, and nineteenth-century sleep research. Her articles on sleep disorders have appeared in the journals *Performance Research* and *Excursions*.

Liz Wan Yuen-Yuk is a DPhil student at the University of Oxford, and a research assistant at Hong Kong Metropolitan University where she has also taught as a lecturer. Her research interests include Mary Wollstonecraft, the Enlightenment, Gothicism, Romanticism, and comparative literature. She has been a contributor to *CHA: An Asian Literary Journal*, *Hong Kong Review of Books*, and *Hong Kong Studies*. Her latest publication is a chapter in *East-West Dialogues: The Transferability of Concepts in the Humanities* (Peter Lang, 2020).

Acknowledgements

I would like to thank Matthew Frost at Manchester University Press for his enthusiasm for this project and his wise advice during the lengthy production process. Tremendous thanks are especially due to the collection's contributors for their innovative scholarly work and commitment to this project during the challenging recent pandemic. Their patience was unflagging. Essay collections are always a team effort and I count myself extremely blessed, under such trying circumstances, to have worked with a wonderfully collaborative and supportive group of international colleagues. A million thank you's are also due to Dorota Babilas who secured permission from the Historical Museum in Sanok for the use of the Zdzisław Beksiński painting for the front cover. I am also grateful to Kasia Ancuta for assisting with that matter.

Introduction – Gothic parasomnias and oneirocriticism: the sleep, dreams, and nightmares of Enlightenment reason and beyond

Carol Margaret Davison

One of the most unexplored regions of art are dreams. (Fuseli, Aphorism 231, *Life* 145)

From John Henry Fuseli's masterpiece *The Nightmare* (1781) – a painting that shocked viewing audiences when first exhibited at the Royal Academy in London in the spring of 1782, among them the godfather of Gothic literature, Horace Walpole[1] – to the screening, two centuries later, of Wes Craven's *A Nightmare on Elm Street* (1984) and beyond, dreams and nightmares have been a persistent and popular topic, possessing tremendous cultural currency, in Gothic literature and horror cinema. As Craig Koslofsky and A. Roger Ekirch have independently recounted, longstanding fears associated with sleep and nighttime in the Early Modern period persisted into, and beyond, the Enlightenment era. While changes had occurred in sleep rituals and nocturnal practices in the wake of broadscale social and technological change, including the development of new means of creating artificial light, sleep remained an experience of potential physical and spiritual danger (Ekirch 43). Where the devil and his disciples (268) were once said to engage in sabbaths at midnight (Koslofsky 28), and sleep's likeness to death required prayer (Ekirch 286), nighttime also came to be seen, in the eighteenth century, as the province of dangerous 'gallants, free-thinkers, and atheists' (260). As darkness lost some of its dominion, cultural attitudes towards dreams and nightmares shifted, the latter known, since the Early Modern period, as a potentially fatal disease called Incubus (Macnish 138) that principally afflicted 'hard students, deep thinkers, and hypochondriacs' (137). Dreams and nightmares became the subject of a rich, varied, gender- and class-directed literature (Ekirch 312–14), and the source of tremendous debate as they were seen to be bound up with 'a whole package of conceptions of the body, the soul, morals and the nature of God' long connected in Western Europe (Pick and Roper 5).

Exploring the matrices of these phenomena in relation to the intellectual and cultural history of the Gothic and tracing some of their transmutations over the course of more than two centuries in different nations, media, and literary forms yield tremendous scholarly dividends. Primary among these is the attainment of a more coherent thematic and theoretical understanding of the ideological investments of Gothic literature and horror cinema and their preeminent psychological, metaphysical, and philosophical concerns. Secondly, as will be delineated in this introduction, an extremely significant and culturally productive cross-disciplinary cross-fertilisation process may be brought into relief around the representation of dreams and nightmares in the visual arts, the Gothic novel, and the horror film that evidences a vital and consistent dynamic between ideas of the sublime and the subliminal. Looking across more than two centuries, the critical eye recognises a pattern whereby actual vivid dreams and nightmares – spawned, occasionally and notably, by illness and the ingestion of alcohol and other drugs – inspired vivid and visual literary and artistic productions that proliferated across media, technologies, and cultural forms. These included etchings, paintings, phantasmagoria, films, Romantic poetry, and the Gothic novel, this last emerging during the era of heated oneirocritical debates and possessing, as will be discussed, its own manifold oneiric aspects and dream/nightmare fixation. A line of inspirational transmission and aesthetic experimentation may be traced, often signposted by the artists themselves, from one artistic work to the other, across two centuries – from Piranesi to Walpole and early Gothic literature, to Romantic poetry, Fuseli, Goya, and late eighteenth-century phantasmagoria, to nineteenth-century Gothic, especially its monsterpieces – into the era of the Surrealists and early twentieth-century silent film and German Expressionist cinema, late twentieth-century horror films, television series, video games, and other media.

In tandem with these rich cultural interfacings is an equally fascinating and informing intellectual history. Given the contentious philosophical, medical, and theological debates about dreams and nightmares during the Enlightenment era and the artistic opportunities offered for the exploration of individual subjectivities, psychic life, and the collective consciousness by dream- and nightmare-inspired scenes and themes, a similar cross-fertilisation process may be traced in the flourishing oneirocriticism and dream-books of that era. Sales of the latter surged in the mid-eighteenth century through to the fin de siècle as they remained extremely popular with women readers (Ekirch 313). Dream- and parasomnia-focused publications continued to inspire and inform artistic productions throughout the Victorian period. They even influenced early psychological theory at the fin de siècle, as evidenced by the work of Frederic W. H. Myers, one of the founders of the Society for Psychical Research (SPR) and theoriser of the concept of the subliminal, and Sigmund Freud, whose landmark study, *The Interpretation of Dreams* (1900), delineated the vital curative and coping role played by dreams in his groundbreaking psychoanalytic conception of the unconscious. Ernest Jones, Carl Jung, and Sándor Ferenczi developed some of these psychoanalytic and oneiric theories and therapies into the twentieth century, a process furthered in neuropsychological studies in more recent decades by university-based divisions of sleep medicine. As Natalya Lusty and Helen Groth have persuasively argued in their magisterial study, *Dreams and Modernity: A Cultural History* (2013), the dream has proven to be a contentious and 'precarious epistemological and scientific object' since the Enlightenment era, one enduring in its fascination, as evidenced by 'a rich tradition of cross-disciplinary theorizing ... [and] historical[ly contextualizing] accounts' (2).

That the Enlightenment era, marked by industrialisation and wide-scale social transformation, also witnessed the efflorescence of parasomnia-inspired and centred Gothic works is a noteworthy cultural phenomenon. Extrapolating from Walter Benjamin's arguments about dreams in twentieth-century art, particularly the work of the Surrealists (236–8), media scholar and dream theorist, Sharon Sliwinski, has claimed that 'Modernity seems to have sapped all significance' from actual oneiric life as a site where we could interrogate our place in the world (xvii). It may be argued, however, that oneiric experiences were transmuted in the face of modernity, assuming a richer, more provocative cultural life, proliferating across literary forms, the visual arts, and media, and were directed towards a variety of ends, including the pleasurable, didactic, political, and the socially critical. As I have argued elsewhere, piggybacking on Franco Moretti's work on the Bildungsroman, the Gothic became *the* symbolic form of modernity (Davison 46), granting expression, from a variety of ideological standpoints, to the dreams and nightmares born of the collision between pre-Enlightenment and Enlightenment belief systems and values (37). Remaining attentive to the aforementioned intellectual and cultural intersections and cross-fertilisations, *Gothic Dreams and Nightmares* examines a range of literary and cultural forms, experimental aesthetics, and narrative strategies through which these phenomena have been variously conceptualised. With an eye to theorising their nature and significance and interpreting this wealth of what Freud would have called cultural dream-work, which requires an ideologically attentive social and cultural contextualisation and unpacking of latent dreams on the basis of manifest dreams, the chapters in this collection draw, where necessary and relevant, on a spectrum of theories about sleep, sleep disorders – generically known as parasomnias – and sleep medicine, across historic eras and nations.

To these ends and to help establish a sense of the major foundations of this subject, a brief overview is needed of some of the varied intellectual and cultural matrices of the eighteenth- and nineteenth-century Gothic, whose oneiric narratives often featured nightmares, were inspired by nightmares, and were frequently compared to realised nightmares. Commentary exists, much of it from Gothic novelists themselves, about the inspirational sources of their work in vivid and haunting dreams, nightmares, waking dreams, and 'hallucinatory states' (Hennessy 49), a phenomenon especially noted in relation to key monsterpieces, including Horace Walpole's Ur-Gothic novel, *The Castle of Otranto* (1764), Mary Shelley's *Frankenstein; or The Modern Prometheus* (1818), Robert Louis Stevenson's *The Strange Case of Dr. Jekyll and Mr. Hyde* (1886), and Bram Stoker's *Dracula* (1897).

According to Walpole, in a letter written in March of 1765 to Rev. William Cole, *The Castle of Otranto* (1764) was inspired by a dream in an ancient castle where 'on the uppermost bannister of a great staircase [he] saw a gigantic hand in armour' (ix). In the 1831 'Author's Introduction to the Standard Novels Edition' of *Frankenstein* (1818), Mary Shelley similarly recounted how her Creature had been formed in the crucible of her subconscious. Following an exciting night of discussion about ghost stories and the possible reanimation of corpses, she experienced a hypnagogic waking dream driven by her imagination – what Robert Macnish would call a 'day-mare' (148). Shelley describes her horrifying vision when, 'with shut eyes, but acute mental vision', she saw 'the pale student of unhallowed arts kneeling beside the thing he had put together' as the foetal monster gained flesh and life:

> I saw the hideous phantasm of a man stretched out, and then, on the working of some powerful engine, show signs of life, and stir with an uneasy, half-vital motion … He sleeps; but he is awakened; he opens his eyes; behold, the horrid thing stands at his bedside, opening his curtains and looking on him with yellow, watery, but speculative eyes. ('Author's' 196)

Terrified yet inspired by 'the spectre which had haunted [her] midnight pillow' (196) just as the Creature later haunts Victor in a mise-en-abîme moment, Mary Shelley crafted what is arguably the greatest monster tale of all time.

Actively seeking artistic inspiration from what he called his 'Brownies', whom he eagerly welcomed to assume control of his consciousness at night, Robert Louis Stevenson likewise recounted in his 'Chapter on Dreams' (1888) how, prior to writing *The Strange Case of Dr. Jekyll and Mr. Hyde* (1886), he 'dreamed the scene at the window, and a scene afterward split in two, in which Hyde, pursued for some crime, took the powder and underwent the change in the presence of his pursuers' (160). Although Bram Stoker's grand-nephew, Daniel Farson, could find no corroborating evidence for the statement (Wilt 9 n.3), Stoker's biographer, Harry Ludlam, claimed that the author of *Dracula* 'after a late night supper of dressed crab'

(100), experienced a similarly inspiring nightmare involving two compelling scenes – of 'a vampire king rising from his tomb to go about his ghastly business' and of Jonathan Harker's seduction in the Count's castle by the female vampire trinity (106–7).

In addition to the aforementioned accounts of the nightmare-inspired Gothic, scholars have likewise recognised the oneiric features of Gothic narratives, acknowledging Patrick Bridgwater's insight that 'the Gothic strives to speak the unspeakable language of the dream' (*De Quincey's* 87), the Gothic being 'essentially a dream literature, its hallmark the realized nightmare' (*Kafka* 58). Indeed, iconic scenes of Gothic terror involving the total loss of control and autonomy are regularly encountered in the world of actual nightmare as illustrated in such spine-tingling episodes as those featuring Ebon Ebon Thalud in Samuel Taylor Coleridge's *Notebooks*, examined by Kirstin A. Mills in Chapter 2 of this collection. Sherry Adler's stark description of the nightmare experience, reminiscent of Fuseli's iconic painting, renders a similarly terrifying vignette:

> Imagine feeling very tired, going to bed, and quickly falling asleep. Your rest is soon disturbed, though, by some sort of rustling noise. You open your eyes and recognize the normal features of your bedroom in the shadowy darkness, but, when you try to sit up, you realize that you are paralyzed; you are unable to move your arms or legs; or even turn your head. With sudden, sickening dread and overwhelming terror, you sense an evil presence approaching. You struggle and try to scream for help, but you still cannot move or make a sound. The sinister being looms over you for a moment, then climbs onto your bed and settles heavily on your chest, crushing the breath out of you. (8)

The Gothic's narrative episodes constitute a symbolic phantasmagoria marked, like Adler's description of sleep paralysis and nightmare, by such shared ingredients as ineffable terror, dreaded and transgressive desires, spectral supernatural creatures and features, self–Other identity confusion, near-death experiences, a hyper-associative state during REM sleep that is similar to, or the harbinger of, mental illness (Pearsall 431; Hobson 89; Appignanesi 148), uncanny elements and encounters, hallucinations, and carceral experiences and imagery. One should also include here the somnial phenomenon when the sleeper enters the hypnagogic state between wakefulness and sleep, or the experience of the hypnopompic state, moving from sleep to wakefulness, that sometimes involves report of hallucinatory ghost-seeing, a phenomenon 'so often reported at bedsides' (Morton 144), especially of the dying. These conspiracy-suffused dream/nightmare-scapes often possess – in the resonant words of Siobhân Kilfeather – a 'dream logic ... [that] is particularly capable of evoking the visual characteristics of shock' (58). The Gothic's often paranoid, epistemologically challenged subject experiences muddled senses and hallucinatory episodes, their self-control frequently being threatened by transgressive, often sexualised and/or racialised, monstrous Others. Such psychological and physiological responses to the Gothic transfer brilliantly to the screen and what Anna Powell calls the 'psychophysiology of cinematic experience' (7), the engendering of 'altered states of consciousness produced by haptic or pathic affect in which the inner body expands to incorporate virtual sensation' (49). Especially as mediated through such cinematic styles as the Gothic-influenced German Expressionist cinema that, in its '[i]ntensive and compressed … use of space and time' offers what Powell describes as 'an objective correlative to altered states of consciousness' (75), the Gothic's evocation of parasomnia-style states found what is perhaps its most suitable technological medium.

Beyond the oneiric nature and sensation of Gothic literature and horror film, scholars have also noted how dreams and nightmares serve as long-standing, readily adaptable, and popular motifs and functional devices in the Gothic novelist's toolkit where they not only 'figure the future or provide an allegorical reading of the plot' (Martin 207) but enable the exploration and expression of the conscious and unconscious aspects of character psychology and subjectivity. The dream not only emerged in the history of modernity, therefore, 'as a social and cultural object as much as a part of individual psychic life' (Lusty and Groth 2), it also served as a means in cultural productions of laying bare – of representing and giving expression to – that psychic life. As Margaret Ann Doody has argued, it was in the eighteenth-century Gothic novel, featuring the 'real world' as 'one of nightmare' (104), that male characters joined their female counterparts in being granted 'a full consciousness' and were shown to be 'self-divided, wary, torn by their own unconscious and divided motives, even weak, erring, and guilty' (121). This literary development was ramped up in the nineteenth century, which witnessed an increased interest in the pseudoscientific study of character through such phenomena as phrenology and physiognomy, a period when 'the lines between the … novel and the new science of mind were particularly blurred' (Lusty and Groth 6). On the basis of these significant developments in literary history, a third activity should be included in Sharon Sliwinski's theory about dreams and social history. To the distinction she draws between *the dream-as-dreamt* – 'the complex mental activity called dreaming' – and *the dream-as-text*, which involves 'the act of disclosing this experience to another person' (xiii) – should be added a third activity, *the fictional dream-as-text*, otherwise known as the act of artistically representing the dream.

The fictional dream-as-text allows for the exploration and expression of character and individual subjectivity that, as Benjamin suggests, is inextricably bound up with the social and the collective. Despite the fact that

Benjamin's oneirocriticism focused on the dream as an actual historical object, his act of 'wedding a psychoanalytic conception of the dream to a Marxist analysis of material and economic culture', was revolutionary. It 'allows us to see', as Natalya Lusty and Helen Groth observe, 'individual consciousness as a part of a wider collective process of historical experience, one that sets in play a dialectic between the repressed and unfulfilled desires of the collective and the historian's critical role as a dream interpreter'. This process, they argue further, 'brings into view the dialectical relationship between sleeping and waking, forgetting and remembering, as central to understanding the social and cultural processes of history' (2). Benjamin's historicised reading of the actual dream-as-dreamt that tethers consciousness to the unconscious and the individual to the collective serves as a sophisticated and useful model for Gothic scholars, provided we remain attentive to the significant paradigm shift between the dream-as-text and the fictional dream-as-text.

In recent years, Chris Baldick and Robert Mighall have rightly censured critics who have, in their quest to expose 'supposed latent fears, desires, and "revolutionary" impulses', misconceived 'Gothic fictions as examples of anti-realist "fantasy" or dream-writing, ... [and, in the process,] repeatedly overlooked their manifest temporal, geographic, and ideological referents' (268). As Benjamin's theoretical model suggests, readings of the Gothic as a dehistoricised type of dream-writing untethered from socio-political realities and intellectual history should be guarded against. This propensity perhaps occurs, in part, because, as Dale Townshend has painstakingly shown, 'Gothic and later psychoanalytic constructions of the subject are inflected with the same set of modern discursive assumptions' (19), an alignment previously discussed by Robert Miles who identified a 'concurrence between psychoanalytic models of the subject and Radcliffe's texts' ('Gothic' 8). The challenging act that Miles advocates of historicising psychoanalysis must be undertaken in cultural criticism, and universalising claims, grounded exclusively in psychoanalysis, must be expressly avoided. In the case of analysing representations of dreams and nightmares in the Gothic, this includes simultaneously considering such phenomena as implied models of subjectivity in cultural productions alongside those theorised in the mental sciences, particularly as they exist in relation to contemporary and relevant philosophical and medical discourses about dreams and nightmares/Incubus.

As the chapters in this volume make clear, the strategies and methods of Gothic writers have varied widely in the creation of the-fictional-dream-as-text. American literary critic Leslie Fiedler advanced the Freudian argument that it was the essential purpose of the Gothic romance, in response to the denial and 'dogmatic optimism and shallow psychology of the Age of Reason', to assert the existence of a 'world of dreams and of the repressed [infantile and ancestral] guilts and fears that motivate them' (140). Fiedler's universalising claim, while applicable to, and illuminating for, certain Gothic texts, does not obtain across the board. More nuanced close readings of individual texts yield more intriguing insights, one outstanding example being Susan Manning's compelling reading of shared parasomnias in Henry Mackenzie's *Julia de Roubigné* (1777) and Charles Brockden Brown's *Wieland* (1798), where she argues, 'Calvinist nightmare[s are] dreamed through Enlightenment minds', playing out 'the ambivalent double consciousness of me/not-me [in] the fiction of enlightened Scotland and America [that] at once acknowledges the shadowy authority of, and disavows responsibility for, the darker self of its bad dreams' (53). Detailed, text-specific analyses are wanted in the critical assessment of some of the most enigmatic dream-turned-nightmare scenarios in the Gothic, such as the bizarre, wild, and vivid parasomnia in *Frankenstein* – examined in several chapters in this volume – that plagues him immediately after he animates and then abandons his creature: Victor's beloved sister/cousin/fiancée, Elizabeth, in the bloom of health, undergoes a horrifying transformation into the corpse of his mother after he kisses her, the grave-worms crawling in the folds of her flannel shroud.

Eighteenth-century oneirocriticism and the Gothic

Sensitive critical and cultural analyses of textual parasomnias that historically contextualise each individual work in relation to the relevant oneirocritical discourses of its era can prove extremely illuminating. Foundational and useful to such analyses is an understanding of the intellectual currents and debates at play around parasomnias at the time of the Gothic's inception. In the watershed movement broadly referred to as the Enlightenment, dreams became, for the first time in centuries, the subject of general interest and contentious debate. Indeed, in the late eighteenth into the early nineteenth century, 'divergent opinions as to the origin and meaning of dreams proliferated in an astounding array of medical, philosophical and poetical writings' (Ford 107). This preoccupation spoke to the challenges faced by, and the limitations of, the new rational empiricist philosophy. Despite attempts to explain and contain their 'supernatural' power by way of 'scientific' theories, dreams and nightmares 'provided the eighteenth-century thinker with a discomforting reminder that many common phenomena remained unexplained by the new [Enlightenment] philosophy' (Powell, *Fuseli* 45). Gothic literature registered these highly contentious debates about the source and meaning of dreams and nightmares during this era of profound cultural transition from old-world, supernatural, pre-Enlightenment value systems into rational, more secular and empirical, Enlightenment value systems.

A noteworthy paradigm shift is discernible in this era's 'oneirocriticism' – dream theory and analysis – that is grounded in a new science of mind that 'included detailed discussion of the intricate connections between mind and body' (Lusty and Groth 5). These new theories contested the traditional interpretation of dreams, dating back to Artemidorus's defence of oneiromancy in *Oneirocritica* (second century CE) as supernatural visions or signs 'sent' from either God or demons. As several chapters in this volume evidence, theories like Andrew Baxter's in *An Enquiry into the Nature of the Human Soul* (1733) that dreams were 'new and foreign impressions' left on the mind by spiritual beings taking over the body (198–201) remained popular in Gothic literature across the eighteenth and nineteenth centuries, being thereafter adapted in twentieth-century Gothic horror and horror cinema. Although 'many spiritualists followed Swedenborg in this model of the dream as a form of nocturnal communion' with God and other spirits (Hayward 163), such theories were being increasingly elbowed aside during and after the Enlightenment era, replaced by medical interpretations of dreams as emanations of physical problems, signposts of 'a corporeal disorder' (Dacome 397), the general consensus being that the dreaming body was a sick, unhealthy body (410). Thus did William Cullen in his *Synopsis Nosologicae Methodicae* (1769) place dreaming 'firmly within a category of the pathological, the "Oneirodynia"' (Manning 43). Following in the path of Thomas Hobbes who claimed that dreams were 'caused by the distemper of some of the inward parts of the body' (qtd. in Powell, *Fuseli* 47), John Bond, in *An Essay on the Incubus, or Night-Mare* (1753), ascribed nightmares to circulatory problems (46). While the 'Night-mare' is 'generally the offspring of excess', according to Bond, its source was 'not a Daemon' (62) but 'a real Disease of the Body' (5). In his *Observations on Man, His Frame, Duty, and Expectations* (1749), David Hartley argued, similarly, that the body's position in sleep 'suggests such ideas, amongst those that have been lately impressed, as are most suitable to the various kinds and degrees of pleasant and painful vibrations excited in the stomach, brain, or some other part' (qtd. in Ford 108). In this theory, which came to be known as associationism, Hartley drew on the Lockean notions of a physico-psychological interpretation of mental activity (Glance 33).

Thus did the study of dreams and nightmares come to constitute a field of medical enquiry in its own right during this period, generating theories that became popular throughout the Victorian age and well beyond. To trace, briefly, but one example, Bond's claim that the victims of nightmare were 'in the jaws of death' (2) anticipated Wes Craven's *A Nightmare on Elm Street* (1984) and recent clinical studies by Sherry Adler evidencing the potentially fatal power of parasomnias (2011).[2] Bond's comparison between sleep and death aligned with the Christian idea that sleep resembled death, an idea adapted by later thinkers. Scottish physician Robert Macnish characterised sleep as 'the intermediate state between wakefulness and death', a type of 'temporary metaphysical death, though not an organic one' (9), where habitual nightmares could actually be fatal (138). In such a manner could Macnish simultaneously uphold interpretations of both a medical and theological nature, the latter reading the sleeping self as 'transition[ing] from a finite self rooted in the world to a transcendent soul caught up within the Universal Spirit' (Hayward 161). Such theories of nightmare stood in stark opposition to those like Immanuel Kant's that, while maintaining the sleep–death association, ascribed a teleological function to Incubus whereby it served to warn its victims of their possible, impending death, 'that the body was in mortal danger due to insufficient blood flow' (Sharpless and Doghramji 68).

Harry Ludlam's intriguing claim that Bram Stoker had consumed 'a too generous helping of dressed crab at supper one night', an event that spawned the nightmare that inspired *Dracula* (99), is in keeping, notably, with such empirical, medically based Enlightenment theories relating to food consumption, indigestion, and the generation of nightmares. It was also a widely held belief that dreams both 'revealed the power of the imagination and ... [were] a form of poetic inspiration' (Ford 107). Claims circulated about writers and authors who went to outrageous lengths to induce Incubus. Macnish infamously claimed in his popular study, *The Philosophy of Sleep* (1830), for example, that Ann Radcliffe's Gothic fictions owed their origins to the fact that she 'supped upon the most indigestible substances; while Dryden and Fuseli, with the opposite view of obtaining splendid dreams, are reported to have eaten raw flesh' (57). While Judith Wilt provocatively claims that Ann Radcliffe 'wouldn't tell us her dreams, wishing, as Montague Summers puts it, to be thought a lady' (8), Rictor Norton and Elizabeth Napier both relate the rumour that Radcliffe deliberately consumed undercooked pork chops prior to bed in order to stimulate nightmares (215–16; 'Ann' 365). Fuseli's 'nightmarish visions' were rumoured to have been fuelled by the same diet (Frayling 73),[3] in combination with opium, 'to induce [his] imagination to greater excesses' (Myrone, 'Fuseli' 36), a theory referenced as fact in De Quincey's *Confessions* (71–2). While Poet Laureate, Robert Southey, was 'reputed to have used laughing gas' to induce inspirational nightmares (Frayling 73), such Gothic-influenced and interested artists, authors, and intellectuals as Piranesi, Coleridge, Théophile Gautier, Stevenson, Freud, and Benjamin were said, in some cases for medical reasons, to have ingested and injected other dream-inducing drugs.[4]

As 'the mechanical and associationistic explanations of dreams, by John Locke (1632–1704), David Hartley (1705–57) and George Berkeley (1685–1753) [that connected dreams to sensory and physiological experiences] came to be perceived as unsatisfactory and in need of challenge' (Ford 107), dreams and nightmares became increasingly regarded as symptoms of varied states of consciousness. During this Enlightenment era, '[i]nterest in the forces and features of psychic life was growing, along with thinking that pointed towards the early twentieth-century identification of the "unconscious" mind, especially the notion that there are parts of consciousness and of identity that are unknown, hidden and dynamic' (107). European thinkers like Georg Christoph Lichtenberg, Gotthilf Heinrich Schubert, and Friedrich August Carus interpreted dreams and nightmares as guides to greater self-consciousness (Powell, *Fuseli* 51), which was one of the common 'techniques of self' in the ancient world, as Michel Foucault notes in his last book, *The Care of the Self* (Sliwinski xvii). While, according to Schubert, dreams are significant as they 'are a way of reckoning ... a higher kind of algebra, briefer and easier than ours, which only the hidden poet knows how to manipulate in his mind' (qtd. in Kent and Knight 13), in Carus's words, nightmares were an attempt 'to rouse us and bring us suddenly to a full consciousness of our self, even if it be a hideous one' (qtd. in Kaufmann 82). John Locke's equation of the dream with the absence of reason[5] and Scottish Enlightenment philosopher Dugald Stewart's view that dreams involved the suspension of the will fed into a related theory that deemed dreams to be 'encounters with an inner form of "otherness"' – sometimes the repressed dark side of the self – which linked them with the more exceptional experiences of madness, ecstasy, and intoxication (Dieterle and Engel 9). These phenomena supported or challenged various nineteenth-century models of the mind and competing models of selfhood (Wigginton 11–12), while simultaneously generating vexing legal and ethical questions about the suspension of the judgment and one's moral accountability for actions undertaken while sleepwalking. Indeed, somnambulism was 'treated as a special form of dream disorder' that signified a disease of the moral sense (Manning 44). Such a diagnosis was in keeping with the promotion of 'temperance, virtue, and pious thought as the recipe for "sweet slumber and easy dreams"' advocated by Scottish Enlightenment thinker, Dr James Beattie, an idea that aligned with the ideas of Benjamin Franklin (qtd. in Manning 45).[6] Gothic literature and the Gothic-inspired visual arts also engaged with such thorny ethical issues about sleepwalking and subjectivity, agency, gender, and the will, as is evidenced in both Charles Brockden Brown's *Edgar Huntly, Or, Memoirs of a Sleepwalker* (1799) and his first, now lost, novel, *Somnambulism*.

The oneiric legacies of Fuseli and Goya

Two iconic visual images exemplify the Enlightenment era's fascination with the dreaming, unconscious self – John Henry Fuseli's painting, *The Nightmare* (1781), a copy of which hung in Freud's apartment in Vienna in 1926 (Frayling 54–5), and plate forty-three of Francisco de Goya's famous eighty-print aquatint etching series, *Los Caprichos*, entitled *The Sleep (or Dream) of Reason Produces Monsters*, which was privately published in the 1790s. Each is worthy of consideration in any study of parasomnias and the Gothic not only because each subsequently influenced other works of Gothic literature and horror film but because each stages a collision between pre-Enlightenment and Enlightenment belief systems that was simultaneously being played out in Gothic literature and contemporary oneirocriticism. Their gendered semiotics also possess noteworthy ramifications for representations of nightmares through to the present day. Despite the different genders of their sleeping subjects, each could be described as portraying Enlightenment dreamers haunted by the ghosts of a superstitious, pre-Enlightenment past. Both images also lay important groundwork for theorising the sublime and the subliminal, connected concepts fundamental to the discussion of parasomnias in Gothic literature and horror cinema.

Goya's famous painting, *The Sleep of Reason Produces Monsters* (see Figure 0.1), is a self-portrait of the artist, then beset by a protracted illness and menaced by bats and owls, signs of mindless stupidities in Spanish folklore during Goya's time (Hughes 171). This haunted, assaulted figure, asleep at his desk beside his painting materials, has been interpreted as the symbolic staging of Goya's confrontation with the menacing forces of his own life and his growing sense of personal, political compromise: while being the court painter to King Carlos IV, he remained dedicated to the cause of the Spanish peasantry. The gestural semiotics of the image – and, more specifically, the sign language of the sleeper's hands – have been interpreted as being connected both to Goya's deafness (Tal 116) and his melancholy, the latter illness having been medicalised with a detailed symptomatology in the eighteenth century by such medical authorities as Robert Burton, Richard Baxter, and Richard Mead. All of these writers maintained that the primary symptom of melancholy was delusion. With the imagination diseased and the reason unsound, the victim fancied, in Mead's words, that there were 'hobgoblins haunting him' (qtd. in Tal 119).

Contrary to interpretations of this captivating painting by Robert Miles and other poststructuralist critics who see it as expressing the ambiguities of the Enlightenment in its questioning whether monsters emerge from the *sleep* of reason or the *dreams* of reason – its 'fantasies of utopias, successful revolutionary actions, where evil is extirpated and the good inherit the

Figure 0.1 Plate 43, Francisco de Goya, 'Los Caprichos' – *The Sleep of Reason Produces Monsters* (*El sueño de la razon produce monstruos*) (1799)

earth[,] as superstition is banished and reason reigns in peace' ('Brown's' 412)[7] – Goya rendered explicit its import when he wrote, 'Fantasy abandoned by reason produces impossible monsters. United with her, she is the mother of all arts and the source of their wonders' (qtd. in Powell, 'Fuseli' 91). Monsters, in Goya's illustration, described as 'hobgoblins' by Mead (qtd. in Tal 119), are the product of the disease of melancholy, 'the tacit condition that implicitly binds sleep, dream, and illness' where the boundary between sleep and dream becomes indistinguishable, the individual, 'when he dreams, ... [believing] he is broad awake and sees visions' (119).

While, in its staging of a battle within the artist between his rational and imaginative selves, Goya's etching visualises a traditional

Enlightenment-based division, in its focus on a male figure, it runs counter to the established socio-cultural gendering of states of unconsciousness in the eighteenth century. As Margaret Ann Doody has written, in the novels of that era, especially the Gothic novel, it was women, then considered to be 'weaker than men, not in control of their environment, [who were] ... permitted to have dreams' (84). Countless paintings of the period likewise figured women in the acts of sleeping, dreaming, and daydreaming, as inherently irrational, a stereotype mirrored in contemporary oneirocriticism where women were featured as natural victims of nightmare (Dacome 401). Henry Fuseli's iconic and scandalous painting, *The Nightmare* (1781–2), with its recumbent and vulnerable female sleeper, grotesque, crouching incubus, and spectral mare, is the preeminent example (see Figure 0.2). Like Goya's image, Fuseli's blends pre-Enlightenment and Enlightenment ideas: superstitious German folklore and Enlightenment medical theory (Shackelford 19) coalesce in the grotesque imp-like incubus who signals and enacts the medical condition of Incubus. Contemporary medical ideas directed the victims of Incubus 'to lie as little as possible upon the back' (Macnish 139) in order to avoid, in the words of Samuel Johnson's *Dictionary*, 'a morbid oppression in the night, resembling the pressure of weight upon the breast' (n.p.).

Figure 0.2 Henry Fuseli, *The Nightmare* (1781)

Two centuries later, in Ernest Jones's 1931 study of the phenomenon, one of the 'cardinal feature[s] in the attack' was said to be 'the sense of stifling oppression on the chest as of an overpowering weight that impedes the respiration often to the extreme limit of endurance' (21).

In stark contrast to Goya's mental landscape portrait of the melancholic artist as a delusional, irrational victim of Incubus, Fuseli's portrait of the female victim has been said to be a 'direct and daring ... foray into the subconscious' that represents the *sensation* of nightmare (Powell, 'Fuseli' 17). It foregrounds female sexuality and libidinal desire, which is demonised in the form of the grotesque, leering incubus, crouching astride the languorous sleeper's pelvic region. The woman on her back is positioned, significantly, in a 'normally receptive sexual attitude' (55) and interpreted in relation to the mare, 'a very ancient masculine sexual symbol ... frequently associated with the devil' (56). The longstanding 'intimate connection between the devil, nightmares and sex', subsequently theorised by Carl Jung (56), is evoked by Fuseli's portrait of the folkloric experience of Hag-riding or Mare-riding (54), symbolically connected to nocturnal female emissions, an association that dates back, at least, to the early sixteenth century. According to Dutch theologian and medical student, Levinus Lemnius, unmarried women 'pollute themselves in the nighte season' (Duffin 59) through nightmares that result in 'a naughty vapour that ascendeth upward and disturbeth their brayne' (58–9). Hereupon, he continues, 'commeth trembling & quaking of the heart by reason of grosse fumes, which invade the panicle or coffyn of the heart, called *Pericardion*, and lye heavelye upon the body pressing it downe as though they were night Hegges, or Hobegobblins' (59). Robert Burton's claim in *The Anatomy of Melancholy* that 'stale maids, nuns, and widows' were subject to terrible nightmares that could be cured by marriage (354–5) – by which was implied regular, legally sanctioned, sexual activity – was in keeping with this idea. John Bond also referenced a clinical case about a young woman affected by nightmares at the time of her menses (47–9), which was popularly believed to be the time of a woman's greatest sexual arousal. That Fuseli's unconscious female may be suffering from nightmare-inducing menses is suggested by the bottle of laudanum evident on her bedside table, a popular treatment for both Incubus and debilitating menses during this era. As the tragic cases of the nightmare-plagued Coleridge, John William Polidori, and De Quincey illustrate, however, laudanum actually exacerbated Incubus.[8]

Goya's melancholic 'hobgoblins' (Tal 119) and Fuseli's lusty, leering hobgoblin are not the same order of beast, as men and women – then, as now – have been interpreted, culturally, through the gender-skewed lens of subject–object, mind–body binaries. While nightmares may be experienced by men who are rendered emotionally unhealthy by external phenomena, they especially plague women's menstruating, maternal bodies, which were considered to be naturally unruly. Regarded as irrational by nature and, like the 'primitive', incapable of mental reflection (Connelly 14), women are portrayed as inherently prone to Incubus. The location of Fuseli's imp-like incubus atop the recumbent woman's uterus forges the established association, as delineated by Marie Mulvey-Roberts, between the 'unnatural' female body and monstrosity (106). As such, these two figures – the woman and the incubus – are essentially coextensive, their positioning suggesting that women, sexually monstrous by nature, may give birth to – are the mothers of – monsters.

While the aetiology of the externalised monsters may seem to reside *within* both sleepers, a significant distinction exists. In Goya's work, the visual focus of the ailment is the melancholic, delusion-plagued male sleeper's mind, but in Fuseli's, they emerge in a more intimate and libidinally associated manner, from within the female sleeper's sexualised body. As Nicolas Powell has argued, 'there can be little doubt that the girl in Fuseli's painting is experiencing an imaginary sexual assault' (60); however, it is likewise intimated by Fuseli's gendered and sexualised iconography that such an assault, in keeping with much Renaissance and Enlightenment oneirocriticism, is unconsciously desired by the female figure. Her body is portrayed, therefore, as naturally monstrous, her potent sexual drives rendering her a magnet for, and a progenitor of, both monsters and nightmares.

Fuseli's hypnotic and oppressive hobgoblin-incubus subsequently migrated into some of Étienne-Gaspard Robertson's phantasmagorias where the demon was menacingly equipped with 'a dagger suspended over her heart' (Castle 149). That Fuseli's eroticised sleeper was also imported into Gothic literature, popularly known in the late-eighteenth century as the 'hobgoblin romance' (Clery and Miles 182–3), where she was adapted and featured in key passages in Mary Shelley's *Frankenstein* (Andres 262; Gerhard 109; Mellor 121; Mishra 222), Thomas De Quincey's *Confessions* (67), and Edgar Allan Poe's 'The Fall of the House of Usher' (Shackelford 19), illustrates the cross-cultural transmission involving Gothic dreams and nightmares previously referenced.[9] Equally significant is the expression in both iconic images – Goya's and Fuseli's – of the interconnected roles of the sublime and the subliminal. According to Judith Wilt, two discrete paths fundamental to the Gothic, both of which evoke terror, lead out of Goya's *Sleep of Reason* – one to the external Gothic sublime; the other, to the internal Gothic sublime, this latter avenue being popularly referenced, post-Freud, as the uncanny, the realm of the subliminal. Goya's arresting image, Wilt argues, 'bred both the eighteenth-century dream of being shaken in a giant hand and the nineteenth-century dream of being transfixed by the alien eye from within' (9). Notably, Wilt's delineation of the Gothic's shifting fixation over those two centuries, identified in her oneirocritical interpretation as co-existing in Goya's painting, applies equally to Fuseli's. The leering incubus both externalises the Gothic sublime while serving as an emanation of the female sleeper's internal encounter with it.

The sublime, the subliminal, and the Gothic novel

While Wilt rightly identifies the two key avenues in the Gothic – the sublime and the subliminal – it is a commonly accepted idea in Gothic studies that, over the course of the nineteenth century, the external sublime mutated into, or was increasingly displaced by, an internalised sublime – sublime terror went inside. In *Radical Gothic* (2000), his painstakingly detailed study of the Gothic sublime, Andrew Smith charts this progressive internalisation process – what he describes as destabilising encounters with the psychological sublime (175). The sublime, Smith demonstrates, transmogrified into the uncanny (6) – across nineteenth-century literary works written by such authors as Edgar Allan Poe and Robert Louis Stevenson, works that Smith claims anticipated Freudian analysis (6). Although it shares with Vijay Mishra's *The Gothic Sublime* (1994) and other studies the problematic issue of being overdetermined by Freudian psychoanalysis, Smith's book serves as an astute historicising corrective to Mishra's overdetermined proto-postmodern reading of the Gothic's 'fascination with fragmentation and the collapse of meaning' (4), a misguided standpoint also advanced – and reiterated – by various critics.[10]

Smith may not identify Mishra's interpretation of the relationship between the sublime and the subliminal as an aspect of Mishra's problematic reading, but it is arguably a key element. Piggybacking on the critical work of such authors as Jørgen Andersen and Mario Praz, Mishra describes the Gothic sublime as 'pure Piranesi; not the vast oceans and tempests of Longinus or Kant, but the subterranean passages and the grotesque deformations contained in the dreamscape of the Gothic imagination'. Mishra extrapolates, calling the Gothic sublime 'the *sub*, not as "up to" (as in *sub* + *limen*, the Latin etymology of sublime), but rather as the *below*, the underneath, of the *limen*, of the limit of one's perception' (39). Gesturing backwards historically and describing the Gothic sublime as 'pure Piranesi', Mishra characterises it as being more akin to the Gothic subliminal – labelled by him as an energy of the unconscious – that erupts from a type of underground, psychic and otherwise, that moves beneath perception. In this definition, Mishra seems to conflate 'terror Gothic' and 'horror Gothic', the two Gothic types distinguished by Ann Radcliffe in her famous posthumously published essay, 'On the Supernatural in Poetry' (1826).

Radcliffe problematically yet intriguingly genders each Gothic type, characterising 'terror Gothic' as 'feminine' and intended to expand the soul by bringing it into contact with sublime objects of terror, and 'horror Gothic' as 'masculine' in its focus on encounters with gruesomely detailed mortality. Radcliffe also underscores their different affective impacts: 'Terror and horror are so far opposite, that the first expands the soul, and awakens the faculties to a high degree of life; the other contracts, freezes, and nearly annihilates them' (168). In Mishra's reconceptualisation, the soul is expanded in the face of sublime objects of terror only to be horrified by the ultimate recognition, engendered by the subliminal, that no transcendence is possible. Thus does Mishra's portrait of the Gothic sublime run counter to the sublime as Romantically conceived. He describes how '[f]rom the depths of the underworld/abyss/*unconscious* the Gothic invades the discourses of the sublime' (39; emphasis added). Electing to reference the Freudian concept of the unconscious, as opposed to the subliminal, Mishra suggests that the unconscious essentially hijacks the Gothic sublime. The manifestation of the sublime in the Gothic mode, he argues, revels in the subterranean and non-transcendence, an experience he describes in masculine and Freudian terms as involving the humiliating yet – putatively and surprisingly – *pleasurable* threat of castration (40).

Although only defined and theorised in the late nineteenth century by F. W. H. Myers as a psychological concept, the idea of the subliminal, along with that of the subliminal self, which 'function[ed] within a composite human personality' (Keeley 772) and survived bodily death, actually predated Freud's theory of the unconscious and the role of dreams in psychoanalysis as delineated in *The Interpretation of Dreams* (1900). Notably, Freud wrote 'A Note on the Unconscious in Psycho-Analysis' in 1912–13, over a decade after Myers's death, to distinguish his ideas from Myers's notion of the subliminal because he was concerned about being seen as a 'junior partner' (Keeley 190). Myers had, in fact, regarded Freud as 'a late entrant into a field that Myers, [Edmund] Gurney, [Frank Podmore,] and [Pierre] Janet, had already explored in some detail' (Hamilton 190). Despite this history, Freudian discourse and theory have been, to date, privileged in discussions of the Gothic, the idea of the uncanny being theorised as a transmogrified and internalised sublime, and the return of the repressed serving as a domineering commonplace, a dynamic that generally carries with it negative associations. Alongside this erasure of Myers's conception of the subliminal self, what has gone unnoted is the fact that this concept, broadly defined, pre-dates Myers's research, being not only inextricably bound up with the sublime but fundamental to the Gothic since its inception. Reconsidering the intellectual and cultural history of the subliminal, especially in its relationship to the sublime, enhances the theorisation of

the Gothic sublime and is fundamental to any study of Gothic dreams and nightmares.

The subliminal from Piranesi and Walpole to Myers and Breton

To date, examination of the vital role played by the subliminal in the Gothic and its relationship to the sublime has either been missing from a theorisation of the Gothic sublime or been skewed in that theorisation, usually in a problematically Freudian way, as the works of Mishra and Smith, among others, illustrate. Reconsidering Gothic cultural history with a focus on the subliminal helps to crystallise the significance of both its mutating nature and role in the history of Gothic literature and horror cinema and its relationship to the sublime. The overwhelming focus in Gothic scholarship has been on the sublime, despite the fact that the subliminal has been inextricably bound up with the sublime since its inception and has shadowed it consistently across centuries. Indeed, it is my contention that it is the Gothic's consistent engagement with the subliminal and the sublime's association with the subliminal in Gothic cultural productions that renders the Gothic sublime radically distinct from the Romantic sublime. It is this fundamental connection that constitutes, I believe, what Mishra refers to as 'the Gothicness of the Gothic sublime' (22). Bringing the subliminal to the forefront of the theorising process, in connection with the Freudian concept of the unconscious that it helped to engender, which emphasises the uncanny and the return of negative, repressed energies and histories, a dynamic that has been privileged in the field of Gothic literary criticism, allows for a more complete re-envisioning of the Gothic's changing face over centuries and across cultural forms and media. It also serves to illuminate some of the Gothic's most significant cultural cross-fertilisations over the centuries.

The degree to which the Gothic is grounded in dreams, nightmares, and the subliminal has yet to be fully recognised and theorised. Indeed, the significant and inextricable bond between the subliminal and the sublime not only informed Gothic literature from its inception but served to inspire it. Horace Walpole, father of the literary Gothic, who lamented in the first Preface to *Otranto* that 'miracles, visions, necromancy, *dreams*, and other preternatural events [were] ... exploded ... from romances' (4; emphasis added), claimed that an incomparable wisdom inhered in dreams (Andersen 52). In tandem with this, he made the striking and passionate recommendation in the fourth volume of his *Anecdotes of Painting in England* (1771) that English painters study 'the *sublime dreams* of Piranesi' (vii; emphasis added). Indeed, no work of art better captures a sense of sublime oneiric encounter than Giovanni Battista Piranesi's *Carceri d'Invenzione* (1745–61)

(see Figure 0.3), the artistic series to which Walpole specifically referred
in his commentary. Originally etched in 1745 and possibly the product
of malarial illness and the impact of medicinal opiates, Piranesi's *Carceri*
rendered Edmund Burke's claims about the sublime effect of infinity and
things multiplied without end into visual artistic – and, more specifically,
architectural – form. In 1761, Piranesi radically reworked his renowned
series of etchings of seemingly endless, inescapable, and illusory architectural structures that, in thwarting, confounding, and dwarfing their various
human captives, remove them, in unsettling ways, from the centre of the
universe. When he reworked his etchings in 1761, as Marguerite Yourcenar
has claimed in what is arguably the most enlightening commentary on the

Figure 0.3 Giovanni Battista Piranesi, 'The Round Tower', *Le Carceri
d'Invenzione*, First Edition, 1749–50

Carceri, 'like his entire century, [Piranesi] was swept by the current which drew Baroque out towards what we call pre-Romanticism, and ... deliberately modified his work in the direction of the gothic novel' (108).

The Italian architectural engraver's impact on the Gothic has been variously recognised by its practitioners and critics alike. Jørgen Andersen rightly observed in 1952, for example, that 'there is a passage still unexplored leading from the *Carceri* into the strangely echoing vaults of the English Gothic novels' (50). Walpole's subliminal Piranesian dreams inspired the imaginative architectural marvels of Manfred's castle, the first Gothic locale (53). Mario Praz reiterated this claim, arguing that Walpole's imagining of the sublime in *Otranto* is akin to Piranesi's madness-inducing *Carceri* with their 'mighty daedalean buildings and the little figures of men at the foot of them' (17). The Gothic's continued fascination with Piranesi's *Carceri* is evidenced in Beckford's *Vathek* and De Quincey's *Confessions of an English Opium-Eater* (1821), among other works.[11]

What has not yet been noted about Walpole's reference to the '*sublime dreams* of Piranesi' is that it explicitly conjoins the ideas of the sublime and the subliminal. Connected by way of the notions of the threshold (Latin *limen*) and transgression, the sublime and the subliminal denote passing under, through, or over a metaphorical threshold. Such transgressive threshold crossings constitute a signature trademark of Gothic literature, which interrogates and often violates such boundaries. It is noteworthy that Walpole's characterisation of Piranesi's *Carceri* does not align with Praz's or Mishra's interpretation of those etchings as imprisoning, nightmarish, and non-transcendent. In stark contrast, Walpole interprets and celebrates the daring, revolutionary art of his fellow antiquarian – his 'wild', 'bold', 'savage', 'fierce', 'exuberant', and 'imaginative' visions, his sublimely imagined scenes that, in Walpole's words, 'would startle geometry, and exhaust the Indies to realize' (*Anecdotes* vii). Walpole's viewpoint notably aligns with Yourcenar's study of both Piranesi's original 1745 *Carceri* images and the darker, 'greatly reworked' series of 1761 (106). In her words, both

> bear very little resemblance to traditional images of a prison[, ...] the nightmare of incarceration chiefly consist[ing] in *confinement*, in being shut up in a dungeon which already has the dimensions of a grave ... We are far from that loathsome horror and that sordid hypocrisy with Piranesi's megalomaniac and sublime *Prisons*. (108–9)

What Yourcenar underscores is their dream-like aspect and atmospherics:

> No connoisseur of oneiric matters will hesitate a moment in the presence of these drawings evincing all the chief characteristics of the dream state: negation

of time, incoherence of space, suggested levitation, intoxication of the impossible reconciled or transcended, terror closer to ecstasy than is assumed by those who analyze the visionary's creations from outside, absence of visible contact between the dreams parts or characters, and finally a fatal and necessary beauty. (110–11)

In regard to the revised series, Yourcenar also notes the numerous changes – the multiplied cross-hatchings, darkened shadows, 'more generous inking', and the addition of 'innumerable wheels, pulleys, cranes, winches, and capstans[,] to the mysterious machines sketched in the foreground or in the corners of the halls, details which certainly transform them into instruments of torture rather than seeming the mere engines of construction they might have been' (106) (see Figures 0.4 and 0.5). Yourcenar also comments on their intense presence of space and sense of ascension – of levitation, as she perceptively describes it.

As Walpole suggests in his statement about 'the sublime dreams of Piranesi', the sublime and the subliminal are not discrete but, rather, connected registers in the *Carceri*. Walpole imports these registers into *Otranto*, in a manner both symbolic and material, thus influencing subsequent Gothic fiction. Perhaps most notably, while Piranesi's engravings, originally rendered in his twenties, produce sublime effects on both the figures in the

Figure 0.4 Giovanni Battista Piranesi, 'The Well', *Le Carceri d'Invenzione*, First Edition, 1749–50

Figure 0.5 Giovanni Battista Piranesi, 'The Well', *Le Carceri d'Invenzione*, Second Edition, 1761

Carceri and their viewers, what Walpole celebrates is the fact that for the artist, the subliminal – the matrix of the dream, the imagination, and creative inspiration – engenders the sublime or, at the very least, is inextricably tethered to it. Walpole's subsequent dream that birthed *Otranto*, along with those experienced by Shelley, Stevenson, and Stoker, among others, provides further evidence of how dreams and nightmares have often served to inspire sublime Gothic artistic conceptions.

Perhaps no better evidence of the artistic legacy of Walpole's subliminally inspired *Otranto* exists – a work influenced by Piranesi's similarly subliminally inspired *Carceri* etchings – than the perceptive and provocative commentary advanced more than a century and a half later by Surrealist artist, André Breton. Among Breton's many references throughout his career to the Gothic's tremendous influence on Surrealism,[12] he identifies Walpole's dream-inspired *Otranto* as proto-Surrealist, as approaching 'the surrealist method' (157). The oneiric source of Walpole's novella held the key, in Breton's view, to the Surrealist aesthetic, that consciously rejected, like German Expressionist cinema in the wake of the First World War, 'the Enlightenment tradition's reliance on rationality, positivism and the dominance of the reality principle' in favour of what Breton called 'the revenge of the pleasure principle' where 'the imagination regains its rights as the key locus of creativity' and knows no bounds (Matheson 56). More notable, however, is the fact that Breton suggests a direct line of cultural transmission that connects Walpole's novel, not to Freud and the unconscious, despite Breton's simultaneous embrace of Freudian terms and principles, but to the work of Myers, who first theorised the idea of the subliminal consciousness and the subliminal self in a series of articles in the Society's proceedings in the late nineteenth century. Breton's entry on Myers in the 'Surrealist Glossary', compiled by Franklin Rosemont from Breton's writings, notes explicitly how Myers's 'studies of automatic writing, especially his "beautiful work" (in Breton's words) *Human Personality*, have exerted considerable influence on the origins and development of surrealism' (Breton 370). Significantly, Breton also notes 'the regrettable fact that so many are unacquainted with the work of F. W. H. Myers, *which anteceded that of Freud*' (100; emphasis added).

In citing the Gothic, the work of Walpole, and that of Myers as influences on the Surrealists, Breton followed the lead of psychologist and philosopher, William James (1842–1910), who characterised Myers's pioneering forays into the psychological study of the mind, specifically and significantly, as '*Gothic* psychology' (qtd. in Shamdasani, p. xv; emphasis added) because of its complex and multi-dimensional nature – what Myers himself referred to in various publications as its 'multiplex' nature (Hamilton 155). In a celebratory assessment of Myers's legacy published subsequent to his death in the Proceedings of the SPR, James wrote in detail about Myers's romanticist approach and momentous contributions to 'the study of the Mind':

> their [the SPR's] work is *like going from classic to Gothic architecture*, where few outlines are pure and where uncouth forms lurk in the shadows. A mass of mental phenomena are [*sic*] now seen in the shrubbery beyond the parapet. Fantastic, ignoble, hardly human, or frankly nonhuman are some of these new candidates for psychological description. ... The world of the mind is shown as something infinitely more complex than was suspected; and whatever beauties it may still possess, it has lost at any rate the beauty of academic neatness. (James 14; emphasis added)

That Myers's 'gothic psychology' – his multiplex view of the subliminal mind – should be compared metaphorically by James to the sublimity of Gothic architecture is noteworthy, hearkening back to the mesmerising mid-eighteenth-century work of Piranesi, which inspired the Gothic's initial engagement with the sublime and the subliminal. James's statement also recognises and celebrates the Gothic's transhistorical, cross-fertilising cultural influence. Myers's revolutionary new conception of the subliminal, which had been explored in the burgeoning field of psychology in Victorian England required, Myers felt, the application of more robust scientific data. According to Myers, the subliminal encompassed 'sensations, thoughts, [and] emotions, which may

be strong, definite, and independent, but which, by the original constitution of our being, seldom emerge into that *supraliminal* current of consciousness which we habitually identify with *ourselves*', a self he found 'it permissible and convenient to speak of [as multiple] subliminal Selves' (14–15).

It is unsurprising to discover that, after reading *The Strange Case of Dr. Jekyll and Mr. Hyde*, Myers saw in Robert Louis Stevenson a comrade in arms, to whom he sent a detailed and astute commentary about that novella in February of 1886. Stevenson largely and enthusiastically agreed with Myers's various insights relative to the subliminal self, as illustrated in his responding correspondence.[13] Stevenson's Gothic novella was crafted around the idea of a complex, sedimented self-identity that may be dual or multiple, as suggested by Jekyll's statements 'that man is not truly one, but truly two' (52), and possibly even 'a mere polity of multifarious, incongruous and independent denizens' (53). This idea aligns with Myers's viewpoint, which was shared by William James, although Myers regarded dissociative states as normal and healthy, as opposed to pathological, which was the viewpoint of fellow psychologist, Pierre Janet (Hunter). Dreams were also a vital element of Myers's exploration of what he called the subliminal self (Lusty and Groth 6) that produced and guided 'normal processes such as creative acts … [and] dreams' (Alvarado 9). Stevenson's 'A Chapter on Dreams' (1888) likewise and notably concurred with Myers's view of dreams as inspirational, the source of fictional gold.

If Stevenson, who possessed a lifelong interest in psychology, anticipated Freudian analysis in his act of transforming 'the sublime into the uncanny', as Andrew Smith claims in *Gothic Radicalism* (6), this was either because he had read Myers's work on the subliminal, '[o]ne of the most significant psychological theories produced in England at the end of the century' (Luckhurst xix), or that of other psychologists who had been influenced by Myers and the research of the SPR. Although only published in instalments between 1891 and 1895, Myers's evidence and case histories for 'The Subliminal Consciousness' were more than a decade in the making, dating as far back as 1882, the year that saw the establishment of the Society for Psychical Research, under whose auspices his scholarship, which had a tremendous impact 'not only on Bloomsbury and English psychoanalysis, but on William James at Harvard and various researchers around Europe' (Appignanesi 151), was being conducted and published. Notably, the SPR's 'influential commitment to the empirical explanation of psychic phenomena', including dreams and nightmares (Lusty and Groth 7), was indebted to the many scholarly articles devoted to the new science of psychology that were published in scientific journals and the popular periodical press throughout the Victorian period. As James noted in regard to the idea of the subliminal and Myers's tremendous contributions to the field:

For half a century ... psychologists ... fully admitted the existence of a subliminal mental region, under the name either of unconscious cerebration or of
the involuntary life; but they have never definitely taken up the question of the
extent of this region, never sought explicitly to map it out. Myers definitely
attacks this problem, which, after him, it will be impossible to ignore. (17)

As much scholarship of recent decades has shown, Freud's dream science, as
delineated in *The Interpretation of Dreams* (1900), possesses 'a monumental
status in terms of heralding a new era of dream theory' (Lusty and Groth 7).
Despite his concerted denials in print and elsewhere, however, Freud's work
was likewise grounded in and 'informed by the interdisciplinary approach
to dreams well established in the nineteenth century' (7). Nevertheless, in
his article, 'A Note on the Unconscious in Psycho-Analysis' (1912), Freud
'forcefully denied that Myers' subliminal[, which was grounded in the study
of the paranormal,] was the same as his, Freud's, unconscious' (Hamilton
190). As James P. Keeley has argued, Freud's claim, made eleven years after
Myers's death, during which time he had significantly developed his theories of psychoanalysis and manifest and latent dreams, was largely correct.
There are important distinctions to be recognised between the Freudian
unconscious and Myers's subliminal self. Foremost among these is the
fact that the Freudian unconscious is far more alien to consciousness than
Myers's conception of the subliminal and supraliminal, the operations of the
unconscious only possibly being glimpsed 'by observing the distortion of the
latent dream thoughts when compared to the manifest dream' (Keeley 781).
Freud's conception of consciousness had also undergone radical change
as illustrated by his suggestion that it may not be split but 'might better
be described as [involving] shifts between [states of] consciousness' (781).
Keeley notably identifies Freud's 'analysis of dreams as [the] master key to
the recently discovered – and newly theorized – unconscious' and the basis
upon which 'psychoanalysis leaves behind the world of late-nineteenth-cen-
tury psychology', especially the work of 'Myers and the SPR, a world based
upon investigations of hypnotism, hysteria, and subconscious personalities,
to proceed in a completely new direction' (787). Keeley's characterisation
of Myers's scholarly investigations as a type of supernatural – as opposed
to a scientific – engagement, however, problematically disregards Myers's
evidence-based research, the central role of dreams and parasomnias in that
research, and his various forays into 'the multiple dimensions of the unconscious mind' (Lusty and Groth 7).

In his concerted efforts to further distinguish Freud's theory from that
of Myers, Ernest Jones, Freud's biographer, defined the unconscious as 'a
region of the mind, the content of which is characterised by the attrib-
ute of being repressed, conative, instinctive, infantile, unreasoning, and

predominantly sexual' (Tyrrell 28). Myers's biographer, Trevor Hamilton, foregrounds a noteworthy contrast, claiming that Jones's 'grim definition [of the Freudian unconscious] bears little resemblance to Myers's essentially optimistic, even romantic subliminal realm. Through the key techniques of psycho-analysis (word association, dream analysis, the examination of verbal slips) the unconscious could, with great difficulty, be accessed' (190). While dreams and nightmares offer keys to both the subliminal and the unconscious, Hamilton advances a significant – and contentious – distinction between Freud's unconscious and Myers's notion of the subliminal:

> For Myers, the unconscious [as Freud later termed it] was not a mere repository of rubbish or the source of psychological disease. It contained gold. *The subliminal had elements of the sublime.* From the subliminal emerged the insights, the skills, the inspirations that one associates with genius and the highest creative achievement. (191; emphasis added)

Hamilton notably foregrounds a yoking between the subliminal and the sublime in Myers's conception of the subliminal. On the basis of Myers's own characterisation of the subliminal as an ambivalent phenomenon, however, Hamilton may be criticised for misrepresentation. According to Myers,

> the subliminal self was involved in the production and guidance of normal processes such as creative acts, dreams, the effects of hypnotic suggestion, and a variety of vital physiological regulatory processes. In terms of the abnormal or the pathological, the subliminal also controlled hallucinations and hysteria (including double and multiple personality) … The range of the subliminal was very wide not only in terms of phenomena or processes but in terms of type of phenomena: 'Hidden in the deep of our being is a rubbish-heap as well as a treasure-house; – degenerations and insanities as well as beginnings of higher development; and any prospectus which insists on the amount of gold to be had for the washing should describe also the mass of detritus in which the bright grains lie concealed.' (qtd. in Alvarado 9)

While William James identified what he called 'the Myers problem' as involving the challenge of determining 'the precise constitution of the subliminal' (Breton 100), Myers readily acknowledged its mixed nature. He noted that the subliminal contained detritus – 'a rubbish-heap' – while simultaneously serving as a gold repository. This latter, more positive interpretation of the subliminal, emphasised by Hamilton, feeds into and supports the concept of the sublime emerging from the subliminal.

Myers's suggestion that the subliminal may serve as the source of creative visions notably aligns with Walpole's reading of Piranesi's awe-inspiring, boldly transgressive, and transcendent sublime dreams. These aesthetic and philosophical concepts, however, are entangled in various complex ways in the Gothic. Similar to John Ruskin's famous conception, after the fact, of the quintessentially Romantic poetic convention known as pathetic fallacy where nature is, fallaciously, said to affectively respond to, mirror, and channel the speaker's mood, Gothic-focused artists like Piranesi and Walpole established what might be called mental landscapes wherein various aspects and manifestations of the subliminal are mapped, in an uncanny and/or terrifyingly sublime manner, onto a physical landscape or locale, assuming such forms as the architectural and the geographic. As the canon of Gothic literature and horror film evidence, such psycho-physical landscapes often involve the traversal of genealogical history and are readily transferable across cultural forms where they have proven exceedingly popular over centuries.

Other sublime-subliminal interfacings are identifiable in the Gothic. In advance of the scholarship of Robert Miles and Dale Townshend, Vijay Mishra identified a consanguinity between psychoanalytic and Gothic models of the subject that astutely recognised the process whereby sublime historic events were sublimated into art. As Mishra explains, 'As a dark metaphor of the mind or, more accurately, as the symbolization of the repressed structures of the unconscious, the Gothic is a ready medium through which a reality (such as that of the French Revolution) may be sublimated and fears about it rechanneled through the discourses of art' (14). This conception of the Gothic sublime is taken up in various chapters in this volume and notably concurs, among other artistic conceptions, with Goya's portrait of his politically compromised sleeping subject.

While differentiating between the sublime dreams that inspire artistic productions and the sublime dreams experienced by characters represented within them, the contributions in this volume recognise that oppressive socio-political forces sometimes feed and fuel the Gothic's manifold parasomnias. Moreover, although those parasomnias may gesture towards the ineffable – an ineffable that, while often artistically challenging to capture, has been variously and creatively represented to powerful ends – it is vital to acknowledge in their critical deciphering that these mental landscapes nevertheless speak volumes about the socio-historic moments and culturally inherited value systems to which they are firmly tethered. Just as the Gothic's dark dreams often suggest there is no escape from a work's various contexts of meaning, Gothic dreams and nightmares also often revel in the pleasure-generating 'terror of the unspeakable, of the inconceivable, of the unnameable' (Morris 312) and the suggestion that escape from the incarcerating scene and transcendence of the self may be impossible. Whether or not light and the possibility of transcendence peek through the seemingly impenetrable darkness, one thing is certain: every Gothic dream and parasomnia, regardless of its register of darkness, as Manny Farber has insightfully claimed, transmits the DNA of its time (Sliwinski xii).

It is noteworthy that the aesthetic and philosophical concepts of the sublime and the subliminal have been entirely sidelined in oneirocriticism in recent decades. As previously discussed, they found their way into both the psychological works of Myers and the SPR – specifically in relation to the empirical study of dreams, human identity, and the science of the mind – in addition to some aesthetic theory and artworks that followed. As Neil Matheson has painstakingly and adeptly chronicled and theorised, the Gothic parasomnia was also adapted to film, where it 'provided a powerful stimulus to the surrealist imaginary through such works as Louis Feuillade's *Les Vampires* or F. W. Murnau's *Nosferatu*' (26). The concepts of the sublime and the subliminal were also adapted and developed by Freudian 'dream science' that embraced a mental – as opposed to a brain-based – theory of dreams. Ironically, despite the insistence of both Myers and Freud about producing clinical, evidence-based theories and studies, present-day twenty-first-century university divisions of sleep medicine have ignored – and even ridiculed – Freudian 'dream science', opting instead to focus on brain-based neuropsychology. Scholars like J. Allan Hobson, Professor of Psychiatry at Harvard University, have deemed the Freudian approach to the interpretation of dreams to be obscurantist and pseudo-scientific (Lusty and Groth 12), and have discounted outright the value of studying the cultural hermeneutics of dreams. Notably and ironically, Hobson's own theories, such as his Activation-Synthesis Model of dreaming, have proven useful in analysing Gothic dreams and nightmares in such cinematic productions as the films of David Lynch and Wes Craven.

The Gothic's engagement with dreams and nightmares continues unabated, remaining a rich seam for creative exploration and production, one that allows for the interrogation of cultural, philosophical, psychological, aesthetic, and ideological questions. With the sublime-subliminal dynamic continuing to infuse its mental-physical landscapes, the Gothic remains imaginatively generative, eliciting both pleasure and terror as it explores and lends expression across a range of art forms and media to the complex nature of human consciousness and subjectivity in relation to sleep and parasomnias. Indeed, some of the most compelling and powerful work of Gothic literature and horror cinema involves their innovative expression and exploration of somnial experiences. Across approximately two and a half centuries, the Gothic and its cultural offshoots have scaled the Piranesian heights and depths of these representations, from their exhilaratingly creative and liberating to their terrifyingly non-transcendent and carceral.

Dreams and nightmares remain tantalising phenomena for interpretation in the Gothic, the most protean of modes, often innovatively manipulated to interrogate our epistemological and ontological certainties, unsettling who we are and what we think we know about ourselves and the world around us while probing the nature of mind – especially in its extreme states and *in extremis* – and the frequently confusing relationship between mind and putative 'reality' as it is variously defined – personal, social, political, and cosmic. In combination with the conventional slippage in these works from dream to nightmare, and nightmare to dream, Gothic parasomnias continue to inspire while breaking new aesthetic and ideological ground. As *Gothic Dreams and Nightmares* seeks to illustrate, Gothic parasomnias remain a critically challenging yet richly rewarding domain worthy of scholarly evaluation.

Long driven by a fascination with the sublime and the subliminal, the Gothic's preoccupation with the compelling and contentious subject of dreams and nightmares has yet to be fully mined and theorised. The more pressing and rewarding questions about this subject remain largely unmapped and untapped. With the aim of addressing this gap in Gothic scholarship, the twelve chapters in *Gothic Dreams and Nightmares*, written from a variety of critical perspectives and ranging across literary forms and media, examine the aesthetic, cultural, didactic, and ideological implications of diverse cultural treatments of its subject from the eighteenth century through to the present day.

The three chapters in Part I, 'Gothic Dream and Nightmare Theory', lay important groundwork for the collection, advancing sophisticated theoretical arguments about Gothic oneirocriticism from a broad cross-section of distinct critical standpoints, ranging from the theological and the psychological to the aesthetic, the scientific, and the Marxist. Referencing a variety of novels by Matthew Lewis, Clara Reeve, Ann Radcliffe, Charlotte Dacre, and T. J. Horsley Curties, Sam Hirst starts things off by laying bare the complex minefield of competing oneiric representations and discourses at play in early British Gothic literature in their chapter, 'The Theology of Gothic Dreams'. Hirst advances a corrective reminder about the often overlooked role of theology in the Gothic's early phase, showing how the theological interpretation of dreams co-existed, sometimes symbiotically, sometimes combatively, with an increasingly medicalised and proto-psychologised conception of the dream. Gothic dreams were, as Hirst adeptly illustrates by way of detailed examples, multivalent, serving not only as an index to deep-seated theological concerns, but to broader theological debates about the nature of the soul, free will and determinism, theodicy, and Providence.

Expanding on the topic of competing dream interpretations in this volume's second chapter, 'Morphean Space and the Metaphysics of Nightmare: Gothic Theories of Dreaming in Samuel Taylor Coleridge's *Notebooks*', Kirstin A. Mills examines Coleridge's lifelong goal, in the face of plaguing nightmares, of theorising one of the Romantic period's most haunting concerns: the metaphysics of nightmare. Mills argues that Coleridge's theory of Morphean Space drew on a wealth of contemporary cross-disciplinary studies of sleep and dreaming that were grounded in conflicting theories, ranging from the supernatural to the scientific. Focusing on his nightmare texts – both private and poetic – and especially his *Notebooks*, Mills maintains that Coleridge borrowed the spatial and metaphysical logic of early Gothic novels by Walpole, Lewis, and Radcliffe, importing their models of distorted optical and cognitive perception. Coleridge manipulated the Gothic as a psychological and cultural impulse ideally suited to question, interpret, and theorise nightmare, allowing for the coexistence and interaction between the natural and supernatural, the cognitive and spiritual worlds. Perhaps most importantly for the field of Gothic Studies, Coleridge's theory influenced a seismic shift in later nineteenth-century Gothic and fantastic literature, from outward haunting to more internal mental haunting, as illustrated by the dream-laden works of Romantic period writers like Mary Shelley, the later short stories of Edgar Allan Poe and, at the fin de siècle, the ghost stories of Henry James.

Moving from intensely personal dream theory to social dream theory, the third and final chapter in this part, entitled 'The Devil's Light: Marx, Engels, and Diabolic Enlightenment', by Jayson Althofer and Brian Musgrove, examines the phantasmagorical dreams and nightmares prevalent in the Victorian era of industrial capitalism where night and day were redefined by new technologies of artificial lighting and work was rationalised 24/7. Althofer and Musgrove contend that a 'sleeplessness of reason' was born in the early nineteenth century and not, as Judith Wilt suggests, in the twentieth century when, she claims, it went 'out to conquer day and night' (9). Configured around 'The Working Day' chapter of Marx's *Capital*, Volume 1 (1867), and Engels's *The Condition of the Working-Class in England* (1845), Althofer and Musgrove offer what they poetically describe as 'an excursion through Gothic gas-lit streets depicted by selected literary "fellow-travellers" who darkly reflect on capitalist modernity's mystifying illuminations and "enlightened" mystifications'. Drawing on the theoretical works of Adorno, Horkheimer, and de Sutter, among others, and ranging seamlessly across literary works by Peacock, Byron, De Quincey, Heine, Gogol, Carlyle, and Dickens, this chapter argues that the Victorian era witnessed the commodification of sleep itself and that capital's hegemony was produced and reproduced as recurrent nightmare. The Gothic unconscious became manifested by factories and other terror apparatuses that fulfilled capital's wish for feeding on demand, and the living nightmare of commodity fetishism – 'this religion of everyday life' surrounded by 'magic and necromancy'.

The three subsequent Parts of this volume are arranged historically along chronological lines that move from the early, classical Gothic era of the late eighteenth and early nineteenth century, through the Victorian period, into the twentieth and early twenty-first centuries. While many of these chapters dovetail back to take up some of the theoretical questions raised in the volume's opening section, they also illustrate the powerful currency still possessed by dreams and nightmares, a fundamental component of human experience, in the Gothic, over more than two centuries and across varied national terrain – British, French, German, Polish, Romanian, and American. Tethering the analyses of the Gothic productions under study to their relevant historical, cultural, and socio-political contexts, a movement is chronicled from largely didactic and socially critical ends in the early nineteenth century where the concept of nightmare was associated with such phenomena as the marriage institution, imperialism, and capitalism, to a fascination with mental landscapes, madness, repressed desire, artistic inspiration, and sexuality at the fin de siècle. The fascinating undertaking of the Society for Psychical Research to catalogue hallucinations, examined by Alice Vernon in Chapter 8, illustrates the complex, sometimes contradictory interpretations involved. Despite ostensibly advancing the post-Enlighten-ment empirical imperative to subject the subconscious to scientific investiga-tion and interpretation, superstitious and supernatural ideas prevailed.

Part II, 'Early Classic Gothic Dreams and Nightmares', undertakes an examination of late eighteenth- and early nineteenth-century Gothic works and their engagement with the role and meaning of parasomnias and the sleeping subject. In 'The Monsters of Prophecy in the Gothic Dream, 1764–1818', Richard W. Moore Jr. takes a Burkean lens to some of the texts examined by Hirst – Walpole's *Otranto* (1764), Lewis's *The Monk* (1796), Dacre's *Zofloya* (1806) – and Mary Shelley's *Frankenstein; Or, The Modern Prometheus* (1818). Moore argues that while the Age of Reason diminished the significance of dreams, the Gothic reconceptualised them as temporally and politically charged social phenomena that tapped various key and pro-found questions of the eighteenth and early nineteenth century concerning historiography, revolution, slavery, and empire. In the very early Gothic, dreams were unambiguously prophetic and assumed a teleological quality either to parody or reassert the authority of Whig historiography. Bringing Burkean notions of the sublime and the monstrous to bear on the Gothic subsequent to the French Revolution, Moore shows how prophetic dreams became complicated by a cloud of uncertainty and the emergence of mon-strosity, novels like *Zofloya* evidencing anxieties about slavery in both the colonies and at home.

Liz Wan Yuen-Yuk's 'Haunted Beyond Dreams: The Gothic and Enlightenment in Mary Wollstonecraft's *Mary, A Fiction*' turns its attention to an in-depth examination of the understudied first novel by Mary Shelley's mother, written in the aftermath of the death of a close friend, Fanny Blood, an experience Wollstonecraft described in a letter as 'a terrifying dream'. In exploring the titular character's terrifying dreams on both the literal and metaphorical levels, Wan argues that Wollstonecraft strategically manipulates the Gothic parasomnia – especially its oneiric, phantasmagorical, and thanatological elements – to reveal psychological and sexual repressions, to advocate for Enlightenment values, and to advance a radical feminist socio-political critique. The narrative itself is interpreted as a Gothic nightmare in the sense of its inclusion of chronic deaths, terror around a lack of control, and liminal states of subjectivity. *Mary*'s literary parasomnias are also interpreted in relation to the Female Gothic, a narrative recipe through which, Wan maintains, Wollstonecraft protests the abuse of, and patriarchal domination over, women. The novel ultimately straddles the gap, Wan argues, between the excess emotions of Gothicism and extreme rationalism as Wollstonecraft points to enlightened learning, reason, and refined sensibility as more effective anchors of sanity than religion.

Part III, 'Victorian and Nineteenth-Century European Gothic Dreams and Nightmares', opens with Maria Giakaniki's compelling look at dreams in relation to the female vampire in 'Wide Awake and Dreaming: The Night, the Haunt, and the Female Vampire'. Giakaniki's jumping-off point is European folklore where such supernatural entities as incubi and succubi, always tinged with eroticism, were said to cause nightmares and sometimes even illness and death in their victims, fates deemed inevitable for those who surrendered to the inappropriate nature and socially unacceptable experience of otherworldly nocturnal visits. Following an examination of Coleridge's poetic narrative, 'Christabel' (1797, 1800), Giakaniki traverses more than a century of British and European literature, examining Joseph Sheridan Le Fanu's Victorian Gothic novella *Carmilla* (1872), Théophile Gautier's hallucinatory novella, *La Morte Amoureuse* (1836), and Mircea Eliade's Romanian horror novel *Domnişoara Christina* (1936). Noting the contrast between the representation of female vampires of the same era created by women authors like Mary Elizabeth Braddon, Mary Wilkins Freeman, and Edith Wharton, Giakaniki undertakes a gender-aware comparative reading that interprets dreams and nightmares as revelatory conduits of suppressed, forbidden, and socially unacceptable emotions. She argues that Gothic parasomnias, seeming at times more real than diurnal life, reveal inner truths, often in a disguised form, that require deciphering. They become the means to explore, in a uniquely enlightening manner, desire, sin, trauma, and the closeted self. In the interfacing between dream and reality, they even assume a wish-fulfilment quality that renders dreams preferable to reality, sometimes evoking the blasphemous desire in their subjects for an alternate existence.

Nicola Bowring's 'Spectral Traces: Dream Manifestation in the Gothic Short Story' explores material manifestations of dream figures and the material effects of dreaming in the Gothic at the fin de siècle. That era, Bowring claims, witnessed a significant interest, and shift, in dream interpretation, from the supernatural to the scientific, a viewpoint discussed in Freud's seminal *The Interpretation of Dreams* (1899) and exemplified by Andrew Lang's *The Book of Dreams and Ghosts* (1897), a text that, while not specifically psychoanalytical, linked dreams to repressed memories, the phenomenon of seeing ghosts, and diurnal sleeping. While 'peoples of classical antiquity ... took it for granted that dreams were related to the world of the supernatural beings in whom they believed, and that they brought inspirations from the gods and demons' (3), Freud refuted the theory, claiming dreams to be communications from the unconscious mind within the dreamer themselves. Bringing a post-structural approach to language and deploying the ideas of Jacques Derrida on speech and writing, Bowring lends new insight into the way in which dreams in the Gothic mode blend the imaginary and the real through language and communication. As her four examples of short fiction by Wilkie Collins, Sheridan Le Fanu, Rudyard Kipling, and Henry James demonstrate, the fin-de-siècle Gothic short story explored anxieties around the unconscious dreaming state and its vulnerability to the monstrous, a trace that becomes a presence, the spectral rendered manifest.

Alice Vernon's '"I Have Seen Faces in the Dark": Gothic Visions in the Society for Psychical Research's Census of Hallucinations' extends what Bowring identifies as the drive towards a scientific examination of dreams and nightmares in the late nineteenth century. Despite being entangled in pseudoscience, the Society for Psychical Research, Vernon argues, pioneered early neuroscientific work on sleep disorders that have since proven accurate by modern equipment in sleep laboratories. Their Census of Hallucinations, undertaken between 1889 and 1892, had typically contradictory objectives: while aiming, ostensibly, to ascertain the prevalence of visions in the general public and to dismiss the ideas of ghostly visitors to the bedroom, it sought evidence of telepathic communication. Building on the claim that parasomnias are intrinsically Gothic in their manifestation, Vernon shows that the tropes and symbolism of the Gothic – from monstrous visitors to supernatural mists – influenced the form and content of the Census anecdotes which, in turn, influenced Gothic fiction. By way of Edgar Allan Poe's short stories, which were written prior to the Census, and texts such as Bram Stoker's *Dracula*, which were contemporary with it, her chapter adeptly exposes and explores the fascinating cross-fertilising relationship between cultural and scientific discourses at the fin de siècle.

The fourth and final Part of this collection, 'Twentieth- and Twenty-First-Century Gothic Dreams and Nightmares: Weird Fiction, Horror Film, Television, and Video Games', consists of four chapters devoted to modern and contemporary Gothic parasomnias across different literary modes and media. Elisabete Lopes's 'Stranger Things: Nightmarish Realities in Thomas Ligotti's Fiction' considers dreams and nightmares as a portal into Ligotti's postmodern Lovecraftian-influenced horror tales, a form that came naturally to this contemporary American horror writer who once described himself as 'a professional at bad dreams' for whom nightmares served as 'the first and foremost source' of his horror fiction. By way of a detailed examination of four of his hybrid Gothic/weird tales, Lopes argues that the dream in Ligotti's work shares much in common with Freud's definition of trauma – a powerful overstimulation that is psychically challenging to process. In consistently unsettling tales deploying the Suburban Gothic, a novelistic sub-type that interrogates domestic and national American ideals, Ligotti stages encounters between the supernatural and the self. While consistently playing out ontological crises involving the intrusion of cosmic horror that destabilises the characters' beliefs about the worlds in which they live, nightmares in Ligotti's fiction also reveal the haunting horrors concealed within. As Lopes notably illustrates, Ligotti also actualised psychiatrist Frederik Van Eeden's lucid dreaming principles from his article, 'Study of Dreams' (1913), that claimed dreamers could gain awareness within, and over, their dreams, experiencing transformative revelations that could enable them to tackle their fears and traumas.

Murray Leeder's 'Night Walking: The Oneiric Horror Cinema' also briefly engages with the question of trauma while undertaking the daunting challenge of examining dreams and nightmares across more than a century of big-screen horror, from pre- and early cinema to proto-horror films like *The Avenging Conscience* (1914) and *The Cabinet of Dr. Caligari* (1920), the symbolic Freudian sequences in *Cat People* (1942), *Spellbound* (1945), and *Vertigo* (1958), and late twentieth-century serial horror films. Tracing the oneiric qualities of cinema back to the late eighteenth-century phantasmagoria, Leeder discusses the claim that films often work on 'dream logic'. He considers the longstanding analogy between film and dreams in film theory that dates as far back as Hugo Munsterberg in 1916 and notes linkages with Surrealism and the first attempts to claim horror films as artistically valid – as when *Minotaure* praised the 'oneiric power' of *King Kong* (1933). Leeder adeptly presents an overview of the theorisation of dreams and nightmares in film, ranging from the avant-garde and French apparatus theorists, through to such interpretive analyses as Robin Wood's Freudian-Marxist reading of film as our 'collective nightmare' and Steven Jones's reading of the *Nightmare on Elm Street* franchise that features extensive dream sequences through the lens of the phenomenon known as recurring nightmare. While dreams and nightmares often serve to subvert and/or complicate classical film conventions and allow for a level of formal and aesthetic experimentation, they may possess, Leeder provocatively argues, the special power of bringing to the fore horrifying socio-political realities from which audiences are provoked to awaken.

In 'Building the Gothic Channel: Dreams, Spectral Memories, and Temporal Disjunctions in *The Witcher*', Lorna Piatti-Farnell turns her attention to the Gothic dream on the small screen in the form of a Gothic-inflected Netflix fantasy series by Polish author, Andrzej Sapkowski. She illustrates how dreams work in this series in a multiplicity of ways. As metaphorical channels, they merge and blend to form a bewildering, yet internally logical, path of storytelling. Dreams thus bridge the gap between the Gothic and fantasy genres while serving to mediate and subvert history, rendering it changeable and unreliable. Linking timelines and traversing geographies, dreams in *The Witcher* act as a 'pivotal site of temporal experimentation' that provides a gothicised understanding of experience, self-identity, and memory, projecting time as a negotiable, rather than a cemented, structure. Capitalising on a number of genre-bending techniques involving mutating monsters, dark magic, and horror-style transformations, *The Witcher*'s multi-functional dreams engage with and unsettle our understanding of evil, humanity, and Otherness.

The volume concludes with James Aaron Green's chapter, '"Lest the Night Carry on Forever": The Transcendent Gothic Unconscious in *Bloodborne*', an action role-playing video game by FromSoftware. By way of in-depth textual analyses, Green illustrates how the game blends traditional Gothic elements from such Victorian classics as *Carmilla* and *Dracula* with cosmic horror ingredients inspired by the works of H. P. Lovecraft, especially in its conjoining of two key topoi of the tradition – blood and the unconscious. Green builds upon the emergent scholarship devoted to *Bloodborne* by examining its depiction of dreams, nightmares, and altered states of consciousness, connected ideas whose primacy is signalled in the game's dream-like opening and the fact that the playing experience itself is a form of nightmare affect. Citing Dina Khapaeva's assertion that Lovecraft was formative to the 'creation of a consumer culture for the nightmare' (92), this chapter finds Gothic-influenced video games like *Bloodborne* poised to sustain that culture and perpetuate the oneiric as a culturally resonant force.

As the chapters in *Gothic Dreams and Nightmares* illustrate, the oneiric has remained a culturally resonant force both in Gothic literature and horror film since their advent. Recognising both the powerful and significant role of the subliminal that has developed in tandem with the sublime, and the fact that dreams and nightmares offer a sublime-subliminal experience in their terrifying yet tantalising transgression of traditionally restrictive and forbidding ideological boundaries, the Gothic offers a unique reminder: human beings are complex, imaginative creatures whose dreams and nightmares serve as portals into the intricate consciousnesses and creative possibilities – inspirational and terrifying, overwhelming and tantalising, transcendent and non-transcendent – of the individual, collective, and cosmic unknowns. Whether our nightmares find their source in childhood trauma or, as Karl Marx claims, in 'the tradition of all the dead generations … [weighing] on the brains of the living', the current and prospective terror of annihilation threatened in the Anthropocene, or, as Charles Thorpe has recently argued, in a 'decaying [capitalist] system stubbornly resisting its slow death' (1), the Gothic remains, at its darkest and most bizarre, and as its dream-work gives ample evidence, a malleable and fertile mode in which authors and artists have found singular imaginative expression. Merging the Kantian motto of the Enlightenment, *sapere aude*, 'dare to know', with the Romantic conception of the imagination as another way of knowing, Gothic-influenced authors, artists, and filmmakers have embraced a radical epistemology of *daring to dream*, even and especially when dreams may transmogrify into vivid, spirit-arresting nightmares, lending expression to those forces and messages that defy repression and seem, tauntingly, to be both ineffable and beyond representation.

Notes

1 In 1783, Horace Walpole penned a note on a copy of his catalogue of that year's Royal Academy exhibition referencing Fuseli, among others, for his 'bombast & extravagant [paintings], without true dignity' (Myrone 35).

2 In her provocative 2011 study of 117 Hmong immigrants who experienced unexplained nocturnal death in the United States, Shelley Adler argues that their experience of SUNDS (Sudden Unexpected Nocturnal Death Syndrome) occurred as a result of their shared cultural belief in spirits, in combination with an obscure cardiac arrhythmia prevalent in Southeast Asia.

3 Frayling cites *Public Advertiser*, 31 May 1790, in relation to this idea and notes that '[t]his rumour was evidently still in the ether when one of his biographies appeared in 1830, three years after Fuseli's death; the biographer felt the need to dismiss it' (73).

4 Robert Louis Stevenson reportedly conceived *Strange Case of Dr. Jekyll and Mr Hyde* after a dream he had while taking morphine for pain (Luckhurst xi). In his Introduction to Freud's book *On Cocaine*, David Carter references Jürgen vom Scheidt's study from 1973 'on the possible role of Freud's experiments on himself in stimulating his interest in dream interpretation' (xi). While Walter Benjamin's use of drugs is common knowledge, in the Introduction to Benjamin's book *On Hashish*, Marcus Boon notes, in regard to the Surrealists,

that '[a]lthough a number of [them] … used drugs, contrary to popular belief André Breton was staunchly anti-drugs and the exploration of consciousness using chemicals – and he expelled from the group any members who took drugs' (5).

5 This association between dreams and irrationality persisted into the Victorian era. According to Ronald Pearsall, among Victorian writers '[t]here was not much place … for the dream itself, which was considered evidence of ill health or the harbinger of madness' (431). Dreams were still regarded as 'the province of the ill or the maladjusted' (434).

6 Robert Macnish's Chapter XI, entitled 'Sleep-walking', notes three conditions of this phenomenon, one of which is 'A complete or partial suspension of the judgment' (151). Susan Manning discusses the empirical medical readings of somnambulism in works by both Scottish Enlightenment and American thinkers. Benjamin Rush 'fully pathologized' and medicalised this dream disorder in his 1812 publication *Medical Inquiries and Observations Upon the Diseases of the Mind* as 'the effect of unsound or imperfect sleep … always induced by morbid or irregular action in the blood-vessels of the brain' (300).

7 Robert Miles has gotten a lot of mileage out of this misreading. His essay on 'Seeing Ghosts' in the essay collection *Haunted Europe* likewise deals with Goya's painting and suggests that many have misinterpreted it. Labelling it one of the most iconic images of European haunting, 'an image frequently misunderstood' (24), Miles claims that its meaning turns on the word *sueno*, the painting's significance being that one of the offshoots of reason is monsters (24–5).

8 Both John Bond and Edward Binns (*Anatomy of Sleep* 1842) note that while it was speculated that John Polidori died of suicide, he was also rumoured to have died either of Incubus or the use of laudanum to ward off the attacks (Sharpless and Doghramji 67).

9 Although Martin Myrone notes that Fuseli illustrated 'contemporary sensationalist literature, specifically the gothic novel', he is 'not able to identify simple and direct parallels between Fuseli and the gothic novel, as if the latter were a clearly apprehended literary genre in its own day' ('Henry' 292). Sophia Andres argues, however, that in her death scene in *Frankenstein*, Elizabeth Lavenza could be Mary Shelley's response to the recumbent woman in Fuseli's *The Nightmare*. Similar to the critical readings of Joseph (109) and Mishra (222), who read Elizabeth's death scene as based on Fuseli's painting, Anne K. Mellor argues that Shelley deliberately responds to Fuseli's ambivalent sexualised-terrorised female sleeper, revealing a Victor Frankenstein who is both fearful and desirous – to the point of possible necrophilia – of his wife's sexuality (121). While De Quincey's *Confessions* is not a Gothic novel, it partakes of its atmospherics and themes and even specifically references Fuseli's painting and its sleeper as emblematic of the opium eater's drug-induced paralysis:

> The opium-eater loses none of his moral sensibilities, or aspirations: he wishes and longs, as earnestly as ever, to realize what he believes possible,

and feels to be exacted by duty; but his intellectual apprehension of what is possible infinitely outruns his power, not of execution only, but even of power to attempt. He lies under the weight of incubus and night-mare: he lies in sight of all that he would fain perform, just as a man forcibly confined to his bed by the mortal languor of a relaxing disease, who is compelled to witness injury or outrage offered to some object of his tenderest love: – he curses the spells which chain him down from motion: – he would lay down his life if he might but get up and walk; but he is powerless as an infant, and cannot even attempt to rise. (67)

On *Frankenstein* as eliciting the experience of nightmare, the *British Critic* reviewer, as if still in the throes of distress, described the powerful effects of the tale developed from Mary Shelley's 'waking dream' (Shelley, 'Author's' 195) to be opiate-like: 'we feel ourselves as much harassed, after rising from the perusal of these three spirit-wearying volumes, as if we had been over-dosed with laudanum, or hag-ridden by the night-mare' (qtd. in Wolfson 387). In regard to Poe's use of Fuseli in 'Usher', Lynne P. Shackelford notes how Poe's 'narrator assumes the exact position of Fuseli's dreaming damsel', retiring to his sleeping apartment directly above Madeline's vault (19).

10 Mishra is, however and notably, not alone in his proto-postmodern reading of the Gothic sublime as wrestling with 'the inherent problem of self-transcendence' (40). A decade earlier, David B. Morris argued that the Gothic sublime is 'utterly without transcendence'. It is, according to Morris, 'a vertiginous and plunging – not a soaring – sublime, which takes us deep within rather than far beyond the human sphere' (306). Terry Castle similarly contends that the Gothic sublime plunges us into 'a hag-ridden realm of [the] unconscious' (5). All three of these critics suggest – Mishra, Morris, and Castle – that the *Gothic* sublime plays out a failed transcendence that ultimately and unfailingly results in a psychological descent into the unconscious.

11 Piranesi's visions haunt Beckford in his *Dreams, Waking Thoughts and Incidents* (1783). He builds figurative castles in the style of Piranesi in the mountains on his journey to Bonn (83). In a fitting subsequent moment in Venice, the setting of many Gothic works, he contemplates meetings of the Three Inquisitors and the Council of Ten and draws 'chasms, and subterranean hollows, the domain of fear and torture, with chains, racks, wheels, and dreadful engines in the style of Piranesi' (122–4). In his meditations on the effects of his opium addiction in the latter work, De Quincey describes himself, in language resonant of Fuseli's *The Nightmare*, as oppressed by 'the weight of incubus and nightmare' (67). In chronicling the significant changes in his dreams, he specifically references Piranesi's *Carceri* with its 'endless growth and self-reproduction' as resembling splendid yet tormenting dream 'architecture' (71).

12 In his 1932 essay, 'Surrealism, Yesterday, Today and Tomorrow', for example, in reference to the 'spiritual and lineally most direct forebears' of Surrealism, Breton says he will confine himself to naming a few. To this end, he very notably mentions

the chief representatives of the Gothic novel, Walpole of *The Castle of Otranto*; Mrs. Radcliffe (who Lautréamont calls the 'crazy spectre'); Monk Lewis, looming large in Sade's *Idea on the Novel* and contributing 'the indispensable revolutionary impulses' which had begun to agitate the Europe of that time; Maturin, who, having loomed over Borel and Baudelaire, is called by Lautréamont 'the Godfather-of-Shadows' – not to overlook, in the vanguard of such matters of terror, that prodigy of verbal orchestration who was Young, unquestionably the most authentic forerunner of the surrealist style, whose secret Lautréamont was the first to appropriate: 'O Nights of Young! how many headaches you have given me!' (84–5)

13 Myers's observations about illogicalities in Stevenson's psychological representation of Jekyll/Hyde were painstakingly detailed in two letters he sent to Stevenson in February and March of 1886. Stevenson responded to the first letter thanking Myers for taking such time and recognising the 'cleverness' and insights of Myers's commentary, promising that if his novella were ever to be published in the form of a collected works, he would make editorial changes to the text. While Myers followed up with a second list of issues and importuned Stevenson to make the changes, he never heard from Stevenson again. See pages 212–22 in Maixner.

Works cited

Adler, Shelley. *Sleep Paralysis: Night-Mares, Nocebos, and the Mind-Body Connection*. Rutgers University Press, 2011.

Alvarado, Carlos. 'On the Centenary of Frederic W. H. Myers's *Human Personality and Its Survival of Bodily Death*.' *The Journal of Parapsychology*, vol. 68, 2004, pp. 3–43.

Andersen, Jørgen. 'Giant Dreams: Piranesi's Influence in England.' *English Miscellany*, vol. 3, 1952, pp. 49–59.

Andres, Sophia. 'Narrative Challenges to Visual, Gendered Boundaries: Mary Shelley and Henry Fuseli.' *Journal of Narrative Theory*, vol. 31, 2001, pp. 257–82.

Appignanesi, Lisa. *Mad, Bad and Sad: A History of Women and the Mind Doctors From 1800 to the Present*. McArthur & Company, 2007.

Baldick, Chris and Robert Mighall. 'Gothic Criticism.' *A New Companion to the Gothic*, edited by David Punter. Wiley-Blackwell, 2012, pp. 267–87.

Baxter, Andrew. *An Enquiry into the Nature of the Human Soul*. James Bettenham, 1733, 2 vols.

Benjamin, Walter. 'Dream Kitsch: Gloss on Surrealism.' *Selected Writings, 1927–1934*, Vol. 2, Part 1, edited by Michael Jennings. The Belknap Press of Harvard University Press, 1999.

Binns, Edward. *Anatomy of Sleep; or, The Art of Procuring Sound and Refreshing Slumber at Will*. John Churchill, 1842.

Bond, John. *An Essay on the Incubus, or Night-Mare*. D. Wilson and T. Durham, 1753.

Boon, Marcus. 'Walter Benjamin and Drug Literature. Introduction.' *On Hashish* by Walter Benjamin. The Belknap Press of Harvard University Press, 2006, pp. 1–12.

Breton, André. *What Is Surrealism: Selected Writings*. Pluto Press, 1978.

Bridgwater, Patrick. *De Quincey's Gothic Masquerade*. Rodopi, 2004.

Bridgwater, Patrick. *Kafka, Gothic and Fairytale*. Brill, 2003.

Carter, David. 'Introduction.' *On Cocaine* by Sigmund Freud. Hesperus Press, 2011, pp. vii–xiv.

Castle, Terry. *The Female Thermometer: Eighteenth-Century Culture and the Invention of the Uncanny*. Oxford University Press, 1995.

Connelly, Frances S. *The Sleep of Reason: Primitivism in Modern Art and Aesthetics, 1725–1907*. Penn State University Press, 1994.

Dacome, Lucia. '"To What Purpose Does It Think?": Dreams, Sick Bodies and Confused Minds in the Age of Reason.' *History of Psychiatry*, vol. 15, 2004, pp. 395–416.

De Quincey, Thomas. *Confessions of an English Opium-Eater*. Oxford University Press, 1996.

Dieterle, Bernard and Manfred Engel. 'Introduction.' *The Dream and the Enlightenment*, edited by Bernard Dieterle and Manfred Engel. Honoré Champion Éditeur, 2003, pp. 9–18.

Doody, Margaret Anne. 'Deserts, Ruins and Troubled Waters: Female Dreams in Fiction and the Development of the Gothic Novel.' *Genre*, vol. 10, 1977, pp. 529–72.

Duffin, Christopher J. 'Night-Mare and Its Treatment.' *Pharmaceutical Historian*, vol. 40, 2010, pp. 58–61.

Ekirch, A. Roger. *At Day's Close: Night in Times Past*. Norton, 2005.

Fiedler, Leslie A. *Love and Death in the American Novel*. Dell, 1966.

Ford, Jennifer. 'Samuel Taylor Coleridge and "The Pains of Sleep."' *Dreams and History: The Interpretation of Dreams from Ancient Greece to Modern Psychoanalysis*, edited by Daniel Pick and Lyndal Roper. Routledge, 2004, pp. 105–23.

Foucault, Michel. *The History of Sexuality, Vol. 3: The Care of the Self*. Vintage, 1988.

Frayling, Christopher. *Inside the Bloody Chamber: On Angela Carter, the Gothic and Other Weird Tales*. Oberon Books, 2015.

Freud, Sigmund. *The Interpretation of Dreams*, translated by Joyce Crick. Oberon Books, 2015.

Fuseli, Henry. *The Life and Writings of Henry Fuseli*, edited by John Knowles, vol. 3. Henry Colburn and Richard Bentley, 1831.

Glance, Jonathan C. '"Beyond the Usual Bounds of Reverie?" Another Look at the Dreams in Frankenstein.' *Journal of the Fantastic in the Arts*, vol. 7, no. 4, 1996, pp. 30–47.

Grubrich-Simitis, Ilse. 'How Freud Wrote and Revised His *Interpretation of Dreams*: Conflicts Around the Subjective Origins of the Book of the Century.' *Dreams and History: The Interpretation of Dreams from Ancient Greece to Modern Psychoanalysis*, edited by Daniel Pick and Lyndal Roper. Routledge, 2004, pp. 23–36.

Hamilton, Trevor. *Immortal Longings: F. W. H. Myers and the Victorian Search for Life After Death*. Imprint Academic, 2009.

Hayward, Rhodri. 'Policing Dreams: History and the Moral Uses of the Unconscious.' *Dreams and History: The Interpretation of Dreams from Ancient Greece to Modern Psychoanalysis*, edited by Daniel Pick and Lyndal Roper. Routledge, 2004, pp. 159–77.

Hobson, J. Allan. *Dreaming: A Very Short Introduction*. Oxford University Press, 2002.

Hughes, Robert. *Goya*. Knopf, 2004.

Hunter, Jack. 'Gothic Psychology, the Ecological Unconscious, and the Re-Enchantment of Nature.' *Gothic Nature*, 26 March 2020. https://gothicnaturejournal.com/gothic-psychology-the-ecological-unconscious/. Accessed 31 May 2021.

James, William. 'Frederic Myers's Service to Psychology.' *Proceedings of the Society for Psychical Research*, vol. 17, 1901, pp. 1–23.

Johnson, Samuel. *A Dictionary of the English Language*. W. Strahan, 1755, 2 vols.

Jones, Ernest. *On the Nightmare*. Liveright Publishing Corporation, 1951.

Joseph, Gerhard. 'Frankenstein's Dream: The Child is Father of the Monster.' *Hartford Studies in Literature*, vol. 7, 1975, pp. 97–115.

Kaufmann, Doris. 'Mapping the Mind in the Late Eighteenth and Early Nineteenth Centuries.' *Biographies of Scientific Objects*, edited by Lorraine Danston. University of Chicago Press, 2000, pp. 67–85.

Keeley, James P. 'Subliminal Promptings: Psychoanalytic Theory and the Society for Psychical Research.' *American Imago*, vol. 58, 2001, pp. 767–91.

Kent, L. J. and E. C. Knight. 'Introduction.' *Selected Writings of E. T. A. Hoffmann*, edited and translated by L. J. Kent and E. C. Knight. Chicago University Press, 1969, pp. 9–45.

Khapaeva, Dina. *Nightmare: From Literary Experiments to Cultural Project*, translated by Rosie Tweddle, Brill, 2013.

Kilfeather, Siobhán. 'Terrific Register: The Gothicization of Atrocity in Irish Romanticism.' *Boundary 2*, vol. 31, 2004, pp. 49–71.

Koslofsky, Craig. *Evening's Empire: A History of the Night in Early Modern Europe*. Cambridge University Press, 2011.

Luckhurst, Roger. 'Introduction.' *Strange Case of Dr. Jekyll and Mr. Hyde and Other Tales*. Oxford University Press, 2006, pp. vii–xxxii.

Ludlam, Harry. *A Biography of Dracula: The Life Story of Bram Stoker*. Published for the Fireside Press by W. Foulsham, 1962.

Lusty, Natalya and Helen Groth. *Dreams and Modernity: A Cultural History*. Routledge, 2013.

Macnish, Robert. *The Philosophy of Sleep*. W. R. McPhun, 1930.

Maixner, Paul, ed. *Robert Louis Stevenson: The Critical Heritage*. Routledge & Kegan Paul, 1981.

Manning, Susan L. 'Enlightenment's Dark Dreams: Two Fictions of Henry Mackenzie and Charles Brockden Brown.' *Eighteenth-Century Life*, vol. 21, 1997, pp. 39–53.

Martin, Philip W. 'Nightmare.' *The Handbook of the Gothic*, edited by Marie Mulvey-Roberts. Palgrave Macmillan, 2009, pp. 206–7.

Matheson, Neil. *Surrealism and the Gothic: Castles of the Interior*. Routledge, 2017.

Mellor, Anne K. *Mary Shelley: Her Life, Her Fiction, Her Monsters*. Routledge, 1989.

Miles, Robert. 'Brown's American Gothic.' *The Oxford Handbook of Charles Brockden Brown*, edited by Philip Barnard, Hilary Emmett, and Stephen Shapiro. Oxford University Press, 2019, pp. 411–25.

Miles, Robert. *Gothic Writing 1750–1820: A Genealogy*. Manchester University Press, 2002.

Miles, Robert. 'Seeing Ghosts: The Dark Side of the Enlightenment.' *Haunted Europe: Continental Connections in English-Language Gothic Writing, Film and New Media*, edited by Evert Jan Van Leeuwen and Michael Newton. Routledge, 2020, pp. 17–35.

Mishra, Vijay. *The Gothic Sublime*. State University of New York Press, 1994.

Morris, David B. 'Gothic Sublimity.' *New Literary History*, vol. 16, 1985, pp. 299–319.

Morton, Lisa. *Ghosts: A Haunted History*. Reaktion Books, 2015.

Mulvey-Roberts, Marie. 'The Female Gothic Body.' *Women and the Gothic: An Edinburgh Companion*, edited by Avril Horner and Sue Zlosnik. Edinburgh University Press, 2016, pp. 106–19.

Myers, F. W. H. *Human Personality and Its Survival of Bodily Death*. Cambridge University Press, 2011, 2 vols.

Myrone, Martin. 'Henry Fuseli and Gothic Spectacle.' *Huntingdon Library Quarterly*, vol. 70, 2007, pp. 289–310.

Napier, Elizabeth R. 'Ann Radcliffe.' *DLB 39. British Novelists: 1660–1800*, edited by Martin C. Battestin. Gale, 1985, pp. 363–72.

Norton, Rictor. *Mistress of Udolpho*. Leicester University Press, 1999.

Pearsall, Ronald. *The Worm in the Bud: The World of Victorian Sexuality*. Pimlico, 1991.

Pick, Daniel and Lyndal Roper. 'Introduction.' *Dreams and History: The Interpretation of Dreams from Ancient Greece to Modern Psychoanalysis*, edited by Daniel Pick and Lyndal Roper. Routledge, 2004, pp. 1–21.

Powell, Anna. *Deleuze and Horror Film*. Edinburgh University Press, 2005.

Powell, Nicolas. *Fuseli: The Nightmare*. The Viking Press, 1972.

Radcliffe, Ann. 'On the Supernatural in Poetry.' *Gothic Documents: A Sourcebook 1700–1820*, edited by E. J. Clery and Robert Miles, Manchester University Press, 2000, pp. 163–72.

Robertson, Ritchie. 'Introduction.' *The Interpretation of Dreams* by Sigmund Freud, translated by Joyce Crick. Oxford University Press, 1999, pp. vii–xxxvii.

Rosemont, Franklin, comp. 'Surrealist Glossary.' *What Is Surrealism: Selected Writings*. Pluto Press, 1978, pp. 359–76.

Rush, Benjamin. *Medical Inquiries and Observations Upon the Diseases of the Mind*. Kimber & Richardson, 1812.

Ruskin, John. 'The Relation to Art of the Science of Light.' *The Eagle's Nest*. 2nd edn, George Allen, 1891, pp. 114–37.

Shackelford, Lynne P. 'Poe's "The Fall of the House of Usher."' *The Explicator*, vol. 45, 1986, pp. 18–19.

Shamdasani, Sonu. 'Introduction.' *From India to the Planet Mars: A Case of Multiple Personality with Imaginary Languages: A Case of Multiple Personality with Imaginary Languages*, by Théodore Flournoy. Princeton University Press, 1994, pp. ii–li.

Sharpless, Brian A. and Doghramji, Karl. *Sleep Paralysis: Historical, Psychological, and Medical Perspectives*. Oxford University Press, 2015.

Shelley, Mary. 'Author's Introduction to the Standard Novels Edition.' Frankenstein. Oxford University Press, 1994, pp. 192–7.

Shelley, Mary. Frankenstein; or, *The Modern Prometheus (The 1818 Text)*. Oxford University Press, 1994.

Sliwinski, Sharon. *Dreaming in Dark Times: Six Exercises in Political Thought*. University of Minneapolis Press, 2017.

Smith, Andrew. *Gothic Radicalism: Literature, Philosophy and Psychoanalysis in the Nineteenth Century*. Palgrave Macmillan, 2000.

Stevenson, Robert Louis. 'Chapter on Dreams.' *Strange Case of Dr. Jekyll and Mr. Hyde and Other Tales*. Oxford University Press, 2006, pp. 151–61.

Stevenson, Robert Louis. *Strange Case of Dr. Jekyll and Mr. Hyde. Strange Case of Dr. Jekyll and Mr. Hyde and Other Tales*. Oxford University Press, 2006, pp. 5–66.

Stoker, Bram. *Dracula*. Oxford University Press, 1992.

Tal, Guy. 'The Gestural Language in Francisco Goya's *Sleep of Reason Produces Monsters*.' *Word & Image*, vol. 26, 2010, pp. 115–27.

Thorpe, Charles. *Necroculture*. Palgrave Macmillan, 2016.

Townshend, Dale. *The Orders of Gothic: Foucault, Lacan, and the Subject of Gothic Writing, 1764–1824*. AMS Press, 2007.

Tyrrell, G. N. M. *The Personality of Man*. Penguin, 1946.

Walpole, Horace. *Anecdotes of Painting in England*. 2nd edn, vol. 4, J. Dodsley, 1772, 4 vols.

Walpole, Horace. *The Castle of Otranto*. Oxford University Press, 1982.

Wigginton, Rebecca. *Twilight States: Sleepwalking, Liminal Consciousness, and Sensational Selfhood in Victorian Literature and Culture*. University of Pittsburgh PhD dissertation, 2014.

Wilt, Judith. *Ghosts of the Gothic: Austen*, Eliot, & Lawrence. Princeton University Press, 1980.

Young, Robert J. C. 'Freud's Secret: *The Interpretation of Dreams* Was a Gothic Novel.' *The Interpretation of Dreams: New Interdisciplinary Essays*, edited by Laura Marcus. Manchester University Press, 1999, pp. 206–31.

Yourcenar, Marguerite. 'The Dark Brain of Piranesi.' *The Dark Brain of Piranesi and Other Essays*, translated by Richard Howard. Farrar, Straus, Giroux, 1984, pp. 88–128.

Part I

Gothic dream and nightmare theory

1

The theology of Gothic dreams

Sam Hirst

> There may be Dreams without Apparitions, as there may be Apparitions with-
> out Dreams; but Apparition in Dream may be as really an Apparition as if the
> Person who saw it was awake: The difference may be here, that the Apparition
> in a Dream is visible to the Soul only, for the Soul never sleeps. (Defoe 201)

Writing in 1727, Daniel Defoe paints a picture of the dream as a privileged
space for engagement with the spiritual world. Free of the imprisoning cage
of the body, the soul's communion with the demonic, the divine, and the
other-worldly is possible, and the visions of sleep, far from being dismissed,
are privileged over the perceptions of the waking mind. Margaret Doody
suggests that Defoe's theologised conception of the dream represents the
last vestiges of an 'old tradition which relates the dream to the promptings
of God or the Devil' that, by the late eighteenth century, had been relegated
to the superstitious past (85). It had been replaced, in fiction at least, Doody
argues, with an interest in 'the psychology of the heroine [whose] subjective
life has meaning, and [whose] dreams cry out for interpretation, but not the
old religious meaning or spiritual interpretation' (85). The reality, however,
is that both contemporary dream discourse and dreams in Gothic literature
have a more complex relationship with the theological than Doody suggests.
Her psychological readings of Gothic dreams offer valuable insights into the
subtexts of Gothic novels and unveil dreams as powerful tools of characterisation. However, like Diane Long Hoeveler's and Elisabeth Bronfen's psychoanalytic readings of the dream or Emma Clery's and Devendra Varma's
focus on Gothic dreams as narrative devices, these readings, by focusing on
an assumed secularisation of the understanding of dreams, elide the ways in
which Gothic dreams both reflect and engage meaningfully with a contemporary theologised dream discourse.[1]

Secular readings of the Gothic dream argue that the Gothic must be read
'in the context of the Western secularisation process' with Hoeveler going
so far as to assert that Gothic novels were not only a reflection, but in
fact a tool, of this secularisation process, broadly understood as an oscil-
lating but constant movement away from supernatural belief ('*Children*'
139). This understanding of the 'secular', however, does not accord either
with the Taylorian model Hoeveler references or the reality of the period.

Secularisation, Charles Taylor suggests, is not the absence or eradication of theological belief and interpretative frameworks, but rather a 'pluralism of outlooks, religious and non- and anti-religious' (437). Secularisation involves a proliferation of multiple co-existing discourses as 'different construals, views which intelligent, reasonably undeluded people, of good will, can and do disagree on' (11). The fundamentally theological reading offered by Defoe did not disappear with him. Indeed, as Jason Ā. Josephson Storm argues there was never a 'hegemonic ontology' in which 'spiritualised interpretations' and 'enchanted ontologies' were completely eradicated in relationship to the dream or more broadly the supernatural (5). A theologised conception of the supernatural potential of the dream survived not only in the form of folk belief but also in later works on the dream, such as Reverend Saalfeld's *Philosophical Discourse on the Nature of Dreams* (1764) and Malcolm Macleod's *The Mystery of Dreams Revealed* (1794). These theological understandings of the dream did not dominate the discourse but did co-exist, sometimes symbiotically and, at other times, combatively, with the development of an increasingly medicalised and proto-psychologised conception of the dream. However, as this chapter will demonstrate, the early British Gothic as a genre is most frequently engaged with theologised conceptions of supernatural dreams. By tracing a history of theological dream belief, this chapter will show how Gothic texts reflect and interrogate theological conceptions of the dream. It will also suggest that while medicalised conceptions of the dream increasingly influenced their depiction in the Gothic, this influence resulted not in the eradication of the supernatural but rather a focus on ambiguity and indecipherability, in which multiple competing interpretations are offered by the texts and left ultimately unresolved.

The dark dreams of the Gothic

> The Night is the Divells Blacke booke, wherein he recordeth all our transgressions ... when Night in her rustie dungeon hath imprisoned our ey-sight, and that we are shut seperatly in our chambers from resort, the divell keepeth his audit in our sin-guilty consciences. (Nashe 12)

The Early Modern period inherited from the Medieval a conception of both the dream and sleep as 'replete with earthly and spiritual dangers' to the 'body and soul, both of which required protection during the defenceless hours of sleep' (Handley 69). In his 1594 treatise *The Terrors of the Night*, Thomas Nashe lays out this conception of the dream as a state in which people, their reason and will dormant, are most endangered by the Devil, who, 'busie to disturbe us and torment us' (5), manipulates our dreams to draw us into sin. It should be noted, however, that even at this early stage, theological conceptions coexist alongside 'natural' explanations. As Charles Stewart articulates, in the conception of the dark dream 'evil thoughts were simultaneously exogenous and endogenous; demons activated what was already there' (289). For Nashe, the endogenous element was linked to a body's prevailing humours, and dreams functioned predominantly as the 'eccho of our conceipts in the day' (15). However, these natural catalysts for dreams could be activated, enlarged upon, or utilised by demonic forces.

The idea of dreams as open to demonic influence was particularly prevalent in the immediate Post-Reformation period until the early to mid-seventeenth century. In this period, the 'demonological explanation' (Bath and Newton) of spiritual phenomena predominated among Protestant denominations. In the immediate aftermath of the rejection of Catholicism, the denial of miracles and dreams as divinely ordained signs, and the rejection of the Catholic conception of the ghost as the spirit of the dead returning from purgatory, proliferated. Such signs and apparitions were frequently reinterpreted as the result of demonic activity. However, the connection between dreams and the demonic did not disappear along with the predominance of the demonological interpretation but came to be placed alongside other possible external origins of the dream. In 1727, Defoe notes the possibility of the influence of the demonic, the divine, lesser angelic spirits, and even the dead in *An Essay on the History and Reality of Apparitions* (207). In the 1764 translation of Reverend Saalfeld's *A Philosophical Discourse*, Saalfeld differentiates between 'domestic' (wholly natural), natural (angelic or demonic), and supernatural (originating in God) dreams (11). In 1794, Malcolm Macleod accuses those who do not believe that God and 'spirits, good or evil, operate on the minds of men, when sleep prevails over the senses' (42) of an atheistic 'Sadducism'. While each of these writers emphasises the existence of wholly 'natural' dreams, they leave open the possibility of demonic intervention.

While we might expect the Gothic, with its interest in the transgressive and the darkly supernatural, to be deeply engaged with this particular theological conception of the dream, the demonic dream is largely confined to the horror Gothic of writers such as Matthew Lewis and Charlotte Dacre. Dacre's *Zofloya, or The Moor* (1806) offers a paradigmatic example of the demonic dream. The dreams of the protagonist Victoria play an important role in her fall and are explicitly identified as demonically influenced. In the final moments of the text, the devil himself confronts Victoria and reveals that '*I* it was, that under semblance of the Moorish slave ... appeared to thee first in thy dreams, luring thee to attempt the completion of thy wildest wishes' (267). The devil's boast underlines two key elements of the idea of demonic dreams. First, it reveals the dream as a space that is particularly vulnerable to spiritual attack, as it is within the dream that the devil initiated his temptations. Second, it demonstrates the ability of the demonic dream to act as a catalyst for moral decline by building upon pre-existing desires.

A fuller example of the potential complexity of the demonic dream, its function, and its theological valence is to be found in Matthew Lewis's *The Monk* (1796) where the question of dream interpretation becomes more vexed for both character and reader. The most obviously demonic dream in the novel is that of Elvira, the mother of the persecuted Antonia, when Antonia is at risk of rape from Ambrosio's midnight intrusion:

> A frightful dream had represented to her Antonia on the verge of a precipice. She saw her trembling on the brink: every moment seemed to threaten her fall, and she heard her exclaim with shrieks, 'Save me, mother! Save me! – Yet a moment, and it will be too late!' (261)

The dream proves prescient and allows Elvira to intervene in Ambrosio's plan; however, her intervention fails ultimately to save her daughter and leads to her own death at the hands of Ambrosio, who will later be revealed as her son.

While, at first glance, the warning of the dream suggests a divine or angelic origin, the devil later claims responsibility for it as he taunts Ambrosio: 'It was I who warned Elvira in dreams of your designs upon her daughter, and thus, by preventing your profiting by her sleep, compelled you to add rape as well as incest to the catalogue of your crimes' (375).[2] The dream reveals its origin by its consequences. In discussions of dream interpretation, the results of the dream are frequently foregrounded as interpretative tools. For Defoe, the purpose of demonic dreams is 'inticement to commit an unlawful action' (207), while Saalfeld points more generally to 'unhappy' consequences (61). In both cases, Defoe and Saalfeld point to the possibility of 'diabolical deception' (Saalfeld 61). Elvira's dream fits in with one of the demonic models explored and systematised by Saalfeld in his *Philosophical Discourse*, namely that demonic dreams 'reveal things of no manner of service, what appearance soever they may put on' (39). Dream warnings, this suggests, which have no 'purpose' and cannot be positively acted on serve a demonic, not divine, purpose. The price for misinterpretation of a dream's origin, as in Elvira's case, can be steep.

Dreams are central to Ambrosio's fall in *The Monk*. After he learns that 'Rosario' is 'Matilda', he is beset by dreams that blasphemously mingle the image of the Madonna with that of Matilda in an erotic montage in which 'his unsatisfied desires placed before him the most lustful and provoking images' (61). On the following night, he dreams of Matilda again and 'already was on the point of satisfying his desires, when the faithless form disappeared, and left him to all the horrors of shame and disappointment' (76). These dreams clearly lay the foundation for his fall into sexual temptation, blurring the dream state and waking worlds, with his dream frustration being assuaged by a waking accession to passion in Matilda's arms. Erotic dreams have a long history of association with demonic promptings. As Charles Stewart articulates, 'erotic dreams have raised perennial questions about the boundaries of the self and the individual's ability to control and produce this self', which leads to questions about their origins: Do they emanate from 'an immoral life, or recent memories' or demonic interference (279)? In Ambrosio's case, these possibilities merge together and create ambiguity around the question of culpability and the precise point of his fall. The dream content could originate with the dreamer. If so, it implies existing sinful desires and suggests a certain measure of pre-existing guilt. Ambrosio's dreams, however, are framed as potentially demonic in origin. The emphasis on the fact that 'he rioted in joys *till then unknown* to him' (61; emphasis added) and an earlier assertion that he is 'so strict an observer of chastity, that he knows not in what consists the difference of man and woman' (19) suggest the demonic introduction of new 'sins' or desires into his soul's registry. Demonic or human in origin, Ambrosio's dreams are repeated and long-lasting and his waking reaction of 'shame and disappointment' (76) points to a willing engagement in the dream that is both frustrated by waking and leads to self-condemnation. This places our interpretation of Ambrosio's dreams at the centre of one of the fiercest controversies of theological dream discourse: the possibility of dream sin. As Stewart notes, in his historical overview of beliefs about erotic dreams in both the Western and Eastern Churches from the Middle Ages on, 'excusable nocturnal emissions became sinful erotic dreams if one entertained them, allowed them to linger, and, most importantly, if one consented to them' (290). The question of 'will' is key to the issue of responsibility. Lewis's depiction of Ambrosio's seemingly demonic dreams, the role they play in facilitating his downfall, and his own willing engagement in the dream's sexual content suggest an affirmation of the concept of what might be called 'dream sin' and places the start of Ambrosio's fall in a 'thought crime', rather than a physical act.

The first dream depicted in *The Monk* offers another distinctive interpretative dilemma to the reader with wider theological implications. After falling asleep in the church, Lorenzo dreams about Antonia. This prescient dream presents an allegorical representation of the later events of the novel: the love of Antonia for Lorenzo; her persecution by an 'unknown' monster whose crimes are 'Pride! Lust! Inhumanity!'; her death; and her ascent to heaven all prefigure her tragic fate (27–8). The origin and purpose of this dream remain obscure to the reader. At the level of narrative, it foreshadows one of the central plots of the novel, producing a sense of inevitability around both Ambrosio's fall and Antonia's fate. However, this dream cannot be extricated from the theological context informing the novel's depiction of dreams and should not be read only in terms of narrative function. If we judge the dream's origin from its results, its purpose is ambiguous. Lorenzo almost immediately dismisses his dream, seemingly negating some of its importance as either a demonic or divine intervention. Despite this, it could be read as a preparatory and consolatory dream from a divine, omniscient source. However, in keeping with a novel whose dreamscape is almost exclusively demonic and similar to the other abortive dream warnings of the text, this dream can be said to function demonically. In a demonic reading of the dream, the act of foretelling, far from spurring Lorenzo to action, provides a framework of inevitability which contributes to his lack of action. The dream becomes, effectively, a catalyst of inaction, which serves the demonic schemes for Ambrosio's fall and Antonia's role as victim within it.

The interpretation of the dream's origin has theological repercussions beyond the act of interpretation and the presumption of the possibility of demonic influence. A divine interpretation presumes divine total omniscience, knowing both the future and the present, and a determinism which not only foresees but predestines the fates of both Ambrosio and Antonia. While this interpretation raises the spectre of a wrathful Calvinist God and the absence of meaningful free will, a demonic interpretation of the dream conversely suggests the possibility of changing the predicted future, the dreamer's culpability for not doing so, and the importance of the individual will. A secondary, connected question is the nature of the devil's omniscience. Saalfeld echoes a common view when he suggests that the devil is a 'sagacious but yet a limited spirit' (62) whose ability to foretell the future is limited to the natural consequences of pre-existing causes and based on present circumstances (61). The devil, if responsible for Lorenzo's dream, uses the dream to provide a version of the future based on the current placement of the main players, but it is Lorenzo's reaction and the dream itself which determine the outcome rather than divine pre-determinism. Lorenzo's misinterpretation of the dream, therefore, like Ambrosio's misinterpretation of his own dreams as 'natural' and Elvira's interpretation of her dreams as divine, has significant consequences. The interpretation of dreams in the novel has narrative repercussions, highlights theological subtexts pivotal to understanding the ideological concerns of the novel – namely, questions around free will, determinism, theodicy, and demonic and divine activity – and represents specific theological stances in relation to dreams, demonic influence, and demonic knowledge.

The dream as spiritual state

> But the Eye of the mind and soul is Incorporeal, and therefore it can well see, apprehend and comprehend things Incorporeal and Spiritual, especially when it shakes off, and as it were quits itself of the Chains and heavy fetters of its earthly Tabernacle, and the sensual Faculties of the external palpability, as comes to pass in Visions and Dream. (Tryon 178–9)

A dark or demonic conception of the dream does not dominate in Gothic fiction more broadly, despite its importance to the horror Gothic. As has been noted, other supernatural sources for the dream were provided by dream theorists: angelic visitation, divine intervention, providential guidance, or spiritual communication. Theological valence continued to be ascribed to the dream. There are numerous reasons for this, including the failure of proto-psychological and medicalised explanations to fully explain dream function or provenance; the mundanity of dreams as an almost universal experience within the context of Christianity as a 'lived religion' in the period (Shaw 9); and the importance of dreams as evidence for the immateriality and immortality of the soul and the functioning of Providence. Thomas Tryon's assertion that the 'soul is incorporeal' (178) and freed in sleep was a standard interpretation. The dream was used as evidence of the soul's ability to function without the body, suggesting the immateriality and immortality of the soul, in popular works as diverse in both origin and content as French Reformed Church theologian Charles Drelincourt's wildly popular *The Christian's Consolation Against the Fears of Death* (1641), Presbyterian Andrew Baxter's *An Enquiry into the Nature of the Human Soul* (1733), and Catherine Crowe's *The Night-Side of Nature* (1848). These texts all emphasise a conception of body/soul duality rooted in a Christian understanding of the immortal and immaterial soul as an 'image of the divine Eternal Spirit' (Tryon 31), which in dreams is 'to a certain degree freed from its impediments [and] may enjoy somewhat of its original privilege' (Crowe 47). This reverses the conception of the dream as a space of particular danger, instead foregrounding the dream as a space of communication between the dreamer and the spiritual world.

As Tryon and, later, Malcolm Macleod, both emphasise, this idea of the dream as a space of communication may include communion with the dead. As Tryon argues,

> By reason of that Affinity or Similitude between incorporeal Beings, and the Soul of man ... it comes to pass, that Souls departed or separated from their Bodies (which divorce we call Death) do often Communicate their desires, and

reveal various Secrets unto their Friends; for Dreams are Incorporeal and the Souls deceased have no other way to impart their Secrets. (68)

The modern delineation between a 'real' ghost-sighting and the dismissal of an apparition as 'just a dream' is not a firm boundary replicated in the eighteenth century. As Defoe notes, an 'Apparition in Dream may be as real an Apparition as if the Person who saw it was awake' (201). Gothic texts abound with ghosts who appear primarily in dreams but whose reality is attested to by the consequence of the dreams. In Clara Reeve's *The Old English Baron* (1787), the hero Edmund is visited in dreams by his parents who reveal their own murders. The dream unveils the truth and allows for a retributive justice. Reeve famously sought to correct Horace Walpole's supernatural excesses in *The Castle of Otranto* (1764) by keeping her supernatural appearances within the 'verge of the probable' (3). Included in this idea of the 'probable' are dreams as points of communion with the dead, in which an assumption of the immateriality and immortality of the soul is supported by its action in sleep, the ability to communicate with the dead in dreams, and the spirit survival represented by the ghosts. The dream also provides evidence of an active Providence. Edmund's dreams are one of the evidentiary proofs of the text which 'when taken together furnish a striking lesson to posterity, of the over-ruling hand of Providence' (Reeve 136). The supernatural nature of the dreams reinforces a concept not only of a natural Providence, worked out through natural laws, but an active Providence in which the divine intervenes directly in the mortal world. The theologised concept of the dream as space of spiritual communion here is essential not only to the development of the plot but to its underlying theological and providential subtext.

Reeve is not the only Gothic writer to include the dream as a space of communication with the supernatural. Texts such as Ann Radcliffe's *The Romance of the Forest* (1792) and T. J. Horsley Curties's *Ethelwina; or, The House of Fitz-Auburne* (1799) incorporate this underlying conception of the dream but also foreground the question of interpretation. In *Ethelwina*, the eponymous heroine, imprisoned by the villainous Leopold, having learnt the tragic fate of her dead father and the current parlous condition of her brother, is beset by guilt, self-blame, and despair. She holds herself partly responsible for her family's fate, believing them murdered or imprisoned 'for her sake' by Leopold who seeks to marry her and thereby inherit the family property. In sleep, 'dreams of torment pursued her' (234), including visions of Leopold's persecution and her brother's danger. They are fears which arise from her current situation and guilty conscience. But dreams soon become a contested space between different points of origin. Her father enters the dream and 'she was again in her present prison in comparative safety' (234). Returned to her place of imprisonment, it remains unclear whether this 'return' is within the dream or a return to consciousness. The dream here changes in tone and content as her father appears in a quasi-angelic guise, 'countenance illumined by a smile of transport' (234) and proceeds to offer counsel, comfort, and absolution from her 'imaginary guilt' before warning her to prepare for 'the momentous crisis of thy fate' (235). The last words are so loud that they wake Ethelwina, who hears the same voice once again after waking and sees the door close through which her father had entered her room in her dream. The line between dream and waking reality is blurred and Ethelwina is concerned with the question not of the source of the dream but of its reality, wary of being 'bigotedly superstitious' in her response (237). Ultimately, Ethelwina takes a cautious and evidence-based approach. She views the dream as 'of so extraordinary a nature' that it was not to be 'passed lightly over' (237), compares the dream to scriptural concepts of providential divine control, and notes the 'powerful effect' of the dream in 'restoring consolation' (238) before deciding on its divine, or divinely influenced, origin. The dream's contested space has become dominated by a providential force, expressed through a visitation of the dead allowed to fulfil specific providential purposes. In comparing the message of the dream to already known or accepted theological principles, Ethelwina, to some extent, enacts the interpretative practice of Wesleyan Methodism. Often associated with an Enthusiastic and misguided acceptance of all dreams as divinely sourced, Wesley's own teaching emphasises that all spirits, dreams, and visions should be 'brought to the only certain test, the law and the testimony' (86). This echoing of Wesleyan thought in the novel does not suggest a Wesleyan alignment in the staunch Anglican, Horsley Curties, but rather points to an overlap between Enthusiastic and moderate Anglican discourse in relation to the interpretation of potentially supernatural dreams.

In *The Romance of the Forest*, the question of interpretation is similarly foregrounded, with Radcliffe providing a model that avoids the sceptical, Enthusiastic, and superstitious excesses deplored by dream theologians such as Saalfeld. The heroine Adeline has four dreams. The first, while she is being held in a cottage by the man she believes to be her father, includes a vision of herself as beaten and bloodied with a warning voice crying, 'Depart this house, destruction hovers here' (41). The last three dreams occur in quick succession when she is staying at the ruined abbey where her real father, of whose existence she is at the time unaware, was murdered on his brother's order. In the first of these dreams, she enters a previously unknown chamber, where she finds a dying man. In the second, she wanders the abbey and sees a figure who chases her. In the third, she follows the man into a room containing a coffin holding the dying man from the first dream, weltering in blood, and hears a voice speaking 'in the voice she had heard before' (110). This voice appears to connect the first dream to this later series, allowing the dreams to be connected as tools of an active Providence. The dreams are clearly supernatural in origin. Radcliffe foregrounds the fact that the dreams contain previously unknown places and information, which allow Adeline to become an agent of Providence in 'punish[ing] the murderer of her father' (343). It is also possible to interpret the dying figure not only as a dream representation of her father but as her father's spirit, although this is left ambiguous. The dream is clearly presented, however, as a space of supernatural communication and in Adeline's response, Radcliffe offers a model of appropriate interpretative practice. The reader is told that 'The longer she [Adeline] considered these dreams, the more she was surprised: they were so terrible, returned so often, and seemed to be so connected with each other, that she could scarcely think them accidental; yet, why they should be supernatural, she could not tell' (110). Leaving open the possibility of supernatural meaning, Adeline avoids a fanatical scepticism which, as Saalfeld warns, 'reject[s] all dreams, as insignificant sallies of our imagination' (116) while equally avoiding a superstition which holds 'all dreams to be significative' and seeks to interpret them using set systems (111). Many accounts of the Gothic focus on the genre's dismissal of 'superstition', but it is worth noting that the discourse of the period differentiated between superstitious and Enthusiastic interpretative frameworks, frequently condemning both. While superstition was connected to fear, inherited religious frameworks, and external priestly manipulation, Enthusiasm was understood in relation to 'hope, pride, presumption, warm imagination together with ignorance' (Hume 82), and the idea of privileged access to the supernatural and the divine. Saalfeld is particularly harsh in his condemnation of Enthusiastic dream interpretation, stating that 'all dreams, which pretend to reveal new articles of faith or practice, are diabolical temptations' (127). Adeline, by withholding judgement, waiting on the results of the dream, and admitting a lack of knowledge, avoids Enthusiastic as well as superstitious extremes. Her response, while seemingly simple, is a carefully calibrated middle ground between the interpretative excesses which haunted theologised conceptions of the dream and underlines Radcliffe's consistent attempts to map a *via media* between them in relation to understandings of the supernatural.

The ambiguous dreams of the Gothic

There is no dream or vision which the wildest or most heated imagination can invent, which an ingenious man, and one who is 'fortified' with a pre-acquired aptitude in these studies, will not make applicable to any subject he pleases. (*Enquiry* 12)

As in the case of *Ethelwina* and *The Romance of the Forest*, within wider dream discourse the possibility of a natural explanation was mooted alongside theologised conceptions of the possibility of the supernatural dream. As the eighteenth century progressed, a range of medicalised and proto-psychological conceptions of the dream proliferated. The humoral theories of Nashe and Tryon were replaced, thanks to the 'neurological turn' (Handley 20) heralded by the pioneering work of Thomas Willis, William Cullen, and George Cheyne, with approaches which focused on the neurological foundations of the dream. Associationist theories, based on John Locke's *An Essay Concerning Human Understanding* (1690) and David Hartley's *Observations on Man* (1749), increasingly dominated the discussion of natural dreams in both theologised dream theories, such as Saalfeld's, and more openly sceptical work such as that of John Ferriar. Ferriar's *Theory of Apparitions* (1813) also points to the ways in which narratives of madness, mental disturbance or imbalance, and auditory and visual hallucinations were frequently applied as possible explanations for seemingly supernatural dreams. However, as Handley notes, there was a 'persistent fusion of natural and supernatural explanations of sleep' (28).

Deists, atheists, and critics of Enthusiasm often pointed to the essential indecipherability of miraculous signs and dreams. This is a key motif in Radcliffe's *Gaston de Blondeville* (1826), in which each supernatural sign pointing to the guilt of the defendant is reread, according to the prejudices of the interpreters, as proof of the plaintiff's complicity with witchcraft. The anonymous author of *An Enquiry into the Pretensions of Richard Brothers*, which deals with a man claiming to be a prophet and nephew of Christ, highlights this concern in relation to dreams, arguing that 'there is no dream' which an interested party 'will not make applicable to any subject he pleases' (12). In later Gothic texts, rather than seeing an entirely secular scepticism or the evacuation of theological valence for Gothic dreams, as many critics suggest, we find the influence of this ever-increasing proliferation of natural explanations alongside various supernatural interpretations. A multiplicity of meanings is offered, including theological interpretations. To some extent, this multiplicity points towards an inherent indecipherability and the potential for dreams to be interpreted according to the desires of the dreamer. However, this multiplicity can also be read as a demonstration of the proliferation of different views and interpretative frameworks suggested by Taylor's model of secularisation, with Gothic texts deliberately creating and reflecting on the ambiguity of supernatural signs and the overlapping spaces of the borders of the supernatural, madness and deception.

Mary Shelley's 'The Dream' (1831) foregrounds such a multiplicity of interpretations in a polyphonic text in which the heroine, Constance, seeks guidance in dreams on her potential marriage by following a folkloric tradition of sleeping on 'St Catherine's Shelf', a dangerous cliff-side ledge, to receive a desired vision. Before Constance seeks her dream, alternative interpretations of such dreams are contested. The king suggests that an 'infatuated' Constance will 'take the disturbed visions that such uneasy slumber might produce for the dictates of heaven' (220). The narrator appears to align themselves with this sceptical reading by interjecting that 'there is no feeling more awful than that which invades a weak human heart bent upon gratifying its ungovernable impulses in contradiction to the dictates of conscience' (221). These voices offer both a medicalised (disturbed sleep) and psychological explanation (suppressed desires and self-deception) for the dream; however, the construction of the narrative deliberately revokes the pre-eminence of these two voices, allowing them to stand as a dissonant polyphonic chorus questioning, but not entirely negating, Constance's later experience and interpretation of the dream as supernatural. The dream foretells a future for Gaspar of imprisonment and suffering. At this point, 'a veil fell from Constance's eyes; a darkness was dispelled' (225), and she has a moment of revelation in which she realises the false principles under which she has been acting in rejecting Gaspar. While this dream can be read sceptically, it may equally be read as a monitory dream, including a prescient vision of an avoidable future, with visible 'waking' effects in Constance's revolution of feeling and thought. The fact that the text allows Constance's version of the dream to close the narrative, ending with her act of testimony with no sceptical reply, leaves these different interpretations of the dream in an unresolved tension.

A similar ambiguity is foregrounded in the anonymously published 'The Astrologer's Prediction, or, The Maniac's Fate' (1826). This interpretative conundrum is apparent in the title itself, which focuses on a fantastic uncertainty between a natural explanation of madness, and an emphasis on the possibility of fortune-telling and a supernaturally understood concept of deterministic fate. The story focuses on the narrative of Reginald, who meets an astrologer who predicts a dark fate for him. In an attempt to avoid his destiny, Reginald, who is depicted as unstable throughout the text, leaves his home and marries. After returning home years later, however, his mental health begins to decline, though he affirms to his wife that she is safe and that 'thy Reginald cannot harm thee; he may be wretched, but he never shall be guilty!' (68). It is at this point in the narrative that a pivotal dream or vision occurs, which is the catalyst for Reginald's murder of his wife and which is worth quoting at length:

Twas not a dream ..., I have seen her [his mother] and she has beckoned us to follow ... Listen while I repeat the horrid narrative. Methought as I was wandering in the forest, a sylph of heaven approached, and revealed the countenance of my mother; I flew to join her but was withheld by a sage who pointed to the western star. On a sudden[,] loud shrieks were heard, and the sylph assumed the guise of a demon. Her figure towered to an awful height, and she pointed in scornful derision to thee; yes, to thee, my Marcelia. With rage she drew thee towards me. I seized – I murdered thee; and hollow groans broke on the midnight gale. The voice of the fiendish Astrologer was heard shouting as from a charnel house, 'The destiny is accomplished, and the victim may retire with honour.' (68)

This narrative itself gestures towards a number of different possible interpretations of the dream. The narrative's insistent reference to Reginald as 'the maniac' and the opening declaration that 'the deadliest madness' (68) was in his eyes when recounting the dream, prefaces the importance of the dream's relation to madness, but the exact nature of this relationship remains unclear. Theological and supernatural interpretations of the dream are not erased from the text.

Reginald's opening declaration that the dream was 'not a dream' and his subsequent description of the changing face of the apparition (demonic, angelic, and ghostly) points back towards the conception of the dream as a space of communication. The reference to 'sylphs' also potentially encodes a reference to Emanuel Swedenborg's angelic communications, functioning as a satirical swipe at Enthusiastic visions by depicting them as self- or demonic deceptions. The revelation of the 'sylph's' identity as a demonic entity, after its metamorphosis into the image of his mother, suggests a demonic interpretation of the dream. The fact that the dream not only presents a vision of the criminal acts but places Reginald in the role of perpetrator is reminiscent of the 'dream guilt' associated with figures like Ambrosio or Victoria. This demonic reading of dream as instigator of 'sin' both through temptation or through complicity in dream sin, is also integrated with a concept of the nightmare as a tool used to discompose the mind, thus leading to madness. The demonic interpretation of the dream is somewhat problematised by the appearance of the astrologer, and more specifically, the motif of fortune-telling and the emphasis on an inescapable fate. This brings us back either to the demonic dream using prediction and a subsequent fatalistic determinism to influence events, as in *The Monk*, or to an understanding of the dream as a warning of an inescapable, divinely ordained destiny, which bears within itself a potential critique of Calvinist predeterminist theologies. Interpretations and possibilities proliferate within the dream and the relationship of the dream to madness becomes increasingly ambiguous.

The dream becomes both potential cause and symptom of madness, with the dream itself a demonic tool or a reflection of mental distress. The parallel emphasis on the astrologer's prediction and its ultimate fulfilment introduces and sustains a supernatural counternarrative, although the relation of the dream to this supernatural narrative is equally vexed. While the dream's role in the fulfilment of prophecy can be read as a validation of the astrologer's claims, it can also be understood as a self-fulfilling prophecy. The last line of the story suggests that the location of the astrologer's death and of Reginald's ultimate murder of his wife is one where 'bigotry [may] weave a spell to enthrall her misguided votaries' (69). The status of the astrologer's prediction as fact or chicanery is made uncertain by this apparent judgement on Reginald's belief in the prediction, but this sceptical reading is undermined by the accuracy of his prophecy in the text and the fact that the dream, based on its features and content, can be easily diagnosed as either supernatural or natural. The text weaves together both sceptical and theological interpretations of the dream, but even if our supernatural interpretations are discarded, the theological valence of the dream does not disappear. It remains a commentary on Enthusiasm, theological self-deception, and the dangers of erroneous dream interpretation, whether or not it also points towards the existence of active demonic intervention in these areas.

As these texts suggest, despite the influence of an ever-growing empiricism and materialism, combined with the rise of cynicism, atheism, and deism in the period, theological conceptions of the dream continued to influence Gothic texts and contemporary discussions of the dream. Gothic texts frequently represent depictions of the dream that can only be understood with reference to the theological paradigms which continued to inform dream interpretation. The revelation of knowledge in Radcliffe's *The Romance of the Forest*, the demonic intervention of *Zofloya*, or the ghostly appearances of *Ethelwina* cannot be fully understood without reference to the frameworks of belief that underpin supernatural conceptions of the dream. The dream and its meaning are not, however, static within the Gothic. Different texts reflect different understandings of the dream, its relation to Providence, demonic activity, the immortality and immateriality of the soul, the questions around total omniscience and demonic foreknowledge connected to predictive dreams, and varied understandings of life after death. Gothic dreams were written against a background of changing beliefs and a secular (in the Taylorian sense) proliferation of multiple viewpoints and interpretative strategies. The Gothic reflects this multiplicity in the theological frameworks that underpin specific depictions, in the frequent emphasis on the question of interpretation, and in a dedication in later works to interpretative ambiguity, which juxtaposes natural and theological explanations. What remains constant, however, is the importance of engaging with the potential theological valence of these portrayals of the dream. Only thus can we understand the complexity encoded within them, and the richness of the theological and the ideological subtexts connected to them.

Notes

1 See Bronfen and Hoeveler ('Heroine'), who both offer psychoanalytic readings of Adeline's dreams in *The Romance of the Forest*. See also Clery, who suggests that dreams were essentially a 'softening device' for the introduction of the supernatural as narrative effect, and Varma, who suggests that the Gothic dream's primary function is to reveal the plot.
2 The devil's interpretation rests on a contemporary definition of rape far different to our current understanding, in which 'rape' can only be judged to have occurred if the victim is awake and actively resisting.

Works cited

A Freethinker. *An Enquiry into the Pretensions of Richard Brothers*. J. Parsons, 1795.

[Anon.]. 'The Astrologer's Prediction, or the Maniac's Fate.' *The Oxford Book of Gothic Tales*, edited by Chris Baldick. Oxford University Press, 1992, pp. 63–9.

Bath, Jo and Newton, John. '"Sensible Proofs of Spirits": Ghost Belief during the Later Seventeenth Century.' *Folklore*, vol. 117, no. 1, April 2006. www-tandfonline-com.ezproxy.mmu.ac.uk/action/aboutThisJournal?show=aimsScope&journalCode=rfol20. Accessed 23 December 2020.

Bronfen, Elisabeth. *The Knotted Subject*. Princeton University Press, 1998.

Clery, Emma. *Women's Gothic: From Clara Reeve to Mary Shelley*. 2nd edn, Northcote House, 2004.

Crowe, Catherine. *The Night Side of Nature*. G. Routledge, 1854.

Dacre, Charlotte. *Zofloya, or The Moor*, edited by Kim Ian Michasiw. Oxford University Press, 1997.

Defoe, Daniel. *An Essay on the History and Reality of Apparitions*. S. Roberts, 1727.

Doody, Margaret Anne. 'Deserts, Ruins and Troubled Waters: Female Dreams in Fiction and the Development of the Gothic Novel.' *The Eighteenth-Century English Novel*, edited by Harold Bloom. Chelsea House, 2009, pp. 71–111.

Ferriar, John. *A Theory of Apparitions*. Cadell and Davies, 1813.

Handley, Sasha. *Sleep in Early Modern England*. Yale University Press, 2016.

Hartley, David. *Observations on Man, His Frame, His Duty, and His Expectations*, 2 vols. S. Richardson, 1749.

Hoeveler, Diane Long. 'The Heroine, the Abbey and Popular Romantic Textuality: *The Romance of the Forest* (1791).' *Ann Radcliffe, Romanticism and the Gothic*, edited by Dale Townshend and Angela Wright. Cambridge University Press, 2014, pp. 100–17.

Hoeveler, Diane Long. 'Regina Maria Roche's *The Children of the Abbey*: Contesting the Catholic Presence in Female Gothic Fiction.' *Tulsa Studies in Women's Literature*, vol. 31, no. 1–2, Spring/Fall 2012, pp. 137–58.

Horsley Curties, T. J. *Ethelwina; or, The House of Fitz-Auburne*. Vol. 2, Minerva, 1799.

Hume, David. 'On Superstition and Enthusiasm.' *The Philosophical Works of David Hume*, Vol. 3. Adam Black and William Tait, 1826, pp. 77–85.

Josephson Storm, Jason Ā. *The Myth of Disenchantment: Magic, Modernity, and the Birth of the Human Sciences*. University of Chicago Press, 2017.

Lewis, Matthew. *The Monk*. Penguin Classics, 1998.

Locke, John. *An Essay Concerning Human Understanding*, 4 vols. H. Saunders, W. Sleater and others, 1777.

Macleod, Malcolm. *The Mystery of Dreams Revealed*. J. Roach, 1794.

Nashe, Thomas. *The Terrors of the Night: Or, A Discourse of Apparitions*. John Danter for William Jones, 1594.

Radcliffe, Ann. *Gaston de Blondeville* in *The Posthumous Works of Ann Radcliffe with A Memoir of the Authoress*, 4 vols. Henry Colburn, 1833.

Radcliffe, Ann. *The Romance of the Forest*, edited by Chloe Chard. Oxford University Press, 1986.

Reeve, Clara. *The Old English Baron*, edited by James Trainor. Oxford World Classics, 2003.

Saalfeld Reverend, Adam Friedrich Wilhelm. *A Philosophical Discourse on the Nature of Dreams*. T. Becket and P. A. de Hondt, 1764.

Shaw, Jane. *Miracles in Enlightenment England*. Yale University Press, 2006.

Shelley, Mary. 'The Dream.' *Mathilda and Other Stories*. Wordsworth, 2013, pp. 213–25.

Stewart, Charles. 'Erotic Dreams and Nightmares from Antiquity to the Present.' *The Journal of the Royal Anthropological Institute*, vol. 8, no. 2, June 2002, pp. 279–309.

Taylor, Charles. *A Secular Age*. The Belknap Press of Harvard University Press, 2007.

Tryon, Thomas. *A Treatise of Dreams and Visions*. Tho. Fabian, 1689.

Varma, Devendra P. *The Gothic Flame*. Arthur Barker, 1957.

Wesley, John. *The Journal of John Wesley*, Vol. 1. Charles H. Kelly, 1903, 8 vols.

2

Morphean Space and the metaphysics of nightmare: Gothic theories of dreaming in Samuel Taylor Coleridge's *Notebooks*

Kirstin A. Mills

Samuel Taylor Coleridge spent his life haunted by nightmares. Suffocating, claustrophobic, peopled with clawing, biting, and attacking fiends, and often accompanied by deep physical and mental anguish, these nightmares were a frequent source of immense terror and anxiety. Characteristically, Coleridge's response to this terror was to attempt to understand it. Throughout his adult life, he obsessively turned to his notebooks to document these 'night-horrors' (*Notebooks* 2: 2398), '[d]reams damnable' (5: 5805) and 'grievous and alarming <Scream-> Dreams' (4: 5360).[1] He researched their possible causes through a vast body of contemporary literature on dreaming that ranged from the supernatural theories of Andrew Baxter's *An Enquiry into the Nature of the Human Soul* (1733) and Emanuel Swedenborg's *De Coelo et Ejus Mirabilibus, et de Inferno ex Auditis & Visis* (1758), which built on folkloric ideas about the soul communing with the spiritual world in sleep, to the emerging medical and biological theories of dreaming delineated in such works as David Hartley's *Observations on Man* (1749) and Erasmus Darwin's *Zoonomia* (1794–6), which sought to explain dreams as the biological products of digestion or bodily disease. Coleridge's notebooks attest to his extensive yet often dissatisfied engagement with these competing theories of dreaming, which failed to fully account for his deeply disturbing, haunting, and frequently physical experiences of nightmare. For Coleridge, contemporary biological models of dreaming were limited by their Lockean approach involving the 'Jack of all Trades, Association' (4: 5360), which reduced the rich products of the mind to material mechanisms independent of the will and Imagination, and thereby threatened the soul's existence. On the other hand, while supernatural theories of dreaming affirmed the soul, they were also terrifying as they connected nightmare with demonic possession, which implied the soul's proximity, in sleep, to Hell.

Plagued by these fears, which intensified the innate horrors of his nightmares, Coleridge spent his life grappling with conflicting dream theories, extending his investigations into his letters, marginalia, lectures, poetry, and lengthy discussions with friends as he gradually developed his own unique, evolving theories of dreams and nightmares. Central to these theories is his concept that dreams occurred within a unique space termed 'Somnial or Morphean Space,' which was opened paradoxically both within, and yet beyond, the brain and body, positioned liminally between the material and immaterial, and natural and supernatural, worlds (4: 5360). Despite his attempts to locate the causes of his nightmares in his minutely detailed digestive and bodily distempers, one of Coleridge's most persistent and terrifying notions, developed from Baxter, was that demonic spirits entered and took possession of the brain and body during sleep while the unconscious mind moved through the realms of Morphean Space. Morphean Space, under such conditions, became a hellish, labyrinthine prison stalked by the tormenting, demonic spirits who possessed the body. While waking to consciousness delivered the dreamer from these spiritual confines, still more terrifying was the potential for the mind to become trapped within Morphean Space and for temporary demonic possession in sleep to descend into complete bodily possession – for the nightmare to become permanent madness.

Coleridge's theories of nightmare represent an extraordinarily wide-ranging and cross-disciplinary understanding of historical and contemporary notions of the mind, brain science, and dreaming. As I have argued elsewhere, they also underpin his highly influential, published oneiric poems and are arguably the single most important influence on the conception and use of dreams in later nineteenth-century Gothic and fantastic literature.[2] With an immediate impact on the dream-laden Gothic of Romantic period writers like Mary Shelley, yet also lasting well into late Victorian Gothic, Coleridge's Morphean Space provides a model of mind that allows for the interaction and overlap between the natural and supernatural and the cognitive and spiritual worlds, without dismissing the reality of either set of phenomena. This model of mind and dreaming, insofar as it allows for such a co-existence, is decidedly Gothic in nature, where pre-Enlightenment and Enlightenment value systems and ideas are brought together. In this model, the seemingly irrational supernatural jostles against the rational and scientific, and the authority of modern rationalism is undermined by the haunting continuation of older superstitions. While Gothic fiction turned upon this nexus of the rational and supernatural, Coleridge's Morphean Space provided a potentially medical, scientific explanation for a genuine rather than illusory supernatural presence in Gothic fiction. As such, while Terry Castle has argued for the Enlightenment 'spectralization or "ghostifying" of mental space', where the supernatural was displaced from external reality to internal delusion (*Female* 141–2), Coleridge's writing both exemplifies and destabilises this claim. In Coleridge's nightmare texts – both private and poetic – the supernatural is experienced as a contemporary concern in ambiguously diseased states of mind. Coleridge's work thus participates in, and influences, the Gothic's move from the earlier geographically and temporally distanced supernatural to the later nineteenth-century Gothic's modern haunting of psychological space. At the same time, however, this ambivalence between supernatural and psychological explanations of the haunted mind, where Morphean Space allows for the simultaneous – and often terrifying – existence of both interpretations, undermines critical attempts to generalise and universalise the move from outer to inner spectres within both Gothic literature and broader philosophical and cultural accounts of supernatural and mental phenomena. In Coleridge's haunted nightmares, the ghosts are at once external and internal, visions prompted by supernatural influence.

Despite the influence of Coleridge's dream and nightmare theories on Gothic literature, critics have yet to acknowledge that these theories, and the many personal nightmare accounts through which Coleridge explores them, are themselves Gothic in nature.[3] This chapter's arguments are, like Coleridge's Morphean Space, multidimensional, but they centre around the claim that despite Coleridge's conscious attempts to distance himself from the Gothic in his literary criticism, his private writing about dreams and nightmares and his attempts to scientifically qualify and quantify his own mind are unsettlingly infused with and informed by this same mode.[4] In particular, I argue that Coleridge's theories of Morphean Space and nightmare constitute an inherently Gothic theory of mind which draws on the spatial and metaphysical logic of earlier Gothic novels. In this way, the topography and architecture of Morphean Space and its relationship to the conscious and unconscious mind, the body, and the external, material world can be mapped onto similar spatial constructions of the haunted castle and labyrinth – and the distorted perception and embodiment of fear that they engender – in Gothic novels by writers like Horace Walpole, Ann Radcliffe, and Matthew G. 'Monk' Lewis.

Moreover, while Morphean Space mirrors Gothic space, rendering Coleridge's mind a Gothic, haunted labyrinth – a thought that was deeply unsettling to him – Coleridge also turns to the language, architecture, and narrative form of the Gothic to construct written accounts of his nightmares. The Gothic, therefore, functions in his notebook writings as more than a conceptual model for the nightmare-haunted mind. In addition, Coleridge consciously adopts the Gothic's narrative form and literary techniques, considering that form the most ideal through which to evoke the emotional experience of his nightmares. As such, I argue here that not only should Coleridge's private notebook writings about nightmares be considered extensions of his literary oeuvre – narrative texts in their own right – but also, more importantly, that these nightmare writings should be, quite specifically, classified as *Gothic* texts. At the same time as it engages with the topography of Gothic novels, therefore, Coleridge's writing – personal, scientific, theoretical, and exploratory – demonstrates the Gothic's mutable power and breadth of application as a shifting, rather than a stable, mode or aesthetic limited to the generic confines of the novel.[5]

The defining feature of eighteenth-century Gothic novels is a profound emphasis on space and place, particularly spaces that intersect with the realms of death and the supernatural, exemplified by the haunted, labyrinthine castle and subterranean passages of Horace Walpole's *The Castle of Otranto* (1764), the cloistered graveyards and burial vaults of Ann Radcliffe's *The Mysteries of Udolpho* (1794), and the subterranean pacts with the devil in M. G. Lewis's *The Monk* (1796).[6] As Fred Botting argues, 'heterotopias – the temporally and geographically distinct locations such as the castles, abbeys, ruins, dungeons, burial vaults and, of course, labyrinths – endow the genre with its most distinctive features' ('Power' 245). In these spaces, the protagonists of Gothic novels experience 'the pleasurable and terrible loss of rational understanding to imaginative excess, a suspension of mastery or knowing subjectivity in an abandonment to the vicissitudes and uncertainties of the narrative' (245). As Castle puts it, in 'Gothic fiction's relentlessly "architectural" obsessions' we see not only the 'Gothic linkage between buildings and stories but the genre's presiding fantasies of self-enclaustration, physical debilitation and psychic surrender' ('Gothic' 689). Gothic space – particularly the labyrinthine, subterranean vaults and passages that imply infinite expansions and compressions of space – is often implicitly hostile. It undermines the protagonist's authority over both the mind and the body: in the former, by way of distorted, hallucinatory perception; and in the latter, by way of the protagonist being pursued and threatened within these spaces by the demonic, haunting supernatural, the tyrannical usurper, or both. Terror in the Gothic often arises from the sense of passive vulnerability experienced by the victim within these confined, haunted spaces, which are 'utterly resistant to the individual's attempts to impose his or her own order' (Punter and Byron 262). The demonic and supernatural are unconstrained by the architectural limits that disorient and imprison the victim, while the victim, in turn, suffers from the claustrophobic sense that the haunted labyrinth will become their tomb.

Coleridge's response to the Gothic was ambivalent. On one hand, his notebooks and letters register thrilling and enthusiastic readings of German Romances, and his best-known poems, *The Rime of the Ancient Mariner* (1798) and 'Christabel' (1816), are, as I have delineated elsewhere, distinctly Gothic narratives (Mills, 'Poetics' 326–33). On the other hand, as 'an hireling in the Critical Review' he also penned vigorous critiques of Gothic fiction, becoming 'almost weary of the Terrible' in which 'dungeons, and old castles,' and 'all the tribe of Horror & Mystery, have crowded on me – even to surfeiting' (*Letters* 1: 318). His review of what he called Lewis's *'pernicious'* novel is perhaps illustrative of why Coleridge found fault with the 'multitude of manufacturers' of '[s]ituations of torment, and images of naked horror' ('Review' 194–7). According to Coleridge, '[t]he sufferings which [Lewis] describes are so frightful and intolerable, that we break with abruptness from the delusion, and indignantly suspect the man of a species of brutality, who could find a pleasure in wantonly imagining them' ('Review' 195). Coleridge's abrupt withdrawal from Lewis's 'fright-ful' 'delusion' mirrors the sensation of waking suddenly from the horrific nightmare delusions Coleridge 'suffered in distempered Sleep' (*Notebooks* 4: 4846). It is precisely the similarities between Coleridge's labyrinthine nightmares and Lewis's hellish 'delusions' that cause Coleridge such discom-fort. The Gothic, for Coleridge, is not cheap trickery for entertainment but a deeply personal mode through which to explore and verbalise the real-life 'dreadful labyrinth of struggling, hell-pretending Dreams' that he suffered throughout his life (*Notebooks* 4: 5375).

Coleridge seems to have recognised the connection between Gothic space and his own theories of mind: in the spectral thirteenth chapter of his *Biographia Literaria* (a textual ghost, present only in the form of a fictitious letter about the *experience* of reading this missing chapter), Coleridge resur-rects the Gothic ruin from Radcliffe's *Udolpho* as a metaphor and model for the expansive spaces and sublime, haunting experience of the Imagination.[7] The Imagination is of course intimately linked with dreams and nightmares, and Coleridge's architectural model of Imagination was likely informed by his developing dream theories, which involved even more literal construc-tions of Gothic space.[8] Central to Coleridge's theories of dream and night-mare, developed extensively in his notebooks, was his concept of 'Somnial or Morphean Space'. A unique space entered in dreams and nightmares, Morphean Space was located paradoxically within and yet beyond the con-fines of the mind, brain, and body, 'below […] consciousness' (1: 1554), and on 'the other side of the confine of Dozing' (2: 2542). In Morphean Space, the will was suspended: in notably Gothic terms, bodily sensation becomes 'the Usurper' of Volition, and the dreamer passively accepts the reality of the dream. Importantly, however, Coleridge distinguished between dreams and nightmares: in the latter, the

> volitions of *Reason* i.e. comparing &c, are awake, tho' disturbed. […] In short, this Night-mair is not properly *a Dream;* but a species of Reverie, akin to Somnambulism, during which the Understanding & Moral Sense are awake tho' more or less confused, and over the Terrors of which the Reason can exert no influence. (3: 4046)

The nightmare is, then, a horrific state of powerless awareness of imprisonment within Morphean Space, where the sleeper is vulnerable to its 'Terrors'.
It is the 'Life-stifling fear' of 'the powerless will / Still baffled, and yet burning still!' that Coleridge records in his poem, 'The Pains of Sleep' (32: 21–2),
and which decades later, still plagued by horrific nightmares, he personifies
as the 'Night-mare Life-in-Death' in his 1834 revision of *The Rime* (193).

The cause of these 'Terrors' was a problem that haunted Coleridge, and
one for which he entertained multiple, competing theories, often simultaneously. Despite his best efforts to resist it, one of the most persistent was an
idea he called 'the Spirit-theory' in which nightmares could be caused by the
invading presence of demonic or 'Malignant Spirits' who took advantage of
the will's passive state in Morphean Space to possess the dreamer's mind and
body, directing and influencing the dream (*Notebooks* 4: 5360). According
to Ronald R. Thomas, 'accounts of dreams and dreaming' in Romantic
writing 'characteristically assume the shape of a possession' (21). Jennifer
Ford likewise notes that supernatural theories of dreaming were popular
'during the latter part of the eighteenth century' and common amongst
Coleridge's friends (142). In his theorising about the possible supernatural
causes of nightmare, Coleridge drew especially on Baxter, whose *Enquiry
into the Nature of the Human Soul* (1733) proposed that '*dreaming may
degenerate into possession*; and that the cause and nature of both is the
same, differing only in degree; for *dreaming* is but *possession in sleep*, from
which we are relieved again when we awake' (2: 131–2).[9] Although the
theory of demonic possession was being replaced by Enlightenment medical
and psychiatric models of insanity initiated by William Battie's *A Treatise
on Madness* (1758), with which Coleridge was familiar, it persisted among
eighteenth-century explanations of madness. The nightmare, then, presents
the terrifying potential for temporary possession to descend into permanent possession in the waking world. In this model, the nightmare threatens
the loss of the dreamer's self-identity and autonomy as the soul becomes
trapped within the labyrinthine realms of Morphean Space while the brain
and body are usurped by the invading, possessing demonic spirits responsible for the mind's torment.

In his 'most grievous and alarming <Scream-> Dreams' Coleridge supposed 'the Figures in my Dream to *be*, or to be assumed by, the Malignant
Spirits themselves – for it is very curious, that they are more or less malicious' (*Notebooks*, 4: 5360). In another entry, Coleridge notes the dramatic
quality of dreams by terming these figures '*Dreamatis* Personae' but any
connection with the illusory narratives of the stage is undermined by his
consideration of their possible supernatural reality as he asks, 'in what
sense the Dream Persons may be deemed Spirits?' (5: 5670). These nightmare creatures often reappeared in multiple nightmares as if stalking the

realms of Coleridge's unconscious, waiting for the chance to possess him in Morphean Space. A common fiend was a stalking 'figure of a woman of a gigantic Height, dim & indefinite & smokelike' who later reforms as 'three old Women, the dim Apparitions of three', who 'attacked me in that dark passage' (2: 1998). More terrifyingly, these frequent attacks were often characterised by a palpable sense of physical touch that threatened to break through the limits of Morphean Space into the material world: Coleridge records 'a claw-like talon-nailed Hand' which 'grasped hold of me' (3: 4046), and similar sensations of 'actual grasp or touch contrary to *my* will, & in apparent consequence of the malignant will of the external Form, actually appearing or (as sometimes happens) believed to exist' (2: 2468). The idea that demonic possession might break the limits of Morphean Space and materially affect the dreamer was an idea that Coleridge found particularly terrifying.

Coleridge's 'Spirit-theory' of dreaming was also partially informed by Swedenborg's theories of spirits inhabiting the body and influencing the mind, which, Coleridge writes, 'haunted me ever since I first read' them (5: 5640). To Swedenborg, Coleridge felt himself 'indebted for imagining myself always in Hell, i.e. imagining all the wild Chambers, Ruins, Prisons, Bridewells, to be in Hell' (4: 5360). Coleridge's rapid listing of the classic Gothic spaces which formed the landscape of his nightmares, and his connection of these rapidly shifting, labyrinthine spaces with the overarching realm of Hell, emphasises the Gothic nature of Morphean Space as 'a dreadful labyrinth of struggling, hell-pretending Dreams' (4: 5375). Architecturally mirroring the landscapes of Gothic fiction, and similarly haunted by malignant spirits, the nightmare's Morphean Space is a place of demonic possession that 'becomes doubly other', like the heterotopia of the Gothic labyrinth:

> literally constituted of detours, repetitions, and duplications which traverse the same space with an interminable criss-crossing of differences and divergences, a space that is other to, constitutive of, and resistant to, the known limits of society and subjectivity; it also forms a dense metaphorical complex woven of figures, traces, and signifiers, a complicated condensation of a multiplicity of conflicting associations, functions, and meanings. (Botting, 'Power' 249)

In his desperation to escape the terrors imposed by the 'Spirit-theory' of dreaming, Coleridge scrutinised the physiological conditions of his dreams and nightmares and engaged with many of the leading contemporary medical, scientific, and philosophical thinkers, for whom the nature and biology of dreaming were some of the Romantic period's most central and haunting ontological questions.[10] Suffering from chronic pain and disease since childhood, Coleridge's minutely detailed physiological experiences are often bound up with the effects of the opium he took as a remedy, but which came to exert an even more painful influence over his body and mind. These medical conditions appear – often in excruciating detail – throughout most of Coleridge's notebook writings about nightmare, but far from dispelling the grip of Coleridge's 'Spirit-theory', these biological accounts are frequently haunted by the lingering possibility of the supernatural and are also expressed with recourse to the language and spaces of the Gothic. An 1832 entry, written two years before his death, expresses Coleridge's relentless mental and bodily anguish where '<month after month, week after week, ever &> ever the Disease KEEPS HOLD, like a *hand grasping*, the contents of the space from the pit of the Stomach to the Navel—' (5: 6648). Coleridge's typographical emphasis indicates the physical power of this disease, recalling the 'grasping' hands and talon-clawed beasts of his earlier nightmare entries. Likewise, referring to opium as an 'evil Spirit' (4: 5001), Coleridge characterises his addiction in terms of demonic possession, employing once more the spaces of the Gothic to describe his pathological experiences: 'the deep Yearning will not die, but lives & grows as in a charnel house – and all my Vitals are possessed by an unremitting Poison' (2: 3075). In an earlier entry of 1806, terrified of the 'spectres' and 'horrors in *Sleep*', Coleridge is driven 'to purchase daily a wretched Reprieve from the torments of each night's Daemons/selling myself to the Devil to avoid the Devil's own Visitations, & thereby becoming his *Subject*' (2: 2944). Coleridge's theories of nightmare, then, spiritual, biological, and medical, are suffused with the language and topography of the Gothic. Morphean Space functions for Coleridge much like the Gothic ruin or labyrinth in Radcliffe and Lewis – namely, as a liminal space both within and yet separate from the external, material world, one that is unsettlingly permeable, haunted by terrifying supernatural intrusions that also provoke the horror of potential entrapment within this space. Haunted, labyrinthine, and ensuring the passive victimhood of the dreamer at the hands of hellish, irrational, tormenting, and possessing spirits, Coleridge's Morphean Space can be read as an inherently Gothic theory of mind and body.

The Gothic nature of Coleridge's theories of Morphean Space and nightmare means that the Gothic was ideally suited as a language, mode, and narrative form through which to record and attempt to understand his frequent and terrifying 'Afflictions of Sleep' (*Notebooks* 4: 5360). Across multiple notebook entries made over the course of his life, Coleridge created powerful narrative accounts of his dream and nightmare experiences. These nightmare writings, I argue, are not only informed by the Gothic's topography, language, and aesthetic mode but can be themselves most productively read as Gothic texts, often employing highly stylised and controlled narrative and linguistic forms in an attempt to evoke – as did other Gothic literature and media – an emotional response of terror in the reader. Historically, most critical considerations of Coleridge's notebooks have treated them as supplementary material to be mined for what they might reveal about Coleridge's poetry, rather than as texts – let alone *literary* texts – in and of themselves (Dixon 77). However, though they do not connect the notebooks with the Gothic, recent critics such as Kathleen Wheeler caution against reading Coleridge's prose 'as if it were merely discursive and logical argumentation, rather than rhetorical and poetic in substantive, irreducible ways' (25). While Coleridge's notebooks certainly differ from his published writing, 'in both', argues Wheeler, 'he draws on his quite phenomenal knowledge of the literary and critical tradition before him' and these 'private jottings are no less rhetorical and strategy-laden than his public, published writings' (22). Likewise, in his recent edited selection of Coleridge's notebooks, Seamus Perry claims that they constitute 'perhaps the unacknowledged prose masterpiece of the age' (vii), while Josie Dixon suggests that some 'of the most vivid' entries in the notebooks are the 'highly dramatic narrative renditions of dreams' (77). Yet Dixon also asserts that while the 'semantic energy of the writing, instilled in its mimetically disordered syntax, is distinctively literary', these 'private, occasional writings-without-a-genre' offer 'only the formalism of formlessness, enacting the generic impossibility of channelling that associative stream into any controlled system of literary expression' (77–8). While this statement might be true of the expansive, fragmented notebooks as a whole, I argue that in the narrative accounts of nightmares, we can clearly see the Gothic as a guiding, shaping mode.

Coleridge's reasons for writing in the Gothic mode during such personal, deeply unsettling moments are twofold: firstly, the Gothic mode allows Coleridge to evoke the atmosphere and emotional affect of his nightmares, and secondly, the Gothic affords Coleridge an authorial position of authority from which to wrest back control of the narrative, and through it, his mind and body, from their passivity and loss at the hands of the demonic, possessing terrors within Morphean Space. Referred to by Coleridge as 'my only Confidants' (3: 3342) and 'the history of my own mind for my own improvement' (2: 2368), the notebooks were produced as aids for the personal study of Coleridge's mind and particularly the mental phenomena like nightmares that continued to haunt him partly because they eluded satisfying explanation. As Paul Cheshire points out, 'it is important to remember that Coleridge will have spent more time *reading* his notebooks than he did *writing* in them' (293). Drawing on the emotional power of narrative – and particularly Gothic narrative – then, was a technique by which Coleridge could capture the unique experience of his nightmares and regain control as both author and reader of his own mind. Without addressing the Gothic or the nightmare texts specifically, Wheeler asserts that 'Coleridge's rhetorical strategies create a poetic prose which seeks to reflect its subject matter in the style' and to 'arouse the reader to a corresponding "passion"' (34). Indeed, as John Worthen argues, Coleridge's notebooks demonstrate how he 'was impelled not only to find language for experience but to create the feeling of feeling. It was how he located himself in the world, as observer and interlocutor' (51). Nowhere did Coleridge's linguistic, textual attempts to locate himself within the world matter more than in those terrifying moments upon waking from a nightmare when his very grasp on material reality and his hold over his mind were under threat of slipping away. In these moments, Coleridge's careful narrativising of his nightmares through the Gothic mode reasserts his authorial control over his mind and experiences.[11]

In the Gothic, labyrinths are 'spaces of inversion, spaces in which the traditional poles of good and evil are reversed: evil has power, good is the victim' (Botting, 'Power' 251). This clear reversal of the moral order in Gothic space signals the Gothic's appeal for Coleridge. In his notebook nightmare writings, the Gothic mode partially functions to imply, and thereby in some ways to reinstate, the moral order that the nightmare disrupts, casting Coleridge firmly in the position of the Gothic protagonist – the persecuted hero – who must eventually be returned, according to the logic of Gothic novels, to his rightful place in the moral order. However, the nature of Morphean Space, perpetually holding open the possibility of an external supernatural realm while also undermining clear distinctions between the waking and nightmare worlds, makes return to this order problematic. While Coleridge's nightmare texts evoke the Gothic in terms of their topography, language, and mood, their return to moral order depends on waking into rational consciousness, and many of them involve several stages of Coleridge's attempts to draw himself out of the labyrinthine Morphean Space while invisible, seemingly demonic forces seek to pull him back in.

An illustrative example is an entry written in the early hours immediately upon waking from a nightmare: 'Wednesd. Morn. 3 °clock, Dec. 13, 1803. Bad dreams / How often *of a sort* / at the university – a mixture of Xts Hospital Church / escapes there – lose myself / trust to two People, one Maim'd, one unknown' (1: 1726). Finding himself once more within the familiar hellscape of the uncannily merged structures of Christ's Hospital and university, Coleridge becomes immediately lost and at the mercy of the strange dream creatures who 'Hustle against' him, '*biting*', 'insult[ing]', and 'attack[ing]' him (1: 1726). An architectural space haunted by malicious, attacking creatures, the dream continues with rapid shifts of character and scene until Coleridge realises, terrifyingly, that he 'cannot awake' (1: 1726). Thus trapped, space continues to unfold in labyrinthine fashion as Coleridge continues his Somnial 'wanderings thro' the Hall' and 'wanderings thro' Streets', 'noticing the Complex side of a Noble building' and 'turning up a Lane' (1: 1726). These shifting architectural foldings are then layered over by cognitive repetitions: the nightmare doubles back on itself as Coleridge, still dreaming, 'literally and distinctly remembered a former Dream, in which I had suffered most severely' (1:1726). The architectural labyrinth is doubled and expanded by concentric layers of Morphean Space, and the nightmare becomes a palimpsest of present nightmare and remembered nightmare, experienced as a double vision, a nightmare within a nightmare.

In this doubled Morphean Space, which amplifies the terror experienced within it, Coleridge is attacked yet again, initiating his concerted effort to break out of the hellish prison:

> —My determination to awake, I dream that I got out of bed, & volition in dream to *scream*, which I actually to[o] did, from that volition/& the strange visual Distortions of all the bed Cloaths [...] all which, I in my dream explained as the effects of my eyes being half-opened, & still affected by Sleep/in an half upright posture struggling, as I thought, against involuntary sinking back into Sleep, & consequent suffocation/twas then I screamed, by will/& immediately after really awoke/

> I must devote some one or more Days exclusively to the Meditation on Dreams. Days? Say rather Weeks! (1: 1726)

Attacked by a host of beings in this space, Coleridge desperately attempts to awaken, finding himself in a disconcerting and terrifying simulacrum of reality – a nightmare version of the real, waking world, while the deeper Morphean Space claws at him, drawing him back in. His powerlessness against the sucking draw of the nightmare world is indicated by his 'struggling [...] against *involuntary* sinking back into Sleep, & consequent suffocation'. Coleridge characterises the nightmare world as claustrophobic, suffocating, malignant, and tormenting, affording it an almost autonomous, conscious power that both emphasises his passive victimhood in this space and also suggests the potential presence of the supernatural behind it. More terrifying is the power of the nightmare – felt here and in countless other nightmare accounts in the notebooks similarly characterised by 'dreadful dreams, & screaming, screaming, or preparation to scream' (2: 1863) – to torture Coleridge with the illusion that he is awake, so that his screaming from inside the nightmare world only barely echoes into the material, waking realm. Climbing back out from the depths of the labyrinthine, doubled Morphean Spaces, Coleridge must also double his scream, screaming twice before he is able to properly awake; the first scream is swallowed by the suffocating nightmare world that is at last shattered by the second.

Ford notes the way the solidus (the oblique stroke '/') acts in this dream text as 'a physical mark upon the page' not only 'to separate ideas, but to prevent some of them from further elucidation', blocking 'further potentially stressful self-exploration' (73). We might take this idea further to note that with such punctuation, Coleridge's writing itself appropriates and attempts to reclaim the architectural, labyrinthine quality of his nightmares. The solidus, fragmenting and dividing the winding, shifting sections of the nightmare, also allows Coleridge to impose his own architectural order on his ideas and to confine and enclose the Morphean Space that had so recently enclosed him. In a later notebook entry, Coleridge refers to his similar habit of digressions and 'parenthetical parentheses' as 'having thus belabyrinthed myself' (2: 2431). Coleridge's syntax itself, then, characterised by winding, shifting ideas and disruptive, dividing punctuation, architecturally embodies the labyrinthine structures of the nightmares he writes about. This textual attempt to restore conscious order and control over his nightmare is mirrored by his abrupt tonal shift in the final, truncated line of the entry, which imposes a detached, analytical rejoinder onto the trailing space left after the final wall/solidus. Reading like the moral at the end of a fable, Coleridge's narratorial tone radically shifts from the breathless, terrified dreamer to the wise sage in order to fully inhabit, at last, the waking world. However, the magnitude of the topic of dreams and nightmare – requiring weeks rather than days to investigate – threatens to spill over beyond reasonable bounds, undermining the certainty of Coleridge's cognitive and linguistic control.

Coleridge's destabilising of his transition from nightmare to waking is a recurring element in his notebook entries. Some of his most chilling nightmare accounts are those that most powerfully deploy narrative techniques to ultimately evoke a terrifying sense that the supernatural is no longer safely confined within the Morphean realm. In the following two examples, both masterpieces in the short-form prose evocation of Gothic fear – narrative feats which would decades later characterise Poe's Gothic – Coleridge not only undermines any clear sense that he has actually awoken but also suggests the continued presence of the supernatural after waking. The ambiguity created by these dissolved boundaries between the waking and sleeping worlds suggests two terrifyingly tautological possibilities: either the transition from Morphean to waking space remains incomplete and the dreamer has descended into madness, trapped within the Morphean world, or the demonic spirits that stalk his nightmares are not restricted to the dream space, but instead stalk the material, waking world, in which case their continued ability to possess Coleridge potentially signals descent into madness-as-demonic-possession anyway.

The first example, dated Sunday, 21 October 1810, is written, as usual, in the breathless moments immediately after waking from the nightmare it attempts to record and evoke:

> Saturday Night, at Mr Butler's at Ridding – the Nightmair – so near awaking and my saying – Yes! Dreams, or Creatures of my Dreams, you may make me feel you as if you were keeping behind me / but you cannot speak to me – immediately I heard impressed on my outward ears, & with a perfect sense of *distance* answered – O yes! but I can— (3: 3984)

Recording his experience in a single, breathless sentence mapped across the borderland between Morphean Space and consciousness – 'so near awaking' – Coleridge employs a fast-paced narrative, mounting suspense, and multiple narrative gaps to evoke a powerful sense of genuine interaction with a sentient, malignant supernatural whose power extends beyond the confines of the nightmare world to terrorise the material, waking realm. The narrative setup is brief and perfunctory, establishing the quick pace that will increase over the short text. The 'nightmair' itself slips into a narrative gap, remaining at a distance within the invisible abyss of Morphean Space. Coleridge's refusal to disclose the contents of this nightmare create a Gothic sense of concentric narratives – at the heart of this entry is an invisible text – while also establishing a powerful sense of space and 'perfect *distance*' between the waking and dreaming worlds. Coleridge, 'so near awaking,' is climbing out of Morphean Space, leaving it behind as he moves towards the 'solidity' of his 'outward' senses that signal his relocation within the outward, material world. Coleridge's silence about the nightmare itself, and his shift into direct, active speech – an indication of his returning willpower and conscious mind as well as a quality associated with the waking world – lulls the reader into a false sense of confidence that Coleridge is safe from the creatures he rebukes, even while he admits his impression – distrusted as a lingering fancy of Morphean Space but not to be countered in the waking world – that the creatures keep close 'behind' him. Likewise, the single solidus in this entry once more performs an architectural function, representing the barrier Coleridge attempts to construct between himself and the demonic creatures: 'you were keeping behind me / but you cannot speak to me'.

Through these careful narrative techniques, Coleridge creates an uncanny, eerie suspense that primes the reader for the sudden, shocking twist when these invisible, immaterial, and apparently voiceless creatures suddenly assert their presence in the material world by speaking to his 'outward ears'. The terror in this moment is amplified by the fact that the creatures assert their presence by usurping the very same tool – the spoken word – that

Coleridge had confidently used to reclaim his ostensible control over his mind. Indeed, rather than concluding, as he does elsewhere, with his own commentary or note on the dream – an attempt to step away from the terror of the nightmare narrative into the safety of verbal analysis – Coleridge instead allows the spoken words of the creature to hover unchallenged. The following silence, emphasised by the trailing dash, resonates with the eerie, unnatural voice, implying the lingering, haunting presence of the demonic creatures. Rather than the passive silence of these creatures in the face of Coleridge's authoritative speech, it is Coleridge who remains silent, his implied passivity presenting the unsettling possibility that he never actually woke up from the labyrinth of Morphean Space.

An earlier entry from 28 November 1800, employs similar narrative techniques to evoke the same effect, where the demonic dream-creature manages to transgress the boundary between Morphean Space and the waking world with terrifying consequences:

> Friday Night, Nov. 28, 1800, or rather Saturday Morning – a most frightful Dream of a Woman whose features were blended with darkness catching holding of my right eye & attempting to pull it out – I caught hold of her arm fast – a horrid feel – Wordsworth cried out aloud to me hearing my scream – heard his cry & thought it cruel he did not come / but did not wake till his cry was repeated a third time – the Woman's name Ebon Ebon Thalud – When my I awoke, my right eyelid swelled— (1: 848)

This dramatic, narrative text, albeit brief, is utterly terrifying. From its first words, the reader is plunged, like Coleridge, straight into the demonic attack in the haunted space of the nightmare. With features 'blended with darkness', as if she embodies the nightmare space itself, the demonic Woman attempts to tear out Coleridge's eye as if in anger that he dares peer into her realm. Another manifestation of the feminine demonic figures and grabbing and clawing talons that repeatedly stalked Coleridge's nightmares, this Woman has such reality and force that she is named ('Ebon Ebon Thalud'). Coleridge's act of recording her name in his conscious writing gives her a tangible, terrifying reality, as if identifying her in this way might arm him against her should he ever again encounter her in Morphean Space. Kathleen Coburn notes the demonic woman's connection with a literary source – a druggist, Ebn Thaher, in the *Arabian Nights* (Coleridge, *Notebooks* 1: 848n). The association is one that compounds the underlying opium addiction that so often caused his nightmares, but once more, the dangerous hold of this substance is figured in both supernatural and material terms – quite literally in this case – as the demonic woman grabs hold of Coleridge's eye, seeking to possess that material organ of vision just as she possessed his passive, immaterial mind while his soul traversed the realm of Morphean Space. The visionary properties of the eye link the external body with the internal world of the dream space, underscoring the demon's terrifying transgression of the boundaries between sleep and waking, illusion and reality, and spiritual and material realms.

Interestingly, Coleridge attempts to wrest control back from this clawing, grasping demon by catching 'hold of her arm fast', but his emphasis on the 'horrid feel', with its disturbing sense of material touch, plunges Coleridge into renewed horror and passivity, drawing from him the screams that are characteristically powerless to break the spell of Morphean Space. The agony of Coleridge's torturous imprisonment within the labyrinthine depths of Morphean Space, where he is powerless to escape the horrifically violent clutches of this 'horrid' demon, is palpable, and Coleridge notes his sense of 'cruel' abandonment in this place when Wordsworth 'did not come' to his rescue. The most terrifying aspect of Coleridge's nightmare tale, however, is in its final, awful, masterfully Gothic twist: Coleridge has finally awakened, screaming, from his nightmare only to be met by the horrific realisation that his eye remains swollen in the waking world too. Instead of the reassuring knowledge that it was only a dream, Coleridge is left instead with the disturbing possibility that the demon has also crossed the liminal boundary between the sleeping and waking worlds. Coleridge offers no analytical comment but is instead rendered silent, stupefied by the terrifying presence of the demonic in his increasingly unstable waking world. Once again, Coleridge's abrupt silence creates the eerie possibility that despite waking from the nightmare, the demon still stalks the material world, unseen in Coleridge's waking state yet still capable of rendering him further harm. The disturbing suggestion is that waking does not dissolve the supernatural spectres but merely renders them invisible.

In these nightmare narratives, Coleridge produces a particular style and form of literary text that both draws on and yet clearly differs from lengthy, moralising Gothic novels, turning instead upon the evocative power of the short form and the single, haunting idea. In this condensed, visionary style, these nightmare narratives approach more closely the later short stories of Edgar Allan Poe, particularly such mesmeric, nightmarish tales as 'Ligeia', and the ghost stories of Victorian writers like Henry James that develop out of this Romantic Gothic context. These later masters of the Gothic short form evoke terror through the concentrated exploration of a single concept, often ambiguously supernatural and psychological, suggesting the possibility of madness, and turning upon narrative twists and ambiguous, suspended endings to amplify the reader's fear. In style, Coleridge's private nightmare writings are literary experiments that anticipate these later Gothic forms, and the works of all three writers emerge from the same impulse to employ the Gothic as a mode through which to investigate the haunted workings of the mind. While Poe and James did not access Coleridge's notebooks directly, in their literary and theoretical explorations of supernatural psychologies, they were both heavily influenced by Coleridge's published theories of the Imagination, and no doubt his well-circulated poems, 'The Rime' and 'Christabel', all of which publicly modelled his theories of Gothic mental space (Mills, 'Poetics' 321–34).[12]

This style of condensed and vivid narrative, approaching poetry, was also a powerful feature of the Gothic ballads that had risen to prominence in the 1790s – a tradition in which both *The Rime* and 'Christabel', originally written for the *Lyrical Ballads*, participate. By sharing these stylistic features, Coleridge's nightmare entries take on the haunting, evocative quality of his oneiric poems, just as those poems are informed by Coleridge's nightmare experiences. These shared stylistic qualities underscore the fact that Coleridge's nightmare writings were constructed – and should therefore be read – as literary texts. Coleridge's nightmare writings therefore demonstrate the broad application of the Gothic as an aesthetic and mode well beyond the generic form of the Gothic novel.

It is through this shared territory of Coleridge's notebook writings about nightmares and his published poetry that Coleridge's ideas of an ambiguously supernatural-psychological Morphean Space enact their extensive influence upon later writers and particularly upon the development of the Gothic. Major novelists writing in the Gothic mode across the nineteenth century, from Mary Shelley in the early decades to Lucas Malet at the fin de siècle, take up the idea that dreams function as a spatial portal through which to access – or be accessed by – the supernatural world, and they likewise preserve the simultaneously supernatural and psychological possibilities of the nightmare, bringing the biological and supernatural dream discourses into fractious dialogue with each other.[13] Shelley in particular was instrumental in transposing Coleridge's concept of Morphean Space back into the form of the Gothic novel from which he partly drew his inspiration, thereby paving the way for the concept's continued influence on later forms of Gothic.

Coleridge's formative influence on Shelley is perhaps most immediately felt in her novel *Frankenstein* (1818, revised in 1831), which explicitly embraces and expands upon Coleridge's Morphean theories. Shelley benefited from close personal association with Coleridge. As a girl, she was aware of and occasionally involved in the many philosophical discussions that emerged from the friendship and correspondence between Coleridge and her father, William Godwin. Any discussion of dreams would have been galvanised by hearing Coleridge, one night, recite *The Rime* for

Godwin and the young Mary. In her adolescence, Shelley attended some of Coleridge's lectures and read *The Friend*. The recitation of 'Christabel' at the Villa Diodati during the 'ghost story' writing competition that would produce *Frankenstein* is the stuff of legend. *Frankenstein* itself is littered with direct and indirect references to Coleridge's *The Rime* and builds particularly on his spatial theories of the haunted mind and demonic possession through nightmare. Like Coleridge, Shelley multiplies layers of Morphean Space. In her framing narrative of the novel's inspiration, added as an Introduction to her revisions of the novel in 1831, Shelley describes writing the tale as one 'possessed' and 'haunted' by the 'hideous phantasm' who appeared to her in a nightmare, and who now stalks the nightmare-space of the novel (9). Frankenstein too is trapped 'in trance' like a passive dreamer within this space, wandering through the increasingly nightmarish landscapes, unable to escape his torment by the demon to whom his fate is tethered as his 'own spirit let loose from the grave' (78).[14] Thereby ambiguously supernatural and psychological, verging on madness, this layered, nightmarish space is enfolded still further as Victor Frankenstein, approaching the mountainous and polar limits of the natural world, like the Ancient Mariner before him, drifts in and out of Morphean Spaces in which he is 'possessed by a kind of nightmare' and within which, like Coleridge's own accounts of demonic nightmare attacks, he 'felt the fiend's grasp in my neck' (188). In these multi-layered, demon-haunted spaces of Gothic consciousness, Shelley transmutes Coleridge's dream theories back into the Gothic novel tradition from which Coleridge had derived his nightmare language and topography.

Through his theories of Morphean Space and nightmare, and his narrative explorations of them, Coleridge's dream-writing acts as a bridge between earlier and later forms of Gothic space, Gothic literature and Romantic-period science, and public and personal forms of writing. In Coleridge's theorising and Gothic-style writings about the dreams and nightmares that haunted him throughout his life, his mind becomes a Gothic space subject to the spectral influences he sought to describe and understand in scientific terms. In addition to dissolving the distinctions that literary critics have traditionally drawn between the Romantic and Gothic as separate and opposing literary categories, and likewise blurring the traditionally assumed boundaries between literature and science, Coleridge's nightmare theories and writings extend the remit of the Gothic mode beyond novels and even beyond the literary. His notebooks illustrate that the Gothic was, even in its earliest moments, less a literary genre and more a psychological and cultural impulse ideally suited to questioning, interpreting, and even theorising one of the Romantic period's most haunting concerns: the metaphysics of nightmare.

Notes

1 My quotations from Coleridge's *Notebooks* adopt the punctuation used by their editors, Kathleen Coburn et al., to indicate the composition of Coleridge's handwritten entries. Angle brackets, <word>, denote a later insertion by Coleridge. Square brackets, [word], denote my own editorial insertions. Strokes, dashes and other punctuation marks are Coleridge's own.

2 See Mills, 'Poetics' and 'Frankenstein in Hyperspace'.

3 Webster offers insight into Coleridge's later notebooks but does not touch on the Gothic. Similarly, while Coleridge's dream theories have received much critical attention (see especially Ford, Vallins, Richardson, and Beer's *Coleridge's Play of Mind*), these studies do not explicitly connect Coleridge's nightmare theories with the Gothic.

4 On Coleridge's critical distancing from the Gothic, see especially Michael Gamer's discussions of the *Lyrical Ballads* and Coleridge's reviews of Gothic novels (90–126).

5 In considering the Gothic as a shifting mode or aesthetic more than a stable genre, I draw on arguments made by critics like Miles, Gamer, and Botting ('Gothic').

6 This architectural quality, intimately bound up with a sense of the supernatural and the confounding of spatial perception, is central to the mythology surrounding the Gothic's emergence, where these 'Gothic' spaces are first mediated, significantly, by a dream. The Gothic's first novel, Walpole's *The Castle of Otranto*, was, according to its author, inspired by a dream set within the labyrinthine space of his castle Strawberry Hill, itself a complicated Gothic construction blending narrative and architecture (Mills, 'At the Limits'). The rhetorical device of the dream-inspired Gothic novel would be repeated at many of the Gothic's most formative moments, most especially Mary Shelley's *Frankenstein* (see following discussion).

7 See Mudge 183, and Mills, 'Poetics' 323–5.

8 On the links between Coleridge's Imagination, dreams, and nightmare, see Ford and Shultz.

9 For detailed accounts of Coleridge's engagement with Baxter, see Ford and Beer ('Coleridge and Andrew Baxter').

10 On the depth and breadth of Coleridge's engagement with medical models of mind, see especially Ford and Richardson.

11 Ford argues that this 'need to impose certainty and control upon the forthcoming dream account is typical of the notebook dream entries' (73), though she does not identify the Gothic as part of Coleridge's rhetorical strategy for wresting back control of his nightmares.

12 For Coleridge's influence on Poe and James, see Stovall and Lustig, respectively.

13 See for example Lucas Malet's references to Coleridge in her fin-de-siècle Gothic explorations of supernatural higher dimensions, as discussed in my essay 'The Supernatural Fourth Dimension in Lucas Malet's *The Carissima* and *The Gateless Barrier*', pp. 616–18.

14 All *Frankenstein* quotations are from Shelley's 1831 revised edition in which Shelley refines and expands her earlier concepts and prefaces her narrative with a new Introduction, locating the origins of the novel in a possessing nightmare. The intensifying of the novel's emphasis on dreams, nightmare, and possession, particularly in its additional framing narrative, indicate the continuing resonance of these topics for Shelley.

Works cited

Baxter, Andrew. *An Enquiry into the Nature of the Human Soul; Wherein the Immateriality of the Soul is evinced from the Principles of Reason and Philosophy,* 3rd edn. London, 1745. 2 vols.

Battie, William. *A Treatise on Madness.* London, 1758.

Beer, John. 'Coleridge and Andrew Baxter on Dreaming.' *Dreaming,* vol. 7, no. 2, 1997, pp. 157–69.

Beer, John. *Coleridge's Play of Mind.* Oxford University Press, 2010.

Botting, Fred. *Gothic.* Routledge, 1996.

Botting, Fred. 'Power in the Darkness: Heterotopias, Literature and Gothic Labyrinths.' *Gothic: Critical Concepts,* edited by Fred Botting and Dale Townshend, vol. 2. Routledge, 2004, pp. 243–68.

Castle, Terry. *The Female Thermometer: Eighteenth-Century Culture and the Invention of the Uncanny.* Oxford University Press, 1995.

Castle, Terry. 'The Gothic Novel.' *The Cambridge History of English Literature, 1660–1780,* edited by John Richetti. Cambridge University Press, 2005, pp. 673–706.

Cheshire, Paul. 'Coleridge's Notebooks.' *The Oxford Handbook of Samuel Taylor Coleridge,* edited by Frederick Burwick. Oxford University Press, 2012, pp. 288–306.

Coleridge, Samuel Taylor. 'Christabel.' *The Complete Poems,* edited by William Keach. Penguin, 2004, pp. 187–205.

Coleridge, Samuel Taylor. *Collected Letters,* edited by Earl Leslie Griggs. Oxford University Press, 1956, 6 vols.

Coleridge, Samuel Taylor. *The Notebooks of Samuel Taylor Coleridge,* edited by Kathleen Coburn et al. Routledge, 1957–2000, 5 vols.

Coleridge, Samuel Taylor. 'The Pains of Sleep.' *The Complete Poems,* edited by William Keach. Penguin, 2004, pp. 328–29.

Coleridge, Samuel Taylor. 'Review of *The Monk.*' *Critical Review,* vol. 19, 1797, pp. 194–200.

Coleridge, Samuel Taylor. 'The Rime of the Ancient Mariner.' *The Complete Poems,* edited by William Keach. Penguin, 2004, pp. 167–86.

Darwin, Erasmus. *Zoonomia, or the Laws of Organic Life,* 2nd edn. London, 1794–6, 4 vols.

Dixon, Josie. 'The Notebooks.' *The Cambridge Companion to Coleridge.* Cambridge University Press, 2002, pp. 75–88.

Ford, Jennifer. *Coleridge on Dreaming: Romanticism, Dreams and the Medical Imagination*. Cambridge University Press, 1998.

Gamer, Michael. *Romanticism and the Gothic: Genre, Reception, and Canon Formation*. Cambridge University Press, 2000.

Hartley, David. *Observations on Man, His Frame, Duty, and Expectations*, 3rd edn. London, 1749, 2 vols.

Lewis, Matthew. *The Monk*. Oxford University Press, 2016.

Lustig, T. J. *Henry James and the Ghostly*. Cambridge University Press, 1994.

Miles, Robert. *Gothic Writing 1750–1820: A Genealogy*. Routledge, 1993.

Mills, Kirstin A. 'At the Limits of Perception: Liminal Space and the Interrelation of Word and Image in Walpole's Strawberry Hill, *The Castle of Otranto* and *The Mysterious Mother*.' *Image [&] Narrative*, vol. 18, no. 3, 2017, pp. 5–17.

Mills, Kirstin A. 'Frankenstein in Hyperspace: The Gothic Return of Digital Technologies to the Origins of Virtual Space in Mary Shelley's *Frankenstein*.' *Global Frankenstein*, edited by Carol Margaret Davison and Marie Mulvey-Roberts. Palgrave, 2018, pp. 265–81.

Mills, Kirstin A. 'The Poetics of Space, the Mind, and the Supernatural in S. T. Coleridge.' *The Palgrave Handbook of Gothic Origins*, edited by Clive Bloom. Palgrave, 2021, pp. 321–41.

Mills, Kirstin A. 'The Supernatural Fourth Dimension in Lucas Malet's *The Carissima* and *The Gateless Barrier*.' *The Palgrave Handbook of Steam Age Gothic*, edited by Clive Bloom. Palgrave, 2021, pp. 613–29.

Mudge, Bradford K. '"Excited by Trick": Coleridge and the Gothic Imagination.' *The Wordsworth Circle*, vol. 22, no. 3, 1991, pp. 179–84.

Perry, Seamus. 'Introduction.' *Coleridge's Notebooks: A Selection*. Oxford University Press, 2002, pp. vii–xiv.

Punter, David, and Glennis Byron. *The Gothic*. Blackwell, 2004.

Radcliffe, Ann. *The Mysteries of Udolpho*. Penguin, 2001.

Shelley, Mary. *Frankenstein*. Penguin, 2003.

Shultz, Alexander. 'The Dangers of Imagination: Coleridge's Dreams and Nightmares.' *The Coleridge Bulletin*, vol. 25, 2005, pp. 46–53.

Stovall, Floyd. 'Poe's Debt to Coleridge.' *Studies in English*, no. 10, 1930, pp. 70–127.

Swedenborg, Emanuel. *De Coelo et Ejus Mirabilibus, et de Inferno, ex Auditis & Visis*. London, 1758.

Thomas, Ronald R. *Dreams of Authority: Freud and the Fictions of the Unconscious*. Cornell University Press, 1990.

Vallins, David. *Coleridge and the Psychology of Romanticism*. Palgrave Macmillan, 2000.

Walpole, Horace. *The Castle of Otranto*. Penguin, 2001.

Webster, Suzanne E. *Body and Soul in Coleridge's Notebooks, 1827–1834*. Palgrave Macmillan, 2010.

Wheeler, Kathleen. 'Coleridge's Notebook Scribblings.' *Prose Studies*. vol. 13, no. 3, 1990, pp. 18–35.

Worthen, John. *The Cambridge Introduction to Samuel Taylor Coleridge*. Cambridge University Press, 2010.

3

The devil's light: Marx, Engels, and diabolic Enlightenment

Jayson Althofer and Brian Musgrove

It is not the slumber of reason that engenders monsters, but vigilant and insomniac rationality. (Deleuze and Guattari 112)

There are those who have hitherto only enlightened the world in various ways; the point is to darken it. (Culp 14)

Introduction

Karl Marx and Friedrich Engels illuminate bourgeois society's Gothic dreaming and realised nightmares through an oneiro-critique of the 'day-for-night' inversions that perpetually revolutionise life under capital. This chapter reads their critique in relation to the epochal conquest of night by technologies of artificial light. It is configured around 'The Working Day' chapter of Marx's *Capital*, Volume 1 (1867), Engels's *The Condition of the Working Class in England* (1845), and an excursion through Gothic gas-lit streets depicted by selected literary 'fellow travellers' who darkly reflect on capitalist modernity's mystifying illuminations and 'enlightened' mystifications. It argues that from the early 1800s, industrialised light – omnipresent in today's so-called 'late capitalism' – augurs 'day without end' (De Sutter 45–65), an endless day always already immanent to capital's revolutionary genesis. Recalling Eve Kosofsky Sedgwick's precept to explore Gothic conventions 'that point the reader's attention back to surfaces' (141), the chapter considers artificial light as *the* naturalised, industrial-age surface-appearance of modernity – simultaneously constituting, concealing, and exhuming some of bourgeois society's most telling dreams and nightmares.

Capital's machinations depend on the 24/7 'ends of sleep' (Crary) transmogrifying into all-encompassing living nightmares. Its Promethean power to light the world – to masquerade as *the* light of the world – is predicated on its monstrous theft of sunlight and sleep from the labouring classes: the wilful disruption, derangement, and destruction of circadian rhythm by shift work. Walter Benjamin's study of artificial light in nineteenth-century Paris links J. J. Grandville's 1844 lithographs of the Milky Way 'as an avenue illuminated at night by gaslamps' to bourgeois society's self-image of a second nature that outshines and ousts the first: 'the collective dream energy of a society has taken refuge ... in the mute impenetrable nebula of fashion' (Benjamin B1a,2) – the zenith of commodity fetishism – creating an alternative galaxy. As Benjamin implies, this transfixes an apparitional reality, a Promethean artifice, superseding nature. For Theodor Adorno, this modern Prometheanism generates the recurrent nightmares of capital's dream world – a bourgeois firmament under which sublunary 'Dreams are as black as death' (119).

Ghost-walking in gaslight

From the late 1600s, Marx observes in 'The Working Day', capital extends the working day 'to the limit of the natural day' and progressively transgresses that limit. Then, from the 1770s, 'the birth of machinism and modern industry' obsolesces traditional boundaries between diurnal and nocturnal modes of existence. This 'violent encroachment' is historically unprecedented: 'All bounds of morals and nature, age and sex, day and night' break down; 'ideas of day and night, of rustic simplicity in the old statutes' are categorically confused. 'Capital celebrated its orgies' in an artificial glare (35: 283).[1] The momentous encroachment is essential to the capitalist mode of production's 'complete mystification', Marx concludes in *Capital*, Volume 3 (1894). Supernaturalism is naturalised by 'an enchanted, perverted, topsy-turvy world, in which Monsieur le Capital and Madame la Terre do their ghost-walking as social characters' in a pageant enacting the new 'religion of everyday life' – commodity fetishism (37: 817).

Capital's ghost-walking is 'enstaged' (Leslie 15), but not in dark or archaic settings customarily associated with Gothicism. It is set in factories, streets, shop windows, and arcades where artificial lighting appears dreamy, magical, devilish, nightmarish, and yet modern, or *new*, as Heinrich Heine stresses in his 1828 *dérive* through London, which is discussed below. Marx 'draws upon a gothic literary imaginary' to publicly anatomise 'capitalism as secretly possessed'; however, 'unlike in the gothic', the form and force that predominantly possess the stage of modern life – the commodity-form and its fetishism – do not lurk 'repressed beneath the surface of modernity' (Osborne 16–17). They ghost-walk in broad daylight and artificially lit night – the *ne plus ultra* of an inverted capitalist 'enlightenment'.

Documenting the horrific consequences of extending the working day to its natural limit – the desire to turn 'idleness' into industry, 24/7, whatever the cost to labouring life – Marx cites *An Essay on Trade and Commerce* (1770), which imagines 'an *ideal workhouse*' functioning as a 'House of

Terror' (35: 281, original emphasis), recognising that the anonymous essay-
ist's dream rapidly materialises in the form of the modern factory. Eric
Hobsbawm demonstrates how industrialists absorbed 'innovations with
great speed', applying 'a rigorous rationalism to their methods of production such as is highly characteristic of a scientific age'. Cotton masters, for
instance, quickly 'learned to build in a purely functional way' and, from
1805, 'lengthened the working day by illuminating their factories with gas.
Yet the first experiments in gaslighting went no further back than 1792'
(43). The terrific speed of innovations constituting the Industrial Revolution
heralds an age of science and sorcery, perversely yet rationally inter-bred.

The stupendous dialectical interplay of these apparent opposites, sorcery
and science, is manifest in the figure of Faust, whose story, 'retold endlessly',
refracts the development of capitalist modernity (Berman 38). Goethe's
Faust, Part II (written between 1825 and 1831), 'ends in the midst of the
spiritual and material upheavals of an industrial revolution' (Berman 45).
Faust metamorphosises into an industrial developer, who scientifically and
devilishly organises his workforce to undertake night work and construct
mighty projects. Overnight, by firelight, a dam and a canal appear. 'Human
lives were sacrificed' to terraform a wasteland into an industrial spectacle
at Faust's command (Goethe, line 11,127). Humane values are expelled;
navvies gutter into early graves. In his germinal analysis of Faust 'the developer', Marshall Berman spells out the violent encroachments of his dreams
and deeds: 'The crucial point is to spare nothing and no one, to overleap
all boundaries ... not only traditional moral limits on the exploitation of
labor, but even the primary human dualism of day and night. All natural
and human barriers fall before the rush of production and construction'
(64). But what Faust unwittingly conjures is a nightmarish return of the
repressed, introjecting 'the wasteland inside the developer himself' (Berman
68). As Berman's incisive summary of *Faust*'s oneiro-critique of the dynam-
ics of capitalist development concludes,

> Goethe plunges us into the symbolist ambience of Faust's inner world.
> Suddenly four spectral women in gray hover toward him, and proclaim them-
> selves: they are Need, Want, Guilt, and Care. All these are forces that Faust's
> program of development has banished from the outer world; but they have
> crept back as specters inside his mind. (70)

Ultimately, then, Faust is not the master sorcerer but, rather, the terrified
inept novice of Goethe's *Der Zauberlehrling* ('The Sorcerer's Apprentice',
1797).

As Max Horkheimer and Adorno argue, the processes of Enlightenment,
its technological rationality, and its mental-moral rationalisations have a

dialectical flip-side – evincing unreason, monstrosity, and terror. Ghost-walking in the costume of science, industrial gaslighting also has mythic, magical, and demonic dimensions. Rigorous, rapid absorption of scientific 'innovations' – *novelty* – will propagate Houses of Terror and wider horror shows.

Thomas Love Peacock's *Nightmare Abbey* (1818) anticipates Horkheimer and Adorno's 'dialectic of Enlightenment' by expressing an 'unsettling critique' of its own 'purportedly "enlightened" era' (Davison 178). Peacock's character Mr Toobad laments

> our calamity. The devil has come among us, and has begun by taking possession of all the cleverest fellows. Yet, forsooth, this is the enlightened age. Marry, how? Did our ancestors go peeping about with dark lanterns; and do we walk at our ease in broad sunshine? Where is the manifestation of our light? (158)

Foreshadowing Marx's history of the unmaking of natural boundaries to establish capital's nightmarish system, Toobad continues: 'We see five thousand in the workhouse, where [our ancestors] saw one. ... We see children perishing in manufactories, where they saw them flourishing in the fields' (159). In Marx's parallel terms, the emerging factory system darkens the day and lights up the night, confounding older 'rustic' verities.

Artificial lighting is a necessary condition of both nightwork in the new, industrialising economy – in Marx's words, 'To appropriate labour during all the 24 hours of the day' (35: 263) – and nocturnal displays of 'the magic and necromancy' that imbue and surround commodities (35: 87). Capital conducts its physical and psychic orgies, of production and consumption, through artificial lighting's *glamour* – with the archaic sense of faery enchantment and the modern connotation of allurement or seduction inseparable. Its glamour epitomises the Gothicisation of science, enterprise, and everyday life, emanating from what Marx calls 'the magic of the bourgeoisie' (4: 283). This magic means that the bourgeois, like Faust, is susceptible to 'ghosts in the night' (Berman 70). Marx and Engels develop *Faust*'s oneiro-critique of the bourgeoisie's sorcerous-scientific formation, and despoliation, of the proletariat in the *Communist Manifesto* (1848), using the Spectre of Communism to induce the Faustian bourgeois to live 'in fear of his own night terrors' (Riley 34). To portray that class's magic as infernal, bewildering, and beyond its control, they retool 'The Sorcerer's Apprentice'. 'Modern bourgeois society', they write, 'is like the sorcerer [*Hexenmeister*], who is no longer able to control the powers of the nether world whom he has called up by his spells' (6: 489; see Pignarre and Stengers 51–5). This recasts the master sorcerer as powerless to undo his hexes, with capitalists as a class haunted by ever-present, revenant, and revolutionary proletarians. Living-dead workers unbury themselves collectively by revolution from below: 'What the bourgeoisie, therefore, produces, above all, is its own grave-diggers' (6: 496). A grave is being dug, Peter Riley argues, 'by the increasingly united workers of the world, but also by the bourgeois himself, as the various self-summoned nightmares eat away at him' (34).

Forty years after co-writing the *Manifesto*, Engels finds the bourgeoisie's infernal magic and its glamours of artificial lighting naturalised in a new 'capital of Capitalist Production' – New York. 'We got into New York after dark and I thought I got into a chapter of Dante's Inferno', he relates during his 1888 North American tour: 'everything there, made by man, is horrid ... naked electric arc-lights over every ship, not to light you but to attract you as an advertisement, and consequently blinding you and confusing everything before you' (48: 211).

Engels first spots the inseparability of tourism and 'blinding' interpellation, even torture, in an infernal setting under 'naked' artificial lighting, when he explores Manchester in the 1840s. There, he finds that such nakedness means peril, deception, and nightmarish bondage to cathemeral shift work for factory labourers while, for manufacturers and factory tourists, naked light is a glamorous veil, forming the caring, protective, and seductive surface of their fantasies of progress and dreams of 'enlightenment'. The enchanted and enchanting society that 'conjured up', in Marx and Engels's expression, 'gigantic means of production and of exchange' (6: 489) depends on the innovation of artificial light and its mass invasion into every pore of production, exchange, and consumption. Speedily absorbed and spread, artificial light becomes the horrid yet normalised surface appearance of bourgeois society. Every scientific-sorcerous artificial light installed during the Industrial Revolution instantiates one of 'the tiny catastrophes of which everyday existence is made up' (Kracauer 62). Their cumulative effect presents a contemporary calamity: 'the deceptive clarity of this upside-down world' and 'the present system of floodlit enlightenment' (Debord 20).

Gothic 'gaslighting': tourism and torture

Capitalism manufactures material commodities and commodified consciousness-corporeality, whereby the circadian rhythm is inverted by the machine's supra-human demands. 'Gas-lighting', Engels reports in 'The Condition of England' (1844), creates 'an enormous demand for cast-iron pipes' (3: 483). It also enforces capital's insatiable demand for minds and bodies in thrall to the commodity form's artificially lit hegemony, incessantly spawning Gothic morbidities such as those Thomas Carlyle reveals and reviles in

Past and Present (1843). Decrying the condition of industrialised England as a crisis of consciousness, or 'spirit', Carlyle thunders at the invasive ideological piping of industrial capitalism's workplace apparatuses, developed into everyday human conduct and consciousness, sparing not even the most intimate sanctum – the soul. His coruscating prose silhouettes the invaded spaces as 'waste latitudes', or spiritual *terra incognita*, 'where the men go about as if by galvanism' (*Past and Present* 187). This recalls Goethe's allusions to the galvanising currents of scientific-sorcerous modernity: 'I felt a shock that went all through me', 'Somehow my feet are as heavy as lead' (lines 2,324 and 2,331). Engels's 1844 review of Carlyle's book renders 'as if by galvanism' as 'like galvanised corpses' (3: 454). Industrialised somnambulants, or zombie-like automata, wander 'with meaningless glaring eyes, and have no soul, but only a beaver-faculty and stomach! The haggard despair of Cotton-factory, Coal-mine operatives', Carlyle reflects, 'is painful to behold' (187). Standing-dead and sleep-walking workers have been drained by work, overwork, and machinic enslavement to the cash nexus, and Carlyle the sorcerer would incant them out of nightmarish oppression and into prelapsarian sentience: 'Awake ye noble Workers ... It is you who are already half-alive, whom I will welcome into life, whom I will conjure in God's name to shake off your enchanted sleep, and live wholly!' (272) The spectacle of 'nightmare sleepers' is not 'playhouse poetry' (270), Gothic diversion, or cathartic entertainment like a phantasmagoria show. It is an everyday experience and a recurrent nightmare. Carlyle communicates its collective reality by staging a Gothic interfusion of the actual and the phantasmic: 'our real-phantasmagory' (124), a rubric readily applicable to, because critically re-enacted by, Engels's *The Condition of the Working Class in England*. Carlyle's horrified apprehension of England's unreasoned modernity – 'behold, some baleful fiat as of Enchantment has gone forth' (1) – echoes throughout Engels's own documentary-apparitional account of industrialism's grimoire.

Following the damned, down-going footsteps of Carlyle's living-dead workers – 'Sooty Manchester, it too is built on the infinite Abysses' (227) – *Condition* is a katabasis into Manchester's Industrial Gothic depths and a proto-sociology of the capitalist uncanny. Engels's reportage of Britain's industrial movement and its seeming sorcery – 'giant cities', he writes with awe, 'spring up as if by a magic touch' – shades into menacing visions (4: 313). At one stage, the 'background' to his vertical travel 'is furnished by old barrack-like factory buildings', 'the pauper burial-ground', and 'the Workhouse, the "Poor-Law Bastille" of Manchester, which, like a citadel, looks threateningly down from behind its high walls and parapets on the hilltop, upon the working-people's quarter below' (4: 352). This shock city houses a new 'Hell upon Earth': 'Everything which here arouses horror and indignation is of recent origin, belongs to the *industrial epoch*' (4: 355, original emphasis). Even Engels's recourse to the mundane – newspapers, official statistics, government reports – summons phantasmal alterity: he decrypts utilitarian facts and figures as multiple signs of workers disfigured and dead on their feet in servitude to capital. *Condition* also traverses the discursive terrain 'discovered' by Thomas De Quincey's *Confessions of an English Opium-Eater* (1821–2), the city imaged as *terra incognita* where 'dreamy lamp-light' is more likely to confound than to clarify the denizens' life-ways (De Quincey 305, 337).

The fabulised discourse of urban-industrial exploration overlaps that which developed more specifically around the factory system. The language registers of these variegated discourses encompass the awe-struck or spiritually uplifted sublime, the biblical, classical mythology, the folkloric, the fairy tale, and the Gothic. Their governing lexicon is phenomenologically enchained to marvel and its double – shock – at capital's magical re-invention of the world. Humphrey Jennings's anthology, *Pandæmonium*, provides examples, from both these discourses, of Gothic dreams and nightmares aroused by the industrial illumination of factories and other urban-industrial stages. Fanny Kemble (1827), descending into the newly completed Thames Tunnel, believes its subterranean engineers are guided by 'God's inspiration': 'the whole lighted by a line of gas lamps, and as bright, almost, as if it were broad day. It was more like one of the long avenues of light that lead to the abodes of the genii in fairy tales' – which, perplexingly, is also 'the beautiful road to Hades' (qtd. in Jennings 168–9). James Nasmyth (1830) witnesses a 'marvellous' if hellish nocturne: blast-furnacemen 'running about amidst the flames as in a pandemonium; while around and outside the horizon was a glowing belt of fire, making even the stars look pale and feeble' (qtd. in Jennings 171). Gaslight's appearance of 'broad day' and the pandemoniacal enfeeblement of starlight presage the ascendancy of capital's second nature.

Thus, by the 1840s, Marx and Engels can *détourne* an available super-naturalised discourse on the industrial scene. Charles Dickens's *Hard Times* (1854) ironically articulates its unstable range – from the glamorous to the ghastly. His fictional Coketown's factories are 'Fairy palaces burst into illumination' (56) but the adjacent workers' brick-built, smoke-blighted quarter is 'unnatural red and black like the painted face of a savage' (20). Dickens – himself a factory tourist – atypically crystallises the opposition of enlightened middle-class dreaming and its obverse: the dark, waking nightmare of working-class barbarity.

Engels's *Condition* critically disassembles the insouciance of 'factory tourism'. Factories have become glamorised bourgeois destinations – tourist spectacles or places of pilgrimage – as well as carnival sites of popular public entertainments such as 'daredevil' acts (Freeman 22). The factory is not only a marvel but also a synecdoche, or model, for the more general regulation and superintendence of contemporary life. For many factory tourists, new mills are exemplars of progress, civility, and care. However, as Horkheimer and Adorno argue, capitalism's 'managed provision of friendly care, administered by every factory as a means of increasing production, brings the last private impulse under social control' and 'such care is transferred in totalitarian style from the factory to society itself' (121).

William Beckford eerily foreshadows Horkheimer and Adorno in his grim vision of a *ville universelle*. In the 1780s, Beckford seeks frisson through technologies of light: machineries of illusion such as the camera obscura, the magic lantern, and, specifically, the proto-cinematic Eidophusikon. A press announcement describes the latter, invented by Philippe Jacques de Loutherbourg, as 'Moving Pictures, representing Phenomena of Nature' (qtd. in Davison 141). In 1782, Beckford personally commissions an Eidophusikon spectacle that conjures Milton's Pandemonium. He vividly recounts 'that strange necromantic light which de Loutherbourg had thrown over what absolutely appeared a realm of Fairy, or rather, perhaps, a Demon Temple deep beneath the earth set apart for tremendous mysteries … glowing haze investing every object' (qtd. in Davison 141–2). This hallucinatory marvel, as Carol Margaret Davison spotlights (141), partly inspires Beckford's writing of *Vathek* (1786). If the Gothic novelist is seduced by the necromantic-light aesthetic of de Loutherbourg's entertainments, fifty years later he is shocked by the application of scientific-sorcerous lighting technologies to globalise capitalist modernity.

In a letter of 1833, Beckford anticipates another paradise lost. In an epochal displacement, industrial capital's gigantic artifice destroys nature and, naturalising itself, becomes second nature – a universal, artificially lit habitat. He foresees a world where locality, community, and humanity become undifferentiated:

> a kind of universal city [*ville universelle*] that extends from one end of Europe to the other and even in Asia and on the coasts of Africa … There is no more countryside anywhere – we cut down the forests, we violate the mountains – we only want canals – we don't care about the rivers. (our translation from the French qtd. in Jennings 187–8)

From there, he rhetorically shifts into a full-scale, Gothic-prophetic mode, in the manner of Carlyle. Also, he almost certainly draws upon another of de Loutherbourg's 'inventions' – the historically pivotal paintings depicting awesome assemblages of industry, precursing Gothic encounters with the factory system, which Marx later describes as a 'demon power' (35:

385). De Loutherbourg's celebrated canvas *Coalbrookdale by Night* (1801), showing the Bedlam Furnaces in Madeley Dale, with open coke hearths emitting an infernal firelight, seems to directly cue Beckford's frightful view: 'everywhere Gas and steam – the same smell, the same whirlwinds of execrable, thick, fetid smoke'. This is the template for a nightmarish new world order, producing 'the same common, mercantile look on whatever side you are on – a boring monotony, and an impious artifice spitting every minute in the face of Mother Nature, who will soon find her children changed into Automata and Machines' (translated from Jennings 188). In 'A Plea for Gas Lamps' (1878), Robert Louis Stevenson electrifies Beckford's universal city: 'A sedate electrician somewhere in a back office touches a spring – and behold! from one end to another of the city, from east to west, from the Alexandra to the Crystal Palace, there is light! *Fiat Lux*, says the sedate electrician' (293). Stevenson's electrician represents the technical sorcerers whose monotonous magic touch illuminates a metropolitanised Hyde: built upon 'the infernal regions' (296), 'the design of the monstrous city flashes into vision' (293–4). Beckford's hideous 'universal city' is prescient of Horkheimer and Adorno's 'totalitarian' conceptualisation of the factory as the emergent model of a 'universal' city-state of human society and being.

In a broad sociological sense, writes Joshua B. Freeman, 'the giant factory helped produce modernity, the now we inhabit still, even if it no longer has the awe-inspiring novelty it once had [it] has made dreams reality, but it has rendered nightmares real, too' (319). The sense of proprietorial 'care' for workers that could be admired in 'progressive' factories – amenably clean, ventilated, and, most particularly, well-lit – is perverse bourgeois fancy.

The scale, machinery, and 'modernity of the mills', Freeman recognises, 'mesmerized' and 'dazzled' middle-class visitors: 'To lengthen hours of operation, in the early nineteenth century mill owners began installing gaslights, a spectacle that drew visitors from near and far' (21–2). What enchants the tourist enrages Engels: 'Work at night is impossible without a very powerful light produced by concentrating the rays of the lamp, making them pass through glass globes, which is most injurious to the sight' (4: 479). By this inversion, shift workers are creatures of the night blinded by light. Artificial illumination becomes infrastructural atrocity; industrial workshops morph into torture chambers. 'Pure brightness is a kind of *light torture*. In [terrestrial] nature', Thomas Posch reflects, 'light never shines continuously from a fixed direction' (50, original emphasis), whereas 'modern society is subject to a kind of "light compulsion" [*Lichtzwang*]' (56). The genesis of 'light compulsion' lies, in Marx's analysis, in the 'dull compulsion of economic relations' that completes 'the subjection of the labourer to the capitalist' and represents 'the "natural laws of production"' (35: 726). Compulsory lighting systems to maximise the working day and obliterate night are literally built into the 'grotesquely terrible ... discipline necessary for the wage system' (35: 726). In capital's perverted theology, as Lord Byron grasps in *Don Juan* (1819–24), *fiat lux* – 'Let there be light' – is scripturally displaced by a dark new fiat: Let there be gaslight!

Upending bourgeois paeans that enchant the industrial landscape, Engels makes *Condition* a psycho-geographic exploration of baleful but bright netherlands. Directed in part by Carlyle's persona 'the picturesque Tourist' – torpid, 'enchanted' workhouse inmates 'reminded me of Dante's Hell' (*Past and Present* 2) – Engels explicitly rebuts 'the English bourgeoisie's fine phrases by means of their ugly deeds' (4: 585). He demystifies the leisured, bourgeois aestheticisation of artificial light as both torture by light and the making light of torture. He counters bourgeois fairy tales, such as one told by Andrew Ure, with 'the barbarism of single cases' of capitalist praxis (4: 457). In *The Philosophy of Manufactures* (1835), the physician-scientist Ure theorises a 'great doctrine' – 'when capital enlists science in her service, the refractory hand of labour will always be taught docility' (368) – and counts 'the number and brilliancy of the gas-lights in a cotton-mill' (375) among the conditions to habituate children to docile labouring. Yet, he also spins science as a sorcery that elevates child labour into a supernatural realm: 'The work of these lively elves seemed to resemble a sport, in which habit gave them a pleasing dexterity' (301). Ure thus aestheticises the mill as a theatre for his gas-lit midsummer night's dream. Engels quotes this noxious fantasy about elf-child workers, only to record how somnambulant children are battered in their nightmare existence: 'how their sleepiness is driven off with blows, how they fall asleep over their work nevertheless, how one poor child sprang up, still asleep, at the call of the overlooker, and mechanically went through the operations of its work after its machine was stopped' (4: 457–8). Inside capital's malignant underworld, it is the worker's 'mission' to endure stupefying and deadening, if not lethal, stress-tedium,

> every day and all day long from his eighth year. Moreover, he must not take a moment's rest; the engine moves unceasingly ... and if he tries to snatch one instant, there is the overlooker at his back with the book of fines. This condemnation to be buried alive in the mill, to give constant attention to the tireless machine is felt as the keenest torture by the operatives. (4: 466)

Ure's 'lively elves' are enslaved by Engels's 'vampire property-holding class' (4: 526). Industrial Manchester is a conflict zone where capital performs its nightmarish dream work and Engels's dissecting gaze exposes infra-ordinary darkness – vampirism, vivisepulture, Victorian hypocrisy – in its 'very powerful light'.

In *Condition*'s Postscript, Engels relates the 'time immemorial' custom amongst Manchester carpenters of

not 'striking a light' from Candlemas [February 2] to November 17, i.e., of working from six in the morning till six in the evening during the long days, and of starting as soon as it was light and finishing as soon as it began to get dark during the short days.

This '"barbaric" custom' is attacked by exasperated building contractors, determined to end it as a 'relic of the "Dark Ages" with the help of gas lighting, and when one evening before six o'clock the carpenters could not see any longer and put away their tools and went for their coats, the foreman lit the gas and said that they had to work till six o'clock' (4: 585–6). Engels draws back the curtain on what the factory tourist might have apprehended as care and improvement – a Dark Age eclipsed by enlightened modernity, with the 'help' of gaslight. He mocks the make-believe philanthropy of the building contractors, whose aim is not to promote the workers' well-being but, rather simply, to rob them of wages, time, and sleep.

By 1845, when *Condition* is published, the unnatural light of capital's enchanted night has irrevocably altered the sleepless practices of both commodity production and consumption. While commodities circulate as beacons of economic enlightenment in proliferating gaslight, critical-cultural awareness is awakening to the kinship between commodity culture and, in Carlyle's phrase, an 'eye-bewildering *chiaroscuro*' (*Sartor Resartus* 141) – the eye-tantalising, eye-torturing interanimation of capital's blinding glare and dark glamour. The working day and the shopping day are artificially extended, with gaslight condensing workplace and marketplace in a unitary capitalist dream – a universal dream city, or utopia, no less. Within the literary-documentary form of 'Commodity Gothicism' (Lootens 132–5), an emergent tendency views commodity culture's nightlife as a creation of 'light'. Light, however, uncannily engenders existential disturbances, symptomatic of an unprecedented relation between the human subject and capital's objects.

'try not to look at the objects'

Capital, Volume 1, identifies the Gothicism of the commodity from its very first sentence. However, Samuel Moore and Edward Aveling's classic translation of that opening – 'The wealth of those societies in which the capitalist mode of production prevails, presents itself as "an immense accumulation of commodities", its unit being a single commodity' (35: 45) – misses

Marx's Gothic evocation. As Ann Cvetkovich explains, the original German phrase rendered as 'immense accumulation of commodities' – *ungeheure Warensammlung* – 'carries the connotation of a "monstrous" collection of commodities, the first instance of the Gothic rhetoric that Marx frequently uses to suggest that personal agency has been replaced by the apparent agency of objects, which, like animated monsters, begin to control human beings' (175).

Across *Capital*'s three volumes, from *monstrous* assemblies of commodities, through the *Frankenstein*-influenced *danse macabre* of factory workers undergoing torturous experiments – 'like those of anatomists on frogs' (35: 460) – to the revelation of capital's 'enchanted, perverted, topsy-turvy world' (37: 817), Marx thematises 'the necessary inversion of capitalism's abstract, Enlightened secularism into a thoroughgoing fetishism that endows both the products and the process of production with uncanny powers' (Murray 256). The transition from feudalism to capitalism does not involve an enlightening passage from superstition to reason. Rather, it annunciates the revolutionary supersession of outmoded religions by a magical new one. In Eugene McCarraher's lapidary phrase, 'the Enchantments of Mammon' (passim) encompass capital's promises, promiscuities, and predations. To Carlyle, dread and diabolism shadow 'enchantment': 'Industrial Work, still under bondage to Mammon, the rational soul of it not yet awakened, is a tragic spectacle. Men [are] restless, with convulsive energy, as if driven by Galvanism, as if possessed by a Devil' (*Past and Present* 206). And Marx equates Mammon with the typical capitalist 'Moneybags' (35: 176–86), for whom capital's enchantments are optimised by its denaturalised conquest of night for 'the working day'.

Gothicism galvanises Marx's critique of an inverted political economy, where Enlightenment secularism is overturned by supernaturalism, particularly in his reading of the commodity as possessing 'metaphysical subtleties and theological niceties' (35: 81). Every commodity is a catastrophic fragment of a calamitous, universal cult-worship: 'The whole mystery of commodities, all the magic and necromancy that surrounds [them]' (35: 87), is capital's 'religion of everyday life' (37: 817). To reprise Horkheimer and Adorno's argument, as summarised by Esther Leslie: 'Enlightenment goes under the guise of science, but is, in fact, irrational, magical and trapped within myth. This magic that subtends but is repressed in industrial modernity converts, it seems, into a malignant force' (9). For Carlyle and Marx alike, the age of capitalism is not a rationally enlightened one but, rather, an epoch of new superstitions and mystifications. Its hegemony is a naturalised supernaturalism; apparently pleasurable 'enchantments' have *doppelgängers* in horror, and night-light technology invests the 'metaphysical' commodity with a new aura. Gothic representations of capital's immense, monstrous accumulation of commodities, seen in a literal new light, become a transnational literary topos – a chimeric imaginary – by which visions of capital's dream world, especially in its cities of dreadful light, are elaborated.

De Quincey's *Confessions*, an internationally circulated sensation, initialises the terms for navigating the bafflements and inscrutabilities of artificially illuminated urban nightscapes – 'these *terrae incognitae* … that brought confusion to the reason' (305). This provokes nightmares of Piranesian labyrinths, circling on themselves; 'engines and machinery … wheels, cables, levers' and interminable 'labours' (330). His *Autobiography* (1853–54) recalls a first walk in London's streets, discombobulated – 'perhaps terrified' – by their 'Babylonian confusion' and 'hurrying figures of men and women … like a pageant of phantoms' (139). In *Confessions*, both the stage and 'the backdrop of the Urban Gothic environment of London, with its dark alleys and labyrinthine streets' (Davison 206), are layered by oneiric light: 'I walk', De Quincey confesses, 'by dreamy lamp-light'. Dreamy Gothic light suffuses his noctivagations and apprehension of objects of desire: the commodities that are his narrative's hero and heroine – opium and the streetwalker Ann: 'lamp-light fell upon her face, as for the last time I kissed her lips' (337).

In *Don Juan*, De Quincey's contemporary Lord Byron imitates modernity's perplexity and perversity by casting artificial light as the aggrandised revenant of a fatal folkloric figure: the will-o-the-wisp. Byron's narrator recalls 'travellers to mighty Babylon' in the 1790s being dazzled by oil-fuelled streetlamps and the novelty of nocturnal window-shopping (Canto XI, stanza 23). 'There barbers' blocks with periwigs in curl / In windows; here the lamplighter's infusion / Slowly distilled into the glimmering glass / (For in those days we had not got to gas)' (XI, 22). Getting to gaslighting does not signal reason or progress, however, and its spectacular use for 'grand illumination' on public anniversaries 'Is of all dreams the first hallucination' (VII, 44). 'The line of lights … up to Charing Cross, / Pall Mall, and so forth', cues images of French revolutionaries hanging 'gentlemen' on 'their new-found lantern' (lamp-posts) and anti-industrialisation protestors turning English 'country seats' into 'bonfires' (XI, 26–7). Lamplighters' infusions, grand light-shows, lamp-posts-cum-gallows, burning estates – these 'may illuminate mankind', but they also manifest an uncanny, inhuman will: 'A sort of *ignis fatuus* to the mind, / Which, though 'tis certain to perplex and frighten, / Must burn more mildly ere it can enlighten' (XI, 27). *Don Juan* performs the inversion-vision of artificial light as a moral-political darkness made hegemonic by capitalism's 'alienation and dismantling of the divinely singular command of the *Genesis* ur-fiat' – *fiat lux* (Lindstrom 197).

A direct precursor of Marx and Engels, Heine, presents ironically disarrayed, Byronised impressions of London-Babylon's artificial illumination in *English Fragments* (1828). The Tower rises 'like a spectral, gloomy dream above the cloud-covered London', wherein he apprehends an Urban Gothic transposition: the fairy-tale motifs of woodland and brook reified, or petrified, into 'the stone forest of houses, and amid them the rushing stream of faces [in] machine-like movement'. Heine stereotypes himself as a German poet, 'a dreamer, who stares at everything, even a ragged beggar-woman, or the shining wares of a goldsmith's'. In London's main streets, 'the eye of the stranger is incessantly caught by the new and brilliant wares exposed for sale in the windows'. Every astral lamp, boot and tea kettle 'shines out so invitingly':

> even the most commonplace necessaries of life appear in a startling magic light through this artistic power of setting forth everything to advantage. Ordinary articles of food attract us by the new light in which they are placed; even uncooked fish lie so delightfully dressed that the rainbow gleam of their scales attracts us.

He contrasts this incessant kaleidoscopic attraction with one of its gravest afflictions: 'the human beings whom we see ... sell the jolliest wares with the most serious faces' (344–9).

In Nikolai Gogol's De Quincey-inspired Petersburg tales, the apex city of Russia's Europeanised modernity is a microcosm of capital's world of gas-lit dreaming. Like London's supernaturalised thoroughfares in De Quincey and Heine, the eponymous street of 'Nevsky Prospect' (1835) involves a crowded apparition of flashing speed and fragmentation – another uncanny spectacle of humanity in machine-like motion. Gogol's narrator *qua* natural historian spots a new species of extremophile in its diabolically lit habitat: 'What does this street – the beauty of our capital – not shine with!' he exclaims, observing a human heliotrope, the modern consumer, turning 'her head to glittering shop windows as a sunflower turns toward the sun'. Nevsky Prospect itself is an enchanted, shape-shifting realm: 'What a quick phantasmagoria is performed on it in the course of a single day!' At dusk, it is marvellously yet horrifically recast by 'deceitful light' from streetlamps. The free dis-association of Gogol's oneirism conveys capital's enstaged ghost-walking. St Petersburg's 'brightly lit' concourse of people, shops and commodities appears as a bricolage of objects and body parts on a dis-assembly line, 'as if some demon had chopped the whole world up into a multitude of different pieces and mixed those pieces together with no rhyme or reason'. 'I always', the narrator protests, 'try not to look at the objects I meet at all' – as if they are empowered to hypnotise and possess. 'Everything is deception, everything is a dream, everything is not what it seems to be! [For] the devil himself lights the lamps only so as to show everything not as it really looks' (245–78). Dark morbidities shade the illuminated commodity.

From the gallimaufry of gas-lit Commodity Gothicism he arrays in *Nicholas Nickleby* (1839), Dickens alights on a pre-Enlightenment *memento mori*, warning of London's demise, if not capital's too. London's 'noisy, bustling, crowded streets', 'displaying long double rows of brightly-burning lamps', are 'illuminated besides with the brilliant flood that streamed from the windows of the shops' piled with commodities 'in rich and glittering profusion'. 'Emporiums' and 'tempting stores' jumble-sell 'clothes for the newly-born, drugs for the sick, coffins for the dead'. 'Life and death went hand in hand', inextricably inverted, in a fugitive 'motley dance like the fantastic groups of the old Dutch painter' – an imprecise reference to Hans Holbein's *Totentanz* woodcuts. The title character catches this optical orgy – 'a strange procession' of 'quickly-changing and ever-varying objects' – from a moving coach (307–8). Dickens evokes the illusions of a phantasmagoria show, as Gogol has done and Marx will do with regard to commodity fetishism: 'a definite social relation between men, that assumes, in their eyes, the fantastic [*phantasmagorische*] form of a relation between things' (35: 83). Flooded by artificial light, consumer capital dances towards death in a maelstrom of the vanities.

Gaslight, in Egon Friedell's haunting summation, 'took possession of all streets and public localities. By 1840 it was flaring everywhere … this strident and gloomy, sharp and flickering, prosaic and ghostly illumination' (qtd. in Benjamin T1a,10). As gaslight flooded 'everywhere', Gothic renderings of the devil's light and its saturation of commodity culture proliferated. To name just three canonical texts of the 1840s that deal in dreams, nightmares, and endarkment rapt in gas-lit studies: Edgar Allan Poe's 'The Man of the Crowd' (1840), whose progeny, Charles Baudelaire's study of Poe (1852) and Stevenson's *The Strange Case of Dr Jekyll and Mr Hyde* (1886), also depict artificial light as deceptive, satanic, and nightmarish; Nathaniel Hawthorne's 'The Celestial Railroad' (1843); and, of course, Engels's *Condition* (1845). In 1848, Marx sees lighting technology, typified by a commodity that Heine had mentioned, as a symbol of triumphalist bourgeois magic and the political overthrow of the feudal ruling class and its 'rustic' order': 'The bourgeoisie turns … the royal sun into a civic astral lamp' (8: 16).

Artificial light reveals the commodity yet conceals its artifice. The auratic commodity and its generative human activities portend *something* globally, beyond reason's reach: the sense of 'being', simultaneously, seduced and shocked by the commodity's life-ways. There is a creeping perception of historically jolted relations between the human subject and objects – dreamy, irrational, and phantasmal. All 'goods' – gold, dead fish, coffins – shine brighter than the shadowy crowds who seem spellbound by them in the carnival of consumption. This alienation exemplifies Horkheimer and

Adorno's argument that the factory's carcerality bleeds into society at large – as in Heine's image of Londoners' 'machine-like movement'. Under the infrastructural ukase of artificial light, worker and consumer are equally obeisant to the commodity, becoming sleep-disordered cogs in capital's perpetual-motion machine. Factory 'hand' and faceless crowd: both are oppressed by the dreamy light cast by the monstrous production and accumulation of commodities.

Recalling Engels's apprehension of light utilised 'not to light you but to attract you as an advertisement' and Ernst Bloch's 1959 verdict on the 'light of advertising' – designed to entice 'dream-birds' – the consumer is a shape-shifted soul, 'the most sacred thing there is next to property' itself; 'gleaming and acclaimed commodities' are the regalia of a profane religion, immanent in 'a parade of Christmas and Easter values throughout the whole year' (Bloch 344). Bloch envisions an inverted capitalist orgy, where the lights of advertising and the shining object 'only serve to increase' an existential 'darkness' (344) – a neat fore-gloss of the twenty-first century's 'fluorescent world of screaming commodities' (Leslie 20) and its incessant commodification of human subjectivity.

'House of Terror'

Although Moore and Aveling's translation of *Capital* overlooks the monstrosity of its Commodity Gothicism, they do transmit the monstrous, diabolical, and uncanny connotation of capitalism in Marx's rich personification of machinery:

> An organised system of machines, to which motion is communicated by the transmitting mechanism from a central automaton, is the most developed form of production by machinery. Here we have, in the place of the isolated machine, a mechanical monster [*mechanisches Ungeheuer*] whose body fills whole factories, and whose demon power, at first veiled under the slow and measured motions of his giant limbs, at length breaks out into the fast and furious whirl of his countless working organs. (35: 384–5)

Marx excoriates the structural demand of such monsters and their capitalist owners that this 'demon power' should not 'lie "idle" during the night' (35: 269). He quotes a cotton magnate's economic rationalisations: 'When one of our people leaves the mill, he renders useless a capital that has cost £100.' He then imaginatively paraphrases that same capitalist: 'Only fancy! making "useless" for a single moment, a capital that has cost £100! It is, in truth, monstrous, that a single one of our people should ever leave the factory!' (35: 409). As another of capital's inversions, the cotton labourer is the *real* disruptive monster for needing sleep and leaving machinery 'idle'. In the bourgeois dream world where workers labour non-stop, capitalists themselves are left sleepless when the nightmare of workers leaving the 'mechanical monster' to sleep is realised.

'Sleep is much modified by habit', Robert Macnish observes in *The Philosophy of Sleep* (1830), and so the habit or dull compulsion of commodity production transforms sleep, dreams, and nightmares for capitalists as well as their 'monstrous' human workforce in a dreadful inversion of psycho-physiological responsiveness:

> silence itself may become a stimulus, while sound ceases to be so. Thus, a miller being very ill, his mill was stopped that he might not be disturbed by its noise, but this, so far from inducing sleep, prevented it altogether; and it did not take place till the mill was set a-going again. For the same reason, the proprietor of some vast iron-works, who slept close to them amid the incessant din of hammers, forges, and blast furnaces, would awake if there was any cessation of the noise during the night. (31–2)

In this oppressive, topsy-turvy vignette, the mechanical monster's cacophony is an aural incubus that *induces* restorative sleep instead of screaming night terror. It primes Chris Baldick and Robert Mighall's contention that, for the 'restlessly dynamic' bourgeoisie, 'everything is a source of profit except perfect stasis' (284). The phantasmagorical reality of incessant commodity production is the structural bedding for what Baldick and Mighall call 'good practical reasons why the middle class should sleep more soundly than other social groups can' (284). Macnish's 'philosophy' of sleep modification – or the commodification of sleep itself – clarifies, but cannot resolve, the contradiction between Moneybags's restless dynamism and biologically necessary quietude. Like its proletarian sleepwalkers, Macnish suggests, the bourgeoisie is also in thrall to the commodity form and its fetishism: the risk of stasis – the cessation of industrial pandemonium – haunts its sleep.

Commodity production assumes and demands a lethal, transmogrifying force. Marx's history of the working day's prolongation into night via new lighting technology represents capital, among its multiple forms, as a mechanical monster shape-shifting into the vampire, werewolf, and 'flesh agents', as the procurers of 'hands' for factory work were called (35: 384, 273). The vampire figure pervades 'The Working Day', from beginning – 'Capital is dead labour, that, vampire-like, only lives by sucking living labour, and lives the more, the more labour it sucks' – to end: 'the vampire will not lose its hold', Marx quotes Engels, 'so long as there is a muscle, a nerve, a drop of blood to be exploited' (35: 241, 306). Capital's vampirism is not of the folkloric kind – killed by light – but a modern neoplasm that feeds in endless artificial day.

Artificial light materialises the commodity, its production, and its consumption, and simultaneously dematerialises the abject human subject in a sleepless, endless day. Emulating Carlyle's and Engels's infernal travelogues and finding 'common ground with Gothic literature' that appeared in the dawn shadows of the Industrial Revolution, Marx 'takes us on a journey through hell' – 'the night spaces of the capitalist underworld' (McNally 138). This katabasis does not occur in darkness. From its artificially lit Inferno, capital produces the circadian arrhythmics of Macnish's miller and ironmonger, the eternally wakeful, hollowed-eyed wanderers of Carlylean wastelands, and Engels's sleepless children tortured by wage slavery, 'tireless' machinery, and 'very powerful light'.

Throughout his Dantean descent into capital's workshops of creation, Marx vivisects the apparent improvements and modernisations that mesmerised the bourgeois factory tourist. By the mid-1800s, the factory system's compulsive practices are perceptually re-viewed as scenic novelties, marvels, where the boundaries between material-metaphysical 'creation' and fantasies of 'recreation' blur, and the chimera of enlightened 'care' is spot-lit and broadcast. Plotting the development from 'Bastille' workhouse to factory, Marx discovers no motive of benevolence or care – only punitive deceit and vampiric passion. Ostensibly, the original late-1700s conception was to extirpate 'idleness, debauchery and excess' – folklorically and ideologically endemic to lower orders – and thus 'to shut up such labourers as become dependent on public support, in a word, paupers, in "an *ideal workhouse*"' (35: 281, original emphasis). However, citing the 1770 *Essay on Trade and Commerce*, Marx exposes the real deception: the dream workhouse is always already intended for a rapid, innovative conversion into something other. Such

> ideal workhouse must be made a 'House of Terror', and not an asylum for the poor, 'where they are to be plentifully fed, warmly and decently clothed, and where they do but little work'. In this 'House of Terror', this 'ideal workhouse, the poor shall work 14 hours in a day'.

The dream comes true as a living nightmare: 'The "House of Terror" for paupers of which the capitalistic soul of 1770 only dreamed, was realised a few years later in the shape of a gigantic "Workhouse" for the industrial worker himself. It is called the Factory. And the ideal this time fades before the reality' (35: 281–2). For Marx, the reality is the cybernetic reconstitution of the human body-as-machine and the commodity form's colonisation of human psychology:

in its blind unrestrainable passion, its were-wolf hunger for surplus labour, capital oversteps not only the moral, but even the merely physical maximum bounds of the working day. It usurps the time for growth, development, and healthy maintenance of the body. It steals the time required for the consumption of fresh air and sunlight. It higgles over a meal-time, incorporating it where possible with the process of production itself, so that food is given to the labourer as to a mere means of production, as coal is supplied to the boiler, grease and oil to the machinery. (35: 270–1)

Thus capital 'reduces the sound sleep needed for the restoration, reparation, refreshment of the bodily powers to just so many hours of torpor as the revival of an organism, absolutely exhausted, renders essential'. Marx concludes, 'it is the greatest possible daily expenditure of labour power, no matter how diseased, compulsory, and painful it may be, which is to determine the limits of the labourers' period of repose' (35: 271). This is a raw vision of capital's aspirational domination of both workday consciousness and the private unconscious – Romantic 'repose'.

In Marx's social anatomy, the confounding of waking life and sleep, day and night, are reductive requirements for the transubstantiation of the human being into mere instrumentality. Industrial capitalism's abolition of 'rustic' statutes means that 'repose' – the need to sleep – is a psycho-biological relic of a dark, pre-modern age. 'Sleep is an uncompromising interruption of the theft of time from us by capitalism', Jonathan Crary argues, 'an irrational and intolerable affirmation that there might be limits to the compatibility of living beings with the allegedly irresistible forces of modernization' (10, 13). Capital's homogenising force sublimates any differentiating structure; archaic binaries such as 'sacred-profane, carnival-workday, nature-culture, machine-organism', figuratively melt into air or turn into gas, and 'any persisting notions of sleep as somehow "natural" are rendered unacceptable' (13).

Conclusion

Capitalism's quotidian psycho-physical operations compel its leaching of working energy and theft of sleep under artificial light. Sleep is dormant and relatively motionless, and to the bourgeoisie – with its unconscious, systemic drive for constant motion and aversion to stasis – nothing, except proletarian social revolution, could be more troubling. The artificially lit conquest and surveillance of night invert regenerative slumber-time into a regime of dominative hyper-activity. In light of the class upheavals, 'the "revolutions" and organizational forms thrown up by the working class' from the early 1800s, capital must re-superintend a proletariat that itself is 'on the move, scheming, energetic, and volatile … to transform their energy and revolutionary heat into work' (Caffentzis 13). Ultra-mobile capitalism fights to confine the proletariat to a terrorising factory system of ceaseless, illuminated activity – an insomniac engine-regime, in which *rigorous rationalism* creates living nightmares. The sleeplessness of reason and dreams of endless day, for the fulfilment of a 24/7 rationalisation of work, produce and reproduce capital's hegemony as recurrent nightmare.

From the early 1800s, the technology of artificial light seeks to accomplish a totalisation. Technological and ideological 'light' will minister life under capital. 'Light' will be a unifying techno-principle, essential to capital's praxis. As Fredric Jameson glosses Marx's observation that the wealth of capitalist societies presents itself, or appears, as an immense/monstrous collection of commodities, 'we can put the emphasis decisively on the ambiguous philosophical verb "appears" (*erscheint*). This is indeed nothing but an appearance, the surface mirage of a market system' (43). Capital is apparitional, and its governing principle – 'light' – doubles as the Gothic surface appearance of its modernity. Light will govern the production and consumption of 'goods', joining factory to arcade, workplace to shopping strip, as processes and sites that are sutured in a holistic dreamscape, veiled by the light of capital's second nature. The principle of 'light' animates capital's endless reproductive cyclicity – a cyclicity manifest in De Quincey's Piranesian dreaming as the 'endless growth and self-reproduction' of vast Gothic architectures (330). Engels's observation that gaslighting 'created an enormous demand for cast-iron pipes' is also brilliantly nightmarish, conjuring the image of a prison house of terror as an artificially illuminated system, inhumanly reproducing itself like a gigantic parthenogenetic organism by the light of its own established needs and structural artifice.

Note

1 All references to Marx and Engels are from their *Collected Works* (Lawrence and Wishart, 1975–2004, 50 vols); volume number precedes page number.

Works cited

Adorno, Theodor W. *Dream Notes*, translated by Rodney Livingstone. Polity, 2007.
Baldick, Chris, and Robert Mighall. 'Gothic Criticism.' *A New Companion to the Gothic*, edited by David Punter. Wiley-Blackwell, 2012, pp. 267–87.

Benjamin, Walter. *The Arcades Project*, translated by Howard Eiland and Kevin McLaughlin. Harvard University Press, 1999.

Berman, Marshall. *All That Is Solid Melts into Air: The Experience of Modernity.* Verso, 1983.

Bloch, Ernst. *The Principle of Hope*, translated by Neville Plaice et al., vol. 1. MIT Press, 1995.

Byron (Lord). *Don Juan*. Penguin, 1977.

Caffentzis, George. *In Letters of Blood and Fire: Work, Machines, and the Crisis of Capitalism*. PM Press, 2013.

Carlyle, Thomas. *Past and Present*. Boston, 1843.

Carlyle, Thomas. *Sartor Resartus*. Oxford University Press, 1999.

Crary, Jonathan. *24/7: Late Capitalism and the Ends of Sleep*. Verso, 2013.

Culp, Andrew. *Dark Deleuze*. University of Minnesota Press, 2016.

Cvetkovich, Ann. *Mixed Feelings: Feminism, Mass Culture, and Victorian Sensationalism*. Rutgers University Press, 1992.

Davison, Carol Margaret. *Gothic Literature 1764–1824*. University of Wales Press, 2009.

Debord, Guy. *In girum imus nocte et consumimur igni*, translated by Ken Knabb. The Anarchist Library, 2010.

Deleuze, Gilles, and Felix Guattari. *Anti-Oedipus: Capitalism and Schizophrenia*, translated by Robert Hurley, Mark Seem, and Helen R. Lane. University of Minnesota Press, 1983.

De Quincey, Thomas. *Confessions of an English Opium Eater with Selections from the Autobiography of Thomas De Quincey*, edited by Edward Sackville-West. Cresset Press, 1950.

De Sutter, Laurent. *Narcocapitalism: Life in the Age of Anaesthesia*, translated by Barnaby Norman. Polity, 2018.

Dickens, Charles. *Hard Times*, edited by Fred Kaplan and Sylvère Monod. Norton, 2001.

Dickens, Charles. *The Life and Adventures of Nicholas Nickleby*. London, 1839.

Freeman, Joshua B. *Behemoth: A History of the Factory and the Making of the Modern World*. Norton, 2018.

Goethe. *Faust I & II*, edited and translated by Stuart Atkins. Princeton University Press, 2014.

Gogol, Nikolai. *The Collected Tales of Nikolai Gogol*, translated by Richard Pevear and Larissa Volokhonsky. Vintage Books, 1999.

Heine, Heinrich. *The Works of Heinrich Heine*, translated by Charles Godfrey Leland, vol. II of vol. III. London, 1893.

Hobsbawm, Eric. *Industry and Empire: An Economic History of Britain since 1750*. Weidenfeld and Nicolson, 1968.

Horkheimer, Max, and Theodor W. Adorno. *Dialectic of Enlightenment: Philosophical Fragments*, translated by Edmund Jephcott. Stanford University Press, 2002.

Jameson, Fredric. *Representing* Capital: *A Commentary on Volume One*. Verso, 2011.

Jennings, Humphrey. *Pandæmonium 1660–1886: The Coming of the Machine as Seen by Contemporary Observers*, edited by Mary-Lou Jennings and Charles Madge. The Free Press, 1985.

Kracauer, Siegfried. *The Salaried Masses: Duty and Distraction in Weimar Germany*, translated by Quintin Hoare. Verso, 1998.

Leslie, Esther. *Synthetic Worlds: Nature, Art and the Chemical Industry*. Reaktion Books, 2005.

Lindstrom, Eric Reid. *Romantic Fiat: Demystification and Enchantment in Lyric Poetry*. Palgrave Macmillan, 2011.

Lootens, Tricia. 'Commodity Gothicism.' *The Encyclopedia of the Gothic*, edited by William Hughes, David Punter, and Andrew Smith. Wiley Blackwell, 2016, pp. 132–5.

Macnish, Robert. *The Philosophy of Sleep*. Glasgow, 1830.

Marx, Karl, and Frederick Engels. *Collected Works*. Lawrence and Wishart, 1975–2004, 50 vols.

McCarraher, Eugene. *The Enchantments of Mammon: How Capitalism Became the Religion of Modernity*. Harvard University Press, 2019.

McNally, David. *Monsters of the Market: Zombies, Vampires and Global Capitalism*. Brill, 2011.

Murray, Patrick. 'The Illusion of the Economic: The Trinity Formula and the "Religion of Everyday Life"'. *The Culmination of Capital: Essays on Volume III of Marx's* Capital, edited by Martha Campbell and Geert Reuten. Palgrave, 2002, pp. 246–72.

Osborne, Peter. *How to Read Marx*. Granta, 2005.

Peacock, Thomas Love. *Nightmare Abbey*. London, 1818.

Pignarre, Philippe, and Isabelle Stengers. *Capitalist Sorcery: Breaking the Spell*, edited and translated by Andrew Goffey. Palgrave Macmillan, 2011.

Posch, Thomas. 'From the Magic of the Light to the Destruction of the Night.' *Awakening the Night: Art from Romanticism to the Present*, edited by Agnes Husslein-Arco, Brigitte Borchhardt-Birbaumer, and Harald Krejci. Prestel, 2012, pp. 50–7.

Riley, Peter. 'Before the *Manifesto*: Märchen and the Impulse to Exorcism.' *Understanding Marx, Understanding Modernism*, edited by Mark Steven. Bloomsbury Academic, 2021, pp. 30–9.

Sedgwick, Eve Kosofsky. *The Coherence of Gothic Conventions*. Methuen, 1986.

Stevenson, Robert Louis. 'A Plea for Gas Lamps.' *Virginibus Puerisque and Other Papers*. London, 1881, pp. 288–96.

Ure, Andrew. *The Philosophy of Manufactures: Or, An Exposition of the Scientific, Moral, and Commercial Economy of the Factory System of Great Britain*. London, 1835.

Part II

Early classic Gothic dreams and nightmares

4

The monsters of prophecy in the Gothic dream, 1764–1818

Richard W. Moore Jr

According to Steven Kruger in *Dreaming in the Middle Ages*, because we live in a post-Freudian world, we often forget or neglect what dreams meant in earlier periods: 'The confinement of dreaming to a psychological or physiological realm is, of course, relatively recent' (2). Before Freud, dreams had for centuries been understood to have a variety of causes and functions. 'For most of its long history', Kruger explains, the dream was 'treated not merely as an internally-motivated phenomenon ... but as an experience strongly linked to the realm of divinity: dreams were often thought to foretell the future because they allowed the human soul access to a transcendent spiritual reality' (2). In the medieval and early modern periods, dreams were seen as having the potential to grant a glimpse of what was unknown or outside the dreamer's body. Prophetic dreams were believed to possess spiritual, philosophical, and political meaning.

But in the long eighteenth century, realism and Enlightenment thinking introduced both a sense of scepticism about the putatively divine significance of dreams and an interest in natural causes for them. Thomas Hobbes and John Locke, for example, explained dreams as merely internal phenomena, the result of disorders of the body or mind. Hobbes, writing in *Leviathan* (1668), stated that the dream 'proceeds from the agitation of the inward parts of the man's body' (9). Similarly, in an oft-quoted statement on dreams in *An Essay Concerning Human Understanding* (1690), Locke wrote that the 'dreams of sleeping men are ... waking man's ideas ... oddly put together' (117). As Janine Rivière aptly puts it, Hobbes and Locke consider dreams 'neither mystical nor mysterious' (137). Despite – and perhaps owing to – Enlightenment scepticism, a growing curiosity emerged about why people had dreams and if science could find neuro-physiological causes. Examining them from the standpoint of medical science, for example, Dr John Bond in *An Essay on the Incubus, or the Night-Mare* (1753) concluded that nightmares were the result of problems with blood circulation between the brain and the heart (19–20). More generally, as Jonathan Glance explains, scientists assumed that dreaming was due to 'an aberrant state of mind' during 'an imperfect sleep' caused by physical, mental, or emotional distress (34). In this way, under the influence of Enlightenment rationalism and medical science, because dreams were considered to be aberrations – evidence of temporary internal disorder – they were removed from social and political importance. As a result, these internal phenomena seemed, paradoxically, outside of time and reality.

Concurrent with this diminished significance and increased interest was the rise of the Gothic, and fundamental to that rise was the narrative/poetic dream scene. This chapter examines the centrality of dreams and their significant transformations across British Gothic novels from Horace Walpole's *The Castle of Otranto: A Gothic Story* (1764) to Mary Shelley's *Frankenstein; Or, The Modern Prometheus* (1818). In the Gothic, dreams and dream-like states serve as spaces in which characters confront the unfamiliar, the unknown, and the unseen future. At the same time, these spaces also seem to contain remnants of the familiar, the known, and the previously seen and experienced past. While the first dreams in Gothic novels are clearly prophetic and providential, prophetic moments in later novels become ambiguous as characters experience hypnagogic or liminal states. To examine these changes, I employ the Burkean concepts of the sublime and the monstrous because the contrast between them provides a framework for understanding the relationship between the dreamer and the dream. Both the dream and the sublime are predicated on the need for separation between the dreamer and the dream or nightmare. The dream and reality must be kept separate, along with the person and the sublime object. Moreover, the distinction between the sublime and the monstrous helps to illuminate the ways in which dreams in Gothic novels dramatise anxieties about Britain's perceived domestic and foreign threats.

Edmund Burke defines the sublime and its causes as 'Whatever is fitted in any sort to excite the ideas of pain, and danger … [and] is productive of the strongest emotion which the mind is capable of feeling' (*Philosophical* 86). Characters in – as well as readers of – Gothic novels often anticipate future terror because of some real or ostensibly real, supernatural, or similarly inexplicable event or occurrence. The sublime may arise from the anticipation of pain in a future event or the escape from pain in a past event. The fear comes from the glimpse of something excessive, powerful, or uncertain and beyond what human beings can imagine or comprehend – 'the Chaos' or 'the Absolute', as Jeffrey N. Cox refers to it when he explains that Gothic novels enact the eruption of the natural order and an 'unveiling' and 'explor[ing] of the Absolute or the Chaos that can never be contained by those orders' (7). The Gothic revelation of a sublime power or force calls into question the attempts of realist novels to contain and explain the order of the world.

However, as Burke explains, this experience of chaos must remain at a distance: 'When danger or pain press too nearly, they are incapable of giving any delight, and are simply terrible; but at certain distances, and with certain modifications, they may be, and they are delightful, as we every day experience' (*Philosophical* 86). The sublime requires distance – either spatial or temporal. When the distance is lost and the danger or threat becomes real, the experience becomes monstrous. Mark Neocleous has argued that the 'danger or pain' that 'press[es] too nearly' is the monstrosity that Burke continually attributes to the French Revolution in his *Reflections*: 'Burke invokes the monster as a way of disengaging the sublime from the horror and terror emerging in France' (76). Burke did not want England to view the Revolution as sublime – that is, from a distant perspective – because France, in his assessment, had created a monster by severing itself from its past. Burke and later alarmists feared that that monstrosity could spread to England. These fears arose concurrently with an interest in prophecies and the use of apocalyptic rhetoric in England among both opponents and supporters of the Revolution.

During and after the Revolution, prophetic dreams in British Gothic literature are complicated by a cloud of uncertainty and the emergence of monstrosity. Although the monstrous seems buried at the end of Matthew Lewis's *The Monk: A Romance* (1796), it emerges and garners proximity in oneiric encounters in Charlotte Dacre's *Zofloya; Or, The Moor* (1806) and Mary Shelley's *Frankenstein; Or, The Modern Prometheus* (1818). The Gothic dream scene comes to be a liminal space for the dramatisation of imperial fantasies and prophetic nightmares. Because Britons viewed slavery and the colonies as remote, the repeated movement from sublimity to monstrosity during these oneiric moments suggests disturbances of the fantasy of empire. Thus, through dream scenes, the novels dramatise the collapse of the geographical and imaginary boundaries between Britain and its colonies. In the process, the Gothic counters Enlightenment philosophy by continually reimagining the dream – considered an internal phenomenon delimited by the dreamer's mental associations – as an external phenomenon caused by unknown forces outside of the dreamer, thereby invoking the return of the social, political, and historical significance of the dream.

The Gothic dream's journey in British novels began when Horace Walpole famously identified in a letter to William Cole, friend and fellow antiquarian, the creative inspiration for *Otranto* as 'a very natural dream for a head filled like mine with Gothic story', a dream in which he was haunted by 'a gigantic hand in armour' (qtd. in Clery, 'Introduction' vii). It is easy for readers of *Otranto* to see the connections between Walpole's dream and the novel. What has been overlooked, however, is that the actual dreams in Walpole's novel do not resemble the dream that inspired it. Walpole's dream, as reported to Cole, would have been viewed, generally, as disordered thoughts from the past and, more specifically, classified in the eighteenth century as a nightmare, a dream experience caused, possibly, by poor blood circulation or by Walpole's irrational associations. In contrast, the dreams in *Otranto* are highly significant and prophetic and draw from an early modern or pre-Enlightenment notion of dreams as potentially possessing political power. Walpole's dream conjures up fearful images and thoughts of chaos or disorder from the past, and yet, the dreams in the novel gesture towards stability and order in the future.

The novel is bookended by two similar yet significantly different statements of the same prophecy. The story opens with preparations for the marriage between Prince Manfred's son, Conrad, and Isabella, the daughter of Frederic. While Manfred's wife, Hippolita, rarely raises any concerns for fear of offending Manfred, the people of his principality seem to know that Manfred fears the fulfilment of the 'ancient prophecy' that 'the castle and lordship of Otranto should pass from the present family, whenever the real owner should be grown too large to inhabit it' (17). While it is clear that Manfred is afraid of losing his power owing to this 'ancient prophecy', the connection between the prophecy and the marriage remains unclear to everyone until Manfred later explains that during the Crusades, his grandfather, Ricardo, killed Prince Alfonso, the father of Father Jerome and grandfather of Theodore, and usurped power to rule over the principality. Ricardo was visited by Saint Nicholas in a dream in which he (Ricardo) was 'promised that [his] posterity should reign in Otranto until the rightful owner should be grown too large to inhabit the castle, and as long as issuemale from Ricardo's loins should remain to enjoy it' (114). Revealed here is the required gender of the heir – the *son* of Manfred – for the family's continued illegitimate rule over Otranto. Notably, because the prophecy is Manfred's grandfather's dream, it is far from 'ancient' when considered in relation to the setting of events – that is, only two generations earlier. Thus does the ancient and public prophecy find its source in a private prophetic dream from the recent past.

This idea of the ancient revealed as recent recalls Walpole's elaborate hoax surrounding the book's publication and his stated objectives for writing *Otranto*. In the first preface, Walpole pretends to be a translator of a found manuscript who speculates that its possible author, an 'artful priest' living around the time of the Protestant Reformation, hoped to aid 'the empire of superstition' by using the innovative and modern style of letter-writing (5). Walpole thus attempts to persuade eighteenth-century readers that 'the artful priest's' style of writing is enlightened, persuasive, and believable, or relatively modern in contrast to the contents of the novel. The supernatural aspects of the story would have deluded readers of that earlier era, but not, Walpole winks, readers of the eighteenth century, the Age of Reason. His fake speculation about the writer of *Otranto* resonates with Thomas Hobbes's real complaint a century earlier that the superstitious masses had been led astray by unscrupulous people. Writing after the English Civil Wars and alluding to the propagation of prophecies during the Interregnum, Hobbes argues in *Leviathan* (1668) that 'men would be more fitted than they are for civil obedience' if there existed no belief in 'prognostics from dreams, false prophecies' (11). While Hobbes did not think that dreams should be significant, he did believe that because of 'crafty ambitious persons' (11), explanations about dreams had been, in the past, and could be, in the future, socially and politically destabilising forces. By warning about the social and political dangers of dreams and prophecies, Hobbes aimed to distinguish the reason and order of the present day from the superstition and disorder of the past.

Because of a perceived incongruity between the Middle Ages and the eighteenth century, Walpole's affixing of his name and the subtitle 'A Gothic Story' to the second edition of *Otranto* caused contemporary critics to be collectively offended to learn that a man of Walpole's social stature would write such an improbable story. E. J. Clery has explained that by confusing readers about the circumstances of the book's publication, Walpole exposed eighteenth-century assumptions about his era's literary and historical superiority (*Rise* 54–5). This theory of British historiography, grounded in a commitment to reason and realism, has been called the Whig interpretation of history. Jonathan Dent argues that Walpole undermines this historiographical standpoint in *Otranto*. Juxtaposing a representation of the Whig historiographical approach, as exemplified by David Hume's *History of England* (1754–61), with *Otranto*, Dent maintains that 'the Gothic rejects the Enlightenment meta-narrative of History' (25). Walpole countered Hume's reverence for broadness, continuity, and homogeneity by publishing *Otranto*, a putatively found and translated manuscript in which a short, fragmentary history is told, thereby drawing attention to what Hume hides – the nature of transmission of historical materials and the construction of the narrative itself. Walpole thus criticises Whig historiography, according to Dent, by fragmenting its fictitious continuity.

In contrast to Dent's argument, I suggest that Walpole parodies the driving narrative of Whig historiography by ultimately unifying fragmented historical materials in a hyperbolic way. Central to the parody is the prophetic dream that lends the novel the appearance of a providential fairytale, in spite of the story's confusing origins and chaotic events. This movement from temporary chaos and terror – the sublime – to order is analogous to the shift from nightmarish inspiration to prophetic fulfilment. Just as its source is a nightmare, Walpole implies that his story, set in the barbaric, distant past, is also a kind of nightmare, and yet the ending depicts not the fear of a nightmare, but the hope of a prophetic dream. In this way, Walpole not only poses as a translator in the first preface but actually works to translate his nightmare into a prophetic dream. It is in this translation that the novel mocks Whig historiography. First, stability is achieved not through reason but through revelation. Instead of rationality winning out over superstition, divine Providence – in the form of prophetic revelation – defeats tyrannical power. Second, prophetic dreams are uniquely capable of parodying the teleology of Whig historiography, where the present is regarded as the inevitable endpoint. Likewise, prophetic dreams from the past are teleological in nature because they are guides to a fixed fate. They evidence what I term *Gothic foresight*: the perceived power of the past to foresee the future. In both prophetic dreams and Whig historiography, there is an overriding certainty about what has happened, what will happen, and what it all means. In *Otranto*, the proof comes in the form of Alfonso's ghost as Manfred acknowledges that 'the vision we have but now seen, all corroborate thy evidence beyond a thousand parchments' (114). In adherence to an unflinching faith in teleology, an apparition stands as evidence that requires no other evidence.

While prophecy is certain in *Otranto*, it is decidedly less so in *The Monk*. Lewis's novel contains many prophetic moments, all of which concern the death of Antonia, the young woman whom Ambrosio eventually rapes and murders and later discovers is his sister. Lewis's novel continually offers readers and characters glimpses of the future but complicates those moments so that both the experience of prophecy and the anticipation of the future become uncertain. This occurs, most elaborately, in Lorenzo's dream. In the novel's first chapter, Lorenzo appears to fall asleep in the Capuchin Church and dream of the same church. Antonia and Ambrosio are there for a wedding ceremony. Lorenzo is called to be the bridegroom, and he steps forward. With this apparent acceptance of destiny, the dream initially presents a pleasant joining of a young couple until an 'unknown', a 'monster', attacks the bride (55). She escapes and ascends; the monster descends. Lorenzo awakens confused as to whether or not he has been dreaming.

D. L. Macdonald recognises a doubleness in the dream as it both engages the past – Ambrosio's sermon earlier in the chapter – and points to the future, with Antonia's death (157–8). While Macdonald moves away from the unresolved doubleness of the dream to the dream's literary connections to Richardson's *Clarissa*, I read the dream as a monstrous dream about a monster. Asa Simon Mittman defines a monster as something cognitively threatening and disturbing to 'our ... epistemological worldview' because it defies categorisation and 'ask[s] us ... to acknowledge the failures of our systems of categorization' (8). Outside of categorisations and definitions, the monstrous invokes fear not just because it is frightening, but because it disturbs our understanding of the world. Likewise, Lorenzo's dream may be said to be hybrid as it eludes definition: it is a combination of both natural and supernatural elements, and there is an in-betweenness to it that complicates the experience of prophecy for the dreamer. First, there is a long prelude. With 'a disposition to melancholy', Lorenzo drifts into a reverie, having 'abandoned himself to the delusions of his fancy' and 'a thousand changing visions' (54). Once alone in the church, Lorenzo seems to be in a liminal state influenced by his mood and surroundings. When he awakens, the line between dream and reality remains blurred. He is confused because the lights are lit, the church is filled with people, and the music is playing, as in the dream. In other words, the conditions of the dream church resemble those of the actual church in which he awakens and, as a consequence, it is difficult to tell exactly when his dreaming begins and ends. Because Lorenzo foresees the future but does so in a liminal state, the experience is difficult to understand and to classify.

The emergence of the 'monster' calls attention to the way that the terms 'monster' and 'monstrous' had become politically charged in the 1790s. Lorenzo's dream is a response to the proliferation of monsters and the apocalyptic rhetoric used in relation to the French Revolution controversy in Britain. The monster, at this point in British history, embodies the Burkean monsters of the future – the unmoored forces of the Revolution – as well as Mary Wollstonecraft's and Thomas Paine's monsters of the past – the tyrannical aristocracy and Catholic Church. Is the monster in Lorenzo's dream a degenerate institution, or is it a monster because it has been severed from the past? Just as the Revolution assumes religious meaning for both sides of the debate, the dream's imagery and setting portend a scene of biblical proportions. In this way, the dream casts Revolution as apocalypse. Monster and Antichrist become different terms for the same purposes as religious and political fears and hopes are rendered inextricable. The dream mixes political and religious hopes and fears and, in the process, the dream, like the 'debate', pulls the Revolution closer to Britain. Revolution – and, by extension, revolutionary violence – and the dream become monstrous.

The ending of *The Monk*, however, suggests a movement away from the monstrous dream to sublime violence, as the climactic events seem to fall short of the apocalyptic dream. Some may argue that the dream cannot be hyperbolic because the ending of the novel is so shocking and disturbing, and consequently, the violence actually exceeds anything foretold in the dream or other prophetic moments. But the novel diminishes the chaotic and violent events, circumscribing them by way of time and space, making them local and contained, short-lived, and forgotten. In terms of time, forgetting pervades the novel: Lorenzo forgets his dream and Antonia and, like the dream and Antonia, Ambrosio is 'soon forgotten as if he never had existed' (360). Despite the shocking crimes, Madrid's memory of Ambrosio and the violence is consigned to a forgotten past. The events promise neither reform nor destruction in the future as, in the end, order and tranquillity are restored (329). Spatially, the violence and chaos remain contained within Madrid. It is a local phenomenon handled by church authorities. Ultimately, the violence and horror are limited to individuals and contained within a particular city, a particular convent and monastery, and a particular family. Rather than threatening and proximate, the events become entertaining and distant, just as Burke worried Britons would view the events across the Channel. In this way, the novel brings together revolutionary and counter-revolutionary forces, religio-political hopes and fears, and pulls them closer, only, ultimately, to expel them.

Because of the popularity of *The Monk*, the novel's plot and themes were adapted into many works, most notably Charlotte Dacre's *Zofloya*. Besides the pacts between their main characters and Satan, *The Monk* and *Zofloya* contain similar dream scenes. Jonathan Glance locates Lorenzo's dream and Victoria's in *Zofloya*, along with Victor's in *Frankenstein*, within a larger group of conventional literary dreams, a group that includes Lovelace's in Samuel Richardson's *Clarissa; Or, The History of a Young Lady* (1747–8), Osmond's in Lewis's play *The Castle Spectre* (1797), and Matilda's in Percy Bysshe Shelley's *Zastrozzi, A Romance* (1810). Writing on *Frankenstein*, Glance argues, 'Mary Shelley skillfully suggests the scientific explanations of dreams, and creates a convincingly "realistic" literary dream, but she derives Victor's dream essentially from previous literary models of dreams which forewarn, but do not prevent, a later tragedy' (37). Victor's dream and others in the novel are often unheeded, premonitory, or supernatural dreams disguised as natural dreams triggered, as Locke theorised, by previous associations. While these dreams do share this doubleness, I suggest that Victoria's and Victor's dreams add an element that places them in a new category of dream, one also found in William Godwin's *Things as They Are; Or, The Adventures of Caleb Williams* (1794) and Ann Radcliffe's *The Italian; Or, The Confessional of the Black Penitents, A Romance* (1797). In this new type of dream, the dreamers awaken only to see someone or something staring at them, dream and reality becoming even less distinct than in earlier Gothic novels. Moreover, a new focus later emerges in *Zofloya* and *Frankenstein*. Whereas earlier Gothic novels explore the tyranny of the Ancien Régime and the unfathomability of Catholic institutions, in later novels like Dacre's and Shelley's, the emphases shift to imperial concerns as the presence of 'otherness' after the dream disturbs the dreamer. The remainder of this essay will examine the ways in which these dream episodes in *Zofloya* and *Frankenstein* expose British attitudes and anxieties about the future of slavery and empire.

The first half of *Zofloya* details the disintegration of the Loredanis, an aristocratic Venetian family. The second follows the daughter, Victoria: her marriage to Berenza; her desire for Berenza's friend, Henriquez; her hatred of Lilla, Henriquez's fiancée; her relationship with Satan in the guise of Zofloya, Henriquez's servant or slave; and her consequent death and damnation. In the novel's second half, Victoria experiences a series of dreams or dream-like scenes. In the first, '[a] group of shadowy figures' floats towards her, one of whom is 'a Moor of a noble and majestic form', as though from an Oriental Tale (135–6). He kneels to her, and she awakens, terrified. The dream, she reasons, must be the result of 'the disturbed state of her mind' (136), an effect of recent unhappiness in her marriage. She quickly falls back to sleep. In a church, Lilla and Henriquez stand at the marriage altar where 'the Moor' interrupts the ceremony and 'beckon[s] her towards him; involuntarily she [draws] near' (136). The scene borrows the wedding scene and interloper from Lorenzo's dream but, unlike the oneiric monster in *The Monk*, the dream Moor in *Zofloya* attracts Victoria and asks her twice whether she will pledge to be his, promising that if she consents, she may have Henriquez. Victoria is hesitant but agrees and immediately takes the place of Lilla, who becomes 'a pallid spectre' and flees (136). Berenza is 'suddenly wounded by an invisible hand' (136), and Victoria exults; however, Henriquez, too, becomes a skeleton. After waking, she, unlike Lorenzo, interprets her dream, but does so incorrectly: she will eventually marry Henriquez, the skeleton merely signifying 'till death' (137). Victoria recognises the dream as prophetic, but realises neither the fate of Henriquez nor the role of this mysterious 'Moor'.

Victoria's first two dreams resemble Lorenzo's in *The Monk* in their prophetic nature, but they also revise Eve's and Adam's dreams in *Paradise Lost* (1674). First, as Glenn Brewster asserts, Victoria's dreams echo Eve's archetypal dream of demonic possession. In Book 4, Satan is 'found / Squat like a toad, close at the ear of Eve' (lines 799–800), infiltrating her mind during sleep and enticing her to eat from the Tree of Knowledge. In Book 5, Eve reports to Adam that her dream begins with someone 'close at [her] ear' (line 36). Her temptation begins in the dream with close whispers. Similarly, in *Zofloya*, Victoria's dreams serve as the space in which 'the Moor' – soon, Zofloya and, ultimately, Satan – first appears and begins 'luring [her] to attempt the completion of [her] wildest wishes!' (267). The foundation for Victoria's formal pact for her soul is laid in the dream. Second, Victoria's dreams subtly allude to Adam's dream. In Book 8, Adam recounts his dream to the archangel Gabriel: 'whereat I waked, and found / Before mine eyes all real, as the dream / Had lively shadowed' (lines 309–11). What Adam dreams appears as real when he awakens, implying a continuity between the two states. This dream is cited by John Keats as the power of the Romantic imagination: 'What the Imagination seizes as Beauty must be truth – whether it existed before or not ... The Imagination may be compared to Adam's dream – he awoke and found it truth' (54). In Keats's definition, the imagination has the power not only to discern truth and beauty but also to shape reality, as in Adam's and Victoria's dreams.

In Dacre's novel, these confluences of dream and reality become more noticeable on the second night that Victoria dreams as Zofloya appears both in her dreams and in her room. In one, she follows Zofloya across a variety of sublime landscapes (143–4) and awakens, her horror intensified because Zofloya stands 'a few paces from her bed' (144). She sees him 'turn, and walk slowly and majestically towards the door' (144), but hopes his perceived presence is just part of 'a delusive dream' (144). This liminal state continues as she becomes paralysed with 'her eyes half-opened involuntarily' and sees Zofloya holding Berenza and Lilla, both of whom are wounded, before they disappear, replaced by a wounded Henriquez, and then reappear (144). Only after the three ascend upwards can Victoria, 'incapable of volition', move again (144). Subsequent to the characters' actual deaths, when Victoria experiences something like a waking dream induced by opium, a similar confusion occurs where she has 'strange visions' and hears 'the ringing of bells' (228). Transported to the room that hides the chest containing Berenza's skeleton, Victoria witnesses the discovery of Berenza's remains by servants (228). They 'rush to drag her from her bed' (228); however, Zofloya appears, the mob disappears, and she awakens. Once again, Zofloya is seen 'standing in fixed attitude at the foot of her bed' (228). The dream, he says, is 'no fable' (229). It proves to be prophetic as Antonio, Berenza's servant, subsequently has a dream that leads him and others to find Berenza. The dreams continue to predict the multiple deaths that follow. However, even more strikingly, Victoria dreams about, and then immediately sees, Zofloya: the unreality of the dream transforms into the reality of Zofloya's presence. In other words, these scenes depict a nightmarish version of Keats's notion of the imagination shaping reality. Victoria's imagination changes the sublime Zofloya into a monstrous Satan: safe, distant sublimity becomes dangerous, proximate monstrosity.

But to understand this transformation from Zofloya to Satan in Victoria's mind, the reader must consider the position and status of Zofloya. Because the titular character is a black African and the novel was published in 1806, the year before the abolition of the British slave trade, the novel has often been read in the context of slavery in the colonies. However, as Kim Ian Michasiw notes, Zofloya's status is ambiguous: he is referred to as both a servant and a slave. This fact leads Michasiw to ask, 'Is [Zofloya] a free man who is acting as a servant to Henriquez, or is he owned by the Spaniard?' (49). It is difficult to answer this question because, as Michasiw explains, the relationship between Henriquez and Zofloya is nowhere identified and we only know about Zofloya through Victoria (49). Although Dacre's novel takes place in late fifteenth-century Italy – like many early British Gothic novels set in Catholic countries in the distant past – this ambiguity concerning Zofloya's status suggests a lack of distinction between servant and slave in Britain before, and at the time of, the novel's publication, a crucial moment for the Abolition movement. The movement arguably received its legal impetus as a result of the Somerset case of 1772 that involved a slave owner attempting to kidnap a former slave, James Somerset, and send Somerset back to the Caribbean. This action was ruled a violation of English Common Law by Judge Mansfield. According to historian James Walvin, many at the time thought – as some still think today – that the Somerset decision led to the outlawing of slavery in England; however, it, more narrowly, made the kidnapping and transportation of a former slave to the colonies illegal. Owing to the confusion, the decision resulted in black people in Britain attaining a precarious status (65–6). As historian Douglas Lorimer has asserted, black people in England, both before and after the Somerset decision, 'lived in a half-way stage between … two varieties of servitude: chattel slavery and household servitude' (122). They found themselves in a state of limbo as 'slave-servants' (124). To borrow Lorimer's term, the character of Zofloya seems to be a slave-servant. In this regard, the novel takes up questions vital to the court cases: were black people in Britain servants or slaves? Was Britain free soil? Did British soil turn slaves into servants?

Catherine Molineux explains in *Faces of Perfect Ebony* that Britons' ideas about slaves, slavery, and the empire had come, for a couple of centuries, from actual slave-servants at home, as well as from paintings and advertisements. Portraits of aristocrats and their slave-servants adorned domestic interiors and were featured in art exhibits. '[B]lack boy' advertisements had also been popular for a couple of centuries in storefronts in London, particularly those shops that dealt in, or were associated with, 'exotic' products like coffee and tobacco. For viewers, casual or otherwise, these portraits and advertisements were suggestive of 'an idealistic vision of imperial mastery' (21). Molineux adapts Mary Louise Pratt's notion of the contact zone and brings the definition of an encounter abroad 'between peoples geographically and historically separated' (Pratt 8) to bear on those at home in Britain. Rather than just an actual or 'physical encounter' between, for example, a white slave owner and black slaves in the colonies, the contact zone can include daydreaming about the images, stories, and products associated with empire that Britons encountered in London (Molineux

6). As Molineux explains, 'Fantasy was both a form of experience and a framework through which to experience imperialism' (6). In other words, the fantasy of empire that came from representations of colonial subjects and slaves, as well as of black people in Britain, shaped how Britons, especially those who never left England, understood the world and Britain's role within it. Moreover, Molineux explains that images of white aristocrats and black slave-servants in seventeenth- and eighteenth-century Britain were often influenced by southern European painters' styles and the 'models of slavery fashioned by Catholic Continental neighbors' (58). These portraits of aristocrats and slave-servants actually helped to exhibit the wealth and power of aristocrats and the British Empire and 'to obscure the violent origins of imperial wealth' (58). While the empire was represented as powerful, its agents and their actions were rendered benign.

Zofloya both draws upon yet ultimately subverts the representations Molineux analyses. The novel represents slaves and slavery not only abroad but also in the metropole. It performs these dual functions through the setting and with the 'Moor'. Following the British Gothic convention where Catholic countries are often associated with the unenlightened, superstitious, and tyrannical past and contrasted with enlightened, egalitarian, and modern present-day Britain, the story is set in late fifteenth-century Catholic Italy, far removed from nineteenth-century Protestant England. The introduction of Zofloya in the middle of the novel, however, shifts the nineteenth-century British readers' attention to a second opposition – one between the Catholic characters, particularly Victoria, and the 'Moor'. Zofloya is viewed as an 'infidel', a non-Christian, and therefore, an 'inferior', by both the Catholic Victoria and British readers, who were predominantly Protestant. Although 'Moor' was a nebulous term, it was often applied to black Muslims who were, notably, often aligned with Catholics in the British Protestant imagination as tyrannical and cruel, especially in regard to the slavery practices of their countries (Molineux 24, 60). The 'Moors' were powerful in southern Europe and northern Africa for centuries, but their 'presence in Europe had a definite termination date' of 1492 after their defeat in Granada (Michasiw 44).

Set against this historic backdrop but written and published at the time of the abolition of the British slave trade, the novel draws parallels between Britain's own past and its present as the relationship between Victoria and Zofloya reflects the multiple ways that the British imagined black Africans. Victoria's initial perceptions of Zofloya vacillate as his status or position confuses her: in one episode, she considers him 'an inferior and an infidel', but in the next, she considers him 'a superior order of [being]' (149). Because she is a white European and an aristocrat and he is a black African and a slave-servant, she considers him 'an inferior', an inferiority that

British readers in 1806 would associate with black slaves in the colonies. At the same time, Zofloya, a Moor and a slave-servant of noble origin, in association with Victoria, a Venetian aristocrat, resembles the images of 'exotic' slave-servants featured alongside British aristocrats in popular contemporary paintings. They also resemble British aristocrats and their actual slave-servants yet in existence in Britain in 1806. Whereas slavery in the colonies, as historian J. R. Oldfield explains, was 'something shocking and yet at the same time comfortably remote [enough] to unite so many people' (148), slave-servants in homes would have provoked unease given their proximity despite being socially erased. They were present yet in the background. Similarly, being nearby yet unperceived is how Victoria imagines Zofloya prior to her dreams. After she notices him, the sublimity of Zofloya – 'the noble presence of the Moor' (149) – lies partially in what Victoria assumes is his veneer of power. For her, as for British readers, the Moor still retains the mysterious traces of ascendancy, but because that power is associated solely with the past, it is a power that is presumably non-threatening.

The possible reasons for Victoria's desire to meet Zofloya are important to consider. Part of the reason for this attraction is that he is someone to help her carry out her diabolical plans while elevating her status. Importantly, because Zofloya kneels to her in the first dream and during their actual early interactions (136, 147), we see a version of the subservient, 'grateful slave' trope most commonly known through the Josiah Wedgwood medallion depicting a slave kneeling and asking, 'Am I not a man and a brother?' Examining this trope in eighteenth- and nineteenth-century British fiction and writings on slavery, George Boulukos argues that though abolitionists employed the kneeling slave ostensibly to show the humanity of slaves, the trope 'ends with the suggestion of meaningful difference, as the slaves are so overwhelmed by passionate, irrational gratitude that they enthusiastically accept their state of slavery' (4). Their gratitude implies that they lack rationality and the desire for independence. Seen as irrational, the slave is judged to be prone to two extremes: either gratitude or vengeance (22, 232). Owing to their irrational gratitude, slaves were considered different by, and from, whites who would not, whites believed, have willingly accepted the fate of a slave. This trope, Boulukos argues, actually helped support the goal of amelioration rather than emancipation.

Reading the relationship between Victoria and Zofloya in the context of this trope and Molineux's notion of a dream of imperial mastery or 'an exotic fantasy of power' (23) suggests a primary source of her attraction to him. Once the member of a degraded family, she believes she will be socially elevated in status by having Zofloya by her side, like the aristocrats who posed in paintings alongside their African slave-servants. It is only later in the novel when Zofloya shocks Victoria with his declaration that they 'are affianced' (242) that he destroys her delusions of superiority and elevation, enlightening her about who is in control: 'A truce, fair Victoria, to folly! – am I not thy equal? – Ay thy superior! – proud girl, to suppose that the Moor, Zofloya, is a slave in mind!' (242). Reading her thoughts, he mocks her for viewing Zofloya as 'but a menial slave' who is beneath her (234). Up until this episode, he has been very strategic in telling her what she wants to hear. By the end of the novel, ironically, Victoria becomes even more degraded, living among banditti in the mountains where Zofloya reveals that he is actually Satan and that he assumed 'the semblance of the Moorish slave (supposed the recovered favorite of Henriquez)' in her dreams (267). She has been deceived into selling her soul to one she initially thought an inferior, a slave. While the first dream could be read as enacting the 'fantasy of colonial mastery' that Molineux explains, the ending demonstrates his victorious deception of Victoria. The reversal suggests an analogous relationship between enslavement and perdition as Victoria ends up bowing to her master. When she swears allegiance to him, she willingly accepts her fate, but does so, paradoxically, without any real awareness of her vow. In this way, the novel both makes the aristocrat the slave and calls into question the notion of the 'grateful' acceptance of slavery.

In this strategic manner, the novel dramatises the collapse of hierarchies and the erosion of differences. The dominance of the white aristocrat over the black slave disappears, as other hierarchies collapse and differences are eroded, including those involving white Europeans and black Africans, Catholics and Muslims, as well as Protestant readers and Catholic characters. Even more importantly, the focus on Zofloya's actual appearances to Victoria after her dreams is suggestive of the fear that results from the realisation that the metropole is not separate from the colonies and that the homeland is dependent on, and therefore subject to, the colonies. While critics have read in the novel's Gothic distancing a setting remote from nineteenth-century Britain and an engagement exclusively with the colonies, it is possible to see the distance between home and colony being collapsed and Zofloya exposing fears and anxieties relating to the British colonies. His physical proximity to Victoria during and after her dreams suggests that the threat to Britain exists close to home, this threat emanating from the double presence of black people in Britain, at once in the background as signifiers of power, and abroad, by way of the threat of revolution. Whereas *The Monk* casts the monstrosity associated with revolution onto the past to establish a sense of sublimity, *Zofloya* does the opposite. Rather than shift from monstrosity to sublimity like Lewis's novel, Dacre transforms sublimity into monstrosity. Thus, while Dacre sets the Gothic novel in a distant time and place, slavery, also thought remote, becomes a close, contagious nightmare from which it is impossible to awaken.

We see this inescapability of monstrosity in *Frankenstein* as the monster's sudden appearances pervade Victor's narrative not only most conspicuously in two separate mountain scenes, but also more subtly in the dream and reverie scenes. When Victor recounts his solitary wanderings in the Alps, he employs the Romantic language of travel and the sublime. In the first scene, for example, he describes hiking in the midst of 'a beautiful and terrific storm' that he likens to a 'noble war in the sky [that] elevate[s] [his] spirits' (48). In the second, he tries, similarly, to convey the 'sublime ecstacy' of the 'terrifically desolate' scene (64). However, both of these recounted moments, framed by sublimity, are interrupted by the unexpected presence of the monster (48, 65). Similar shifts from sublimity to monstrosity during the dream and reverie scenes surprise Victor. Because he wants to take credit for creating a 'new species' from 'lifeless matter' (32), the dream and reverie episodes, I argue, reveal an imperialist attitude in Victor. While he believes that he can separate himself from both the nightmare that plagues him and his fears, his ever-present living creature continually thwarts this imperialistic scientist's desire for sublime detachment.

Soon after Victor brings the creature to life and becomes horrified by its reality, he falls asleep and dreams initially of Elizabeth, his future bride, who transforms, graphically and terrifyingly, into his dead mother. He describes how 'a shroud enveloped her form, and [he] saw the grave-worms crawling in the folds of the flannel' (34–5). The dream, like those experienced by Lorenzo and Victoria, conflates past and future, nightmare (Victor's mother's death) and prophecy (Elizabeth's death). As in *Zofloya*, the dreamer wakes up to find an animated corpse who assumes the place of another, in this case, Victor's mother: 'I beheld the wretch – the miserable monster whom I had created. He held up the curtain of the bed; and his eyes, if eyes they may be called, were fixed on me. His jaws opened, and he muttered some inarticulate sounds, while a grin wrinkled his cheeks' (34–5). Like Victoria, Victor experiences a conflation of Adam's and Eve's dreams as there is a fusion of past and future: the haunting presence from the past is combined with a sense of instant prophetic fulfilment. The presence of the monster immediately after the dream establishes a continuity between dream and reality. Moreover, in his second creation sequence, the end of Victor's reverie about the prospect of creating a future 'race of devils' notably hearkens back to his initial scene of nightmare: 'I trembled, and my heart failed within me; when, on looking up, I saw, by the light of the moon, the *daemon* at the casement' (114–15; emphasis added). Again, Victor is suddenly confronted with the sight of the monster, and, in a sense, awakened from the reverie by the monster's presence. The 'daemon at the casement' appears – or seems to appear – by an act of the imagination.

The horror Victor experiences in these scenes of nightmare echoes and mirrors the initial revulsion he feels toward his creation. In the case of the latter, Victor repeatedly recounts that he wanted to 'bestow animation upon lifeless matter' (32). Ironically, the source of his revulsion towards his creation is that the being he has animated is 'capable of motion' (35). Dead bodies have never bothered him because he has regarded them – corpses – as basic materials for his work. As he recounts, 'a churchyard was to me merely the receptacle of bodies deprived of life' (30). Though Victor claims these places never frightened him, there is a sense of the Burkean sublime in his approach to work as he arguably takes 'delight in distance' (Burke 86). Not only has Victor been detached from family and society, he has considered his creation, before animation, with scientific detachment, from a distance. At the same time, while he has believed himself to be a rational man of science, he recognises in retrospect that he has in fact been frenzied: 'During my first experiment, a kind of enthusiastic frenzy had blinded me to the horror of my employment; my mind was intently fixed on the sequel of my labor, and my eyes were shut to the horror of my proceedings' (113). His goal is his fixation, and the body parts are just a means to an end he never fully understands. Victor is shocked at the moment of animation because he witnesses the corpse's sudden transformation from an inanimate object to a living being. This initial shock reverberates through the novel as he attempts to evade responsibility for his experiments by distancing himself both physically and emotionally from his creation, but is continually forced to confront its life and its presence. Thus, the moment of animation is analogous to the confrontation between the monster and Victor in the mountains, after the dream, and after the reverie. In each of these instances, sublime detachment gives way to monstrous confrontation.

It is Victor's initial desire to father 'a new species' (32) along with the creature's later exposure to an orientalist text that hints at Victor's imperialist attitude. The creature explains that he learned history from Felix who was reading C. F. Volney's *Ruins of Empires* to Safie (79–80). Volney begins *Ruins* by contrasting the state of the places he visited in the Middle East with their former glories: 'The aspect of a great city deserted, the memory of times past, compared with its present state, all elevated my mind to high contemplations' (4–5). The contrast between 'now' and 'then' leads him to consider what caused the demise of these cities in the Middle East. Volney, as Edward Said explains in *Orientalism*, viewed himself as a scientist and an observer of cultures, but he had imperial ambitions: 'he eyed the Near Orient as a likely place for the realization of French colonial ambition' (81). Volney and other Orientalists provided European powers with some fundamental research necessary for the expansion of empires. Because Western scholars have viewed 'the Orient' as having no modern history, it has 'remained fixed in time and place for the West' – an ahistorical object – available for study and control (Said 108–9).

We find this imperialist attitude of objectification represented in Victor's attitude and intentions toward the creature. Composed of exhumed body parts, the monster is, in a sense, representative, exclusively, of the past. Paradoxically, however, the creature possesses no recognised history. Gayatri Spivak has asserted that the novel is a failure of 'Shelley's emancipatory vision' because 'the master alone has a history' (269). Victor recognises no previous history for his creature until it is animated. Until that time, he is regarded as a blank slate, its narrative beginning only at the moment it is brought to life through Victor's experiment. Likewise, Victor's dream ends with a being, ostensibly without a history, staring at him. Here and before its animation, Victor views the creature as the Western scholar viewed 'the Orient' – namely, as one static, dead object. This lack of understanding and his plan for animation suggest Victor's imperialist attitude.

Challenges to this imperialist attitude, however, are exposed in the change between the first and second rounds of creation. While Victor exhibits a detachment prior to the creature's animation in the first experiment, he feels disgust toward the body parts before the female creature's animation in the second round. One reason for this change is that Victor can now see the materials as a potential living being. Although he refers to the creature's companion as 'the thing on which I was engaged', it is also 'the creature on whose future existence [the monster] depended for happiness' (115). Here, there is a vacillation between object and living being: Victor cleans up 'the remains of the half-finished creature' and admits that he 'almost felt as if [he] had mangled the living flesh of a human being' (118). Victor imagines that what he once saw as basic materials once was/might be a living person.

But what can account for this change in perspective? The main answer is Victor's tacit awareness that the monster has a lived history. First, although Victor may think he awakens from his earlier dream to a being without a history, the scene as a whole complicates that notion as the creature's ostensible lack of a past before its animation is juxtaposed against the images in Victor's graphic dream after its animation. The scene narrates a movement from life to death to rebirth in the three bodies: Elizabeth's body full of life, Victor's mother's drained of life, and a corpse composed of various body parts brought to life. The sequence of bodies also moves from the unknown future of Elizabeth to the known past of his dead mother to the unknown past and future in the form of a living corpse. In this way, by making the monster part of the signifying chain of bodies, the dream seems both to point out what the monster lacks and to endue it with a personal history, albeit one that belongs to Victor. Second, the monster does gain a history independent of Victor. It is the narrative itself – not just the content (for example, the killing of William) but the very telling – that causes Victor's anxieties because it possesses a history and a future at least partly out of Victor's control. Victor learns that he does not and cannot know everything about his creation, and this realisation is juxtaposed with the monster's continual appearances. His anxiety about creating a 'race of devils' in the future is caused in part by the corpse's absence of a past being supplied by the monster's narrative, as well as by the gaps that remain unknown. In both Victor's dream scene and the monster's narrative, an ostensible absence – a lack of history – becomes a permanent presence.

More broadly, an implicit battle over the narrative as a whole – especially, the struggle for the subaltern, the unnamed, to be heard – structures Shelley's novel. On the one hand, the monster does get to speak and outlives Victor and therefore has the final word. On the other hand, even though the monster has a narrative, the narrative is still under Victor's control. Because Victor revises Walton's notes and exerts control over the entire narrative, he also retains power over the monster's account (146). In addition, the monster underscores to Walton that Victor 'could not sum up the hours and months of misery which I endured, wasting in impotent passions' (154). Unseen and unimagined, the monster's sufferings are unrepresented by Victor. In spite of Victor's pyrrhic victory, the two narratives do not demonstrate a clear distinction between ruler and subject. Although a permanent separation between Victor and the monster occurs when the monster floats away from Walton's ship – 'He was soon borne away by the waves, and lost in darkness and distance' (156) – this separation comes only after the destruction of Victor's family and the end of Victor's life. Because the animated corpse stands in the presence of 'the lifeless form of his creator' (153), Victor's death represents a reversal of positions as the experimental scientist now lies in the place of the corpse. For Victor, however, there will be no reanimation.

Mary Shelley's *Frankenstein* ultimately represents empire as a failed experiment. The novel implies that the enterprise of empire-building means a slippage from sublimity to monstrosity and that, therefore, imperialism is monstrous. Victor's assumptions of distance and detachment reflect the desire that home – liberated Britain – and its subjugated colonies remain separate. Both *Frankenstein* and *Zofloya* expose Britain's aim to preserve its supposed position of superiority and control over its subjects and territories while – and by – maintaining a boundary between home and the colonies. In both novels, however, the continuities between dream and reality – particularly, the presence of the monster after Victor's dream and that of Zofloya in the bedroom during Victoria's second night of dreams – are suggestive of disturbances to the fantasy of empire as the violence of the past and present is thrown back on the scientist and the aristocrats, the representatives of imperial power. Unlike in *Otranto* and *The Monk*, there is no restoration of social order in Dacre's and Shelley's novels. Rather, the corpses arise, the buried and repressed violence of the past returns, and the imaginary space between home and colony collapses.

By the time of the publication of *Frankenstein*, the reanimated corpse has become an analogue of the Gothic dream. Both are hybrid – mixtures of past and future, nightmare and prophecy – and liminal, occupying states between dream and reality, death and life. Evidence of this analogous relationship is revealed by the juxtaposition of the dreams that purportedly inspired *Otranto* and *Frankenstein*. Like Walpole, whose dream of a disembodied hand in a medieval castle inspired *Otranto*, Shelley explains in the 1831 Introduction that the pivotal inspiration for her novel was a dreamlike vision of what would become the animation scene where the 'horror-stricken' Victor, 'the pale student of unhallowed arts', realises the folly of his actions and goes to sleep. He hopes that the monster, his creation, will soon 'subside into dead matter' again (172). Instead, Victor awakens to 'behold the horrid thing stand[ing] at his bedside, opening his curtains, and looking upon him with yellow, watery, but speculative eyes' (172). Mirroring the situation of Victor in the novel, that of the 'pale student' in Shelley's oneiric vision involves unavoidable confrontation between creator and creation. Sleep brings neither the student's escape nor the monster's death, and awakening does not distance the student from monstrosity. In this way, Shelley's oneiric inspiration resembles the dream in *Frankenstein* as well as those in *Zofloya*, as the line between dream and reality is indistinct. In Shelley's case, however, she – and not her character – is neither asleep nor awake: 'I did not sleep nor could be said to think' (172). Likewise, although 'the successive images [arise] in [her] head', they do not remain. While she has 'shut eyes, but acute mental vision', she 'sees', using the word 'saw' three times, thereby indicating visual perception (172). Unlike the images in Walpole's dream, a result of his 'head [being] filled with Gothic Story' (qtd. in Clery, 'Introduction' vii), the images here do not seem to be (or do not seem *only* to be), according to the account, inside of Shelley's head. That the images are external suggests that the dream is just that – an external phenomenon. In this and other externalisations of the dream, the Gothic counters the attempts of Enlightenment philosophy and medical science to reduce dreams to mere internal phenomena. In the Gothic, the dream becomes analogous with the corpses Victor assembles and to the imperial subjects of the British Empire: ostensibly atemporal and ahistorical 'dead matter', but revealed to be otherwise. Once thought to be dead and removed from time, the dream, like the reanimated corpse, is revealed to be a phenomenon marked indelibly by liminality, temporality, and history.

Works cited

Bond, John. *An Essay on the Incubus, or the Night-Mare.* D. Wilson and T. Durham in the Strand, 1753.

Boulukos, George. *The Grateful Slave: The Emergence of Race in Eighteenth-Century British and American Culture.* Cambridge University Press, 2011.

Brewster, Glenn. 'Monstrous Philosophy: Charlotte Dacre's *Zofloya; Or, the Moor* and John Milton's *Paradise Lost.*' *Literature Compass*, vol. 8, no. 9, 2011, pp. 609–19.

Burke, Edmund. *A Philosophical Enquiry into the Origin of Our Ideas of the Sublime and Beautiful and Other Pre-Revolutionary Writings*, edited by David Womersley. Penguin, 2004.

Burke, Edmund. *Reflections on the Revolution in France*, edited by J. G. A. Pocock. Hackett, 1987.

Clery, E. J. 'Introduction.' *The Castle of Otranto: A Gothic Story*, by Horace Walpole, edited by W. S. Lewis. Oxford University Press, 1996, pp. vii–xxxiii.

Clery, E. J. *The Rise of Supernatural Fiction, 1762–1800.* Cambridge University Press, 1999.

Cox, Jeffrey N. 'Introduction.' *Seven Gothic Dramas, 1789–1825*, edited by Jeffrey N. Cox. Ohio University Press, 1998, pp. 1–77.

Dacre, Charlotte. *Zofloya; Or, The Moor*, edited by Kim Ian Michasiw. Oxford University Press, 2008.

Dent, Jonathan. 'Contested Pasts: David Hume, Horace Walpole, and the Emergence of Gothic Fiction.' *Gothic Studies*, vol. 14, no. 1, 2012, pp. 21–33.

Glance, Jonathan C. '"Beyond the Usual Bounds of Reverie?" Another Look at the Dreams in Frankenstein.' *Journal of the Fantastic in the Arts*, vol. 7, no. 4, 1996, pp. 30–47.

Hobbes, Thomas. *Leviathan: With Selected Variants from the Latin Edition of 1668*, edited by E. M. Curley. Hackett, 1994.

Keats, John. *Selected Letters of John Keats Based on the Texts of Hyder Edward Rollins*, edited by Grant F. Scott. Harvard University Press, 2002.

Kruger, Steven F. *Dreaming in the Middle Ages.* Cambridge University Press, 1992.

Lewis, M. G. *The Monk: A Romance*, edited by D. L. Macdonald and Kathleen Dorothy Scherf. Broadview, 2004.

Locke, John. *An Essay Concerning Human Understanding*, edited by R. S. Woolhouse. Penguin, 1997.

Lorimer, Douglas. 'Black Slaves and English Liberty: A Reexamination of Racial Slavery in England.' *Immigrants and Minorities*, vol. 3, no. 2, 2010, pp. 121–50.

Macdonald, D. L. '"A Dreadful Dream": Transvaluation, Realization, and Literalization of *Clarissa* in *The Monk.*' *Gothic Studies*, vol. 6, no. 2, 2004, pp. 157–71.

Michasiw, Kim Ian. 'Charlotte Dacre's Postcolonial Moor.' *Empire and the Gothic: The Politics of Genre*, edited by Andrew Smith and William Hughes. Palgrave Macmillan, 2003, pp. 35–55.

Milton, John. *Paradise Lost*, edited by John Leonard. Penguin, 2003.

Mittman, Asa Simon. 'Introduction: The Impact of Monsters and Monster Studies.' *The Ashgate Research Companion to Monsters and the Monstrous*, edited by Peter Dendle and Asa Simon Mittman. Routledge, 2016, pp. 1–16.

Molineux, Catherine. *Faces of Perfect Ebony: Encountering Atlantic Slavery in Imperial Britain*. Harvard University Press, 2012.

Neocleous, Mark. 'The Monstrous Multitude: Edmund Burke's Political Teratology.' *Contemporary Political Theory*, vol. 3, no. 1, 2004, pp. 70–88.

Oldfield, John R. *Popular Politics and British Anti-Slavery: The Mobilisation of Public Opinion against the Slave Trade, 1787–1807*. Manchester University Press, 1995.

Pratt, Mary Louise. *Imperial Eyes: Travel Writing and Transculturation*. Routledge, 2008.

Rivière, Janine. '"Visions of the Night": The Reform of Popular Dream Beliefs in Early Modern England.' *Parergon: Journal of the Australian and New Zealand Association for Medieval and Early Modern Studies*, vol. 20, no. 1, 2003, pp. 109–38.

Said, Edward W. *Orientalism*. Vintage, 2004.

Shelley, Mary. *Frankenstein: The 1818 Text, Contexts, Nineteenth-Century Responses, Modern Criticism*, edited by James Paul Hunter. Norton, 1996.

Shelley, Mary. 'Introduction to *Frankenstein*, Third Edition (1831).' Frankenstein: The *1818 Text, Contexts, Nineteenth-Century Responses, Modern Criticism*, edited by James Paul Hunter. Norton, 1996, pp. 169–73.

Spivak, Gayatri Chakravorty. '*Frankenstein* and a Critique of Imperialism.' *Frankenstein: The 1818 Text, Contexts, Nineteenth-Century Responses, Modern Criticism*, edited by James Paul Hunter. Norton, 1996, pp. 262–70.

Volney, C. F. *The Ruins of Empire*. Black Classic Press, 1991.

Walpole, Horace. *The Castle of* Otranto: *A Gothic Story*, edited by W. S. Lewis. Oxford University Press, 1996.

Walvin, James. *Britain's Slave Empire*. Tempus, 2007.

5

Haunted beyond dreams: the Gothic and Enlightenment in Mary Wollstonecraft's *Mary, A Fiction*

Liz Wan Yuen-Yuk

I am now beginning to awake out of a terrifying dream – for in that light does the transactions of these two or three last days appear. (Wollstonecraft, *Collected Letters* 63)

The years 1785 to 1787 were one of the most traumatic periods in Mary Wollstonecraft's life because she experienced the death of her close friend, Fanny Blood (1758–85). This devastating event, in part, inspired Wollstonecraft to write her first novel, *Mary, A Fiction*, published in 1788. Just as in real life Wollstonecraft compared her life to a nightmare, so too is her novel's protagonist, Mary, frequently haunted by literal and metaphorical parasomnias. Although critics often overlook the novel or categorise it mainly as 'a late work of sensibility' (Todd x), its oneiric, phantasmagorical, and thanatological elements render it Gothic as well. In support of this claim, Michael Gamer notes that Wollstonecraft was a 'reviewer and quasi-editor' of various Gothic texts (292) and Diane Long Hoeveler recognises in *Mary* the ideology of 'Gothic feminism' that focuses on women's victimisation and moral superiority to men ('The Construction' 31). To date, however, there has been a dearth of critical work devoted to the dreams and parasomnias in *Mary*. This chapter contends not only that these phenomena in Wollstonecraft's novel form an integral part of Mary's characterisation and the novel's plot, but that the narrative itself may be interpreted as a Gothic nightmare, in the sense of its inclusion of chronic deaths, terror around a lack of control, and liminal states of subjectivity.

These literary parasomnias are, also and significantly, inextricably bound up with elements of the Female Gothic, a narrative recipe that, generally, 'centralise[s] the imprisoned and pursued heroine threatened by a tyrannical male figure' (Wallace and Smith 3). From Hoeveler's perspective, the Female Gothic often 'presents a blameless heroine triumphing through a variety of passive-aggressive strategies over a male-created system of oppression and corruption, the "patriarchy"' (*Gothic Feminism* 9). Whether Mary prevails or not is a matter of interpretation; what is observable is that she perceives herself as subject to patriarchal forces that threaten to dictate her life, over which she, as if trapped in a dream, can exercise little control. As Carol Margaret Davison has characterised them, Female Gothic fictions are 'oneirically suffused novels featuring female protagonists [that generate] titillating conceptions of the conjunction between love and terror, [and call] women's limited roles and domestic ideals into question' (*History* 89). The 'nightmare' serves in these narratives as a means through which the novelist protests the abuse of, and patriarchal domination over, women. Simultaneously, the work delineates Mary's aspirations and efforts to become an enlightened learner who possesses both reason and refined sensibilities, which ultimately prove to be more effective than religion as anchors of sanity. The novel, therefore, straddles the gap between the excess emotions of Gothicism and extreme rationalism. In exploring Mary's terrifying dreams on both literal and metaphorical levels, this chapter argues that the motif of the nightmare is strategically manipulated to reveal psychological and sexual repressions, in Freudian terms, to advocate for Enlightenment values, and to advance a radical feminist socio-political critique.

Literary dreams have long functioned as a channel for social commentary. As the editor of *Reading Dreams: The Interpretation of Dreams from Chaucer to Shakespeare* (1999), Peter Brown, discusses in his own chapter, the 'numerous advantages' of characters having dreams as a 'means of framing ... narratives': it 'permits the author to disavow responsibility for what follows' and 'provides a way of dealing with a wide variety of subjects' (25). Indeed, literary dreams disguise deeper meanings, possessing an additional layer because they are 'not real dreams ... but conscious imitations of them, rooted in the cultural and historical apprehensions of their cause and content' (Glance 31). As such, dreams are purposefully woven into narratives to convey and engage with certain social issues. *The Handbook to Gothic Literature* defines 'nightmare' as a common 'fictional or dramatic device [used] to figure the future or provide an allegorical reading of the plot' (Martin 164). In *Mary*, although dreams are not prophetic, they may at times function allegorically and didactically. For instance, the corpse of a little girl in the protagonist's recurring nightmares may symbolise the tragic consequences of negligent mothers, thus warning parents not to leave their children unprotected. Likewise, the connotations of nightmares often point to the elephants in the room, with dreams embodying or symbolising what is feared in or abhorred by society. As Davison notes, Gothic narratives often possess a 'dream logic' which frequently shocks, with the texts 'centr[ing] on an often paranoid subject' (*History* 33). Margaret Anne Doody has analysed the dreams in many eighteenth-century Female Gothic novels and theorises that '[i]nstitutions, power, [and] political activities are the nightmarish cruel realities from which no one can escape' (99). The anxieties portrayed in

Mary align with these critical dream interpretations as they do not simply entertain readers with a sense of terror, they also provide an experimental space for addressing real-life concerns, such as coerced marriage, as well as advocate for radical feminist ideas, such as female autonomy and education. A dream-centred analysis of the story can be conducted in tandem with a Gothic-centred criticism given that reality and nightmares are intermixed. As William Patrick Day notes, the Gothic world resembles 'a dreamscape, a land of nightmare' because it blurs the boundary between fiction and reality (30): it is 'an imitation of the world of the dream, the hallucination, in which that which is real and that which is imaginary fade into one, creating a reality that subverts our perceptions' (31). As Doody puts it, in the (Female) Gothic world '[t]here is no longer a commonsense order against which the dream briefly flickers; rather, the world of rational order briefly flickers in and out of the dreamlike' (93). While Mary is troubled by nightmares, the events of her life unfold and form a dream world, transcending the boundaries not only of sleep but of her reality. This phenomenon aligns with the notion that a nightmare signifies 'a state between sleeping and waking, or ... death and life' (Martin 164), as Mary's nightmare visions are oftentimes fused with her subconscious imaginings, and she experiences a liminality between living and dreaming.

These different, frightful mental states lead to another major feature of Gothic fantasy: fears and the ways they are processed. Gothic fantasy is, in part, a 'dynamic literary system' where '[t]he protagonists find themselves in a world created by the circle of their own fears and desires' (Day 4). As the first part of this chapter will show, Mary is trapped in a vicious cycle: the fearful occurrences and desires that she wishes to suppress are always resurrected in her dreams, which in turn cause her to make certain (sub)conscious decisions that unfortunately and indirectly bring her more trauma. As Valdine Clemens argues, the 'return of the repressed' constitutes 'a fundamental dynamism of Gothic narratives' (3–4). This accords with Freud's psychoanalytic theories that make 'fantasy central to the self' (Roberts 225): he sees the unconscious as 'the home of the wishes and ideas that have been repressed, denied access to consciousness' (220), and 'sees human behaviour as driven to a large extent by unconscious fantasies' (225). In Freud's own words, dreams are 'psychical acts; their driving-force is a wish in need of fulfilment; their unrecognizable ability as wishes, and their many oddities and absurdities, derive from the influence of the psychical censorship which they have gone through in the course of their formation; as well as the compulsion to escape this censorship' (346–7). In accordance with this Freudian definition, much of Mary's desires are, paradoxically, what she also fears and wishes to repress due to her yearning for acceptance by society. Reading Wollstonecraft's novel through this

Freudian framework, it will be argued that many of Mary's actions are motivated by her suppressed wishes, dreams, and intentions to release herself from censorship.

Mary's dreams and their aftermath

To facilitate and contextualise my arguments, which are based on specific textual moments, the plot must be briefly delineated. The novel depicts its protagonist, Mary, as a 'genius' who flees from marriage. Having grown up in a loveless patriarchal family, Mary establishes an intense friendship with a neighbour, Ann. At the age of seventeen, due to economic reasons and in adherence to honour her mother's dying wish, Mary is coerced into marrying her neighbour, Charles. While Charles continues his studies on the Continent, Mary accompanies Ann, whose health is failing, to Lisbon, in hopes of her recovery. There she meets Henry, a fellow genius who is also languishing, and the two gradually fall in love, their relationship intensifying after Ann's death. By the time Henry declares his love, Mary has decided to return to England to live with Ann's family. Although Henry follows her and they reunite, he dies shortly thereafter. Mary is traumatised by love but consents to return to live with Charles until her own death, which she forecasts as imminent. Throughout the novel, Mary is seen struggling with her illicit desires for both Ann and Henry, conflicts that are complicated by Mary's Protestant faith and her goal of becoming an educated and enlightened being. The upshot of these tensions is various horrible episodes of madness in Mary's life involving unfulfilled desires and a succession of deaths.

Dreams serve as a key to unpacking the novel because they both reveal and influence Mary's mental state. Nightmares pervade Mary's life, serving, in part, to render the novel Gothic. From a young age, Mary develops a deep sense of compassion for both people and animals, and the text highlights her sensitive observations of the world. These personal characteristics arguably intensify her emotional reactions to unpleasant scenes in her life, that, due in part to the oppressive environment she inhabits, are transformed into nightmares. The most traumatic real-life event, albeit short and seemingly insignificant, is truly Gothic in nature and becomes incredibly influential in her life. It takes place early in the novel when '[a] little girl who attended in the nursery fell sick', and despite the fact that Mary 'paid her great attention', contrary to Mary's wish of looking after the child, the child is 'sent out of the house' to her destitute and negligent mother (*Mary* 8). This is one of the first instances in Mary's life where her best intentions to help others are unrealised. Soon after,

> [t]he poor wretch [the young girl], in a fit of delirium stabbed herself, and Mary saw her dead body, and heard the dismal account; and so strongly did it impress her imagination, that every night of her life the bleeding corpse presented itself to her when she first began to slumber. (*Mary* 8)

This parasomnia, resonant with Matthew Lewis's powerful Bleeding Nun episode, provides ample evidence that Mary is suffering from post-traumatic stress disorder.[2]

The aftermath of the tragedy lies in Mary's constant mental replaying of the scene. As Clemens argues, Gothic protagonists quite often grapple with 'hidden guilt, transgression, and retribution' (6). Mary is clearly traumatised and '[t]ortured' by the experience, and 'the impression that this accident made [is] indelible' (*Mary* 8). Mary's unsatisfied urge to help the girl might have caused her to feel guilty, for the 'bleeding corpse' is not only a sight of horror but also serves as a reminder of Mary's inability to save the child. Almost as reparation, Mary makes the vow that 'if she [is] ever mistress of a family she would herself watch over every part of it' (8). This promise does not relieve her tormented psyche. The nightmare featuring her suicidal friend recurs often, as confirmed by the fact that, even years later, in Lisbon, Mary 'always [sleeps] with Ann, as she [is] subject to terrifying dreams; and frequently in the night [is] obliged to be supported, to avoid suffocation' (20–1). The 'suffocation' here parallels John Bond's 1753 description of the 'Night-mare' that

> generally seizes people sleeping on their backs, and often begins with frightful dreams, which are soon succeeded by a difficult respiration, a violent oppression on the breast, and a total privation of voluntary motion. In this agony they … remain in the jaws of death, till, by … some external assistance, they escape out of that dreadful torpid state. (2)

This description is akin to the definition of nightmare provided in Samuel Johnson's *Dictionary*, an author Wollstonecraft often quotes admiringly in her letters. It also aligns with the representation of the sleeper in the painting, *The Nightmare* (1782), by Henry Fuseli, an artist with whom Wollstonecraft had 'a torrid but apparently unconsummated romance between 1789 and 1792' (Taylor 8).[3] Mary's trauma, which leads her to suffer from nightmares, aligns with popular eighteenth-century notions of this phenomenon.

Just as personal demons 'point to a larger societal need to confront similar issues of social and moral responsibility' (Clemens 6), Mary's trauma subsequently shapes her philanthropic disposition to help the disadvantaged. Perceiving sick and wounded bodies as both a threat and a chance for her to redeem herself from her past futility, she is even driven to risk her life in saving others. One of the people she tries to preserve is a poor, gravely ill woman who lives in a site of ruin, a figurative grave. Her dilapidated house, with 'tattered shreds of rich hangings still [remaining]' but which are 'covered with cobwebs and filth' (*Mary* 40), all create the perfect Gothic setting. As Mary, like a typical Gothic heroine, presses on to provide help, she is forced to inhale 'the most poisonous air' from the patient who is expiring from a 'putrid fever' (41). With her knowledge in medicine, she prescribes for the woman, and leaves with 'a mixture of horror and satisfaction' (41). Her efforts are 'repaid' by the gradual recovery of the patient, but the description of that recovery is more horrific than triumphant: Mary sees her 'rising as it were from the grave' (41). While this occurrence is apparently positive, it can also be interpreted as a ghastly image of a corpse reviving from a coffin, which is typically Gothic and nightmarish. It serves as a harbinger of Mary's near-death experience upon contracting the disease, which is 'so violent' it causes her to become 'delirious' (41). As Clemens stresses how the Gothic heroes' stories 'identify a gap between official ideology and actual reality' (6), this is an instance of the intertwining of real and imagined Gothic horrors, the horror of the social injustice of poverty blending with the horrors associated with a putrid, foul-smelling human body.

The satisfaction Mary obtains from assisting others, however, is not long-lasting. On the contrary, it aggravates Mary's situation by way of the nightmarish realisation that human nature is tainted by ingratitude and even vampirism. Although she survives the illness, she finds, with painful pangs, that her favours are 'forgotten when no more [are] expected' (41). The people whom Mary has helped do not improve in personality but, instead, become Gothic characters. For instance, when on the ship returning to England, after Mary rescues and financially assists a woman, she unfortunately becomes impecunious herself. When Mary thereafter advises the woman to make her own living, much to Mary's horror, the woman 'load[s] her with abuse' (41). The woman hence assumes the role of a Gothic villain, becoming greedy, insatiable, and ungrateful, a person who vampirises other people's resources. It seems as though Mary's attempts to curb her nightly distress by way of good deeds place her in greater danger, her efforts often being counter-productive. As if to accentuate this point, Mary is not spared her nightmares: even towards the novel's end when she is overwhelmed by life and wishes to rest, 'a thousand fearful dreams [interrupt] her slumbers' (49). The frustration and horror of seeing her ideal of humanity as benevolent shattered, cause Mary to compare her life to a horrid dream.

Mary's life as a nightmare

Just as the Gothic sphere is 'a world of utter subjectivity' (Day 22), so does Mary's strong sensibility eventually lead her to perceive her life as a nightmare. As Jane Hodson argues, Gothic novels emerged 'at that historical

moment in which fiction becomes particularly adept at representing consciousness', and, by extension, 'subjectivity' (299). Gothic characters may
feel confused as to whether they are awake or not because 'by articulating
fantasy in terms similar to the world of dreams, the Gothic writers made
dreams and nightmares a part of the real world, ... as an aspect, uncontrolled
and dim, of human desires' (Day 31). This is the world Wollstonecraft creates for her heroine, where reality and dreams are interwoven through one's
subjectivity.

One aspect of subjectivity that perennially threatens Mary is her own
romantic needs, which, forbidden to be satisfied due to social norms, distress her. In the Female Gothic, the nightmare 'is that women frequently
cannot run toward what they claim to desire, the man they want to marry'
(Hoeveler, *Gothic* 10). This claim applies to *Mary*. However, contrary to
the typical Female Gothic novel which convinces readers that the heroine's
rebellion against patriarchy will 'result in an improved home for both their
mothers and themselves' (10), in *Mary* there is only the aggravated repression of her desires, which results in her near-destruction.

One unattainable figure Mary desires is Ann, but Mary is soon inhibited
from a union with her friend as a result, ironically, of her own marriage to a
boy she dislikes, a truly Gothic experience. As in a nightmare in which one
is 'powerless to act' (Day 45), Mary is coerced into tying the knot with her
neighbour, Charles. She is already burdened with care about Ann's dire poverty when she is summoned by her 'very tyrannical and passionate' father
(7), who tells Mary that her mother is dying and that 'the [wedding] ceremony was to be performed directly, [so] that her mother might be witness
of it' (14). Mary's initial response is to succumb to unconsciousness: 'overwhelmed', she 'rolled her eyes about, then, with a vacant stare, fixed them
on her father's face; but they were no longer a sense; they conveyed no ideas
to the brain' (14). As if unable to reconcile herself to her fate, which entails
her transferral from one patriarchal household to another, Mary's 'suspension of thought' continues until she reaches home (14).

Eugenia C. DeLamotte identifies two dominant fears driving the Gothic
romance: 'the fear of terrible separateness and the fear of unity with some
terrible Other' (22). Here, both are present: her mother's decease and the
potential of Charles being like her dictatorial father, a 'terrible Other'. When
Mary's thoughts return, 'a thousand thoughts' rush through her mind: 'her
dying mother, – [Ann's] miserable situation, – and an extreme horror at
taking – at being forced to take, such a hasty step' (14). As Doody puts
it, the Female Gothic 'heroine's relationship to a lover or to marriage may
be fraught with anxiety amounting to dread. The heroine has a strong but
divided sense of self, and the self is usually suffering from something more
complicated than simple desire or simple grief' (74). Here, Mary's self is

tormented by her loss of autonomy and the 'circle of powerlessness that evidences the daughter's inability to escape her mother's fate' in succumbing to patriarchy (Domínguez-Rué 126), resulting in a 'nightmare of repetition which mocks individual intentions and free will' (Meaney 25). Mary's only solace is the notion that marrying Charles entails the union of his property with her father's, meaning that she can continue to live where she is, near Ann, whom she 'love[s] better than any one in the world' (15). Still, this thought does not suffice to alleviate Mary's situation. Typical Gothic excess, when temporality and spatiality collapse (Day 28), is at play in Mary's marriage scene. Time is compressed in a dreadful montage: 'Mary stood like a statue of Despair, and pronounced the awful vow without thinking of it; and then ran to support her mother, who expired the same night in her arms' (15). Mary's marriage, promptly tainted by death, is ominous, with her only hope of finding happiness existing, apparently, outside of it. Justice or gratification for Mary, however, is ultimately impossible, as both of her beloveds are taken by death.

Death serves as another pivotal Gothic element in Mary's harrowing story, resembling a nightmare in which what one dreads becomes one's unalterable reality. Davison notes in the Introduction to *The Gothic and Death* that 'Gothicists readily identify death as one of the foremost terrors at the heart of their cultural field of study' (1). The novel, although short, contains at least eight terrifying instances of death, involving the following characters: Mary's younger siblings who 'died in their infancy'; the self-stabbed girl; Mary's remaining brother; Ann's benefactor; Mary's mother; Mary's father, whose decease triggers the narrative to describe 'Death' as 'a king of terrors when he attacks the vicious man' (17); Ann; and Henry. As Zygmunt Bauman claims, death remained 'unmasterable by the Age of Reason' (qtd. in Davison, *The Gothic and Death* 2). Just as in Gothic fantasy, 'no action can ever achieve its intended result' (Day 44), so too are Mary's efforts to prevent death futile. Consumed by 'the fear of losing [Ann]', Mary studies physic, but her knowledge 'end[s] in vanity and vexation of spirit, as it enable[s] her to foresee what she could not prevent' (16). The chronic deaths and lack of control constitute a torturous and nightmarish experience for Mary.

Ann's abrupt death triggers a series of episodes into Gothic unconsciousness and the return of the repressed. In the Female Gothic, there is 'the pattern of uneasy loss leading to a crisis which precipitates an anguished vision. The bounds of reality dissolve, and the heroine is left alone in delirious terror which is more insistent and prevalent than a dream – the nightmare terror takes control for a while of vision, actions, and speech' (Doody 86–7). When Ann 'died suddenly as Mary was assisting her to walk across the room', Mary is 'stunned', 'unable to reflect, or even to feel her misery'

(28), as if subject to paralysis. Henry's attempts to soothe her and his tender declaration of love for her, contrary to his intentions, cause Mary's mind to become 'unhinged' (30). Reality and dreams then intertwine. 'Lost, in waking dreams', Mary considers confiding in Ann, only to realise that her friend is dead, and, as if aware that she is betraying Ann by harbouring feelings for Henry, Mary 'aloud … beg[s] forgiveness of her' (30). The subsequent night is 'passed away in feverish slumbers' (30). The intensity of Mary's emotions culminates in a Gothic, uncanny, oppressive symphony of suffering and death: 'One instant she was supporting her dying mother; then Ann was breathing her last, and Henry was comforting her' (30). This rapid transitioning of images in Mary's mind will later be echoed in the iconic montage in Wollstonecraft's daughter Mary Shelley's *Frankenstein* when Victor dreams of kissing his beloved Elizabeth but, in horror, finds himself clutching his mother's corpse: 'I thought I saw Elizabeth, … but as I imprinted the first kiss on her lips, they became livid with the hue of death; her features appeared to change, and I thought that I held the corpse of my dead mother in my arms' (Shelley 59). The resemblance between the two texts is striking, especially when both protagonists are helplessly delirious with visions of their desires and fears.

Mary's psychological turmoil stems, in part, from the fact that she wants all three people but is obliged to suppress her yearning for various reasons. Her mother, even if still alive, would never become affectionate towards her daughter. It is also her mother who hastens her daughter's unwanted marriage, a major cause of suffering, yet Mary feels responsibility towards her. Mary also recognises, with disappointment, that 'Ann only felt gratitude' towards her (10) and that 'Ann and she were not congenial minds' (16). Mary still loves Ann unconditionally, occasionally erotically, while refusing to define their relationship. As Claudia Johnson insightfully argues, 'the prose seems to dissolve under the stress of having to describe this relation at all' (194). Henry is a romantic interest, but also a forbidden one, due to Mary's marriage and her self-imposed guilt towards Ann. Simultaneously, the more Mary tries to deny death and censor her desires, mentally, the more those objects of her desire – Ann and Henry – regress as a pseudo-reality into her dreams, which are then transmogrified into nightmares.

Much of the terror of the Gothic atmosphere is characterised by 'the sense of mystery, suspense, and fearful anticipation' (Day 27). Henry's death is an example. Gravely ill, 'his end … approaching', Mary '*wait*[s] to see him die' (51), unable to control the narrative of Henry's life or her own. Instead, she is forced to watch as the scene unfolds, as if unable to wake from a nightmare. There is ominous silence preceding his death: 'a frightful calmness stilled every turbulent emotion' (51). The amount of grief and anxiety Mary experiences, coupled with the possible ambivalence of not wanting her beloved to die, yet hoping he can find eternal comfort, arguably moves beyond the sentimental into the realm of the Gothic. This is especially true when one considers that Henry's adulterous longing might result in his damnation in hell. At Henry's request, he dies in her arms. His soul 'seemed flying to her, as it escaped out of its prison', while 'his hand seemed yet to press hers' (51). This is a liminal life-in-death moment and an almost supernatural vision that resembles sleep paralysis as Mary still lacks control over her mind and body. Soon afterwards, Mary also seems to experience dying herself as '[e]very event of her life rush[es] across her mind with wonderful rapidity' (51). She then gets up in a 'phrensy', whereas the narrative of the next paragraph collapses, ending the chapter with the words, 'her head swum – she sunk –' (52). As Hodson generalises, 'Gothic literature returns obsessively to moments where language breaks down, where sentiment overwhelms the speaker' (292) and 'acts of communication founder' (298). Such linguistic fragmentation, representative of the unspeakable, also signifies the disintegration of the self, along with time and space, much like that in a dreamscape and Gothic fantasy: it is 'one of unresolved chaos, of continuous transformation … and fear' (Day 8).

Enlightenment and the Gothic

Death becomes Mary's only release from the tortures of her living nightmares. In the last chapter, the narrator states that after all she has suffered, her nerves are 'not to be restored to their former state' (53). Mary now longs for death more than ever: the only 'gleam[s] of joy' she can experience arise when she thinks she is 'hastening to that world where there is *neither marrying*, nor giving in marriage' (53). The phrase, which is simultaneously the last line of the novel, alludes to Matthew 22:30: 'For in the resurrection they neither marry, nor are given in marriage, but are as the angels of God in heaven.' Only when Mary is not inhibited by constraining patriarchal institutions – when she is dead – may she finally feel free. This fascinating literalisation of the Biblical phase is a strategic socio-political and radical feminist manipulation of the language, serving, in part, to neutralise gender hierarchies.

This biblical allusion points to where *Mary* both differs from and aligns with the conventional model of Gothic fantasy. On the one hand, 'death is neither an escape nor a door through which one can pass to achieve a final humanity'; it 'results neither in transfiguration, as in a religious vision … nor in a reaffirmation of human identity' (Day 7). That Mary has been deeply religious since she could read (7), coupled with her belief in the Christian afterlife, seems to affirm the hope of her redemption and ascension to heaven. Hence, the novel counters the tradition of Gothic fantasy that '[does] not point toward a higher, spiritual truth' (Day 14). On the other hand, the Gothic world 'traps [its energy] in a closed system' where all attempts of the protagonist, such as escaping from marriage and preventing her loved ones' deaths, in Mary's case, are futile (Day 44); 'there is no ordinary world to wake up in' (Doody 93). Religion is similarly shown to be fruitless. Although Mary's 'recollection' of the day she took her 'baptismal vow' has 'never failed to wake her dormant piety when earthly passions ma[k]e it grow languid' (12), religious rituals do not eradicate her nightly nightmares, nor are her prayers answered. Moreover, the novel is a cliffhanger in the sense that it 'leaves its heroine yearning for death' (Todd xxii) yet it does not confirm whether Mary's wish for heaven is granted.

At the same time, just as Wollstonecraft herself is a disciple of Enlightenment thinkers and as her typical response to sentimental novels is to stress the importance of the cultivation of reason, so does *Mary* emphasise intellectualism and rationality. Barbara Taylor remarks that this novel was 'highly innovative in many respects, not least in its use of fiction to explore female intellectual "possibilities"' (36). Indeed, the narrative highlights Mary's keen interest in training her mind with reason. Neglected by her mother, Mary is taught by an old housekeeper to read, and since then 'peruse[s] every book that [comes] her way', and 'learn[s] to think' (7). She observes that 'apparently good and solid arguments might take their rise from different points of view; and she rejoice[s] to find that those she should not concur with [have] some reason on their side' (21). Mary's open-mindedness, critical thinking, and objectivity may promote not only Enlightenment values but also gender equality, which Wollstonecraft advocated both in her first book, *Thoughts on the Education of Daughters* (1787) and, most notably, in *A Vindication of the Rights of Woman* (1792). By way of displaying the intellectual capabilities of the heroine, *Mary* 'directly challenged the male authors who in their philosophical tracts and sentimental novels depicted women as irrational and infantile beings' (Gunther-Canada 8), suggesting that it is possible for stereotypically emotional females like Mary to reconcile the 'opposites' of reason and feeling.

The tension between rationality and emotions forms an integral constituent of Gothic novels. While the Gothic genre quite often parodies or even undermines 'smug' Enlightenment ideas and 'certainties', many Gothic authors also purposefully counterpoint superstitious and rational phenomena in order, ultimately, to affirm Enlightenment principles and mindsets (Davison, *History* 44–5). Horace Walpole's *The Castle of Otranto* (1764) is said to have 'founded a genre that is consistently self-conscious about playing a double game' of both 'moving its audience' with suspense and 'play[ing] on its readers' readiness to believe' (Lynch 196). The supernatural elements can make even 'the most rational, enlightened, and sceptical reader ... regress to an exhilarating state of "daemonic dread"' (Clemens 2). In other words, the Gothic writer may show an awareness that ghosts do not exist yet still conjure them for pleasurable entertainment.

The novels of Ann Radcliffe are prominent examples of the blending of Enlightenment rationalism and Gothic sensationalism. Numerous critics have noted the origins of the Female Gothic in the Enlightenment period (Spooner 130; Davison, *History* 106). Radcliffe's signature motif is the 'explained supernatural', which Davison terms 'an Enlightenment offshoot' (*History* 106), and William Donoghue interprets as 'a steady rationalization and realization of elements native to the discourse of scepticism – moving out of the dark ... toward knowledge and verisimilitude' (96). In other words, Radcliffe's novels build up a tension involving seemingly supernatural elements, such as ghosts, and then provide logical explanations that deconstruct them.

Although *Mary* was published before Radcliffe's first novel, the textual strategies and effects in the novel that describe Charles anticipate Radcliffe's techniques. Charles 'grows' in power with his absence; he is nonetheless haunting and terrifying. To Mary, Charles is initially a mere 'boy she seldom took any notice of' (15), but she soon sees her marriage as 'a dreadful misfortune' and develops an 'extreme dislike' of him (16). When he mentions his return from his overseas studies, Mary is terrorised by the prospect (17). She 'could not [even] muster up sufficient resolution to break the seal' of Charles's later letter (46). Charles resembles a menacing spectre, representing the terrifying power of 'social forces so vast and impersonal that they seem to have supernatural strength' (DeLamotte 17) – namely, the patriarchal power entailed, and even enforced, by marriage. But immediately thereafter, Mary's reaction is undermined by the statement that 'her fears [of Charles's imminent return] [are] not prophetic' (46). Instead, Charles informs Mary that he will extend his trip to the Continent. When he eventually returns, he is described by their common friend as a 'good-natured, weak man' (52). This description 'disarms' Charles narrative-wise, dissociating him from the notion of evil. It suggests that his Gothic nature only exists in Mary's consciousness. As Nicola Trott argues, such 'explained supernaturalism' aligns with the Enlightenment project of 'search[ing] out the cause of fright', while 'the heroine's sensibility provides the reader with a pleasurable succession of Gothic terrors and uncertainties' (486). In these sequences, the 'nightmare' of Mary's marriage is shown to be imagined.

Nevertheless, having Charles's ghostly oppressive disposition 'explained' does not undermine the Gothic characteristics Mary believes he possesses or the Gothic nature she associates with the institution of marriage. Gary Kelly remarks how *Mary* 'shows that marriage is a business deal between families and a prison for female desire' (44). Indeed, in Anne K. Mellor's words, '*all* marriages contracted under the existing laws of England may *contract into* oppressive prisons or legalized slavery for women' (419). This is the concept conveyed by Wollstonecraft in her second novel, *Maria; or, The Wrongs of Woman* (1798), in her protagonist's powerful statement that '[m]arriage had bastilled [her] for life' (115), an idea 'shown to be universally applicable' (Davison, *History* 85). This quintessentially Female Gothic statement applies to *Mary* as well. Mellor, referring to *Maria*, claims that 'the true horror of Wollstonecraft's story is that the terrors previously identified with the supernatural manifestations of the Gothic romance ... literally exist within the average domestic household in England' (419). Just as *Maria* 'relocates the characteristic pattern of imprisonment and escape found in the Gothic novel from a reassuringly distant past to the eighteenth-century present ... thus reveal[ing] its continuing resonance' (Spooner 131), so too in *Mary* does Wollstonecraft, by employing Female Gothic motifs, present the plight of women in marriage as a universal nightmare.

To convey the horrors of women's lives, Wollstonecraft strategically tweaks Enlightenment concepts of dreaming and blends them with Gothic notions. In the Age of Reason, '[t]he re-codification of dreams as symptoms of corporeal disorder was articulated alongside the conceptualization of dreaming as an instance of madness' (Dacome 397), and '[i]n the literature that medicalized and moralized bodily conduct, dreams unveiled a diseased body' (411). In Wollstonecraft's novels, however, nightmares are much less about physical ailments than a mind deeply disturbed by restrictive social norms that engender distorted Gothic psyches. As 'women were the most likely readers' of popular dream books such as '[t]he 1750 *Dreams and Moles*' (Perkins 128), Wollstonecraft might also have appreciated the trope of dreams as an opportunity to channel radical ideas to her own sex, because *Maria* extends her use of Gothic nightmares to portray madness caused by a diseased society that denies equal rights to women. *Maria* begins with a juxtaposition of '[a]bodes of horror ... filled with spectres and chimeras', which are the 'stuff as dreams are made of' (61), and the stark reality of Maria's imprisonment in an asylum, the horrifying aftermath of her marriage to an immoral tyrant. These dreams accentuate the mental afflictions of women in a sexist world and, in turn, pave the way for future literary works embracing radical feminist ideals.

Much of Wollstonecraft's radicalism lies in her defence of female rights and autonomy. As William Stafford has argued, novels such as *Mary* and *Maria* are '[t]ragic narratives of the 1790s' which 'reveal the tragic structure of reality ... of the social and sexual order' (30). To Wollstonecraft, simply being female already entails dire suffering, even when a woman is above the lower class. Gary Kelly concurs, stating in regard to *Mary* that, compared with other novels in Wollstonecraft's time such as Eliza Warwick's *The History of Eliza Warwick* (1778) and Mrs H. Cartwright's *The Platonic Marriage* (1787), 'Wollstonecraft aims to construct a story at once ... more radical in criticizing the character and condition of women of [the middle] class' (45). Wollstonecraft more explicitly foregrounds the issues of class and gender in *Maria*, as Kelly, Mellor, and other critics have examined. Yet from a young age, Wollstonecraft had always observed, with a sharp mind, various kinds of prejudice and intersectionality in society. In *Mary*, she highlights the potential of one's genius[4] and intellect, as well as the strength of friendship, as in Mary and Ann's case, to transcend class boundaries. While Wollstonecraft was against social hierarchy, she was even more critical of the gender divide. Mary Lyndon Shanley analyses Wollstonecraft's 'biting condemnation of both domestic and political patriarchy' (149), remarking that '[t]he core of Wollstonecraft's feminist vision was her belief in the desirability and moral necessity of women's independence' (159). Susan Ferguson likewise extrapolates, arguing that Wollstonecraft advocates for 'a system based on individual talent and reason' (Ferguson 440) that allows women 'the *opportunity* ... to choose to live as they will' (444). Indeed, Mary wants to live freely, independently, and according to reason. As she is barred from her ideal lifestyle as a result of her imprisoning marriage and the repressive and restrictive society, her life will remain a nightmare. In Wollstonecraft's time, '[i]t *was* radical to argue for women's essential rationality, their right to education and careers' (Ferguson 450). Such an argument was radical because the defence of women's rationality places them on par with men and entails the fight for equality. This egalitarian idea would have seemed to threaten not only the male ego but also the social order, so most people found it shocking and unacceptable.

Mary's consistently apprehensive response to marriage reflects Wollstonecraft's radicalism, and it is through presenting the female perspective of unwanted wedlock as Gothic parasomnias that Wollstonecraft's feminist 'dreams' may be articulated. While Mary's reactions towards Charles resonate with modern symptoms of PTSD – 'when her husband would take her hand, or mention any thing like love, she would instantly feel a sickness, a faintness at her heart' (53) – her sentiments also signal that '[t]he visions of horror are not private – they have become public' (Doody 99). Enforced marriage has stripped Mary of her freedom of choice, for her 'first favourites [are] men past the meridian of life, and of a philosophic turn' (18), and Charles is neither. His wish to 'join in the masquerades, and such burlesque amusements' (46) only renders him shallow-minded and even, possibly, a libertine, a 'classic' kind of Gothic villain. Having such an uncongenial partner engenders a feeling of Gothic, nightmarish oppression. A nightmare for a woman, then, is one in which she has no autonomy and is coerced into marriage with a man she can neither love nor respect, in which any attempt, if possible at all, to escape from such imprisonment is condemned as insane and immoral by her society, including other women. When discussing *Maria*, in which the female protagonist's flight from her husband results in her being treated as a madwoman, Davison argues that Wollstonecraft 'essentially strips away the veneer of Radcliffe's established Female Gothic recipe in order to bring its socio-political agenda into starker focus', and that Wollstonecraft's work 'marshals the Female Gothic's energies in a new, more feminist direction' (*History* 148–9). Indeed, according to Doody, '[i]t is in the Gothic novel that women writers could first accuse the "real world" of … deep disorder. Or perhaps, they rather asked whether masculine control is not just another delusion in the nightmare of absurd historical reality in which we are all involved' (99). To escape from this 'absurd' world, in Hoeveler's words, '[t]he optimistic dream that concludes the female Gothic requires that juridical violence, paranoia, and injustice, coded as the masculine, be brought to heel, punished …, and contained safely in the confines of the fantasy home – the female-dominated companionate marriage' ('Teaching' 108). Only then may the 'recurring nightmare' of patriarchal oppression finally end and the heroines enjoy peaceful slumbers.

Conclusion

When comparing the largely oppositional genres of romance and realistic fiction in relation to wish-fulfilment, Patrick Brantlinger remarks that '[r]ealistic novels are shaped by struggles for rational self-awareness in ways impossible in dreams, … but romances reject the rational and tend to imitate dreams' (17). *Mary*, however, straddles both realms, manifesting both Enlightenment rationality and Gothic sensationalism. With its strategic portrayal of nightmares in which reality and dreams are literally and metaphorically interwoven, *Mary*, as a prototypical Gothic novel, simultaneously expresses matrimonial dissent and feminist values. This chapter is by no means an exhaustive account of the oppressive and traumatic visions that reflect and influence Mary's subconscious. There is much more to explore, such as Nature's alternately healing and maddening effects on Mary. Although Wollstonecraft deemed *Mary* 'a crude production' a decade after its original publication, in 1797 (*Collected Letters* 404), the novel remains admirable for its courageous, radical, and pioneering spirit. Its feminist dreams continue to resonate and germinate, while its nightmares remain terrifying and fascinating.

Notes

My heartfelt gratitude goes to Dr Carol Margaret Davison, for not only her patient, generous, and nurturing guidance, but also her research suggestions and constant inspiration.

1 Notably, even though the girl is innocent in real life, her mutilated self resembles the horrifically threatening Bleeding Nun in Matthew Lewis's *The Monk* (1796). That figure had appeared in German tales such as 'The Elopement' (1782–6) by Johann Karl August Musäus, which features the nightly haunting of the spectre of a 'skeletal-looking nun' (Mulvey-Roberts 37), and Wollstonecraft may have radically adapted the legend of the Bleeding Nun to more realistic ends to capture a post-traumatic-style haunting of her protagonist.

2 Whether the two became lovers is unconfirmed; Godwin's *Memoirs* 'strongly implies not' (Taylor 197).

3 'Genius' is another major topic of the novel. See, for example, Andrew Elfenbein's chapter 'Mary Wollstonecraft and the Sexuality of Genius' in *The Cambridge Companion to Mary Wollstonecraft*, edited by Claudia L. Johnson, Cambridge University Press, 2002, pp. 228–45.

Works cited

Bond, John. *An Essay on the Incubus, or Night-Mare*. D. Wilson and T. Durham, 1753.

Brantlinger, Patrick. 'Romances, Novels, and Psychoanalysis.' *Criticism*, vol. 17, no. 1, 1975, pp. 15–40.

Brown, Peter. 'On the Borders of Middle English Dream Visions.' *Reading Dreams: The Interpretation of Dreams from Chaucer to Shakespeare*, edited by Peter Brown. Oxford University Press, 1999, pp. 22–50.

Clemens, Valdine. *The Return of the Repressed: Gothic Horror from The Castle of Otranto to Alien*. State University of New York Press, 1999.

Dacome, Lucia. '"To What Purpose Does It Think?": Dreams, Sick Bodies and Confused Minds in the Age of Reason.' *History of Psychiatry*, vol. 15, no. 4, 2004, pp. 395–416.

Davison, Carol Margaret. *History of the Gothic: Gothic Literature 1764–1824*. University of Wales Press, 2009.

Davison, Carol Margaret. 'Introduction.' *The Gothic and Death*, edited by Carol Margaret Davison. Manchester University Press, 2017.

Day, William Patrick. *In the Circles of Fear and Desire: A Study of Gothic Fantasy*. University of Chicago Press, 1985.

DeLamotte, Eugenia C. *Perils of the Night: A Feminist Study of Nineteenth-Century Gothic*. Oxford University Press, 1990.

Domínguez-Rué, Emma. 'Nightmares of Repetition, Dreams of Affiliation: Female Bonding in the Gothic Tradition.' *Journal of Gender Studies*, vol. 23, no. 2, 2014, pp. 125–36.

Donoghue, William. *Enlightenment Fiction in England, France and America.* University Press of Florida, 2002.

Doody, Margaret Anne. 'Deserts, Ruins and Troubled Waters: Female Dreams in Fiction and the Development of the Gothic Novel.' *The Eighteenth-Century English Novel*, edited by Harold Bloom. Chelsea House, 2004, pp. 71–111.

Ferguson, Susan. 'The Radical Ideas of Mary Wollstonecraft.' *Canadian Journal of Political Science / Revue canadienne de science politique*, vol. 32, no. 3, 1999, pp. 427–50.

Freud, Sigmund. *The Interpretation of Dreams*, translated by Joyce Crick. Oxford University Press, 1999.

Gamer, Michael. 'Gothic Literature.' *Mary Wollstonecraft in Context*, edited by Nancy E. Johnson and Paul Keen. Cambridge University Press, 2020, pp. 289–96.

Glance, Jonathan C. '"Beyond the Usual Bounds of Reverie?" Another Look at the Dreams in Frankenstein.' *Dream and Narrative Space*, special issue of *Journal of the Fantastic in the Arts*, vol. 7, no. 4 (28), 1996, pp. 30–47.

Gunther-Canada, Wendy. *Rebel Writer: Mary Wollstonecraft and Enlightenment Politics.* Northern Illinois University Press, 2001.

Hodson, Jane. 'Gothic and the Language of Terror.' *Romantic Gothic: An Edinburgh Companion*, edited by Angela Wright and Dale Townshend. Edinburgh University Press, 2016, pp. 289–305.

Hoeveler, Diane Long. 'The Construction of the Female Gothic Posture: Wollstonecraft's *Mary* and Gothic Feminism.' *Gothic Studies*, vol. 6, no. 1, 2004, pp. 30–44.

Hoeveler, Diane Long. *Gothic Feminism: The Professionalization of Gender from Charlotte Smith to the Brontës.* Pennsylvania State University Press, 1998.

Hoeveler, Diane Long. 'Teaching the Early Female Canon: Gothic Feminism in Wollstonecraft, Radcliffe, Austen, Dacre, and Shelley.' *Approaches to Teaching Gothic Fiction: The British and American Traditions*, edited by Diane Long Hoeveler and Tamar Heller. The Modern Language Association of America, 2003, pp. 105–14.

Johnson, Claudia L. 'Mary Wollstonecraft's Novels.' *The Cambridge Companion to Mary Wollstonecraft*, edited by Claudia L. Johnson. Cambridge University Press, 2002, pp. 189–208.

Kelly, Gary Donald. *Revolutionary Feminism: The Mind and Career of Mary Wollstonecraft.* Macmillan Academic and Professional, 1992.

Lynch, Deidre Shauna. 'Early Gothic Novels and the Belief in Fiction.' *English and British Fiction 1750–1820*, edited by Peter Garside and Karen O'Brien, vol. 2. Oxford University Press, 2015, pp. 182–97.

Martin, Philip W. 'Nightmare.' *The Handbook to Gothic Literature*, edited by Marie Mulvey-Roberts. Macmillan, 1998, pp. 164–5.

Meaney, Geraldine. *(Un)Like Subjects: Women, Theory, Fiction.* Taylor & Francis Group, 2012.

Mellor, Anne K. 'Righting the Wrongs of Woman: Mary Wollstonecraft's *Maria.*' *Nineteenth-Century Contexts*, vol. 19, no. 4, 1996, pp. 413–24.

Mulvey-Roberts, Marie. *Dangerous Bodies: Historicising the Gothic Corporeal.* Manchester University Press, 2016.

Perkins, Maureen. 'The Meaning of Dream Books.' *Dreams and History: The Interpretation of Dreams from Ancient Greece to Modern Psychoanalysis*, edited by Daniel Pick and Lyndal Roper. Routledge, 2004, pp. 125–35.

Roberts, Andrew Michael. 'Psychoanalysis.' *Romanticism: An Oxford Guide*, edited by Nicholas Roe. Oxford University Press, 2005, pp. 219–36.

Shanley, Mary Lyndon. 'Mary Wollstonecraft on Sensibility, Women's Rights, and Patriarchal Power.' *Women Writers and the Early Modern British Political Tradition*, edited by Hilda L. Smith. Cambridge University Press, 1998, pp. 148–67.

Shelley, Mary Godwin. *Frankenstein; or, The Modern Prometheus*, 1818, edited by Maurice Hindle. Penguin, 2003.

Spooner, Catherine. 'Unsettling Feminism: The Savagery of Gothic.' *The Gothic and Theory: An Edinburgh Companion*, edited by Jerrold E. Hogle and Robert Miles. Edinburgh University Press, 2019, pp. 129–46.

Stafford, William. 'Narratives of Women: English Feminists of the 1790s.' *History: The Journal of the Historical Association*, vol. 82, no. 265, 1997, pp. 24–43.

Taylor, Barbara. *Mary Wollstonecraft and the Feminist Imagination.* Cambridge University Press, 2003.

Todd, Janet. 'Introduction.' *Mary. Maria. Matilda*, edited by Janet Todd. Penguin, 2004, pp. vii–xxx.

Trott, Nicola. 'Gothic.' *Romanticism: An Oxford Guide*, edited by Nicholas Roe. Oxford University Press, 2005, pp. 482–501.

Wallace, Diana, and Andrew Smith. 'Introduction: Defining the Female Gothic.' *The Female Gothic: New Directions*, edited by Diana Wallace and Andrew Smith. Palgrave Macmillan, 2009, pp. 1–12.

Wollstonecraft, Mary. *The Collected Letters of Mary Wollstonecraft*, edited by Janet Todd. Columbia University Press, 2003.

Wollstonecraft, Mary. *Maria.* 1798. *Mary. Maria. Matilda*, edited by Janet Todd. Penguin, 2004, pp. 55–148.

Wollstonecraft, Mary. *Mary.* 1788. *Mary. Maria. Matilda*, edited by Janet Todd. Penguin, 2004, pp. 5–53.

Part III

Victorian and nineteenth-century European
Gothic dreams and nightmares

6

Wide awake and dreaming: the night, the haunt, and the female vampire

Maria Giakaniki

Vampire myths and literature have always been closely associated with strange nocturnal visions and the concept of nightmare. Moreover, nightmares caused by supernatural presences such as vampires often include the element of eroticism. Such supernatural entities as incubi and succubi in early European folklore were supposed to provoke not only sexual pleasure but also illness and death in their victims, an inevitable fate for those who gave in to the inappropriate nature and socially unacceptable experience of otherworldly nocturnal visits. Furthermore, the connection between sexuality and dreams caused by fiendish mythological entities has been insightfully explored in such classic psychoanalytic works as *On the Nightmare* by Ernest Jones (White-Lewis 49–50). As with the parasitic demons of European folklore, sexuality is at the core of classic vampire fiction and its representations of dreams and nightmares. In this respect, the mysterious nightly dream sequences that are depicted in classic vampire works are distinguished by singular traits that render them much more than what they initially seem to be to the dreamer-protagonist: most often, these bizarre nocturnal phenomena are not exactly dreams, but unusual erotic experiences during which the dreamer is suspended between sleep and wakefulness, or experiencing different states of sleep, ranging from deep sleep to hypnagogia – the transitional state between wakefulness and sleep – and diverse forms of lucid dreams, including wakeful dreaming. In this last case, the subject enters sleep without losing consciousness (Gish 1) and experiences the dream as a second life, a state that completely blurs the boundary between reality and nocturnal vision.

In Samuel T. Coleridge's Romantic poetic narrative 'Christabel' (1797, 1800), and Joseph Sheridan Le Fanu's Victorian Gothic novella *Carmilla* (1872), the unsettling dreams experienced by the female protagonists are simultaneously erotic and repulsive, sometimes even resembling the state of trance. They belong to the hazy realm of sleep and the authors describe them in an abstract and suggestive manner. In Théophile Gautier's hallucinatory short story 'La Morte Amoureuse' (1836), and Mircea Eliade's Romanian horror novel *Domnișoara Christina* (1936), the nocturnal vampiric contact is, for the male protagonist, part of either a repetitive, often lucid, vivid dream or the uncanny experience of wakeful dreaming. Thus are the romantic and sexual desires sovereign, the protagonists unable to distinguish facts from illusion since the dreams are too real, a simulation of real life. This chapter constitutes a close and, in part, comparative analysis of the dreams and nightmares in these four literary works focused on female vampires. It adopts a basic psychoanalytical approach while remaining attentive to their different historical-cultural contexts. Particular attention will be paid to the ways in which the erotic vampiric dreams or nightmares are employed by each author to depict concealed or suppressed desires. It will also demonstrate how the complex figure of the female vampire represents diverse forms of sexual attraction, including parasitic otherness, and how these features are especially conveyed through the use of dreams and nightmares. Finally, consideration will be given to the different approaches to same-sex and heterosexual vampiric relationships and to the authorial perspective on gender, as the female vampires are considerably eroticised.

In the extended poetic narrative 'Christabel', written in two parts, in 1797 and 1800 respectively, the dividing line between external reality and somnial experience seems to be rather indistinct. Coleridge himself was deeply preoccupied with the field of 'nocturnal visions' – namely dreams, and their symbolic significance. Often troubled by horrible recurrent nightmares, connected with both juvenile traumas and his later infamous opium addiction, he undertook extensive research on the topic of parasomnias. This interest often inspired his poetry, especially in such renowned works as 'Kubla Khan, Or, A Vision in a Dream: A Fragment' (1797), *The Rime of the Ancient Mariner* (1798), and the more directly autobiographical 'The Pains of Sleep' (1803), which is a vivid poetic testimony of night terrors rooted in feelings of guilt and anxiety that disrupt the natural process of sleep and physical rest. Furthermore, Coleridge was profoundly intrigued by certain theories that attributed the existence of dreams to the interference of spirits that are supposed to bring punishment for past sins, while also considering these demonic entities to have a divine source (Ford 147).

The complex, multi-layered, almost cryptic text that constitutes 'Christabel' tells of a young, noble, motherless heroine who lives with her father in a castle. The flirtatious or even erotic nature of Christabel's nocturnal encounter with an unknown young lady named Geraldine is manifested from the beginning of the narrative: Christabel 'happens' to meet beautiful white-clad Geraldine in the moon-lit forest subsequent to dreams of her beloved knight the previous evening. Thus is an implicit association forged between dreams and sexual awakening. In this respect, Geraldine initially makes her appearance as a type of surrogate lover in the place where

Christabel roams – the dark, mysterious forest, 'reminiscent of a child's nightmare' (Twitchell 44), that signifies the subconscious mechanisms during sleep. Thus, from the outset, the whole scene of Christabel's meeting with Geraldine resembles a strange dream.

A short while after their random encounter in the woods, Christabel invites Geraldine to her castle, offering a warm shelter to the apparently deserted maiden. Although there are several signs indicating that Geraldine is a creature of demonic origin, Christabel soon permits her to invade her personal domain and space, leading her to her own bedroom and agreeing to lie in bed with her, unconsciously conceding to her own seduction while her mother's vivid memory seems invisibly present. Christabel thus submits to Geraldine's bidding, as if she is already under her hypnotic spell.

In Christabel's chamber, Geraldine asks her young hostess to disrobe while she does the same, in a ritualistic simulation of a preliminary stage of a sexual encounter. Geraldine's naked bosom, which is revealed at this point, is 'A sight to dream of, not to tell!' (line 253), an allusion to a kind of deformity never actually described, that invokes a vague sense of 'defilement' and 'horror' (May, 709). Geraldine herself refers to the particular spot in her bosom as 'the mark of my shame, this seal of my sorrow' (lines 269–70), an enigmatic phrase that can be considered as an insinuation of sin, guilt, and transgression. The female breast, both a symbol of maternity and sexuality, can exert, in the case of Geraldine, a supernatural power to anyone who touches it, since 'in the touch of this bosom there worketh a spell' (line 267); Christabel indeed touches it, and this is an action that 'seals her fate' (Twitchell 42), enticing her to lie down and be seduced by Geraldine.

The conclusion to part 1 of the poem includes the emblematic wakeful sleep scene of the text, when Geraldine and Christabel lie together in bed, which the narrator describes as follows:

> With open eyes (ah woe is me!)
> Asleep, and dreaming fearfully,
> Fearfully dreaming, yet, I wis
> Dreaming that alone, which is
> O sorrow and shame! (lines 292–6)

These lines allude to a state of wakeful dreaming for Christabel, which is marked by intense unease and abashment, while the ardent wish of the omniscient narrator is that this is only a dream for Christabel and nothing more. The next lines indicate a paradoxical mix of horror and maternal warmth:

And lo! the worker of these harms,
That holds the maiden in her arms,
Seems to slumber still and mild,
As a mother with her child. (lines 298–301)

These lines highlight Geraldine's dual function: she serves both as a lover and a surrogate mother for Christabel, in a forbidden contact possessing homoerotic and incestuous overtones. The encounter is distinguished by a feeling of degradation but also tenderness, demonstrating Christabel's simultaneous conflicting emotions of repulsion and attraction towards Geraldine.

Figure 6.1 'Christabel and Geraldine in the Chamber' by H. J. Ford and Lancelot Speed, 1891, created for Andrew Lang's *The Blue Poetry Book*

After the pivotal erotic dream scene, Christabel 'gathers herself from out her trance' (line 312) and expresses her emotional tension by shedding tears while her countenance is both 'sad and soft' (line 314). The use of the word 'trance' underlines the state Christabel is in – namely wakeful but not fully conscious, possibly an altered state of consciousness related to hypnosis. Nevertheless, the fact that at the same time 'she seems to smile / As infants at a sudden light! / Yea, she doth smile, and she doth weep' (lines 317–9) underlines that she experienced a joy mixed with horror and sorrow in her contact with Geraldine, language that perhaps alludes to an uncomfortable coming-of-age experience. The tears of Christabel, in this context, might be an expression of both sadness and relief.

When Christabel awakens in the morning and enters the realm of the conscious self, she seems to have feelings of ambivalence and uncertainty regarding what took place during the night. Soon thereafter she exclaims, 'Sure I have sinn'd!' (line 381), implying that something transgressive occurred, which remains vivid in her memory either as emotions or images, possibly some sort of improper physical contact. This is never actually described, belonging to the hazy realm of sleep, where inappropriate, socially unacceptable acts may be concealed. It is noteworthy that Coleridge himself associated nightmares with the feeling of having sinned and somnial manifestations as 'the troubled outpourings or reflections of his psyche' (Ford 144). In this respect, Christabel's dream can be regarded as the projection of her subconscious thoughts and forbidden yearnings. Her feelings of shame and guilt in the morning are most possibly related to a taboo experience of some form of infantile sexuality: Geraldine may have corrupted Christabel by inducing her into a 'contact' both motherly and erotic, of both an incestuous and homosexual nature. Christabel's seduction seems also to be more psychological than sexual (Strickland 651). Geraldine seems to be primarily a psychic vampire as there is no allusion to blood draining or other physical contact except for their sleeping embrace. Their vampiric/sexual contact mainly takes the form of energy exchange/draining, with Geraldine becoming stronger and Christabel becoming enfeebled and confused (Twitchell 44). The reference to myth, which connects Geraldine with lamias, is only a pretext to transfer the supernatural traits of the former to the psychological realm: Geraldine is not only a succubus but also a 'vampiric', thus parasitic, mother or lover who gradually dominates Christabel, mostly through her trance-like sleep, during which the latter experiences both pleasure and horror, without being able to react.

In the second part of the poem, when Christabel presents her new friend, Geraldine, to her father, Sir Leoline, another dream of symbolic connotations is described by the bard, Bracy. In his nightmare, which transpires when Christabel is under Geraldine's spell, a snake throttles a dove, thus signifying the unhealthy, improper bond between the two women. Moreover, even after she is awake, Christabel remains partly immersed in a dreamy or trance state; Geraldine's spell, which involves the domination of both a mother and a lover, is extended into the daylight. Soon, Geraldine bewitches Sir Leoline too, as a female companion/wife surrogate, while in one of the alternate endings, Geraldine transforms into Christabel's beloved knight, which lays more emphasis on the theme of transgressive sexuality and presents the vampire as a possibly hermaphroditic creature.

Sleep and dreaming in 'Christabel' are related to the state of hypnosis and bewitchment. During Coleridge's era dreams were associated with both of these notions, more particularly with witchcraft practices and animal magnetism or mesmerism, circumstances in which the human will is supposed to be paralysed and the subject can be at the mercy of malignant forces (Ford 100). Coleridge explored different approaches to the mystical realm of dreams, considering them as either caused by external stimuli or the subject themselves. The latter explanation gestures towards later psychoanalytic interpretations according to which dreams are the product of subconscious mechanisms related to suppressed desires and fears. In this respect, dreams are considered to be the most profound 'reality' of the human psyche, and a dream may be regarded as 'sinful' or transgressive, representing deeply coveted emotions and desires. In the case of 'Christabel', it seems that an inner reality is presented under the guise of a dream so as to render it more acceptable. Thus, Geraldine is a projection of Christabel's fears and inmost desires that are materialised in her wakeful sleep. Geraldine is the maternal abject, inspiring the contradictory emotions of attraction and fear, as she is both a familiar and unfamiliar/uncanny figure. Notably, the fearful knowledge she imparts can come only through dreams, and the intricate, riddle-like paths of the subconscious self.

It is very possible that the Irish author Joseph Sheridan Le Fanu, in writing the seminal vampire novella *Carmilla* (1872), was inspired by Coleridge's 'Christabel' since the similarities between the plots of the two works are striking. Most importantly, the central theme of the heroine's sexual awakening by a female parasitic figure/mother surrogate is present in both texts and is also expressed through the symbolic use of dreams and nightmares.

In several of Le Fanu's short stories and novels such as the famous *Uncle Silas* (1864) and 'The Room in Le Dragon Volant' (1872), the latter published alongside *Carmilla*, there are often instances of real-life experiences which are presented as dreams, or cases where dreams are fused with facts, provoking a sense of disorientation and uncertainty regarding the nature of reality itself. Towards the end of his life, Le Fanu had become deeply preoccupied with the works of the Swedish theologian Emmanuel Swedenborg, according to whom every person has an 'inner eye' that enables them to see beyond the physical world into the world of the spirits that exist among humans (Tracy xiii). Swedenborg experienced strange religious and meta-physical visions, and his personal 'otherworld' prompted Le Fanu to plunge into his most mystical phase, with *Carmilla* being a product of that period. In this respect, the ethereal, elusive content of visions and dreams and the indistinct boundaries between the material and immaterial world play a particularly valid role in *Carmilla*. Moreover, this is the mid-Victorian era when romantic friendship between females and the passionate, suppos-edly spiritual, love between women was legitimised as something pure and poetic (Faderman 157–62). Nevertheless, the 'phantom' of lesbianism, as an 'unnatural' sexual tendency that is also physical and not just spiritual, hovered in the Victorian mind.

Whereas in 'Christabel' there is one pivotal somnial experience, *Carmilla* is abundant in unusual dreams and bizarre nightmares experienced by Laura, the female narrator. The first memorable experience Laura has as a child, which also anticipates the later remarkable events, is regarded as a dream by her family, although she believes it was real. This episode involved her initial meeting with the vampire Carmilla, who attacks Laura for the first time when she is only six years old in an episode when Laura believes she is fully awake. When years later, Laura meets Carmilla again, suppos-edly by chance, when Laura becomes Carmilla's hostess and companion, she immediately recognises the female face. She tells her new friend that 'twelve years ago, in vision or reality, I certainly saw you', while Carmilla claims, 'twelve years ago, I saw your face in a dream' (Le Fanu 242), mirroring Laura's statement in a purposeful attempt to blur the boundary between dreams and reality.

After their first encounter and while their relationship evolves, with Carmilla's behaviour often being romantic and erotic towards Laura, the latter has a second somnial experience which frightens her in a similar man-ner to the incident from childhood, which she later considers a dream. In this second nocturnal incident, Laura narrates that she was sleeping but that she was conscious, in a type of hypnagogic state, involving a lucid dream where she sees a large feline animal. After being attacked and pierced by this creature, she awakens in terror. In this second stage of the nocturnal incident, when Laura believes she is actually awake, she notices the mys-terious figure of a woman who quickly disappears (259) (see Figure 6.2). Once more, dream and reality are confused. Laura sees the female vampire, although in different forms, both in her sleep and when she wakes up. After this horrible experience, Laura has strange repetitive dreams that she can-not explain, dreams that make her ill; nevertheless, she does not attempt to resist them or ask for help. This is the most important phase of Laura's

Figure 6.2 'Laura in Bed' by David Henry Friston for 'The Dark Blue'
(February 1872)

somnial experiences as they become more distinctly connected to her sexual restraint and, possibly, the repression of old memories belonging to a traumatic childhood.

Laura's dreams usually start with a pleasurable sensation but conclude with frightening paroxysms that leave her weak. There is a vague sense of confusion and inscrutability regarding these dreams, which concern people and places Laura cannot remember afterwards, in which a deep female voice dominates that always causes a sensation of 'indescribable solemnity and fear' (263). However hard to decipher, these nocturnal visions are directly connected to her being attacked by the vampire. They may also be related to memories and experiences from her past, incidents and emotions hidden in her subconscious that mingle with her present fears. Part of her dream involves erotic touch as she always feels 'warm lips' kissing her (263). Notably, this apparently pleasurable sensation concludes with a feeling of extreme discomfort, described as a feeling of 'strangulation' bringing about a 'convulsion' (263). Even in her sleep, Laura's queer sexuality is suppressed, as those erotic scenes are always vaguely described, thus censored, with the feeling of pleasure she experiences becoming a terrible feeling of discomfort similar to a kind of punishment by dream's end. Moreover, the young heroine is confronted by this vague matriarchal figure that appears repetitively in her semi-nightmares, a mysterious character whose presence and austere voice represent a form of authority that Laura cannot comprehend, resulting in her feelings of guilt for succumbing to the forbidden sexual contact with a female vampire. Furthermore, the feeling of suffocation Laura experiences at the end of these strangely pleasurable erotic 'sessions' could be associated not just with the stereotypically oppressive feeling of a nightmare, but also with the experience of asphyxiation/strangulation bringing sexual ecstasy (Mason 146).

One of Laura's most significant nocturnal experiences transpires when, in one of her usual strange and frightful dreams, she hears a female voice of unknown origin saying, 'Your mother warns you to beware of the assassin' (Le Fanu 264), and immediately thereafter sees Carmilla 'bathed, from her chin to her feet, in one great stain of blood' (264). In this instance, 'Laura fuses self, killer and mother' (Auerbach 12), meaning that there are no separate identities distinguishing the assassin and the assassinated in the dream and probably in Laura's subconscious. Moreover, this particular nocturnal experience signifies Laura's strong bond with Carmilla as they reflect each other. The dream is symbolic of their close relationship and emotional, though 'unhealthy', connection, while also underscoring their identification as female members of the same family, as Carmilla is Laura's ancestor on her maternal side. Thus the two young girls are relatives and lovers at the same time, with queerness and incest being both prominent Gothic themes.

Laura rejects the sexual advances of Carmilla during the day, yet at night she is passive and accepting, even though she describes the nocturnal experiences in a contradictory manner, presenting them as both repulsive and pleasurable, similar to the state of her feelings towards Carmilla. Laura cannot commit the shameful vampiric act while being fully conscious and awake, thus she unconsciously transfers it to the realm of sleep. An act committed under circumstances when the subject cannot be in full possession of her senses and self-control is under milder moral criticism, especially when that desire is homoerotic and/or incestuous, which are taboo. Laura's nightmares are hazy and indistinct, odd experiences between dream and reality, which she does not associate with her diurnal life. Most of her nocturnal experiences resemble Christabel's dream: she seems to be in a deep state of trance, not realising what is happening to her, believing that what she undergoes is not actual when it is. She considers these strange phenomena to be only incomprehensible nightmares. Thus, it is only during sleep that what is unacceptable or too horrible to happen in full consciousness, can take place.

Furthermore, it is probable that the dreams Laura has when she is being attacked by Carmilla are somehow connected to her own past experiences. In this respect, the vampiric act not only awakens suppressed sexuality but also stirs buried memories of the psyche, which is possibly marked by past trauma. This is suggested by the fact that Laura's childhood trauma only resurfaces after the first attack by the vampire, although this traumatic experience remains only vaguely suggested (Thomas 78). In this case, Laura's memories as a child may not have been merely suppressed but repressed, meaning that they have been buried deep in her unconscious. Yet childhood traumas, like witnessing or experiencing violence and molestation/ abuse, can be channelled into parasomnias, taking the forms of nocturnal terrors (Nader 9). In this respect, Carmilla's vampiric attacks on Laura can be considered as the re-opening of a primal wound through dreams and nightmares.

The common element between dreams in 'Christabel' and *Carmilla* is the fact that they are indistinct and abstract yet revelatory of intense sensations, which range from pleasure to horror, while only hinting at forbidden sexual experiences. Moreover, they are nocturnal experiences that are considered to be distinct from diurnal life and refer to bizarre uncontrollable states that are not fully realised by the subject, suggesting that the latter is in a trance.

Although 'sexual corruption' via sleep in 'Christabel' is subtler than in *Carmilla* where eroticism is somehow more explicit, the heroine in Coleridge's narrative seems to be more conscious of the facts than Laura. Victorian patriarchal values and norms reflected in *Carmilla* indicate that the sexual experience remains either concealed in the subconscious part of the self or at least not articulated by the heroine herself, not only for its queerness but also because of the idea, unacceptable in the Victorian era, of woman's sexual impurity. In either case, Laura remains an unsuspecting victim who does not consent to her own seduction, at least not consciously. The heroine in 'Christabel' on the other hand, a literary work belonging to the Romantic era, admits the fact of her own 'corruption' and, although it upsets her, she appears to acknowledge it.

In both works, sexual urges and human fears are attributed to demonic entities of the night; thus dreams and nightmares nurture and host the concealed desires that cannot be expressed or enacted in any other way: 'Geraldine and Carmilla flourish in the obscure privacy of women's bedrooms and dreams' (Auerbach 50). Indeed, it is through the world of dreams that the queer female vampire mostly acts. Both works are complex representations of the female psyche, involving lesbianism, incest, and the dual self as depicted in instances of symbolic mirroring between victim and victimiser. Whereas 'Christabel' and *Carmilla* refer to queer female sexuality which is subtly explored mainly through dreams and nightmares, 'La Morte Amoureuse' by French author Théophile Gautier and *Domnişoara Christina* by Romanian author Mircea Eliade focus mainly on suppressed male heterosexual desire which is openly manifested in erotic nocturnal 'episodes' of wakeful dreaming. Both of these works feature an utterly seductive female vampire who acts mostly through nightly visions, while the erotic experience might be either a dream, an actual event, or something in-between. In the case of 'La Morte Amoureuse', the dream resembles real life itself, yet it is not.

With the novella 'La Morte Amoureuse' ('The Dead in Love'), Théophile Gautier completely blurs the boundary between reality and nocturnal vision in a tale of dreamlike eroticism and ambiguity (Guiley 12). Gautier's works were part of French Romanticism but they were also connected to later movements such as Symbolism and Decadence, for which he is considered a precursor. He was also a key representative of 'Le conte fantastique' of the 1830s and 1840s. Gautier's works were often distinguished by dreams and nightmares, fantasies, hallucinations, the invisible world, madness itself (Ponnau 38), and the shadowy parts of human existence more broadly, similar to other nineteenth-century French authors such as Gérard de Nerval, Charles Nodier, Prosper Mérimée, and Guy de Maupassant, who were also authors of fantastic tales. Gautier had also delved into the dream-like state produced by the use of such drugs as hashish (James 110), just like other writers and artists of the late eighteenth and early nineteenth century, such as Thomas de Quincey and Coleridge, who made use of narcotics for either medical or recreational purposes, a practice which in certain cases heightened their creative imaginations.

'La Morte Amoureuse' is the strange oneiric story of the forbidden sexual yearnings of a priest named Romuald, who leads a double life: one while he is awake and the other while he is asleep. The paradox, in this case, lies in the fact that the protagonist's real life is the life he thinks he is dreaming about at night, while his life with the vampire Clarimonde, the second life which intrudes on his former existence, is experienced as if it were his regular daily life. In this respect, the life of the dream takes complete possession of the protagonist's mind, displacing his prosaic everyday routine as a priest.

Romuald's first nocturnal visit to Clarimonde's castle on a black horse, whose description is reminiscent of Fuseli's emblematic painting 'The Nightmare', is marked by his reviving the beautiful dead seductress with a kiss, which evokes the Sleeping Beauty motif. Subsequently, the enchanting courtesan visits him in his sleep, inviting him to reject his ascetic existence and live a full life of sensual love and romantic splendour with her, in a completely secular and material world, which seems like a sensational and hedonistic vision according to the protagonist's luscious descriptions.

Although this dream life, to which Romuald easily succumbs, is experienced as actual, the protagonist presents it in his narrative as mostly ideal and visionary. In this second form of existence, Clarimonde is depicted as an almost perfect creature who incarnates all female charms and charisma in one person and can offer her beloved a luxurious prosperous life beyond his wildest imagination. This dualism in Romuald's experience of reality can also be considered a duality of the inner self. All the secret wishes, fantasies, and desires of the protagonist, who feels entangled in his profession as a priest, are materialised via a female supernatural entity. Romuald's repressed self has achieved a complete reversion through wakeful dreaming. He is a kind of 'daydreamer' who has denied prosaic reality in order to live a second parallel life through the abysses of his unconscious mind. The dream here is not a glimpse of another life but a new 'life' itself in all of its elusive grandeur.

In this respect, the vampire Clarimonde is a symbol of forbidden sexuality like Geraldine and Carmilla; however, there does not seem to exist any repulsion or disconcertedness in the protagonist's attraction towards Clarimonde, only religious guilt. While the female vampires created by Coleridge and Le Fanu are ambivalent figures devoid of moral principles, Clarimonde is mostly treated with sympathy by both the hero and the author of the tale. She is an empathetic vampire in love who strives to protect her lover from her lust for blood which is necessary for her existence. Where Geraldine and Carmilla are ambiguous, parasitic, maternal, and lover surrogates, Clarimonde is the fascinating and mysterious representation of all types of women – the materialisation of a stereotypical male fantasy. While everything is presented through Romuald's subjective perspective, Father Sérapion, the elder priest of the tale, is the voice of rationality and conservatism according to whom this charming female is extremely dangerous, a horrendous bloodsucking monster. In this respect, all the misogynistic traits of religion are represented by Sérapion (diLiberti 78), who describes Clarimonde as a vicious destructive demon. Nevertheless, the real concern of Sérapion may not only be the physical decline of his friend but also a fully non-clerical and worldly existence that completely distracts him from his vows of celibacy and sexual abnegation. Romuald's seduction is both sensual and spiritual and it extends, chronically, for years – at least through the protagonist's perception of time. These characteristics constitute it not just as a nocturnal vision but as an alternative existence through continuous and prolonged wakeful dreaming. Moreover, this story is an anxiety dream, a dream of fulfilled desire that ends as a nightmare due to feelings of guilt (Epstein 8–12).

With this unusual and uncanny tale, Gautier challenges the existence of reality itself, making the reader uncertain as to which of the two states constitutes the real life of the protagonist and whether there is only one objective reality or two different subjective states. The most plausible explanation is that the real life of the central character is the dull reality he lives as a priest since this experience precedes his life with Clarimonde. His dream life, however, is so bright and happy that, for a while, it overshadows his sombre commonplace existence. The latter ends up being a series of mundane episodes, almost a lacklustre nightmare he reluctantly experiences. In this respect, Romuald's dream life is more real than his actual life as a priest, since his perception of it is much more intense. This also echoes the author's tendencies in his works towards an ideal illusory life since 'in certain cases a waking dream has as much power as the sleeping one' (Du Camp 168). Indeed, Gautier might have shared the desires and obsessions of the heroes in his fantastic stories, desiring mythical women and extravagant lifestyles that only existed in his mind. Thus these chimaeras become an antidote to 'untrustworthy realities' (168). In this respect, Gautier's tales featuring wakeful dreams are allegories of unfulfilled human yearnings, of real life's ardent daydreamers who cannot conform to the contemporary world.

Another European fantastic novel featuring a female vampire, which obscures the boundaries between dream and reality, is *Domnişoara Christina* (*Miss Christina*) by Mircea Eliade, a twentieth-century philosopher, historian of religion, and author of both realist and supernatural fiction. His theory of 'the sacred and the profane', as well as the notion of 'the eternal return', relate to the significance of myths and archetypes in the history of human civilisation. In *Domnişoara Christina*, he draws inspiration from Romanian folklore and, in particular, the strigoi myth. In a 1978 prologue to the novella, the author draws some parallels between his theory of the sacred and the profane and his uncanny literature, referring to certain analogies between the element of the sacred or the invisible and the element of the supernatural and the uncanny which intrudes into the material world. Moreover, in his work *Myth and Realities* he refers to those uncanny manifestations as 'breakthroughs of the sacred (or the "supernatural") into the World – that is, hierophanies' (6). Likewise, in *Domnişoara Christina*, it is the world of dreams and phantoms of the night that intrudes into and affects the real world.

The female vampire in Eliade's novella enters the dreams of the male protagonist with a romantic disposition and explicitly erotic intentions, bringing to mind Gautier's Clarimonde. At first, Christina appears in Egor's dreams but then dream and reality become one and the same and Christina makes nocturnal visits to her potential lover with the purpose of romantically and sexually seducing him, visits that exit the misty realm of dream, becoming a haunting reality. The first time Egor, the guest of a noble family who dwell in a rural location, sees Christina in his dreams, a long-dead close relative of the family, she is actually an intruder. Initially, other people appear in the dream, some of whom try to warn him against some kind of vague threat, yet the female vampire gets control of Egor's sleep, affecting the scene of the dream, becoming the centre of it, displacing all other influences. She then approaches him romantically and sexually, revealing special feelings for him, and claiming that she will not hurt *him*. Her manner, which seems full of empathy, brings to mind Clarimonde's approach to her lover and potential victim. Egor awakens and sees Christina approaching him, but she soon leaves without touching him.

The second time Christina visits Egor in his sleep, she becomes the protagonist of his lucid dream, magically transporting him to a glamorous ball of another era from his room in the house where he is staying as a guest, the same edifice where she had also lived. In both dreams, Egor's senses are heightened and he can smell the vampire's perfume and feel her sensual touch – her presence prevails, especially the sound of her voice as she tries to convince him of her romantic intentions, which sound sincere. She orders him to wake up and he does; then she exits the dream and enters reality. When Egor sees her in his room, he realises he is no longer dreaming. She touches him and he lies down pale in his bed, at which point the scene is interrupted, suggesting that what must have taken place afterwards is the vampire's erotic attack.

The drama is resolved in the last somnial experience Egor has with Christina. After falling asleep at his desk, unsure as to whether he is dreaming or not, Egor cherishes the hope that he will wake up. Although drawn to Christina, he never wished to succumb to her advances. In this lengthy dream sequence, Christina attempts direct sexual seduction. He is both repulsed and attracted, finding her both eerie and desirable. In an emotional outburst of romantic melancholy, Christina confesses she no longer wishes to be part of a dream. Subsequent to this final encounter with Egor and his discovery of the reason behind her death twenty years earlier, Christina gradually disappears, the whole scene taking place in the nightmarish zone between dream and reality.

Christina represents a sexual temptation for the protagonist, who is becoming romantically attached to Sanda, the eldest daughter of the house and Christina's niece. This fact renders the nocturnal attraction an almost taboo affair. Once again, the forbidden desires can only thrive after dark, either in a nocturnal vision or a strange reality resembling a dream.

Christina's haunting influence extends into daylight, since the family's life itself seems to be plunged into a sinister atmosphere which is apparent from the first day of Egor's visit: the cattle are dying, apparently due to strigoi attacks; Sanda is ill, her mother is acting strangely, and the younger daughter, Simina, is expressing signs of sexual perversion. It is interesting to note that Eliade's great preoccupation with sexuality and its various manifestations is also demonstrated in his other non-supernatural works.

In *Domnişoara Christina*, the otherworldly femme fatale possesses certain traits borrowed from the classic female vampires that preceded her, such as the infatuation, passion, and romantic empathy that distinguish Carmilla and Clarimonde. In particular, there are several parallels between Eliade's novel and Gautier's tale. In both cases, the male vampire is either seduced or nearly seduced while the somnial episodes of wakeful dreaming are experienced as being almost real. In *La Morte Amoureuse*, reality is displaced by the dream, which becomes a new alternate reality and, in Eliade's novel, the dream is so vivid that it gradually becomes real, while the phantom, by its own wish, exits the dream and materialises in front of the central character. In both cases, the dream signifies forbidden desire. The male protagonists violate social norms since Romuald is a priest, while Egor is in love with Sanda, the vampire's niece. Egor is mostly conscious during the nocturnal incidents when he experiences lucid dreaming, while Romuald has difficulty distinguishing between fact and illusion due to his almost continuous wakeful dreaming. Furthermore, both works depict the female vampire as a powerful agent of seduction who obscures the dividing line between dream and reality.

In the four literary works examined, dreams highlight or even reveal the content and/or subtext of each narrative which mainly concerns forbidden or suppressed, thus unacknowledged, desire. In this respect, the dreams serve to shed light on the complex web of contradictory emotions experienced by the central characters. Dreams and nightmares in these tales serve as the subconscious outlets for the heroes' socially unacceptable romantic and sexual tendencies: Christabel and Carmilla have to suppress their strong transgressive emotions for a maternal figure who is also a substitute lover, while Romuald and Egor are tempted to give in to sensuality and eroticism, violating the vows and boundaries set by religion and the standards of romantic fidelity. The common element in all four works is the fact that the dream is the space where internalised emotions and instincts are liberated and expressed, and the site, primarily, where female vampires act. There is a range of different ways in which each subject experiences those dreams: in *Carmilla*, the dream is almost separate from reality, and the heroine does not realise the associations between nocturnal and daily life, while in 'Christabel' dream and fact are closer to each other since the heroine admits to having at least partial knowledge of what took place in the dream and recognises its connection with reality. In 'La Morte Amoureuse', the hero is confused regarding what is a dream and what is not since he allows his dream life to replace his daily life, while Egor in *Domnişoara Christina* is not always conscious of the permeable boundaries between dream and fact. Furthermore, dreams are delineated in their various versions – hypnagogia, states of trance, lucid dreams, and wakeful dreaming. In all of these cases, the line between somnial experience and reality is quite indistinct, allowing the subject to enter an intermediate level of experience and consciousness where nothing is certain and tangible.

Also, through the employment of dreams, four male authors depict female vampires as utterly seductive and dangerous, a stereotypical portrayal of the lethal power of the femme fatale. The authors' visual descriptions of Geraldine, Carmilla, Clarimonde, and Christina sometimes verge on fetishism, especially in their references to their breasts or hair, providing evidence of the male gaze that eroticises the female vampire. In contrast to this tendency, female vampire tales of the same era penned by women authors like Mary Elizabeth Braddon, Mary Wilkins Freeman, or Edith Wharton picture this parasitic presence quite differently. In Braddon's short tale 'Good Lady Ducayne', the female vampire is presented as an old repulsive lady, while in Freeman's 'Luella Miller', the psychic female parasite, though described as very feminine, is devoid of any real sensuality while also acting in a realistic domestic setting far removed from the mysterious sensational haziness of the dream. Moreover, in the ghost story 'Bewitched' by Edith Wharton, although the female apparition haunts and feeds on a man who used to be her lover, there is no explicit description of her external appearance or any sexualisation of her face, body, voice, or movement. In stark contrast, Coleridge, Le Fanu, Gautier, and Eliade adopt a sexually objectifying and voyeuristic male point of view regarding the power of seduction of their female vampires, directly relating female sexuality with draining, destruction, and death, even in the cases where they sympathise with their supernatural heroines.

Sometimes, dreams seem more real than diurnal life, while also revealing inner truths, often in a disguised form that requires deciphering. In this respect, dreams in Gothic literature often signify what is concealed but needs to come to the surface. Uncanny creatures of the night, such as the literary female vampires examined here, represent suppressed and forbidden emotions that are socially unacceptable. In this case, dreams and nightmares become the means to explore, in a uniquely enlightening manner, desire, sin, trauma, the closeted self, and even the blasphemous wish for an alternate existence.

Works cited

Auerbach, Nina. *Our Vampires, Ourselves*. Chicago University Press, 1995.

Braddon, Mary Elizabeth. 'Good Lady Ducayne.' *Children of the Night: Classic Vampire Stories*, edited by David Stuart Davies. Wordsworth Editions, 2007, pp. 171–94.

Coleridge, Samuel Taylor. 'Christabel.' *The Norton Anthology of English Literature*, *Vol. 2*. Norton, 1993, pp. 349–64.

diLiberti, Julia. 'Vampires Suck but Not as Much as the Men Who Use Them: The Narratological Strategy of the Vampire chez Gautier.' *Aimer et Mourir: Love, Death and Women's Lives in Texts of French Expression*, edited by Eilene Hoft-March and Judith Holland Sarnecki. Cambridge Scholars Publishing, 2009, pp. 66–97.

Du Camp, Maxime. *Théophile Gautier*, translated by J. E. Gordon. T. Fisher Unwin, 1893.

Eliade, Mircea. *Miss Christina*, translated by Maria Hymou-Marinescou. Dioni, 2004.

Eliade, Mircea. *Myth and Reality*, translated by W. R. Trask. Harper & Row, 1963.

Epstein, Edna Selan. 'The Entanglement of Sexuality and Aesthetics in Gautier and Mallarmé.' *Nineteenth-Century French Studies*, vol. 1, no. 1, 1972, pp. 5–20.

Faderman, Lillian. *Surpassing the Love of Men*. The Women's Press, 1985.

Ford, Jennifer. *Coleridge on Dreaming: Romanticism, Dreams and the Medical Imagination*. Cambridge University Press, 1998.

Gautier, Théophile. 'The Dead in Love.' *Arria Markella and Other Fantastic Tales*, translated by Effie Yiannopoulou. Agra Publications, 2001, pp. 41–77.

Gish, Elliott. *Lucid Dreaming: A Wake-Initiated-Lucid-Dream (WILD) Approach*. 2014. Saybrook University, PhD Dissertation, www.researchgate.net/publication /318946859_Lucid_dreaming_A_Wake-InitiatedLucid-Dream_WILD_approach. Accessed 1 June 2021.

Guiley, Rosemary Ellen. *The Encyclopedia of Vampires, Werewolves and Other Monsters*. Visionary Living Publishing, 2005.

James, Tony. *Dream, Creativity and Madness in Nineteenth-Century France*. Clarendon Press, 1996.

Le Fanu, Joseph Sheridan. *Carmilla. The Wordsworth Collection of Irish Ghost Stories*. Wordsworth Editions, 2005, pp. 227–96.

Mason, Diane Elizabeth. *The Secret Vice: Masturbation in Victorian Fiction and Medical Culture*. 2003. Bath Spa University College, PhD Dissertation, https:// core.ac.uk/download/pdf/40108683.pdf. Accessed 1 June 2021.

May, Claire B. 'Christabel and Abjection: Coleridge's Narrative in Process/on Trial.' *Studies in English Literature, 1500–1900*, vol. 37, no. 4, 1997, pp. 699–721.

Nader, Kathleen. 'Children's Traumatic Dreams.' *Trauma and Dreams*, edited by Deirdre Barrett. Harvard University Press, 1996, pp. 9–24.

Ponnau, Gwenhaël. *La Folie dans la Littérature Fantastique*. Presses du CNRS, 1987.

Strickland, Edward. 'Metamorphoses of the Muse in Romantic Poesis: Christabel.' *ELH*, vol. 44, no. 4, 1977, pp. 641–58.

Thomas, Ronald R. *Dreams of Authority: Freud and the Fictions of the Unconscious.* Cornell University Press, 1990.

Tracy, Robert, Introduction. *In a Glass Darkly* by Joseph Sheridan Le Fanu. Oxford University Press, 1993, pp. vii–xxviii.

Twitchell, James B. *The Living Dead: A Study of the Vampire in Romantic Literature.* Duke University Press, 1981.

Wharton Edith. 'Bewitched.' *Children of the Night: Classic Vampire Stories*, edited by David Stuart Davies. Wordsworth Editions, 2007, pp. 233–51.

White-Lewis, Jane. 'In Defense of Nightmares: Clinical and Literary Cases.' *The Dream and the Text: Essays on Literature and Language*, edited by Carol Schreier Rupprecht. State University of New York Press, 1993, pp. 48–72.

Wilkins Freeman, Mary Elizabeth. 'Luella Miller.' *The Wind in the Rose Bush: And Other Stories of the Supernatural*, edited by Alfred Bendixen. Academy Chicago Publishers, 1986, pp. 75–106.

7

Spectral traces: dream manifestation in the Gothic short story

Nicola Bowring

> Lay your hand along that hollow in the bed; someone *did* lie there …
> the place is still warm. (Le Fanu, 'Carmilla' 247)

Gothic has, since its inception, been concerned with the liminal nature of dreams, which in Gothic writing regularly transgress boundaries between sleeping and waking, the imaginary and the real. Most often, dreams are forms of communication: warnings, prophecies, or simply the re-emergence of repressed material. They function in the Gothic as a kind of language in themselves, a narrative play around revelation and foretelling, symbolism, and imagining. This chapter focuses on the destabilisation of material/immaterial boundaries in Gothic dreaming through material concepts of language, and the examination of dreams as a form of communication. In doing so, it considers material dream manifestations in the Gothic short story as a kind of writing inscribed upon the body and objects as a type of material language. Such an assessment involves a post-structural approach to language and deploys the ideas of Jacques Derrida on speech and writing and the trace in language, acknowledging influences from earlier psychoanalytic concepts of Freud and Lacan. What the Gothic offers is not simply the idea that dreams may have symbolic meanings, but that they may in fact break down the very barrier between symbol and symbolised, objects becoming dreams and dreams becoming objects. In Gothic writing, 'reality' is not 'privileged' over dream, and in the stories explored here this very dichotomy – of reality and dream – is ruptured. Reading these texts in the light of poststructuralist thinking on speech and writing brings new insights into the way in which dreams in the Gothic mode are used to blend the imaginary and the real through language and communication.

The concept of the dream as a divine message goes back to the earliest civilisations. In his seminal work of psychoanalysis, *The Interpretation of Dreams* (1899), Freud notes that 'peoples of classical antiquity … took it for granted that dreams were related to the world of the supernatural beings in whom they believed, and that they brought inspirations from the gods and demons' (3). Freud's text goes on to refute this concept, claiming dreams

instead as communications from the unconscious within the dreamer themselves. This shift in interpretation became marked in wider culture too. Jill
Matus, in *Shock, Memory and the Unconscious in Victorian Fiction* (2009),
draws attention to this change in how the dream was regarded, from having
been seen as an exterior, supernatural, or divine force to being associated
with the psychological interior (16).

The shift in consideration of the dream, then, from supernatural to scientific,
marks the late nineteenth century as a significant era in the reading and interpreting of dreams. This is due in part to the development of psychology and
psychoanalysis in this period, but also to a more general concern with forward-
looking scientific progress, whilst reflecting back on tradition and antiquity.
Jarlath Killeen, in his study of Gothic writing during this era on the occult,
notes that in that field, 'the Victorians found the best expression of their Gothic
refusal to be either wedded completely to modernity or completely turned
towards the past' (159). The same might be said of interpreting dreams, where
modern psychoanalytic interpretations had begun to hold sway, but the temptation to believe in the external, spiritual visitation could not be fully denied.

There is a clear interest, during this era, in the mechanisms of the dream,
with publications such as *The Saturday Review*, *The Gentlemen's Magazine*,
and Dickens's *All the Year Round* featuring frequent articles on this subject. These articles at times merge scientific discourse, quite comfortably,
with considerations of literature from Shakespeare and Dryden ('Dreams
and Dreaming' 329), illustrating this same oscillation between progress and
the retrospection Killeen considers. Other notable works of the era include
Andrew Lang's *The Book of Dreams and Ghosts* (1897), a text which,
whilst not specifically psychoanalytical, relates dreams to repressed memories, and the phenomenon of seeing ghosts to diurnal sleeping. The fin de
siècle was, therefore, an era of change in terms of the nature of both dreams
and the supernatural. What is significant is that even whilst the differing
approaches to understanding dreams – the scientific/psychological and the
supernatural/religious – may appear in opposition to one another, it remains
that both regard the dream as a form of communication, a message of sorts
that may be deciphered and/or interpreted.

This chapter explores material manifestations of dream figures and
the material effects of dreaming in the Gothic, taking the late nineteenth-
century short story as its focus. Though the realist novel, in both its low
and high literary forms, had been dominant for much of the nineteenth
century, late Victorian Gothic writing saw a move by many writers back
towards the mode of romance. The school of 'sensation fiction', exemplified in the novels of Wilkie Collins, remained a popular alternative
to the strictness of realism through the mid-to-late nineteenth century,
and many of Collins's short stories engaged with Gothic themes, the text
explored here, 'The Dream Woman', among them. Wilkie Collins was a

key contributor of short stories to *Household Worlds* in the 1850s, and his short story 'The Dream Woman' (1876) was a later development of one of these – 'The Ostler'. The narrative portrays the marriage of Francis Raven to Alicia Warlock, a woman who previously appeared to him in a dream, and her subsequent effect on his life.[1] Le Fanu's 'Carmilla', from which my opening epigraph is drawn, offers an alternative to traditional realism in some respects through its engagement with Gothic folklore around the vampire figure. This short story has become one of the defining examples of pre-*Dracula* vampire fiction, showing a clear line of influence in the Gothic genre. The vampire is frequently held up as a paradigmatically liminal figure, positioned between the human and the inhuman, as well as being materially liminal through the process of metamorphosis. As noted by Tim Youngs in his study of late Victorian Gothic writing, *Beastly Journeys* (2014), which focuses on the significance of travel in Gothic narratives of the monstrous, metamorphosis was itself a key concern in this transitional era from the Victorian to the Edwardian sensibility (4).

An engagement with the exotic and the 'foreign', as we see in Le Fanu's stories, also became an increasingly popular focus in the later Victorian period, helped by the attention to issues around colonisation. One writer who engaged with this theme in multiple forms was Rudyard Kipling, who had undertaken extensive travels in India, Africa, and the United States. Kipling's work brought a colonial flavour to the Gothic of the era. His short story, 'At the End of the Passage' (1890), explored the psychological effects of overwork and, it is suggested, extreme heat, on the Engineer Hummil, stationed abroad in India. This impact is especially evident in his dreams. In fact, his story lends a new, mystical/psychological element to the Gothic dream and its embodiment in reality.

The work of one of the most prolific short story writers of the late nineteenth and early twentieth century, M. R. James, also bridges the late Victorian and Modernist periods and exemplifies this increased attention to subjectivity and the unconscious, as well as deep concerns with supernaturalism and scientific experimentation. James was deeply influenced by mid-nineteenth-century ghost stories, but as Luke Thurston notes, took these in new directions for a more modern era, making James one of the best-known short story writers of this transitional period (57). His short story, 'Lost Hearts', was published originally in 1895 in the *Pall Mall Magazine*, and later in his collection *Ghost Stories of an Antiquary* (1905). The focus on ghosts in this narrative allows for an exploration into both another key Gothic figure associated with the semi-material and embodiment through supernatural beings within and outside of dreams.

Each of these four short stories offers a different dream message that may be read as arising from the unconscious of the dreamer or having a ghostly or monstrous conduit. In Le Fanu's narrative, Laura's desire – both sexual and for companionship – is reflected in the appearance of Carmilla. Francis's dream woman is the Freudian death drive personified. For Hummil in Kipling's story, there is a suggestion of subconscious colonial guilt, particularly in the form of the dream being something identified with Indian myth, that kills Hummil. Finally, in 'Lost Hearts', Stephen's subconscious fear of his uncle is manifested in the warnings of the two child ghosts he sees. In all of these stories, then, the communication may come from both within and outside. Between them, the stories explore childhood, adolescent, and adult phases and the fears and desires of each. In all of the stories, this communication leaves a physical trace, a writing upon the body. These stories thus allow for a new way of reading communication in Gothic dreams, as something that is both an internal communication of the unconscious *and* supernatural in origin, as a trace language, combining absence and presence.

Jacques Lacan dates the origin of psychoanalysis – the practice of the subject 'telling' their history – to 1895 and the publication of Freud's *Studies in Hysteria* (Lacan 213). *The Interpretation of Dreams* followed shortly afterwards in 1899. This key text in the development of psychoanalysis focused on dreams as a form of language revealing something of the unconscious. Later, during the mid-twentieth century, Lacan's call for a 'return to Freud' is driven by the call for a return to the centrality of language and speech in psychoanalysis. In 'The Function and Field of Speech and Language in Psychoanalysis', Lacan laments the way in which analysts have 'abandon[ed] the foundation of speech' (202). Lacan's work considers in more depth the material aspect of language. In his words, '[i]t is a subtle body, but body it is' (248). The 'messages' of the unconscious are read by Lacan through their revelation in the hysterical symptom. For Lacan, '[t]he unconscious is that part of concrete discourse qua transindividual, which is not at the subject's disposal in re-establishing the continuity of his conscious discourse'. However, part of discourse can be 'refound' – 'in monuments [and] deciphered like an inscription' (215). The practice of psychoanalysis thus has the aim of recovering and deciphering these inscriptions, which along with the hysterical symptom may include the dream. Dreams, for Lacan, have 'the structure of a sentence, or, rather, to keep to the letter of the work, of a rebus – that is, of a form of writing' made up of a 'simultaneously phonetic and symbolic use of signifying elements' (221). Here, Lacan compares the dream to writing, which we might regard as more material than the spoken word, and the distinction Derrida explores in *Of Grammatology*. Both Lacan and Derrida seek to deconstruct, to some extent, the borders between spoken and written language. Lacan sees language as having a material form, and Derrida stresses the error of seeing writing simply as a physical, secondary, manifestation of spoken language (*Of Grammatology* 37). Gothic dream figures also complicate this boundary, in their interiority/

ries reveal a preoccupation with the boundaries between the imaginary
d the physical and the vulnerability of the unconscious, sleeping state to
solicited messages and invasion and to the visitations of the spectral.

Vision

is manifestation of spectral figures coming from both within and without,
rticularly in terms of dreams that carry messages, has been significant
m the early days of the Gothic. In one of the very earliest examples of
British Gothic novel, *The Old English Baron*, Clara Reeve utilises the
rrier between dreams and reality as a way of framing and containing the
pernatural in her text. Sir Philip, arriving in the region of Lovel Castle,
ich has passed from the Lovel family into other hands, opens the mystery
the novel by dreaming: 'During his sleep, many strange and incoherent
ams arose to his imagination. He thought he received a message from his
nd Lord Lovel, to come to him at the castle' (11). Later, Edmund, the
ung hero, sees this same Lord, his parent, in a similar dream-vision, as 'a
rrior, leading a lady by the hand … their hands met over his head, and
y gave him a solemn benediction' (38). In both cases, a kind of montage
lows, telling the story of the murder and usurpation of the Lord and his
tle, but in fragmented form and whose full meaning both characters fail
the time to grasp. This fragmentation in the dreamscape forms part of
focus of this analysis in terms of the dream acting as a deconstructed
ssage form.

n the two texts I explore here, dreams carry warnings and feature figures
o later become manifest in person; their presence in the dream becomes
actual presence. In a night-time experience hovering between dream/
ernatural visitation, Laura first encounters the vampire in 'Carmilla',
m which the epigraph to this chapter is taken. As a child, she is visited by
trange woman' who appears to comfort, then attack, her. This woman,
annily, comes from without – the vampire Carmilla appearing in Laura's
ne – as well as from within, as a fulfilment of Laura's lack of a mother.
lowing this visitation, the discussion of the nurse and governess makes
r that a physical event has taken place – 'someone *did* lie there' – and
ugh the two seek to reassure the child, the trace of the vampire's presence
ear.

Years later, Laura encounters Carmilla in an even more 'manifest' form
he young woman dependent on them for recovery, who again arrives
n without, but also from within in fulfilling Laura's older desire for a
nd. Peter Day has noted the manipulative power of Carmilla at this point
ersuading her to accept the early visitation as a dream (28), but what

exteriority, like that of writing: 'Now we must think that
same time more exterior to speech, not being its "image"
more interior to speech, which is already in itself a writing
munications of dreams are, strictly speaking, neither speec
they retain aspects of both, in their language-like structure

The question of absence is important to both of these
nificant to dreaming in the Gothic, where one may dream
ure, and may even dream them into presence. 'Through th
a presence made of absence' (Lacan 228), noting the sign
observation of the 'fort/da' game, the game enacted by
which an object is thrown away and retrieved ('gone'/'the
coming to terms with the absence of the parent figure. D
the trace explores in depth a sense of presence-in-absence.
short stories can extend the significance of Derrida's conc
Gothic dreams, alluded to in my title, 'Spectral traces'.
trace, neatly put by Spivak in her translator's preface to
as 'the mark of the absence of a presence, an always a
sent' (xvii), is significant to Gothic dreaming, where p
may relate to absence in reality, yet may bring on or repl
reality. The trace is, through its contradiction and its ref
oppositions, significant to the dream readings here. If a
trace of their opposite, then the dream by its very nature
of the real, and the real is inherent to the dream. The s
for 'dream' and 'nightmare', if we read dream as a pleas
nightmare as not; so many dreams in the Gothic and in
ticular could be categorised as both. The concept of the
fitting to the short story, which is able to infer without
leave a *trace*, or a suggestion, of an idea. Like the drea
latent content may appear 'scant' in comparison to the
pretation of the content itself. I would like to suggest tha
barrier between dream/reality may be precisely permea
retains the trace of reality, and 'reality' the trace of drea

Le Fanu's 'Carmilla' (1874) is a narrative marked by c
the barrier between the immaterial world of dreams and
transgressed. The first section of this chapter, 'Vision', f
vision which later appears in manifest form, through
'The Dream-Woman'. The second section, 'Effect', foc
effects of dreaming and how these represent a crossing
and material worlds, picking up the analysis of 'Carmilla
'The Room at the End of the Passage'. M. R. James's
focus of the final section of this chapter, 'Trace', which
physical trace left by dream figures on the body and m

is particularly noticeable here is the way in which this is done through language and terminology. Upon their meeting, Carmilla immediately exclaims, 'I saw your face in a dream' (Le Fanu 259) with Laura as the mother figure, herself as the child, designating it a dream, whereas Laura phrases it 'in vision or reality' (259), already wavering from her conviction as a child, though not yet convinced. Carmilla says 'I must tell you my vision about you; it is so very strange that you and I should have had, each of the other, so vivid a dream' (259). She asserts it as a dream, a shared experience, marvelling at its vividness, and through her language manipulates Laura into an acceptance of this; Laura then describes to Carmilla 'my corresponding *vision*' (260; emphasis added). Carmilla's words, unlike those of the nurse in Laura's childhood, override even the physical evidence from the time. While Nina Auerbach, in 'My Vampire, My Friend', refers to this as a 'shared childhood dream' (11), this suggests that Carmilla deliberately uses the confusion between dreams and reality and manipulates it through her language and her communication with Laura. In much the same way, however, that the hollow in the bed remains physically manifest, Carmilla's terms 'vision' and 'dream' – despite her very assertive use of the 'so' – maintain this uncertainty, manifest, in a sense, within the language itself. Both 'vision' and 'dream' contain this very trace of 'reality'. In fact, the very term 'vision' can be both actual and imaginary: our vision refers to our ability to see (the real), yet 'a vision' is deemed something unreal. 'Vision', therefore, is a contradictory term.

This contradiction occurs in the nature of deception and of the lie itself. Lacan argues for the importance of the patient's speech during the psychoanalytic process even if their narrative is not honest: 'Even if it communicates nothing, discourse represents the existence of communication; even if it denies the obvious, it affirms that speech constitutes truth; even if it is destined to deceive, it relies on faith in testimony' (209). The lie maintains the trace of its opposite, of truth and of faith in testimony. Carmilla's persuasion of Laura to her version of these visions relies on Laura's faith in her. Here, Laura's dream provided a more honest testimony, whilst Carmilla's words alter this. Laura's second significant dream in the text, of the 'sooty-black animal that resembled a monstrous cat' (278), seems to highlight the potential of the dream to reveal what daylight does not. In the 'dream' – 'I cannot call it a nightmare, for I was quite conscious of being asleep' (278) – she sees her attacker as a cat, seeing Carmilla in her non-human, predatory form which perhaps relates more strongly to her true nature. When Laura awakens, the figure, though terrifying, appears human again.

Wilkie Collins's short narrative in four parts, 'The Dream Woman', also features a materialising dream figure, Alicia Warlock, who appears in dream visions before manifesting in real life. Alicia appears to Francis Raven in a dream, attempting to stab him, before his actual meeting with her many years later. During the dream, Francis is under the impression of wakefulness due to physical sensation. He experiences what he describes as 'a faint shivering that ran through me from head to foot, and a dreadful sinking pain at my heart, such as I had never felt before. The shivering only disturbed my slumbers – the pain woke me instantly' (34). Francis's dream of Alicia, however, unlike that of Laura, is labelled clearly by others as a dream precisely because of the lack of physical trace or evidence. The landlord of the inn in which Francis dreams, angry at being awakened, furiously exclaims, '[t]he Devil fly away with you and your woman with the knife! There isn't a mark in the bedclothes anywhere' (38). Francis, however, feels the reality of the dream, and is almost more horrified at its apparent *un*reality than if it had happened: 'A dream? The woman who had tried to stab me, not a living human being like myself? I began to shake and shiver. The horrors got hold of me at the bare thought of it' (38). The shivering once more reflects his response during the dream itself. This relationship between actual physical sensation and dream is explored in late-Victorian theories on the dream, including Lang's *The Book of Dreams and Ghosts*, which describes the way in which dreams may dramatise 'on the impulse of some faint, hardly perceived real sensation' (15). These literary texts explore a relationship between the physical and the dream world that is prevalent in philosophical writings also.

What is communicated here to Francis, forced back into dream status and repressed, prevents his recognising Alicia Warlock years later upon meeting her in real life. It is left to his mother to do this, from his description of the dream. It is much later, as Alicia really does raise a knife to him, that Francis finally makes the connection: 'The Dream Woman again? No! My wife. The living woman, with the face of the Dream – in the attitude of the Dream – the fair arm up; the knife clasped in the delicate white hand' (68). This relationship between the Dream Woman and Alicia Warlock, in fact, is constantly under question in the narrative. Percy Fairbank, the frame narrator of Francis's story, does not at first believe the two to be the same, stating, 'Francis Raven had, in my opinion, brooded over the misty connection between his strange dream and his vile wife, until his mind was in a state of partial delusion on that subject' (74). Throughout the text, the doubling of these two (one?) figures remains somewhat ambiguous, as Francis continues to refer to them separately, refusing to wholly conflate the two women, dream and real. This kind of opposition and othering is inherent to Derrida's concept of the trace:

> The trace, where the relationship with the other is marked, articulates its possibility in the entire field of the entity [*étant*], which metaphysics has defined as

the being-present starting from the occulted movement of the trace. The trace must be thought before the entity. (*Of Grammatology* 47)

The concept of the trace being 'thought before the entity' is strangely fitting to both stories, where the dream beings are literally 'thought' (or 'dreamt') before becoming entities. This 'occulted movement' of the trace, likewise, might reflect Francis's inability to fully connect the dream woman and his wife. To him, Alicia can seemingly be only one of them at a time; each eclipses the other. After her attempt on his life and subsequent departure, Francis again refers to her as the 'Dream Woman' (70), as though she has reverted to this through her night-time appearance with the knife. The 'Dream Woman' leaves one physical trace, in the form of evidence for her escape from a locked room: 'A picklock lay on the floor, which told me how she had gained entrance in the night. And that was the one trace I could find of the Dream Woman' (70). The term 'trace' crops up again, as Francis aims to locate the wife who has threatened him, 'the law has failed completely to find a trace of my wife' (72) – at which point she is once again his wife, rather than the Dream Woman. Francis's final comment at this point about the woman is likewise telling, 'I don't say I believe in dreams; I only say, Alicia Warlock is looking for me' (73). Here, 'believe' and 'dreams' are presented as an opposition, with 'Alicia Warlock' – now neither the Dream Woman nor the wife, but simply given her own name – occupying a liminal space between the two.

After the murder of Francis takes place, Alicia does leave traces of her movements. 'The investigations pursued on the morning when the crime was committed showed that the murderess, after leaving the stable, had taken the footpath which led to the river' (104). However, the final paragraph maintains her liminal state, between vengeful human and dream-vision: 'So – beginning in mystery, ending in mystery – the Dream Woman passes from your view. Ghost; demon; or living human creature – say for yourselves which she is' (104). Alicia Warlock is, of course, potentially all three. Collins ends the narrative with Shakespeare's famous profession from *The Tempest*, 'we are such stuff / as dreams are made of' – this reference highlights the material again, the sense of what is physically made and present, and the fact that even the 'real' may be of the same material as the 'dream'.

Both Laura in Le Fanu's story and Francis in Collins's story are warned by mothers, though in the latter case, the mother remembers the face of Alicia from the dream, whilst for Carmilla the mother's warning takes place in a dream: 'I heard [a voice], sweet and tender, and at the same time terrible, which said, "Your mother warns you to beware of the assassin"' (283). What is dwelt on here, with respect to communication, is the sound of the

voice itself, and the aural qualities of the dream. The passage is full of oppositions: 'sweet and tender' / 'terrible', 'white' / 'stain'. The significant thing in
this passage is the misinterpretation of the communication. Laura's impression is that it is Carmilla who is in danger, not Carmilla the assassin; despite
the 'warns *you*', she wakes 'possessed with the one idea that Carmilla was
being murdered' (283; emphasis added). In the dream state there is potential
for slippage in meaning, especially given the symbolic nature of the communication. There is also the potential for not remembering, as Francis did
not remember Alicia, and for not fully comprehending the communication
of the dream. Laura remembers from her later dreams 'one clear voice, of a
female's, very deep, that spoke as if at a distance, slowly' (282), but makes
no mention of the actual words spoken, which she appears not to recall.

Effect

For both of these dreamers, the dreaming leaves a physical trace on the body
itself, a form of writing or inscription of this message from the unconscious
or supernatural. Here the body physically tells what the mind cannot, giving
evidence of the testimony of the dream. In Francis's case, this is how we first
encounter him, apparently, suffering from a form of night terror:

> He stops and grows restless on a sudden. We see him writhing on the straw.
> He throws up both his hands and gasps hysterically for breath. His eyes open
> suddenly. For a moment they look at nothing, with a vacant glitter in them –
> then they close again in deeper sleep. Is he dreaming still? (14)

This is, in the context of the Gothic dream, a loaded question, for Francis's
dreams are not just that.

There is a crossover in the effects of the dream, as both physical events
in the world may affect the dream, and vice versa. Nicola Bown discusses
the concept in Victorian theories of dreaming that 'sleep does not prevent
perception, and that dreams are caused by sense-impressions reaching the
mind from the external world during sleep' (160). This raises the question
for Francis of whether his original dream is merely this, or influenced by
an actual figure. In these dreams, the opposite also occurs, with the events
of the dream leaving a physical trace on the dreamer. The physical, bodily
effects of Laura's dreams become more marked as the text progresses. The
dreams focus largely on physical sensations:

> Certain vague and strange sensations visited me in my sleep. The prevailing
> one was of that pleasant, peculiar cold thrill which we feel in bathing, when

we move against the current of a river. … [T]hey left an awful impression, and a sense of exhaustion, as if I had passed through a long period of great mental exertion and danger. … Sometimes there came a sensation as if a hand was drawn softly along my cheek and neck. Sometimes it was as if warm lips kissed me, and longer and longer and more lovingly as they reached my throat, but there the caress fixed itself. (282)

It is here we might note, too, that the first trace of the vampire, in Laura's childhood, was warmth – Carmilla is no cold-blooded killer, and what critics such as Auerbach have drawn on is her intimacy and sensuality. This intimacy, though, draws life from Laura, and the effects of these dreams are telling on her physical condition. Laura notes, later, that '[m]y sufferings had, during the last week, told upon my appearance. I had grown pale, my eyes were dilated and darkened underneath, and the languor which I had long felt began to display itself in my countenance' (282).

Rudyard Kipling's 'At the End of the Passage', the narrative of four men stationed in India, and in particular Hummil, an engineer who has begun to suffer disturbing dreams and nightmares, also explores their effects on the physical body of the individual, in a strange crossing over of dreams and reality. The physical trace left of the dream on the body in this instance becomes death itself, as the mysterious force pursuing Hummil in his dream apparently catches up with him. The communication of this dream is never clear but left ambiguous. 'I've been afraid of it for months past, Spurstow. It has made every night hell to me; and yet I'm not conscious of having done anything wrong' (339).

In this, and more particularly in both the relationship of heat and drugs to the dream state as well as through the apparitions Hummil begins to see during his waking hours, this narrative explores the boundary between the dream world and the physical, revealing it as fluid and permeable. Hummil has been afraid to sleep due to visions of a long passage and trying to escape from something within it. Hummil is given morphine to try to help him sleep, but here the crossover between dreams and reality causes him fear. The morphine is not enough to block the dreams, yet the physical effect of the drug – a numbing of the body – 'slows him down', causing Hummil to feel that he cannot run within the dream: 'It will only take me half-way again, and I shan't be able to get away this time. … Generally I am as quick as lightning, but you had clogged my feet, I was nearly caught' (Kipling 339). Here, rather than the dream seeming to leave the physical body in a particular state, the physical state of the body, caused by the effects of the drug, influences activity within the dream world. Morphine is medically confirmed to have an effect on dreams, often causing 'distressing' experiences (Lane et al. 2003). It can also be a cause of hallucinations (NICE 2021). Whilst the effect on the body then is analgesic, the effect on the mind may be said to be the opposite. Another significant writer of this era, Robert Louis Stevenson, reported conceiving his *Strange Case of Dr Jekyll and Mr Hyde* via a dream, during a time when he was taking morphine for pain (Luckhurst xi).

What is noticeable about Hummil in his return to the room Spurstow is in, after the drugs have failed to send him to sleep, is his voice, his tone, which is compared to that of people 'who speak in the lucid intervals of delirium to their friends a little before they die' (338). Hummil has been infected by the dream state, and is no longer fully intelligible to his friends, but is speaking a dream language that signifies but not fully, one that is not wholly interpretable. Not only are Hummil's words unintelligible to Spurstow at this point, but his appearance speaks the change, too: 'As a sponge wipes a slate clean, so some power unknown to Spurstow had wiped out of Hummil's face all that stamped it for the face of a man, and he stood at the doorway in the expression of his lost innocence. He had slept back into terrified childhood' (339). This concept of regression to childhood through nightmare speaks to dreams as a language of the unconscious. It is as though life were written on Hummil's face, and has been 'wiped clean', the only remaining written evidence being the writing of the dream, its 'telling' on his physical condition. Chuma, the native servant, describes his opinion of the sleep terrors:

> my master has descended into the Dark Places, and there has been caught because he was not able to escape with sufficient speed. We have the spur for evidence that he fought with Fear. Thus have I seen men of my race do with thorns when a spell was laid upon them to overtake them in their sleeping hours and they dared not sleep. (342–3)

Though this interpretation is met with derision by the three English men, it fits precisely with Hummil's earlier fears and descriptions of his dreams. This return to superstition seems, in a Freudian light, to connect to the return to 'terrified childhood', as both superstition and childhood are associated by Freud with a more 'primitive' state and to some extent with the unconscious itself. The concept of night terrors in different cultural belief systems is explored in recent critical work, including Adler's *Sleep Paralysis: Night-Mares, Nocebos, and the Mind-Body Connection*, in which she investigates sleep paralysis and nocturnal death amongst Hmong immigrants in the United States. Her subjects share stories of *dab tsog*, a legendary figure, who suffocates the dreamer during sleep (97), in a similar phenomenon to that which Hummil experiences in Kipling's narrative. This form of sleep terror retains a connection to the idea of displacement, though in Kipling's tale, it is the alienation of the coloniser expressed rather than that of the displaced immigrant.

In Hummil's disturbed mental state, we see dream figures begin to appear – potentially – in reality too. Following his dream, Hummil walks out and 'the first thing he saw standing in the verandah was the figure of himself' (341). Relying on the physical movement of the figure to judge the nature of the apparition, Hummil tells himself, '[i]f the thing slides away from me all in one piece, like a ghost, I shall know it is only my eyes and stomach that are out of order. If it walks – my head is going' (341). Later, the vision 'dissolved' at one time but at another 'rose and walked out hastily', maintaining its liminal status. Hummil is beginning to break down as a person, his sense of identity fractured, due to overwork and the hot conditions. The figure is 'himself' but also a 'thing' that he separates from himself. It is an inscription of himself, both himself and his opposing spectral not-self, resulting from the dissociation caused by his nightmares. Hummil's determination to mark it as either real or not real, based on its bodily materiality, demonstrates his need to restore the boundaries between real/not real, material/imaginary, which is yet shown to be impossible, as he notes '[e]xcept that it cast no shadow it was in all respects real' (341). The figure's lack of shadow marks it as only semi-material, potentially marking Hummil himself as now liminal, positioned between the physical state of living and dead, and the mental state of dreaming and being awake.

Trace

The two dreams discussed above appear to leave a physical trace upon the body. This reflects the dichotomy in this era in reading dreams as either psychological or supernatural. It might seem to suggest a leaning towards the supernatural interpretation if only an actual visitation by an external force could leave a physical trace, yet this reading through language and materiality suggests that the psychological, too, could leave its traces, certainly through the physical effect left on the body of the dreamer. Derrida relates the idea of the trace to work by Emmanuel Levinas, through the relationship to 'the alterity of a past that never was and can never be lived in the originary or modified form of presence' (*Of Grammatology* 70). There is something ghostly about the trace, about the spectral return of the other, the opposite, in language, and in the Gothic, this frequently comes about through the language of dreams, particularly where these dreams relate to ghosts themselves.

M. R. James's short story, 'Lost Hearts', was published some twenty years after 'Carmilla', towards the end of the Victorian era. The narrative tells of a young orphan named Stephen who goes to live with his elderly

distant cousin, Mr Abney, at Aswarby Hall, and features two child ghosts
who communicate with Stephen through his dreams in the first instance,
warning of the terrible truth behind their disappearances, before manifesting clearly enough to attack Abney himself. The children are introduced
to Stephen through their absence. Both were taken in by Mr Abney in the
past, as apparent orphans themselves. Phoebe Stanley one morning disappeared, relates Mrs Bunch, 'she out of her bed afore any of us had opened
an eye, and neither track nor trace of her have I set eyes on since' (27), and
Giovanni Paoli 'was off one fine morning just the same' (28). This makes
their warnings to Stephen and attack on Mr Abney, who is revealed to be
responsible for their deaths, the more significant as material communications. Derrida explores the significance of absence in writing, particularly
through writing functioning as a mark which can still transmit a meaning
after the person who wrote it has gone ('Signature Event Context' 319). The
physical marks left by the ghost/dream children on Stephen and the door
transmit this message after their deaths, and their very presence as dreams
or ghosts highlights the trace of the opposite in the very term 'gone', for
both ghosts and dreams represent that which is gone yet not gone.

The dreams of the young Stephen at Aswarby Hall leave physical traces
on his body as well as the surrounding environment. To begin with, these
traces appear much like those in 'Carmilla' and 'At the End of the Passage'.
The first time that Stephen dreams of the child, the child itself is not there
when he awakes. He does, however, find himself in the passage he traversed
in the dream, when the 'terror of the sight forced Stephen backwards and
he awoke to the fact that he was indeed standing on the cold boarded floor
of the passage in the full light of the moon' (James 29). As in the case of
Laura, Stephen's dream-wanderings become real wanderings by night, the
movement of the dream reflected in physical movement, as happens with
the somnambulist.

Later in the year, however, though Stephen does not recall his dreams
themselves, we see physical evidence of them in his night clothes and bedroom door:

> 'Gracious me, Master Stephen!' she broke forth rather irritably, 'how do you
> manage to tear your nightdress all to flinders this way? Look here, sir, what
> trouble you do give to poor servants that have to darn and mend after you!'
>   There was indeed a most destructive and apparently wanton series of slits
> or scorings in the garment, which would undoubtedly require a skilful needle
> to make good. They were confined to the left side of the chest – long, parallel
> slits about six inches in length, some of them not quite piercing the texture of
> the linen. Stephen could only express his entire ignorance of their origin: he
> was sure they were not there the night before. (30)

The dreams leave their own nightmare trace physically, though no mental trace remains for Stephen, who merely notes that his night had been 'an unusually uneasy and oppressed' one (30). The scratches were made by the ghostly dream manifestations of the two young children, whose hearts Mr Abney had removed to create an elixir which would enable him to attain supernatural powers, and the tearing on the 'left side of the chest' is the first indication of this. Stephen's 'entire ignorance' of the explanation and meaning of this highlights the sense of the dream as partial communication, not fully explained. Just as writing, for Derrida, 'extends very far, if not infinitely, the field of oral or gestural communication' and complicates this through its separation from the addresser/writer ('Signature Event Context' 311), so the dream manifestation both brings closer and separates the addresser from the addressee. The dream is often held in the unknown, and the manifest effects must be connected back to the message of the dream, within which process there is always room for slippage between signifier/signified. To a reader, it may appear as an attack on Stephen himself, though later events suggest it is a warning. The torn nightdress and the move towards the heart point to the absence of the heart in the two young children, which Stephen sees clearly upon their spectral manifestation in the garden towards the end of the story – '[o]n the left side of [Giovanni's] chest there opened a black and gaping rent' (33). This bodily rent, the absence of a heart, points to its opposite – the previous presence of the heart. What is gaping once was closed, what is black (dark, space), once was red and full. The clear repetition of 'left side of the chest' not only directs us to the rent but also back to Stephen's nightdress.

The scratching, of course, is caused by nails, and the appearance of the nails that Stephen notes in the young boy draws attention again to the liminal state of death, in the ghost-figure: 'The moon shone upon his almost transparent hands, and Stephen saw that the nails were fearfully long and that the light shone through them' (33). It was a common myth, widely held in the nineteenth century, that nails and hair continued to grow after death. This spectral figure, the child in death, bears the trace of life, the indication of growth that had begun and should have continued; both Giovanni and Phoebe die in what might be considered a particularly 'liminal' phase of life, early puberty.

Conclusions

Like Carmilla and Alicia Warlock, Giovanni and Phoebe begin as dream creatures, only to become manifest; although spectral and partially transparent, they have a very physical existence, especially in their ability to cause harm.

Their warning to Stephen of what may happen to him becomes a very real happening to Mr Abney, who experiences a brutal death in which 'a savage wild-cat might have inflicted the injuries' (36). In fact, all of the dream-beings in these texts have the ability to cause harm: Carmilla, Alicia, the children, and, we assume, the being that 'catches' Hummil in his dream, Hummil's death seemingly happening within the dream and manifesting in reality.

The crossing of boundaries, between dream and reality, speech and writing, is reflected in the crossing of literal barriers in these texts. The children leave scratches on Stephen's door suggestive of an attempt to enter and later gain entry to Mr Abney's study through an open window (36). Alicia Warlock, likewise, must use a pick-lock, which becomes the physical 'trace' she leaves behind following her night visit to Francis. Mrs Bunch tells Stephen, 'just turn the key of the door when you go to your bed' (30), and Carmilla advises Laura to do the same, though in her case this is done through subtle persuasion again, in her telling Laura of her own habit of doing so (261). The locking in 'Carmilla', of course, is ineffectual. Carmilla – in many respects the most clearly physical being in these four tales, as evidenced in the sensual descriptions of Laura – is in fact the one being who can make her way, it seems, through a locked door.

Lacan draws attention in his work to hypnotic remembering as 'a spoken representation' which 'implies all sorts of presences' (212), noting the potential for speech to re-present the past. As such, it is 'situated in both' the imaginary and reality. Like this hysterical speech, dreams function as a kind of language that is false (imaginary) yet true, something that reflects an absence yet invokes a presence. Both Derrida's refusal to privilege speech over language as a 'purer' form and Lacan's insistence on the materiality of language obscure the boundary between speech and writing, the material and the immaterial. The Gothic dream, as a form of writing as well as speech, both material and immaterial, and its potential for embodiment reflect this concept of these boundaries as permeable. Gothic dreams can represent both internal communications from the unconscious and supernatural visitation since they deconstruct boundaries, allowing for slippage around words, symbols, and meaning. As the four examples by Collins, Le Fanu, Kipling, and James demonstrate, the Gothic short story is utilised to explore anxieties around the unconscious dreaming state and its vulnerability to the monstrous, to a trace which becomes a presence, the spectral made manifest.

Note

1 Though 'The Dream Woman' is a development of 'The Ostler', the version explored here, published in 1876, is significantly expanded, such that Collins asserted it should be read as a new story (Collins 3), and is hence given this date.

Works cited

Adler, Shelley. *Sleep Paralysis: Night-Mares, Nocebos, and the Mind-Body Connection*. Rutgers University Press, 2011.

Auerbach, Nina. 'My Vampire, My Friend: The Intimacy Dracula Destroyed.' *Blood Read: The Vampire as Metaphor in Contemporary Culture*, edited by Joan Gordon and Veronica Hollinger. University of Pennsylvania Press, 1997, pp. 11–16.

Bown, Nicola. 'What Is the Stuff That Dreams Are Made of?' *The Victorian Supernatural*, edited by Nicola Bown, Carolyn Burdett, and Pamela Thurschwell. Cambridge University Press, 2004, pp. 151–72.

Collins, Wilkie. *The Dream Woman*. Alma Classics, 2014.

Day, Peter. *Vampires: Myths and Metaphors of Enduring Evil*. Rodopi, 2006.

Derrida, Jacques. *Of Grammatology*, translated by Gayatri Chakravorty Spivak. Johns Hopkins University Press, 1976.

Derrida, Jacques. 'Signature Event Context.' *Margins of Philosophy*, translated by Alan Bass. Harvester Press, 1982, pp. 307–30.

'Dreams and Dreaming.' *All The Year Round*, edited by Charles Dickens, vol. 4, no. 83. 1890, pp. 109–14, https://ntu.idm.oclc.org/login?url=https://search.proquest.com/docview/7851929?accountid=14693&pq-origsite=primo. Accessed 1 May 2021.

Freud, Sigmund. *The Interpretation of Dreams*. Oxford World's Classics, 2008.

James, M.R. 'Lost Hearts.' *Ghost Stories of an Antiquary*. Dover Publications, 2011, pp. 24–36.

Killeen, Jarlath. *Gothic Literature 1825–1914*. University of Wales Press, 2009.

Kipling, Rudyard. 'At the End of the Passage.' *Victorian Ghost Stories: An Oxford Anthology*, edited by Michael Cox and R. A. Gilbert. Oxford University Press, 1992, pp. 328–45.

Lacan, Jacques. 'The Function and Field of Speech and Language in Psychoanalysis.' *Écrits*, translated by Bruce Fink. Norton, 2006, pp. 197–268.

Lane, M., A. Serrano, S. Walters and G. R. Park. 'Morphine and Remifentanil and Their Effects on Dreams, Nightmares and Hallucinations in Critically Ill Patients.' *Critical Care* vol. 7, no. 2, 2003, p. 97, www.ncbi.nlm.nih.gov/pmc/articles/PMC3301542/. Accessed 4 May 2021.

Lang, Andrew. *The Book of Dreams and Ghosts*. Project Gutenberg, 2004, www.gutenberg.org/ebooks/12621. Accessed 1 May 2021.

Le Fanu, Joseph Sheridan. 'Carmilla.' *In a Glass Darkly*. Oxford University Press, 1993, pp. 244–319.

Luckhurst, Roger. 'Introduction.' *Strange Case of Dr. Jekyll and Mr. Hyde and Other Tales*. Oxford University Press, 2006, pp. vii–xxxii.

Matus, Jill. *Shock, Memory and the Unconscious in Victorian Fiction*. Cambridge University Press, 2009.

NICE. 'Morphine.' https://bnf.nice.org.uk/drug/morphine.html#sideEffects. Accessed 1 May 2021.

Thurston, Luke. *Literary Ghosts from the Victorians to Modernism: The Haunting Interval*. Routledge, 2012.

Youngs, Tim. *Beastly Journeys: Travel and Transformation at the Fin de Siècle*. Liverpool University Press, 2014.

8

'I have seen faces in the dark': Gothic visions in the Society for Psychical Research's Census of Hallucinations

Alice Vernon

Introduction

Prior to modern neurological diagnoses, the representation of and explanations for certain sleep disorders had become entangled with insanity or the occult. Parasomnias – those disorders which produce involuntary movement or hallucinations – are intrinsically Gothic in their manifestation. The symptoms of sleep paralysis, for instance, involve a semi-awakening while the body is still in the paralysed state of REM sleep; the sleeper may often hallucinate a 'hag', incubus, or other monster to explain the feeling of heavy pressure on their chest (Cheyne 169). In the 1834 edition of his treatise, *The Philosophy of Sleep*, Robert Macnish describes the sensation of sleep paralysis as a 'spell' that makes the sufferer feel 'pent alive in his coffin' (122–3). Nineteenth-century newspapers and fiction, in particular, sensationalised stories of sleepwalkers, or somnambulists, who became symbolic of the restless or possessed individual whose ghostly unconscious emerges during the night. In 1885, for instance, the *South Wales Echo* reported that a girl of sixteen had, in her sleep, carried her employer's infant around the house 'with great care and tenderness' (3). This incident happened far away in Lincolnshire but was clearly deemed interesting enough to relay to *South Wales Echo* readers. There are hundreds of similar examples from this period; in many of them, the disturbed sleeper is imbued with the repressed, the dangerous, and the secretive, and medical knowledge could not provide a more concrete explanation than overwork or indigestion. The end of the nineteenth century, however, witnessed an especially noteworthy shift in scientific understanding about sleep and its disorders. Rather than a product of the crypt or the overly indulgent supper, physiologists were beginning to theorise about the brain's function, and malfunction, in sleep.

Some of the most vital early work in this area of neuroscience was conducted by members of London's Society for Psychical Research, a group renowned for its rigorous experiments, both scientific and pseudo-scientific.

In the final decades of the nineteenth century, the Society focused particularly on investigating so-called prophetic or 'inspired' dreams and dream-like visions. Rhodri Hayward, in describing the Society's work at this time, acknowledges the 'statistical, historical, and psychological approaches, intended to demonstrate the continuity of the dream inspiration and the subject's waking life' (167). The Society sought to use current scientific modes of inquiry to demystify the sleep phenomena traditionally attributed to spiritualism and the supernatural.

Indeed, some of our current understanding of parasomnias stems from the research of certain key members of the group. Frederic W. H. Myers, for instance, coined the term 'hypnopompic illusions' in a groundbreaking 1892 essay called 'The Subliminal Consciousness' that appeared in Volume 7 of the *Proceedings of the Society for Psychical Research* (314). He used this term to describe the phenomenon of experiencing tactile, auditory, and sight-based delusions as a 'prolongation of dream-figures into the first waking moments' (314). His theory was accurate: modern equipment in sleep laboratories has shown that these hallucinations occur when a person wakes up while the thalamus – the part of the brain that produces the most activity during sleep – is still active (Waters et al. 1104). In other words, sleep hallucinations occur when a person wakes up before the rest of their brain is ready. It is the Society's research into this parasomnia, as well as its related phenomenon of sleep paralysis, that will be the focus of the chapter.

Between 1889 and 1892, the Society for Psychical Research undertook a large-scale Census of Hallucinations. The aim, they claimed, was to 'ascertain what proportion of persons have had sensory hallucinations while awake, and not suffering from delirium or insanity or any other morbid condition obviously conducive to hallucination; and, further, to enquire into the nature of these hallucinations' (*Proceedings* 33). On one hand, the Society was curious to investigate the prevalence of visions in the general public and to dismiss ideas of ghostly visitors to the bedroom. However, they were also continuing their investigations into telepathy and the psychic sending and receiving of images and thoughts. They were seeking examples of visions they could present, with supporting evidence, as possible proof of telepathic communication. Much of the Society's work bears these contradictions. Rather than dispel ideas of ghosts and ghouls, the anecdotes collected by the Census often served to reflect the supernatural more strongly. While the Census is a fascinating precursor to the boom in sleep research of the mid-twentieth century, it is also an intrinsically Gothic text.

This chapter will examine the relationship between the Gothic and nineteenth-century parasomnias. It will look at the ways in which the cultural prevalence of Gothic imagery, in literature, art, and medicine, is reflected in the sleep-related hallucinations reported in the Census. The first half of the chapter will discuss texts from the short stories of Edgar Allan Poe, prior to the Census, and texts such as Bram Stoker's *Dracula* which were contemporary with the Society's work on visions. As these examples will show, the tropes and symbolism of the Gothic – from monstrous visitors to supernatural mists – seem to have influenced the form and content of the Census anecdotes, which in turn influenced Gothic fiction. Subsequently, the second half will contextualise the Census in relation to cultural and medical debates regarding sight, examining how scientific inquiry into supernatural visions – from sleep studies to reports of haunted houses – influenced the work undertaken by the Society for Psychical Research. In framing the anecdotes of the Census in relation to these relevant scientific and cultural discussions, I will expose and explore the interrelationship between Gothic fiction, art, medicine, and the content of hallucinations experienced by the Victorian public.

'I must be careful of such dreams': the Census of Hallucinations and Gothic literature

The Census of Hallucinations was conducted by members of the Society for Psychical Research between April 1889 and May 1892. The Society received 17,000 responses, of which 2,272 answered positively to the main question, 'Have you ever, when believing yourself to be completely awake, had a vivid impression of seeing or being touched by a living being or inanimate object, or of hearing a voice; which impression, so far as you could discover, was not due to any external physical cause?' (*Proceedings* 33). The findings were collected and analysed in the Society's periodical, *Proceedings of the Society for Psychical Research*, in 1894.

Despite Frederic W. H. Myers' interest in the hallucinations experienced during sleep, the analysis of the Census dismisses visions deemed to be related to sleep and dreams. However, this dismissal is inconsistent, and our modern understanding of hypnopompic hallucinations allows us to see that many of the anecdotes more valued by the Society for their supernatural content are also a result of this parasomnia. Indeed, it seems as though the only hallucinations dismissed are those in which the respondent themselves declares a strong link to sleep. Where the respondent considered themselves to be perfectly awake, the anecdote was accepted. However, the experience of hypnopompic hallucinations and sleep paralysis is such that the line between sleeping and waking becomes blurred and indistinguishable. The sleeper *feels* completely awake despite still being neurologically asleep. Variants of the phrase, 'I knew I was awake', appear throughout the Census in anecdotes that seem to be classic examples of parasomnia. It thus becomes a statement that cannot be considered trustworthy.

What is interesting about the Census in relation to reports of twenty-first-century hypnopompic hallucinations are the images seen in visions. They are unarguably the stuff of the supernatural, of both Gothic horror and contemporary ghost stories prolific at the time of the Census. But they are also the stuff of supernatural investigation and are often presented with a scientific, analytical tone. Luke Thurston notes that 'the ghost story at its most powerful bears the mark of something which the human subject longs to have "theorized away"' (7). The imaginations of Victorian sleepers seem to be preoccupied with death and ghostly visitations from departed loved ones, but there is an accompanying sense of self-analysis and inquiry inspired by the popular supernatural discussions of the era. This is rarely seen in modern reports of parasomnias, which tend to employ the more overtly gruesome imagery and monsters of horror films. As noted by Richard J. McNally and Susan A. Clancy, twenty-first-century episodes of sleep paralysis are often populated instead by narratives of alien abduction (114). This suggests that the cultural discourses of the era contribute to the content of sleep-related hallucinations. In the case of the nineteenth century, as this section will show, the popular Gothic fiction of the time gave birth to equally Gothic visions.

The report shared by Miss E. M. J. is one of the more disturbing hallucinations included in the Census anecdotes:

> One night in the year 1882 or 1883, I awoke completely and sat up in bed. There was light enough in the room to see all the objects in it distinctly. My bed faced the door. Coming from the door, which was shut, I saw distinctly, and noticed the dress she had on, a lady friend staying in the house. She was advancing on her hands and knees. My first thought was that she had lost her reason. I asked her what she wanted. She did not answer but disappeared under the bed. I leaned over the side of the bed to see if I could see her[,] believing her really to be there; almost immediately the room was quite dark. [...] I was teaching at the time, and had been overworking. (*Proceedings* 79–80)

This anecdote bears some similarity to Gothic tropes popularised by Edgar Allan Poe. In particular, it is reminiscent of both 'Ligeia' and 'The Fall of the House of Usher', which both feature women who monstrously linger on a threshold between life and death. In Miss E. M. J.'s story, she tells of her friend – someone she knows well – behaving in a grotesque and animalistic manner while approaching the bed. It demonstrates the ability of hypnopompic hallucinations to defamiliarise, and make us fearful of, everyday objects and people.

Distortion caused by sleep visions is a particular focus of Poe's 'Ligeia'. In this story, the protagonist settles into married life with his new wife,

Rowena. But their marital bliss is haunted by the memory of his first love, an ethereal and extraordinary woman called Ligeia. Soon, Rowena falls ill and, in her illness, seems to take on the shape of the other woman. What is particularly interesting in this story is that there is continual reference to disturbed sleep and troubled visions. For example, Rowena is said to have awoken from an 'unquiet slumber' after which she 'partly arose, and spoke, in an earnest, low whisper, of sounds which she *then* heard, but which I could not hear – of motions which she *then* saw, but which I could not perceive' (235; original emphasis). In a similar manner, numerous reports in the Census include a note to say how E. M. J.'s – the respondent's – bedfellow did not experience the same sights or sounds as she had. Notably, Poe's protagonist describes witnessing strange visions of his own, 'Wild visions, opium-engendered, flitted, shadow-like, before me' (236). It would seem that both Rowena and her husband suffer hypnopompic hallucinations that alter their sense of reality. With this in mind, Rowena's 'transformation' into Ligeia at the story's conclusion could be read as a sleep- and opium-related delusion. What the protagonist relates is not real, but a grotesque hallucination.

Another of Poe's stories, 'The Fall of the House of Usher', illustrates the link between reading and visions, specifically the reading of Gothic tales and the experience of Gothic visions. The protagonist comes to stay at the imposing mansion of his friend, Roderick Usher, whose sister, Madeline, is believed to have died and been sealed up in the tomb during the protagonist's visit. While the narrator reads the '"Mad Trist" of Sir Launcelot Canning', strange noises seem to accompany, in perfect synchronicity, the words from the story (160). As he also, significantly, observes, '[Usher's] head had dropped upon his breast – yet I knew he was not asleep' which, as mentioned above, is an untrustworthy phrase (162). When the narrator reaches the climax of the story, Usher cries, '*Madman! I tell you now that she stands without the door!*' (163; original emphasis). When the door opens, the ghastly figure of Madeline appears, covered in blood, who falls 'heavily inward upon the person of her brother, and in her violent and now final death-agonies, bore him to the floor a corpse, and a victim to the terrors he had anticipated' (163).

Reading provokes the imagination in a similar way to the experience of parasomnia. In *The Philosophy of Sleep*, Macnish warns that reading or discussing 'horrible subjects, such as spectres' will cause them to reappear 'magnified and heightened' in dreams (52). In reading a story, the brain becomes populated with images based on the words on the page. This was theorised by seventeenth-century philosopher John Locke when he described, in *An Essay Concerning Human Understanding*, the ways in which memory and imagination could furnish the material of dreams (44).

In a hypnopompic hallucination or episode of sleep paralysis, the brain casts phantoms and monsters from its bank of imagined threats to create a physical explanation for the odd sensations. It is worth suggesting then, that the supernatural figures in the stories we read can emerge in the visions of the half-awake brain. As respondents to the Census all composed eloquent narratives of their experience, they were members of the reading public. The anecdote given to the Census by Mr J. W. A. demonstrates the relationship between reading and hallucination:

> Over and over again I have seen faces in the dark. Lying in bed, broad awake, faces have come out suddenly in the darkness near my bed, appearing, some hideous, some beautiful, and generally extremely vivid. Here is a particular instance. I had been reading of Brynhilda and lay in bed thinking about her life; when out there came on the darkness a grand face – worth anyone's toil to transfer to canvas – and so vivid that now, after several years' interval, I could make a picture of it if I could only draw. In general, however, these faces seem to have no connection with any particular person or name. They occur most commonly when I am very tired. (*Proceedings* 80)

While sleep-related hallucinations have historically been explained by way of demons, spirits, and witches, there is evidence to suggest that reading, including Gothic fiction, further influenced the shape of those visions. And from them came the inspiration for further stories of night-time terror. Sleep disorders and the Gothic are closely entwined, and the nature of the phantoms reported in the Census provides evidence for the link between the monsters of stories and the monsters of hallucination.

By gathering so many anecdotes in one place, the Census provides ample evidence that sleep is at the root of most hallucinations experienced by healthy people. Sleep itself may be said to be a Gothic site. Gothic stories emphasise the horror of liminality – of in-between spaces and in-between states – and disturbed sleep is both of these at once. To hallucinate is to fall through the trapdoor of a Gothic mansion and discover its secret monsters. While the Census aimed to show that seemingly supernatural visions can be explained through natural causes, it seemed to demonstrate, more clearly, the strength of the link between sleep and the terrors of the Gothic aesthetic.

Many of the anecdotes reported in the Census share connections with the Gothic events of Bram Stoker's *Dracula*. Indeed, *Dracula* and the Census were both created together: Stoker began writing his vampire novel in 1890, the year after the Census began, and published the text three years after the Society's report in 1897. Stoker was certainly aware of the Society and its work. In writing of his friendship with Henry Irving, Stoker recalls attending 'a delightful breakfast in the house of Frederick Myers' in 1898 (396). The pseudoscientific elements of *Dracula*, from mesmerism to telepathy, suggest an awareness of, and keen interest in, the Society's activities. These overlapping preoccupations and the publication of the Census report in 1894, several years in advance of *Dracula*'s publication, make the links between the two texts all the more intriguing.

One of the most intriguing parallels is the recurring hallucination of mist at the sleeper's bedside, a mist that takes the shape of a figure. The following extract from the report in the Census given by Miss H. T. seems particularly comparable to certain events in *Dracula*:

> I have seen a figure three times. I cannot remember the exact dates; the figure appeared to me between the years 1867 and '76. The form appeared each time directly I got into bed. I have always been in good health. [It] always appeared the same way; that is, on getting into bed and putting the light out, there would be a sort of movement in the air, which gradually took the form of mist and then developed into a dark veiled figure, which came nearer to me and when bending over and about to touch me I threw my hands into it, and it vanished. Until it was almost touching me, my terror was so great that I could neither call my sister, who was asleep beside me, nor move hand or foot. (*Proceedings* 120)

In Bram Stoker's novel, Dracula appears to Mina on two occasions in the form of a mist pouring into her bedroom and gathering into the figure of a man. Both scenes bear a marked similarity to Miss H. T.'s anecdote. In the first of these visitations, Stoker complicates Mina's experience by having her describe the event as a result of disturbed sleep. As the mist pours in towards her, Mina describes how 'some leaden lethargy seemed to chain my limbs and even my will. I lay still and endured. I closed my eyes, but could still see through my eyelids. (It is wonderful what tricks our dreams play us, and how conveniently we can imagine)' (215).

In Miss H. T.'s report, however, there is nothing of the rationality with which Mina describes her own encounter. The phrase concerning her good health even suggests that Miss H. T. is dismissing the unreality of her experience. Her account has been written in such a way as to emphasise the supernatural character of the figure. Where Mina's first description still clings to the realm of science and sleep, her second encounter with Dracula is written with a much closer resemblance to Miss H. T.'s anecdote:

> Then indeed my heart sank within me: beside the bed, as if he had stepped out of the mist – or rather as if the mist had turned into his figure, for it had entirely disappeared – stood a tall, thin man, all in black. [...] For an instant my heart stood still, and I would have screamed out, only that I was paralysed. (238–9)

The structure of Mina Harker's anecdote and that of Miss H. T. follow the same pattern: the mist appears, develops into a dark figure that moves closer to the bed, and then the sleeper discovers herself to be paralysed. In both anecdotes, the paralysis seems to be misunderstood as a result of terror. During an episode of sleep paralysis, however, the terror arises *because* of the inability to move, particularly when the sleeper is in a supine position (Cheyne 170). The brain builds a narrative around the sensation, which often leads to a hypnopompic hallucination of a monster or threatening figure. To read Miss H. T.'s anecdote in light of our contemporary understanding of REM and parasomnias, it is clear that she was suffering from sleep paralysis.

Visions of dead relatives thus appear frequently in the Census report, its entries often written with the narrative style of a contemporary ghost story or penny dreadful. The content of a specific anecdote involving this theme seems to be echoed again in *Dracula*. It is recorded by Mr P., and relates to his deceased son:

> Our third child, a boy, lived only 16 days. From the first it was evident that his life would be a short one; but, perhaps all the more on that account, every effort was made to prolong it. I had taken a small share of the watching, and just before the boy died was lying on the sofa in that state of wakeful weariness that comes of death-bed watching. Lying thus, I saw, a few feet above my head, a blue flame. It was about an inch and a quarter long, and surrounded by a slight haze or halo. It hovered above me for a few seconds, then took an irregular diagonal course towards the corner of the room farthest from me, finally seeming to pass through the ceiling. As it vanished a voice from nearly the opposite side of the room said, 'That's his soul.' No person other than myself was in [the room] at the time. A few minutes later the child died. (*Proceedings* 126)

In Stoker's novel, the vision of a blue flame appears to Jonathan Harker during his initial journey to Count Dracula's castle. Before setting off, he is warned by his hotel's landlady that it is the eve of St George's Day, when 'all the evil things in the world will have full sway' (16). He then consults his dictionary to identify words he overhears between the hotel owners and his coach driver: '*Ordog* – Satan, *pokol* – hell, *strogoica* – witch, *vrolok* and *vlkoslak* – both of which mean the same thing, one being Slovak and the other Servian for something that is either were-wolf or vampire', which all produce in him 'ghostly fears' (7; original emphasis). Moreover, the description of the phenomenon is accompanied by a reference to sleep. Stoker writes: 'Suddenly, away on our left, I saw a faint flickering blue flame. [...] I think I might have fallen asleep and kept dreaming of the incident, for it seemed to be repeated endlessly, and now, looking back, it is like a sort of awful nightmare' (12). This passage, as with many instances of the supernatural in *Dracula*, is described ambiguously, using the strange phenomenon of sleep and the influence of suggestion and imagination to question the reality of the experience.

Notably, Mr P.'s anecdote is presented in the Census as part of a group that involves ghostly lights and flames. In analysing these stories, the Society members discuss the prevalence of light as 'a symbol of the soul or spirit – and consequently [associated] with death' that 'prevails among the Tartars' (*Proceedings* 125–6). This section of the Census data, then, is discussed in terms of its links to Eastern European folklore – folklore which, as seen in the example above, is part of the fabric of Stoker's novel.

What Stoker achieves in *Dracula* is to solidify the intangible terrors of sleep. He takes the internal experience of sleep-related hallucinations and makes them external. When Mina is being attacked by Dracula, the description only moves away from the narrative pattern of Census anecdotes when other members of the group arrive to witness the scene. While F. W. H. Myers and other members of the Society sought to use the Census to distinguish sleep-related hallucinations from what they believed to be genuine examples of telepathy, Stoker's *Dracula* rekindles the fear of supernatural apparitions. Dracula is the sleep hallucination made manifest.

In 1904, ten years after the Society for Psychical Research released its Census report, M. R. James published one of his most famous ghost stories, 'Oh, Whistle, and I'll Come to You, My Lad'. In this work, a professor becomes haunted by a ghost in his hotel room. What is interesting about this story is that James seems to show an acute awareness of the relationship between sleep, beds, and the figure of the ghost. In the professor's room are two beds, and there seems to be a disturbance in the vacant bed. Here, the narrator makes a clear reference to the similarity between the story's events and those of the hypnopompic hallucination. James writes:

> I can figure to myself something of the Professor's bewilderment and horror, for I have in a dream thirty years back seen the same thing happen; but the reader will hardly, perhaps, imagine how dreadful it was to him to see a figure suddenly sit up in what he had known was an empty bed. (139)

The figure alights from the bed and approaches Professor Parkins. James writes, 'Parkins, who very much dislikes being questioned about it, did once describe something of it in my hearing, and I gathered that what he chiefly remembers about it is a horrible, an intensely horrible, face *of crumpled linen*' (139; original emphasis). While this scene is a fascinating innovation on the ghost, placing it next to the Census and surrounding work by Myers allows for an interesting dialogue. Myers seems to be drawing attention here to a symbiotic link between the ghostly figure and the bed. Many contemporary ghost stories, and many of the anecdotes in the Census, situate the narrative in a bedroom at night. For example, Fitz-James O'Brien's 'What Was It?' (1859) features an encounter that could be interpreted as sleep paralysis. Edward Bulwer Lytton's story 'The Haunted and the Haunters: or, The House and the Brain' (1859) sees the protagonist lie on his bed at night in order to watch for the ghost. Often in these narratives, the ghost approaches the bed. In James's story, however, he brings the ghost closer and emphasises the bed as an inherently Gothic site. To go further, James suggests that it is sleep itself which is the stuff of Gothic horrors; the ghost *is* the sleeper in the vacant bed. It is draped in a *bedsheet* when it rises up – this fundamental object of sleep is what gives the ghost its form.

This section has demonstrated the influence of Gothic fiction on the contents of the Census, as well as the way hallucinations have influenced Gothic fiction in turn. But it was not merely fiction that provoked startling hallucinations in the public imagination. Extravagant funerals, *memento mori*, and a growing practice in detailed anatomical models contributed to a cultural proliferation of death, decay, and the afterlife. Gothic tropes were not limited to stories but were fast becoming a fundamental part of the cultural fabric. Moreover, as interest in hallucinations, optical illusions, and supernatural encounters grew, so did the Victorian understanding of sight and the eye itself. The next section will explore the ways in which physical objects and the act of looking could give rise to the Gothic and ghostly figures of hallucinations.

The evil eye: seeing ghosts in Victorian science and art

In conducting the Census of Hallucinations, the Society for Psychical Research sought to understand not just the prevalence of visions among the general public, but also the various ways in which human sight could be deceived. The Society wanted to find concrete evidence of genuine visitations from the dead and telepathy between the living, which lead them to advance their understanding of the natural causes of hallucinations. Developments in ocular health, psychology, and the science of light further distanced apparitions from the realm of the supernatural. But not all welcomed this shift in the discussion of sight.

The eminent art critic, John Ruskin, disagreed with the way in which sight was becoming dominated by scientific, rather than aesthetic, discussion. In his lecture, 'The Relation of Art to the Science of Light', Ruskin emphasises the importance of the 'soul of the eye' over the 'lens of the eye'

(116). For Ruskin, advances in understanding sight, perception, and the brain were an affront to artistic appreciation. They reduced aesthetic beauty to colours and textures, the effect of sunlight reflecting from a surface and being translated by the brain. As Srdjan Smajic notes, Ruskin describes a sort of 'double vision' wherein

> the spectator who desires to see things in their true light must learn to switch back and forth between two ways of seeing, to alternate between two conceptual models of vision – or perhaps use both pairs of eyes at once, observing things simultaneously with the 'lens of the eye' and the 'soul of the eye'. (1121)

Further on in Ruskin's lecture, he turns his attention to the concept of the 'evil eye' (123). He wonders what the phrase might mean, and how the language of science might reduce it. He writes, 'How, if evil, can [the eye] fill the whole body with darkness? What is the meaning of having one's body *full* of darkness? It cannot mean merely being blind' (123). In other words, are the hallucinations of fear, grief, paranoia, and madness only to be explained in medical terms? Ruskin seems to want to return the focus of sight to the spiritual; hallucinations may be provoked by an overactive imagination, but as Ruskin argues, such fears should be analysed in an artistic as well as scientific manner. Despite his membership in the Society for Psychical Research, Ruskin criticised the work being conducted in putatively scientific pursuits such as the Census. Where the Society and its contemporaries analysed anecdotes with the view to dismissing the phenomena, Ruskin sought to return such visions to a more ethereal realm.

On the other hand, some of the Society's work around the Census, in particular Edmund Gurney, Frederic Myers, and Frank Podmore's *Phantasms of the Living* (1886) and Myers's *Human Personality and Its Survival of Bodily Death* (1903), seem more akin to Ruskin's esoteric presentation of sight and the soul. As noted by Helen Groth and Natalya Lusty, 'Myers believed that every healthy personality contained multiple selves or personalities, none of which should be privileged over the other, and that these selves struggled to take possession of the conscious self while dreaming, or in analogous dream-like states in which phenomena such as automatic writing occurred' (71).

Ruskin's focus, as an art critic, was solely on visible, *seen* phantoms. But, as discussed in the Census, visions are not purely visual. In considering the evil eye, we must also think about the evil ear and evil touch. For example, the anecdote by Mrs H. R. is a purely auditory hallucination:

> I was in bed, unable to get any sleep. I recollected a bad dream I had had in the same house, and a sudden feeling of fear of the invisible made me pull

the clothes closely round me. As I did so, I distinctly thought I heard a voice behind me say, 'It is of no use doing that.' At the time I was so frightened that I jumped out of bed and lighted a candle. This occurred in July, 1883. I was not in very good health at the time. (*Proceedings* 170)

Here, the inner darkness that Ruskin describes in his lecture is *heard* rather than seen. The evil of Miss H. R.'s poor health manifests into a rather sinister statement, prompting her to banish the darkness of her bedroom with the light of a candle.

Hypnopompic hallucinations can involve any of the senses, but the more senses involved, the likelier it is that the experience will be interpreted as a supernatural encounter. The anecdote recorded by Miss H. Wilson involves both sight and touch and suggests a visitation from a spirit:

A long time ago I was lying asleep, or nearly so, one night, when I felt a hand laid gently on my shoulder. I was not surprised or frightened. I thought it was my sister Alice, who shared the same room with me, and I was too sleepy to rouse myself till I felt the hand pressing more heavily as if to wake me; then I said, 'What is it, Alice? What do you want?' and at the same time opened my eyes. No candle or lamp was in the room, it was quite dark; but close to my bedside stood, enveloped in light, a figure like my sister – it seemed my own sister Alice; there was the golden-brown hair, blue eyes, and fair complexion, and yet it looked like a being from another world, standing in light unlike any earthly light – a beautiful glorified being! It stood for a few moments, then vanished, and the room was all darkness again. I felt deep awe, but no fear. (*Proceedings* 79)

The description of light features in many of the reports in the Census; the sense of the room being illuminated is a key trait of hypnopompic hallucinations. The nature of the glow here is interpreted by Miss Wilson as being other-worldly. While she does not specifically use the term, there is a strong suggestion that she was visited by some sort of spirit or ghost.

Investigation into proof of ghosts and the afterlife was – and still is – a fundamental part of the Society's work. A particular report of a supposed haunting was published in *Proceedings of the Society for Psychical Research* in 1892 and is frequently referenced in the Census analysis as a way of comparing anecdotes to this description of ghostly experiences. The 'Record of a Haunted House' was undertaken by the woman who experienced a series of ghostly visions, Miss R. C. Morton, and is presented with a prefatory note by Frederic Myers. The 'ghost' was believed to be one of the house's previous occupants, the 'second' Mrs S., who roamed the house in search of the hidden jewellery belonging to the first Mrs S. This story in itself bears the traits of a scandalous Gothic story – jealousy, restlessness, and secret compartments in houses. Indeed, while the Society present such documents as the Census and the 'Record of a Haunted House' as serious analyses of data and experiments, their *readability* is worth noting. Their stories are compelling and use scandal and shock in much the same way as they are employed in Gothic fiction. As L. Anne Delgado notes, 'while the narratives compiled and published by the psychical researchers were not purported to be creative endeavours, they were curiously similar in content to fictional ghostly encounters' (242).

The report of Miss R. C. Morton has an investigative tone; she catalogues her experiences objectively, gathers evidence from other members of the household and its staff, and conducts experiments in keeping with the Society's emphasis on obtaining proof of phenomena. However, despite Morton's sincerity in pursuing the 'ghost', many of her anecdotes take place at night and after waking from sleep. For example, she writes, 'On the night of August 1st, I again saw [the ghost]. I heard the footsteps outside the landing about 2 a.m. I got up at once, and went outside. She was then at the end of the landing at the top of the stairs, with her side view towards me' (Morton 315).

Morton's experiences with the ghost build in complexity over several years. Where at first, she is awakened by the noise of 'slight pushes against my bedroom door', she then begins to see the figure of a woman as an accompaniment to these sounds (Morton 315). Interestingly, as she discusses her experiences with her family and members of the staff, these other people begin to report their own encounters. Indeed, it is only her parents who seem unaffected by the experiences and proclaim never to have seen nor heard the figure. In a bizarre anecdote towards the end of the report, one of Miss Morton's friends, Catherine M. Campbell, recalls seeing the ghost 'exactly as described' in her own home one hundred miles away from the Morton residence (Morton 324). It seems clear here that the vision spread through Morton's suggestion – that the nature of her description influenced the shape of her friends' visions. If one of her family or staff experienced a hallucination, their account would be influenced by Morton's recounted sightings of the house ghost.

The anecdotes in the Census are rife with stories of ghosts, bereavement, and the spirits of loved ones. Modern reports of hypnopompic hallucinations, however, often lack such imagery. It is much more prevalent for visions and sleep paralysis to be associated with the monsters of horror movies and alien abduction, where the hallucination of weightlessness common in sleep paralysis becomes explained by way of zero gravity and teleportation. These hallucinations describe modern representations of spaceships, advanced technology, and extra-terrestrial life. As McNally and

Clancy describe, twenty-first-century episodes of sleep paralysis 'usually fit contemporary cultural stereotypes (e.g., thin grey bodies, large heads, dark eyes)' (115).

The difference in content between nineteenth- and twenty-first-century sleep hallucinations suggests that culture plays an important role in shaping the monsters of the night. The Society was aware of this relationship, as Myers reportedly 'embraced the generative connection between literary inspiration and accounts of inspired dreaming' (Groth and Lusty 6). For the participants in the Census, the Gothic imagery of popular fiction was bolstered by the prevalence of death-related objects in everyday life. As described in the report, 'apparitions of the dead are better remembered than apparitions of the living'; the majority of anecdotes received involved deceased friends and family members, some of which took place over a decade before the Census (*Proceedings* 67). Indeed, the anecdotes are dominated by figures of death, either spectral appearances of departed loved ones, supposed visitations by those on the brink of death, or hideous visions that seem to come from the pages of contemporary Gothic fiction.

One possible influence on the content of these anecdotes is the popularity of *memento mori* in the nineteenth century. *Memento mori* were objects which functioned to remind their owner of mortality – their own, especially – and the uselessness of vanity. These objects ranged from large mantelpiece dioramas to small tokens that could fit inside a pocket. It was common for *memento mori* to be grotesque, depicting realistic compositions or posing skeletons in a darkly humorous mimicry of the living. A large collection of these objects was amassed by pharmaceutical entrepreneur, Henry Wellcome (1853–1936), and are currently held by the Wellcome Collection and Science Museum. A comparison of the *memento mori* collected by the Wellcome and the anecdotes presented in the SPR's Census shows a clear correlation in Gothic imagery. For instance, Mrs L. H. relates the following hallucination:

> I was asleep, and I woke with a start, it then being early morning. On looking round the room, I distinctly saw the head of a skeleton floating in the air, about a foot from the ceiling. I gazed at it intently (being now quite awake), when I saw it gradually change to my mother's head and face and float away, seemingly through the ceiling. (*Proceedings* 116)

A recurring trope in *memento mori* is of a human head or figure presenting both life and death: one side shows the colours and vitality of life, and the other side is skeletal. Figure 8.1 provides one such example.

Figure 8.1 Coloured wax model of a half-living, half-skeleton man, 1810–50 (Science Museum Group. 'Coloured wax model of a male, half skeletal, half living and dressed in regency clothing, England, 1810–1850.' A78827. Science Museum Group Collection Online, www.collection.sciencemuseumgroup.org.uk /objects/co77701/coloured-wax-model-of-a-male-half-skeletal-half-living-and -dressed-in-regency-clothing-england-1810–1850-anatomical-figure. Accessed 11 October 2020)

These particular types of *memento mori* present an image of the living face becoming skeletal, and vice versa. It may well be the case that Mrs L. H.'s hallucination emanated from the memory of having seen such an object.

Memento mori could also be highly personal objects, although nonetheless Gothic in their aesthetic. It was a common practice in the nineteenth century to incorporate a part of the corpse of the newly deceased (usually hair, but sometimes also bones or teeth) into a setting, such as jewellery to be worn by the mourning family. As Deborah Lutz explains, 'Nineteenth-century relic culture speaks, on the one hand, of a desire to see death as not permanent, in that material remains might be proof that the loved one still exists somewhere, somehow' (128). This attitude towards death expanded the liminal space of the afterlife and the supernatural. The regular confrontation with death imagery, in objects, images, and texts, including the popular Victorian culture of mourning, brought ideas of ghosts and decay to the forefront of the public imagination. In experiencing a sleep-related hallucination, the Victorian mind had a wealth of phantoms with which to populate it.

Conclusion

In 1894, the Society for Psychical Research published the report of data gathered in its Census of Hallucinations. The Census had two functions: to find evidence of telepathy but also to investigate the prevalence of visions in healthy people. What the Census provides is a large number of anecdotes detailing the contexts and components of actual hallucinations at the fin de siècle. Setting aside the Society's interest in the supernatural, the Census report is a valuable document that showcases certain members' innovative work in the domain of sleep disorders. Throughout the report, sleep and dreams are used to explain some of the anecdotes. Frederic Myers also coined the term 'hypnopompic illusions' – a term that is still used in sleep psychology – in relation to the recorded hallucinations. Even though the dysfunctions of sleep are somewhat disregarded in the Census data, it lay the foundations for Myers's future work.

There has been relatively little scholarship undertaken analysing the Census data. As it provides a wealth of information in regard to aspects of sleep, psychology, and the supernatural, there remains plenty of work to be done. This chapter has aimed to unpick the specific parasomnias underlying many of the anecdotes in the Census and to offer an explanation for these causes. What this analysis has shown is that, in comparison to modern sleep hallucinations of UFOs and horror-film monsters, nineteenth-century hallucinations were largely influenced by the pervasive Gothic imagery in fiction, culture, and science. Furthermore, these hallucinations likewise influenced supernatural tropes in fiction, creating a cycle in which sleep and the Gothic imagination were in constant dialogue with each other. Despite its age and the Society's reputation for questionable scientific theories, the Census offers invaluable data that should not be forgotten by modern sleep science. The ghosts, skeletons, and spectral mists detailed in the Census anecdotes provide an extraordinary glimpse of the intensity with which the Gothic imagination haunted the sleeping public.

Works cited

Cheyne, J. A. 'Situational Factors Affecting Sleep Paralysis and Associated Hallucinations: Position and Timing Effects.' *Journal of Sleep Research*, vol. 11, 2002, pp. 169–77.

Delgado, L. Anne. 'Psychical Research and the Fantastic Science of Spirits.' *Strange Science: Investigating the Limits of Knowledge in the Victorian Age*, edited by Lara Karpenko and Shalyn Claggett. University of Michigan Press, 2017, pp. 236–53.

Groth, Helen and Natalya Lusty. *Dreams and Modernity: A Cultural History*. Routledge, 2013.

Gurney, Edmund, Frederic William Henry Myers, and Frank Podmore. *Phantasms of the Living*. Trübner and Co., 1886.

Hayward, Rhodri. 'Policing Dreams: History and the Moral Uses of the Unconscious.' *Dreams and History: The Interpretation of Dreams from Ancient Greece to Modern Psychoanalysis*, edited by Daniel Pick and Lyndal Roper. Routledge, 2004, pp. 159–77.

James, M. R. 'Oh, Whistle, and I'll Come to You, My Lad.' *Classic Ghost Stories*, edited by John Grafton. Dover, 1998, pp. 125–40.

Locke, John. *An Essay Concerning Human Understanding: In Four Books*. J. Dickson and C. Elliot, vol. 3, 1777.

Lutz, Deborah. 'The Dead Still Among Us: Victorian Secular Relics, Hair Jewelry, and Death Culture.' *Victorian Literature and Culture*, vol. 39, no. 1, 2011, pp. 127–42.

Macnish, Robert. *The Philosophy of Sleep*, 2nd edn. D. Appleton & Co., 1834.

McNally, Richard J. and Susan A. Clancy. 'Sleep Paralysis, Sexual Abuse, and Space Alien Abduction.' *Transcultural Psychiatry*, vol. 42, no. 1, 2005, pp. 113–22.

Morton, Miss R. C. 'Record of a Haunted House.' *Proceedings of the Society for Psychical Research*, Kegan Paul, Trench, Trübner and Co., vol. 8, 1892, pp. 311–32.

Myers, Frederic William Henry. *Human Personality and Its Survival of Bodily Death*. Longmans, Green, and Co., 1920.

Myers, Frederic William Henry. 'The Subliminal Consciousness.' *Proceedings of the Society for Psychical Research*. Keegan Paul, Trench, Trübner and Co., vol. 9, 1892, pp. 298–355.

Poe, Edgar Allan. 'The Fall of the House of Usher.' *Tales of Mystery and Imagination*. Wordsworth Editions, 2008, pp. 148–63.

Poe, Edgar Allan. 'Ligeia.' *Tales of Mystery and Imagination*. Wordsworth Editions, 2008, pp. 226–38.

Proceedings of the Society for Psychical Research. Keegan Paul, Trench, Trübner and Co., vol. 10, 1894.

Ruskin, John. 'The Relation to Art of the Science of Light.' *The Eagle's Nest*, 2nd edn. George Allen, 1891, pp. 114–37.

Smajic, Srdjan. 'The Trouble with Ghost-Seeing: Vision, Ideology and Genre in the Victorian Ghost Story.' *ELH*, vol. 70, no. 4, 2003, pp. 1107–35.

South Wales Echo, 'A Girl Somnambulist.' 27 October 1885.

Stoker, Bram. *Dracula*. Wordsworth Classics, 2000.

Stoker, Bram. *Personal Reminiscences of Henry Irving*. William Heinemann, 1907.

Thurston, Luke. *Literary Ghosts from the Victorians to Modernism: The Haunting Interval*. Routledge, 2012.

Waters, Flavie, et al. 'What Is the Link Between Hallucinations, Dreams, and Hypnagogic-Hypnopompic Experiences?' *Schizophrenia Bulletin*, vol. 42, no. 5, 2016, pp. 1098–1109.

Part IV

Twentieth- and twenty-first-century Gothic dreams and nightmares: weird fiction, horror film, television, and video games

9

Stranger things: nightmarish realities in Thomas Ligotti's fiction

Elisabete Lopes

As evidenced by the publication of Horace Walpole's *The Castle of Otranto* (1764), the first Gothic novel, which was inspired by a dream, and Mary Shelley's *Frankenstein; Or the Modern Prometheus* (1831) which had its roots in the terrors of a 'waking dream', dreams and nightmares have been interwoven in the Gothic imagination since its inception. Alluding to this interconnection between the Gothic and the dream, William Patrick Day observes that '[t]he world of Gothic fantasy is an imitation of the world of the dream, the hallucination, in which that which is real and that which is imaginary fade into one' (30). American horror writer Thomas Ligotti has consistently taken a special interest in dreams, which has been signalled in the titles of some of his short story collections – *Songs of a Dead Dreamer* (1989), *Grimscribe* (1991), and *The Nightmare Factory* (1996). As Ligotti has said in an interview, 'the first and foremost source of horror that preoccupied my mind were nightmares. I've been a professional at bad dreams all my life' (Weirdfictionreview.com).

According to D. W. Behrend, dreams are associated in Ligotti's work with madness; they evoke a kind of psychosis that ultimately leaves the protagonist of the tale with a sense of displacement, disorientation, hopelessness, and of being frightened to death. Dreams are essentially doorways or portals, entry points through which come revelations about the real nature of an otherwise unknown reality. Only by dreaming can the dreamer come into contact with what Ligotti calls in his story, 'Flowers of the Abyss', 'the madness of things', an expression that describes an alternate reality that lies beneath the conventional real world. With an eye to these ideas, this chapter examines the role dreams play in Ligotti's fiction where they have the potential both to subvert and to deconstruct the world in which characters believe they live. Indeed, dreams turn the characters' worlds upside down, carrying out a chilling deconstruction of their realities and exposing them as authentic nightmares. To understand more clearly the implications of dreams and nightmares in Ligotti's fiction, four of his most paradigmatic tales will be examined through a Gothic lens: 'Flowers of the Abyss' (1991),

'In the Shadow of Another World' (1991), 'The Sect of the Idiot' (1989), and 'Dream of a Manikin' (1989).

Although the last three tales appear to take place in an urban cosmopolitan space, 'Flowers' stands as a vivid example of the Suburban Gothic, for which it is important to consider the role of the social and symbolic American suburbs that, in the aftermath of the Second World War, offered a privileged refuge from the city. They became iconic of the American Dream, living in the suburbs becoming an indicator of a prosperous and happy middle-class American life. However, with time, the suburbs became a liminal space possessing a hybrid nature ripe for a Gothic-focused critique that interrogated and undermined both domestic and national American ideals, the paramount suggestion being that the American Dream was actually a nightmare. A natural repository of nightmares, the suburbs are a preeminent locus for subversion in Ligotti's fiction. Time and again, he critically deconstructs their status as a utopia – a putative 'happy place'.

In combination with his engagements with the Suburban Gothic, Ligotti's horror writing incorporates many recognisable Gothic tropes, including the search for forbidden knowledge; encounters with otherness and the unknown; unreliable narrators; doppelgängers; experiences of physical metamorphosis; psychological disturbances, such as trauma and madness; transgression; and grotesque imagery. Ligotti combines these tropes with the popular theme of Gothic dreams and nightmares to destabilise narrative certainties and his characters' worldviews in his compelling fiction.

Firmly rooted in the Gothic tradition, his tales are authentic narratives of darkness in the sense described by Dani Cavallaro in *Gothic Visions: Three Centuries of Horror, Terror and Fear* (2002). They 'nourish our attraction to the unknown by presenting us with characters and situations that point to something beyond the human, and hence beyond interpretation – a nexus of primeval feelings and apprehensions which rationality can never conclusively eradicate' (6). Ligotti's narrative excursions into Gothic horror are invested with a weird quality that contributes to their oneiric nature. Jonathan Newell envisions the weird as 'a tumour of sorts growing out of the Gothic – composed of the same tissues but unfamiliar, alien and yet not – entirely – so, at once part of its progenitor and curiously foreign to it' (4). The weird imbues Ligotti's stories with a dreamlike aura, but also stretches the uncanny to its limits where it entails 'feelings of uncertainty, in particular regarding the reality of who one is and what is being experienced' (Royle 1). This sensation of uncertainty haunts Ligotti's characters, who are assaulted by doubts concerning the nature of their realities. In crafting an atmosphere of uneasiness among his characters, Ligotti seems inspired by episodes of parasomnia, an umbrella term comprising such sleep disturbances as night terrors, sleep paralysis, and sleepwalking. These are used by the author to construct the narrator as unreliable and to imbue the narrative with a dreamy or nightmarish aura. These literary strategies contribute to rendering the tales phantasmagorical and liminal where Ligotti's protagonists may be said to wander between the real world and the dream world. In the symbiosis of both worlds, supernatural phenomena and other unexplained events take root and flourish.

In these encounters with the supernatural, Ligotti relies on the uncanny, the weird, and the intrusion of cosmic horror, aspects that magnify the characters' Gothic experiences since they destabilise the narrators' beliefs concerning the worlds in which they live. Typically, in narratives that feature cosmic horror, characters do not possess a full and true understanding of how the universe works. Howard Phillips Lovecraft, one of the founders of the American Gothic whose literary work greatly inspired Ligotti, described cosmic horror in his famous tale, 'The Call of Cthulhu' (1928), as follows:

> The most merciful thing in the world I think, is the inability of the human mind to correlate all its contents. We live on a placid island of ignorance in the midst of black seas of infinity, and it was not meant that we should voyage far. The sciences ... have hitherto harmed us little; but some day the piecing together of dissociated knowledge will open up such terrifying vistas of reality, and of our frightful position therein, that we shall either go mad from the revelation or flee from the deadly light into the peace and safety of a new dark age. (139)

According to Lovecraft, humans are not able to grasp the full meaning or nature of the universe because they are not in possession of that knowledge. However, if they had the knowledge to process all the world's secrets, they would be thrown into the 'terrible vistas of reality', meaning they would lose their sanity and see their future compromised. It is within this context that Vivian Ralickas defines cosmic horror as 'the fear and awe we feel when confronted with phenomena beyond our comprehension' (364). Given the fact that humans are insignificant before the world's 'terrible vistas', they are not properly equipped to tackle the true nature of the world and as a result, upon a glimpse of the 'true' reality, they are rendered helpless and unable to cope with such overwhelming disclosures. That is the reason why cosmic horror is essentially indissociable from the notion of cosmic indifferentism, which is based on the notion that the universe has a neutral position regarding the pleas, wishes, and designs of human beings. Echoing Lovecraft, Ligotti offers the reader a portrait of a cold, indifferent universe that is uncaring towards people's destinies.

As Jeffrey Andrew Weinstock explains, cosmic indifferentism entails the '[d]read, provoked by the suggestion that humankind is insignificant and adrift through a cold universe of unimaginable and often malign powers and forces' (179). The idea of cosmic horror, allied with cosmic indifferentism, is expressed by Lovecraft when he describes the weird tale as bearing 'a certain atmosphere of breathless and unexplainable dread of outer, unknown forces' (6) aligned with 'a malign and particular suspension or defeat of those fixed laws of nature which are our only safeguard against the assaults of chaos and the daemons of unplumbed space' (6).

Ligotti's fiction can be said to plunge its roots into the tradition inaugurated by Lovecraft in its exploration of cosmic horror and the fear of the unknown. In an interview with Shawn Ramsey, Ligotti openly acknowledged Lovecraft's influence on his oeuvre, saying, 'I hope my stories are in the Lovecraftian tradition in that they may evoke a sense of terror whose source is something nightmarishly real, the implications of which are disturbingly weird and, in the magical sense, charming' (21). Using Lovecraft's narrative recipe, Ligotti suspends the fixed laws of nature in his tales. The realities his characters know are frequently and suddenly disrupted by the intrusion of 'chaos and demons of the unplumbed space', enveloping them in experiences that are shown to be, ultimately, 'nightmarishly real'.

In the fictional Ligottian universe, the interaction between cosmic horror and cosmic indifferentism produces a reality in which humans become similar to puppets as they are manipulated by unknown forces beyond their understanding. They ultimately discover that the lives they believe they are living with a sense of purpose, identity, and autonomy are deceptive lies. In the majority of Ligotti's tales, the umbilical cord that links characters to reality is abruptly severed with devastating consequences. The protagonists of such stories become affected by a sense of alienation and dread of the unknown. By way of dream-like hallucinations, they discover that the real world is a place of chaos and madness, an alternate reality where abomination and disorder rule. Such revelations occur throughout much of Ligotti's fiction and constitute one of his most important and original literary signatures.

Cosmic horror, aligned with the weird and the uncanny, brings to mind the philosophical concept put forward by Eugene Thacker in his work, *In the Dust of this Planet* (2011) – the world-without-us. This concept is intimately connected with cosmic indifferentism as it consists of conceiving of the world in a way that is not mediated by human perception or influence. Thacker observes that 'the world-without-us' is not to be found in the 'great beyond' that is exterior to the world (the world-for-us) or the Earth (the world in itself); rather, it is located in the very fissures, lapses, or lacunae in the World and the Earth. The author alleges that 'the Planet (the world-without-us) is the "dark intelligible abyss" that is paradoxically manifest as the World and Earth' (7–8). The world-without-us ties in with Ligotti's fictional indifferent universe that, as he suggests in 'Dream of a

Manikin', grounds itself upon a 'metaphysics stripped of all that is human' ('Dream' 58).

More than a wish for fulfilment, dreams for Ligotti are, essentially, experiences informed by trauma. On this basis, the definition of the dream in his work appears much closer to the definition of trauma as discussed and defined by Sigmund Freud, as the following passage from 'Introductory Lectures on Psycho-Analysis' (1916–17) illustrates: '[the dream is] an experience which within a short period of time presents the mind with an increase of stimulus too powerful to be dealt with or worked off in the normal way, and this must result in permanent disturbances of the manner in which the energy operates' (275).

Ligotti's popular narrative recipe notably subverts the traditional idea of trauma. His unreliable narrator, a popular figure used in Gothic fiction, is initially depicted as a normal citizen, a person with whom the reader can easily identify. He is typically transformed at a point in the narrative and his beliefs questioned after he experiences traumatic changes to his reality. His confrontation by often disturbing, Surrealist-style landscapes reminiscent of otherworldly dreams and hallucinations, is always portrayed as profoundly uncanny. In Freudian terms, that which was perceived as previously homely becomes unhomely and strange due to the fact that it has 'returned' after being repressed (124). In Ligotti's tales what is repressed is the lingering, underlying fear of death, where the 'I' is threatened with dissolution, of being swallowed by a world without order and destitute of meaning. Confronted by 'intellectual uncertainty' (Freud 125), Ligotti's narrators are plunged into an existential nightmare. Afflicted by an ontological crisis, they become unreliable, hostages in an ambiguous space, in which dreams and nightmares intrude with the purpose of undermining not only their credibility but also that of the narrative itself.

In 'Flowers of the Abyss', a schoolteacher is impelled by the town dwellers to visit a house nested in the woods where a tragedy involving an entire family – the Van Livenns – has occurred. This house is especially intriguing to the narrator because all of the family members have apparently committed suicide. From the outset, the house is depicted in a strikingly Gothic manner by way, particularly, of funereal motifs. He envisions it as 'a ghostly flower' whose entrance is reminiscent of a tomb, the doorway resembling a sepulchre (311). Everything in the house evokes the grim memories of the tragedies that occurred inside. The stranger who opens the door is a sort of interdimensional traveller, 'a vagabond of the universe, a drifter among spaces where the madness of things has no limits' (314).

He explains to the protagonist how the tragedy came upon the Van Livenn family when they encountered an accursed object, a music box, that possessed eerie powers. Its sounds drove people crazy, leading them to a gruesome death. At nightfall, the stranger tells the narrator to look in the direction of the house's garden where he glimpses flickering ghostly figures trying, unsuccessfully, to materialise. The mysterious man then identifies them as the Van Livenn family who, after death, chose to remain in the garden.

Ultimately, the narrator experiences the nefarious effects of the music box and sends a message to the town's dwellers telepathically, by intruding into their dreams, telling them to destroy the house and its contents. This allusion to telepathy connects notably with the principles of lucid dreaming, originally put forward by the psychiatrist Frederik Van Eeden in his article 'A Study of Dreams' (1913) where he argues that 'dreamers' may gain awareness in their dreams and exert a certain control over them. In combination with this idea, the tale also advances the lucid dreaming principle that posits dreams as a transformational experience that enables a deeper understanding of fears and traumas and offers a means for their management. Although the tale concludes with a crowd of people heading to the Van Livenn house with the intention of burning it down, there is an underlying sense that darkness may still linger, the house serving as a type of cosmic portal open to other entities.

In this eerie tale, Ligotti reconfigures the leitmotif of the haunted house and infuses a Suburban Gothic story with supernatural ingredients. As Bernice M. Murphy argues, the Suburban Gothic is a sub-genre that plays 'upon the lingering suspicion that even the most ordinary-looking neighbourhood, or house or family has something to hide, and that no matter how calm and settled a place looks, it is only ever a moment away from dramatic (generally, sinister) incident' (2). This description captures what happens to the Van Livenns, as they see the dream-like normalcy of their family life suddenly and nightmarishly disrupted. They are compared to flowers by the stranger at the house, which operate in this dark narrative as a symbol of purity, hinting that the family members were good, innocent, and well-intentioned people. However, they became victims of an ageless evil that, via the music box, took root in their domestic space. Ligotti plays here with duality, insinuating that light, as represented by the flowers, and darkness, as represented by the house (as mausoleum), form a harmonious pairing amidst the 'madness of things' (313). By playing with the idealisation of the suburban 'dream home', this chilly tale provides an explanation for something that the town dwellers are unable to rationally understand – namely, the unresolved mystery surrounding the collective deaths of an apparently happy family.

While when the corpses are initially discovered, it appears that the family was murdered at the hands of some errant killer, it is subsequently revealed that each family member has, apparently, committed suicide. In Ligotti's fiction, appearances are shown to be potentially deceptive. Even a normal and innocent family can be touched by darkness. Bewitched by the evil powers of a wooden music box with strange glyphs, they begin to display erratic behaviours and are impelled to wreak havoc in their 'home sweet home'.

In 'Flowers', Ligotti also depicts the music box as a motif for a house filled with secrets. It is suggested that the Van Livenns were a dysfunctional family, as the shouting coming from the house after they move in keeps the neighbours away (315). The house subsequently looks unkempt and abandoned (315), resembling a type of mausoleum, signalling the demise of their 'family togetherness', a trademark of suburbia. The intrusion of the madness of things into the placid Van Livenns' homely space signals the emergence of damaging supernatural forces on their family unity. In Ligottian terms, the madness of things suggests the presence of a cosmic reality distinct from that previously experienced, one that causes chaos, disorientation, and psychological disturbance among the characters. In Lacanian terms, it signifies a condition where the Real, which entails a resistance not only to language but to signification, permeates the Symbolic order, equated with language and coherence, and destabilises it. This means that the intrusion of the madness of things upon the characters' domestic environment provokes a disruption, as the Symbolic order is subsequently shaken by the emergence of the Real. An ontological crisis is experienced whereby chaos and disorder enter the narrative. Although this is not explicit in 'Flowers', the reader can extrapolate that the members of the family become possessed and that their collective possession leads them to suicide.

The stranger at the former Van Livenn house explains to the narrator that once he was an ordinary student of philosophy, but after his travels to certain deranged places, the so-called places of madness disturbed by supernatural forces, he has been overtaken by darkness. He tells the narrator, 'With darkness I saw darkness' (316). By being subjected to the nefarious influence of the music box, the protagonist likewise becomes a victim and an emanation of darkness, a doppelgänger of the dark traveller. Friedrich Nietzsche's famous statement, 'when you gaze long into an abyss the abyss also gazes into you' illustrates the lesson at the heart of Ligotti's tale. Underlying Nietzsche's statement lies the trope of contagion. The protagonist also becomes 'infected' by darkness when he accesses the alternate reality of the Van Livenns' house. Ligotti thus combines several Gothic motifs that destabilise the suburban reality: the doppelgänger, the uncanny atmosphere, and the motif of contamination. This echoes Vidler's contention whereby 'the notion of the uncanny aligns itself with defamiliarization and with ghostliness, disturbance and disease' (220). This leads them to a parallel universe comprised of dark nightmares. The apparent 'shiny world' of the American suburbs is revealed only to disclose its photographic negative. Ligotti critiques them as a constructed, inorganic locale haunted by an artificial homogeneity. As Dahlia Schweitzer contends in *Haunted Homes* (2021), the suburbs comprised:

> a carefully constructed house of cards engineered via government policy and racist strategy, built on precarious local agreements, all of which would coalesce to form (on the surface) rows and rows of uniform homes, each promising opportunity and hope for those who were lucky to buy in, while (below the surface) a web of oppression, racism and financial risk lurked and festered. (6)

Extrapolating from this description, the suburbs are a diseased and unnatural site concealed by immaculate lawns. This picture-perfect place is deconstructed and revealed to be illusory. The ghosts of financial difficulties, trauma, and dissatisfied housewives lurk in the shadows, undermining the American Dream. This is the perfect terrain for the stormy emergence of the return of the repressed. Engaging with the Gothic as a type of 'dream/ nightmare fiction', Ligotti extends the Suburban Gothic into the domain of the metaphysical Gothic.

As an expression of domestic horror, 'Flowers' resonates with V. C. Andrews's *Flowers in the Attic* (1979) or Charlotte Perkins Gilman's 'The Yellow Wallpaper' (1892). The mysterious Pandora-like box that appears in the tale also seems to be inspired by Clive Barker's *The Hellbound Heart* (1986). It focuses on a domestic environment disturbed by Lemarchand's box, which unleashes torture and pain on a family and opens into an alternate dimension that vividly summons hell itself. In 'Flowers', Ligotti manipulates the subversive dimension of the Gothic to expose both the fragilities of suburbia and its role as the underbelly of the American Dream. That dream serves as the vehicle through which he dissects the contradictions inherent in American society.

While the destiny of the narrator is not revealed, there are clues that he has died. By consorting with darkness, he has become part of it. The reader may ultimately doubt the narrator's existence but recognises that he operates as the collective spirit of a community striving to understand what happened to the Van Livenn family. On a symbolic level, 'Flowers' can also be understood as a journey of self-discovery that culminates in insanity. The house to which the narrator is drawn operates as a metaphor for his troubled mind. In this reading, the stranger serves as his dark double, whose mind remains 'home to the madness of things' (318).

The darkness and the nightmares lodged within reality put the credulity of the protagonist of 'In the Shadow of Another World' (1991) to the test while threatening his sanity and forever altering his conception of the world. In this story, a man visits a house in the care of Raymond Spare. The home's macabre details resonate with the Gothic description of the Van Livenns' 'embodied' house in 'Flowers'. As the narrator observes, 'There seemed to be the appearance of petrified flesh in its rough outer surfaces, and it was very simple to imagine, an inner framework not of beams and boards, but rather of gigantic bones from great beasts of old' (367). The description evokes the idea of the home as a sacrificial place, composed of the flesh and bones of the sacrificed, those previous visitors who were lured in out of curiosity. The atmosphere of its interior also recalls the sepulchral ambience of the Van Livenns' house that 'exuded the atmosphere ... of a well-tended mausoleum' (368). It once belonged to an individual who dabbled in dark matters and, to ensure secrecy, sealed all of its windows, especially those in the turret, the location of his private workshop where that 'fearful genius had practiced his science of nightmares' (371). In the semantic lexicon of Ligotti's tales, this 'science of nightmares' is the equivalent of the madness of things that killed the Van Livenn family. The narrator is told that this researcher required 'antiseptic surroundings' (369) since he is sensitive to the surrounding ambience and what lies beyond its boundaries. The scientist's intentions are invested with mystery, his nightmares beginning to interfere with his sanity. Having opened a door to another dimension, otherworldly creatures trespass into his reality.

After Spare removes the seals from the turret's windows where the scientist developed his secret research, the environment suddenly changes. As the narrator observes, 'What formerly had appeared as an artist's studio ... was gradually inheriting the aura of a stained-glass cathedral ... that suffered some obscure desecration' (370). The search for forbidden knowledge, a pervasive motif in Gothic fiction and key to the researcher's quest, seems to have profaned the once sacred place that must now be sealed to prevent the entrance of evil forces. Recalling the events of 'Flowers', dark energies try to force their way into the narrator's reality. Astounded, he notes, 'I perceived through those prismatic lenses, vague forms which seem to be struggling towards visibility, freakish outlines laboring to gain full embodiment' (371). These creatures dwell in a dark dimension, eager to penetrate the narrator's reality. Their nature remains obscure, as the narrator remarks, 'whether their nature was that of the dead or demonic – or possibly some peculiar progeny generated by their union – I could not tell' (371). Deprived of its protective seals, which consist of 'crude and cryptic designs' (372) conceived to protect the house against a parallel world of madness and darkness, the alternate reality begins to take over.

During the visit, Spare reads a passage to the narrator taken from the notebooks that belonged to the former owner of the house who, trying to glimpse what lurked beneath the visible world, dabbled in the occult and studied the forces of nature. This passage points to the underlying existence of another world, another reality with which humans are not familiar, a reality comprised of nightmares, demons, and spectres, one lodged in 'the shadows of another world' (372). After the reading, Spare becomes possessed and starts 'opening the shutters like a sleepwalker performing some obscure ritual' (374). The windows then become portals that enable the narrator to catch a glimpse of another reality. As he observes, 'the visions they offered were indeed those of a haunted world, a multifaceted mural portraying the marriage of insanity and metaphysics. In brief, the whole of the world was a pageant of nightmares' (375). While the narrator experiences this dream-like episode and gets lost in a 'maze of illusions' (377), he addresses the house of terror as if it were a personification of himself: 'I have no idea how long I had been enthralled by the chaotic fantasies imposing themselves upon the unprotected rooms of my mind' (376). Like the narrator of 'Flowers', Spare becomes possessed and is unwillingly dragged towards the world of shadows, screaming that the windows are '*pulling me into the stars and shadows*' (378). The narrator undergoes this surreal experience with a feeling of impotence, unable to save Spare.

Recognising that he should abandon the house in order to save himself, the terrified narrator steps outside, noting,

> My intuition was correct. For as soon as I had gone out into the night and turned back to face the house, I could see that its rooms were no longer empty .... And from where I stood, the sights were now inside the house, which had become an edifice possessed by the festivities of another world. (378)

Looking at the house, he sees that the forces of that alternate universe have taken over, the enchanted windows possessing a twofold role, 'for looking *in* as well as out' (378). From the outside, the 'desecration' of the cathedral-like building is now apparent, as it is rife with 'terrible vistas'. Deprived of its protective seals, with time, the house acquires the reputation of an accursed place that held 'festivities of another world' (378). The cathedral serves as a symbol of the sacred 'desacralised' by the weird metaphysical experiments carried out by the scientist. Thus is the quest for knowledge envisioned by the former owner of the castle-like house as a sacred quest, then reversed. This is typical of Ligotti's fiction where the pursuit of knowledge, in true Gothic fashion, is shown to bring suffering and unleash unnamed and unpredictable evils. Also, in accordance with Ligotti's personal beliefs, religion, the need for a God, and science are all shown to be futile and illusory attempts to anchor humankind to this world that ultimately fail to overturn death (*Conspiracy* 116).

Both 'Flowers' and 'Shadow' feature a lurking, underlying reality filled with darkness and madness that superimposes itself on the tenuous reality

of the characters, rendering them overwhelmed and powerless, hopeless
pawns destitute of free will. It is noteworthy, however, that in this particular tale, the narrator who witnesses 'the shadows of another world' is
spared. Reminiscent of Mary Shelley's Victor Frankenstein, Ligotti's narrator chooses not to pursue any further knowledge and to step away from
cosmic, arcane matters. Left alive as a witness to this world of nightmares,
he ends the story in the fashion of a cautionary tale:

> Wisely avoiding the enchantments of hell, the citizens of the town have kept
> to their own little secrets of gently stirring trees and silent houses. And what
> more can they do in the way of caution? How can they know what it is their
> houses are truly nested among? They cannot see ... that world of shadows
> with which they consort every moment of their brief and innocent lives. (379)

Like Victor, Ligotti's narrator abandons the pursuit of knowledge since it
will only bring him pain, disillusionment, and unhappiness. This cautionary
tale also embraces the lesson of *Frankenstein* as its protagonist's search for
the secrets of nature renders him a doomed individual like the student of
philosophy in 'Flowers'. So, the admonishing quality of Gothic fiction nicely
conveys Ligotti's philosophical viewpoint, according to which human consciousness and the desire for knowledge regarding the nature of this world
are conducive to pain.

The protagonist of 'The Sect of the Idiot' unfortunately does not partake
of the fate of the lead character of 'Shadow'. When he witnesses the world
of shadows, he becomes part of it, one of the elect, like the creatures who
dwell there. In this tale, the unnamed narrator describes the old town where
he lives as both a place that 'conveyed an impression of endlessness, or proliferating unseen dimensions, ... [and] the very image of a claustrophobe's
nightmare' (201). This vision resonates with that of the American suburbs
as an ideal place behind whose uniformity and apparent conformity lies a
dismal reality. The suburbs and the American Dream are thus shown to
disguise claustrophobic nightmares.

Shortly after his arrival, the narrator has a strange dream that alters the
way he sees and experiences the old town. He finds himself 'in a small dark
room ... whose windows looked down on a maze of streets which unraveled
beneath an abyss of stars' (202). This intermingling of the urban landscape
with space, a juxtaposition so pervasive in 'Shadow', is also given prominence in this obscure tale. Influenced by the content of his dream, the narrator realises that another reality co-exists with the one he knows, one that
appears to be unravelling before him that can only be sensed or guessed
at, since it cannot be clearly seen. 'Gazing out of the window', he says, 'I
was sure that cryptic proceedings were taking place in sequestered corners

..., [my] vague observances ... were at odds with accepted reality' (202). A powerful sense of cosmic indifferentism emerges from the description of his existential experience within the strange dream: 'I did not feel myself to be of any consequence in this or any other universe. I was nothing more than an unseen speck lost in the convolutions of strange schemes' (203). The overwhelming feeling of cosmic insignificance is magnified as the narrator states, 'In the dream nothing supported my existence, which I felt at any moment might be horribly altered or simply ended' (203). This passage evokes Edmund Burke's aesthetics of the sublime: although overtaken by the instinct of self-preservation, he still appreciates the magnitude of the terrifying experience (168). Notably, Ligotti's conception of the sublime aligns more with Vijay Mishra's theory that connects sublimity to death, where 'in spite of the intervention of the law of reason, the attraction of dissolution in the sublime is ... overpowering ... The abyss is embraced, but not contemplatively' (Mishra 85). According to Ligotti, this abyss, leading into the realm of death, elicits paradoxical feelings in the subject: alongside fear, he experiences an overwhelming desire that impels him to fuse or to dissolve into the unknown.

Within the dream, the atmosphere of the house is likewise depicted as oneiric and uncanny, a place, as the dreaming narrator relates, 'in which time and space had become deranged. A few moments in these rooms might count as centuries or millennia, and their tiniest niche might encompass a universe' (203). One room, in particular, appears to 'border on the voids of astronomy and its windows opened onto the infinite' (203), a description that suggests the possible intrusion of an alternate realm. In this peculiar room, the narrator encounters mysterious robed creatures with bizarre anatomies whose presence leaves him paralysed in horror. These strange beings seem to weave strange conspiracies in a discourse that consists of a 'soft buzzing noise' (204). Initially 'infected' in the dream, the protagonist's infection progresses after he is awakened and finds himself slowly transforming into one of them, a process that requires shifting from the reality he knows to the alternate reality encountered in his dreams. As occurs in 'Flowers', the narrator of this eerie tale is ultimately swallowed up by darkness, becoming part of it.

Once again, Ligotti revisits the practice of lucid dreaming alluded to in 'Flowers', which entails a process of transformation for the dreamer. This is also emphasised in 'Sect'. Following a dreamy nocturnal expedition, the character's physical shape undergoes substantial alterations, as he becomes one of these alien-like creatures who is engaged in creating his own reality. This tale is subversive in its insinuation that the character might be fabricating his own reality without even being aware of it. This ties in with what Ligotti terms Metzinger's paradox advanced by neuro-philosopher Thomas Metzinger in

Being No One (2004). Ligotti, in *The Conspiracy Against the Human Race* (2018), reflects upon Metzinger's idea that the brain is the organ responsible for manufacturing the subjective sense of human existence (92). In these terms, the 'human being is not a "person" but a mechanistically functioning "phenomenal self-model" that "simulates a person"' (92). Then, in line with the philosopher's thought, and, as Ligotti concludes, it is impossible for human beings to achieve any realisation of the true reality due to the 'inbuilt manacles of human perception that keep [their] minds in a dream state' (93).

As 'The Sect' illustrates, Ligotti incorporates into his tales scientific research concerning 'reality', such as simulation theory – first advanced by Nick Bostrom in 'Are You Living in a Computer Simulation?' (2003) and developed by Rizwan Virk in *The Simulation Hypothesis* (2019) – that conceptualises humans as avatars in a computer-fabricated world. It is also resonant of Michio Kaku's multiverse theory from *Parallel Worlds: A Journey Through Creation, Higher Dimensions, and the Future of the Cosmos* (2006), which claims many 'realities' are happening simultaneously. The incorporation of these emerging theories into Ligotti's narratives is not only transformative for the characters and the realities in which they exist but is also key to his Gothic style. His work verges on science fiction due to its speculative nature, a quality that lends the author's Gothic an innovative avant-garde flavour.

Along similar lines, the plot of 'Dream of a Manikin' takes the reader onto the unstable paths of the dream, while engaging with two significant works – Sigmund Freud's psychoanalytic theories and E. T. A. Hoffmann's tale, 'Der Sandmann' (1816). This story features a psychiatrist and his patient, Amy Locher, who is referred to him by an unnamed female colleague. Locher, who seems an honest, emotionally balanced young woman, informs the doctor that she has been having recurrent nightmares that leave her disturbed and confused. Despite working for a financial firm, in her dream she is employed in a fashion shop where she dresses mannequins. Emulating the atmosphere of 'Sect', in 'Manikin', the Lacanian Symbolic where language and signification are nested collapses and gives way to the emergence of the chaotic Real, which begins to intrude in the tale when Miss Locher's conventional language is overtaken by an alternate discourse marked by incoherence. The psychiatrist remarks that the young woman's responses sometimes assume 'the incoherent language of the oneiric' (51). This illogical discourse is connected to the strangeness of Miss Locher's dreams that are plagued, cryptically and significantly, by mannequins. As she notices in one of these episodes:

> all around the room … are people dressed as dolls. Their forms are collapsed, their mouths open wide. They do not look as if they are still alive. Some of

them have actually become dolls, their flesh no longer supple and their eyes have lost the appearance of teary moistness. Others are at various intermediate stages between humanness and dollhood. (48)

The young woman's attitude towards the mannequins that haunt her dreams is revulsion. Their unclothed bodies repel her touch because 'they are neither warm nor cold, as only artificial bodies can be' (46). In this way, the mannequins serve as figures of abjection insofar as they evoke the image of a corpse, which is, according to Julia Kristeva, 'the most sickening of wastes. ... [the] I expelled ... [where we see] death infecting life' (4). Due to its uncanny resemblance to humans, the mannequin mirrors Freud's conceptualisation of the double as a 'harbinger of death' (*Uncanny* 142). It thus serves as a reminder of human mortality and a lack of agency.

After some sessions, Amy Locher stops visiting the psychiatrist, who then decides to assume the role of detective and investigate the reason behind the young woman's disappearance. Like the traveller of darkness in 'Flowers', the psychiatrist essentially pursues forbidden knowledge as he 'penetrat[es] the mysteries of [Miss Locher's] dream' (51). On a rainy night, the doctor drives through the city in search of the address of the financial firm, only to come across a shop with a bright neon sign. In the shop window, he gazes at a mannequin that bears a strong resemblance to Miss Locher. Logically, he dismisses the ridiculous idea that his patient's story might actually be true. However, the seeds of doubt have been planted in his mind and he soon falls prey to similar nightmares. As in 'Sect', these nightmares work as if they were symptoms of a type of psychologically transmitted disease – the disease of dreams infecting his brain – an idea that reiterates the parasitical nature of the dream that is key to Ligotti's literary worldview. This conception of the dream as a parasite surfaces in other of his tales such as 'Mrs. Rinaldi's Angel' (1991), where dreams are literally likened to parasites, 'maggots ... feeding on the mind and soul as ordinary maggots feed on the body' (399). Much like vampires, these dreams are predatory. They sneak into the narrative and assault the characters, just to feed on them. As a passage taken from this tale exemplifies, 'if these dreams have no world of their own to nourish them, they may come into yours and possess it, exhaust it little by little each night. They use your world and use it up' ('Angel' 399). In 'The Mystics of Muelenburg' (1987), Klaus Kingman also introduces himself to the narrator as a 'parasite of chaos' (359), inhabiting a realm made of nightmare.

Equally resonant with others of Ligotti's tales, the characters' reality is breached by unexplained cosmic forces which intrude upon their lives unexpectedly. In one of Amy Locher's dreams, one of the walls in her bedroom is replaced by a great gap with 'a view to a star-clustered blackness', a kind of 'starry abyss' (47). A similar phenomenon strikes the psychiatrist who feels contaminated by his female patient's nightmares. In one of these, he notices that in his hallway 'there are things that look like people dressed as dolls, or else dolls made up to look like people' (57). A critique underlies this haunting by nightmarish mannequins of an America that appears figuratively comatose and in thrall to conformity, in which people seem devoid of critical discernment. Like shop mannequins, they constitute mere bodies, naked of values, mechanised in their actions, and having similar 'programmes' running inside their brains. Ligotti addresses a society in which creativity, originality, and individual agency have become obsolete. Read along these lines, 'Dream' illustrates, with Gothic undertones, this transition from subject to object, where the individual mind surrenders to the pressure exerted by the collective.

In the nightmares that afflict both Amy Locher and the psychiatrist, there are clues that they are actually being transformed into mannequins: after experiencing the dream, the doctor feels paralysed with terror (57) and his patient notices that 'her own mouth is open wide and will not close' (48). In Miss Locher's case, she asserts that her dream feels so real it is a 'dream of flesh' (51). Following these eerie and powerful nightmares, they both turn into mannequins, their identities annihilated as they are drawn into a world of mute objectification. By playing with language – and its absence – Ligotti deconstructs the characters' realities, implying that the world they inhabit is but a fabricated matrix in which they function as mere avatars. As S. T. Joshi adeptly observes about Ligotti's technique in this instance, 'it is not, in the end, a replacement of the real world by the unreal, but a sort of turning the real world inside out to show that it was unreal all along' (139).

Instead of the flimsy figures that appear in previous tales, in 'Dream of a Manikin' there is an evil, lurking presence 'of another character hidden in the background' (52) described as 'unseen' and 'demonic' (47). This insidious presence is believed to have been manipulating the characters' fates all along. The clues indicate that this ominous character is the female psychiatrist to whom the doctor confides his problems and who referred Miss Locher as a patient. Ligotti seems here to deconstruct the Western-based beliefs that envisage God as both creator and supreme being. This tale lifts the veil on a dystopian alternate realm in which the world seems to be ruled by a feminine entity whose nature is described by Miss Locher as something demoniacal. This mysterious female looks down on humans because they live under the illusion that they have both consciousness and free will. In reality, they are mere puppets, actors who labour and act under 'her' or someone else's control.

Infused as they are with cosmic indifferentism and cosmic horror, many of Ligotti's Gothic tales engage with alternate realities where nightmares that may be considered authentic heterotopias of darkness, thrive. According to Thacker, the idea of heterotopia, a concept he borrows from Foucault, entails 'a fluid sense of social space and the processes to which space is subject. ... It is, therefore, a concept which connects material and metaphorical spaces in the literary text in new and illuminating ways' (29). In this sense, a heterotopia can operate as a counter-reality to the extent that it 'inverts and contests real sites' (29). In 'Dream of a Manikin', the narrator describes these areas where reality collapses as 'zones of the unreal' (58) where distortions of the perceived reality of the subject are distilled through a dream/nightmare which operates as a type of inverse mirror that deconstructs and defamiliarises the narrator's reality and becomes that reality. The ultimate terror surfaces when the subject realises that this dream/nightmare is their true reality. According to Stefan Dziemianowicz, Ligotti 'discomposes the certainty of the "real" world of his stories ... [and] characters are forced to redefine what they consider "real" and "unreal," "natural" and "supernatural"' (38). Thus does the dream cease to play the role of an escapist fantasy, becoming manipulated and transformed instead into a dystopian reality – which assumes the true contours of a nightmare – in which characters find themselves at the mercy of unidentifiable forces. When characters realise that they are not who they think they are, that they are devoid of agency and possess an illusory identity, they become paralysed. Summoning Gothic conventions, and particularly the return of the repressed, Ligotti brings them face to face with their mortal, ephemeral reality.

Thomas Ligotti's characters are never at home, either physically or psychologically. At some point in his tales, they suffer the intrusion of other cosmic realms that generate a feeling of estrangement. Like the narrator of 'The Sect', they feel 'homeless amid an alien order of things' (203). They become afflicted by a kind of existential disorientation and displacement, the actual world being exposed as an uncanny, unhomely space that is unstable and on the verge of collapse. Thus they become instilled with fear, terror, and uncertainty after being mercilessly thrown into the claws of the unknown.

Treading an original literary path, Ligotti forges a mythology about 'the madness of things'. The cryptic inscriptions that signal the existence of these parallel realities are present in other tales: in 'Flowers' they appear inscribed in the music box; in 'In the Shadow of Another World', they are used to seal the windows of the mysterious house; and in 'The Sect of the Idiot', these glyphs form part of a mysterious arcane form of communication between the robed creatures encountered by the narrator. Both in 'Shadow' and 'Flowers', the ghostly apparitions strive to be seen to no avail; they remain imprisoned within a darkness that refuses to return them to their previous human shape. This same darkness engulfs both protagonists in 'Manikin' whose fate is to become lifeless objects. Objects are thus used as signs in oneiric landscapes that, at any time, threaten to transform dreams into nightmares: houses and music boxes become metaphors for the human brain and the lethal potential inherent in the imagination. In this light, our soul – the turret of 'Shadow', which serves as a powerful metaphor for the human mind – becomes a forbidden lab where the laborious conjecturing of our consciousness produces ghosts and unnameable terrors. Mannequins work as a powerful reminder of the finitude of the human being and, in this manner, they evoke an encounter with death. The cryptic messages that appear inscribed in the objects the characters encounter contain enigmatic invitations for them to research further.

Many of Ligotti's characters suffer from what might be called 'Frankenstein's syndrome'. From the stranger who welcomes the teacher in 'Flowers' to the mysterious researcher in 'Shadow', each wishes to penetrate the veil of the apparent to find out what is hidden on the other side. In their perilous 'dreamy' journeys, they eventually find themselves and contemplate the horror hidden within their souls. The layered realms encountered by these characters come to assume a double meaning: they can be interpreted as the intrusion of some alternate dimension into their realities, or they can be understood as projections of their tortured brains. In Ligotti's tales, dreams are dismal windows that open onto cosmic, estranged landscapes, ultimately offering visions that radically alter their narrators' lives. Tragically, they become haunted by 'shadows of other worlds' they try, unsuccessfully, to sublimate or dismiss in order to carry on. Ligotti takes the Gothic to his experimental lab and engineers a hybrid genre where the metaphysical encounters the existential. In such metaphysical Gothic narratives, reality is dissected and deconstructed, the path to knowledge shown to lie through death and fusion with a liquid, black, nihilistic sublime that has nothing to offer but the (dis)comfort of oblivion.

Note

I would like to express my gratitude to Carol Margaret Davison for her comments, suggestions, and detailed editorial work on this chapter.

Works cited

Behrend, David. 'I Am Not Dying in a Nightmare: Dreams and Psychosis in the Work of Thomas Ligotti.' https://dwbehrend.files.wordpress.com/2014/12/dreams-and -madness-in-ligotti.pdf. Accessed 9 October 2020.

Bostrom, Nick. 'Are You Living in a Computer Simulation?' *Philosophical Quarterly*, vol. 53, no. 211, 2003, pp. 243–55.

Burke, Edmund. *A Philosophical Enquiry into the Origin of Our Ideas of the Sublime and the Beautiful*. Harper & Brothers, 1984.

Cavallaro, Dani. *Gothic Visions: Three Centuries of Horror, Terror and Fear*. Continuum, 2002.

Davison, Carol. *Haunted Homes*. Rutgers University Press, 2021.

Day, William Patrick. *In the Circles of Fear and Desire: A Study of Gothic Fantasy*. University of Chicago Press, 1985.

Dziemianowicz, Stefan. 'Nothing Is What It Seems to Be: Thomas Ligotti's Assault on Certainty.' *The Thomas Ligotti Reader: Essays and Explorations*, edited by Darrel Schweitzer. Wildside Press, 2003.

Foucault, Michel. 'Of Other Spaces: Utopias and Heterotopias.' *Architecture/ Mouvement/ Continuité*, no. 5, October 1984, translated by Jay Miskowiec, pp. 1–9. https://web.mit.edu/allanmc/www/foucault1.pdf. Accessed 20 October 2020.

Freud, Sigmund. 'Introductory Lectures on Psycho-Analysis (Part III).' *The Standard Edition of the Complete Psychological Works of Sigmund Freud (1916–1917), Volume XVI*, edited by J. Strachey. The Hogarth Press and the Institute of Psycho-Analysis, 1963, 24 vols.

Freud, Sigmund. *The Uncanny*, translated by David McLintock, Penguin, 2003.

Joshi, S. T., *The Modern Weird Tale*. McFarland & Company, 2001.

Kaku, Michio. *Parallel Worlds: A Journey Through Creation, Higher Dimensions, and the Future of the Cosmos*. Anchor Books, 2006.

Kristeva, Julia. *Powers of Horror: An Essay on Abjection*, translated by Leon S. Roudiez. Columbia University Press, 1982.

Ligotti, Thomas. *The Conspiracy Against the Human Race: A Contrivance of Horror*. Penguin, 2018.

Ligotti, Thomas. 'Dream of a Manikin.' *Songs of a Dead Dreamer* and *Grimscribe*. Penguin, 2015, pp. 45–59.

Ligotti, Thomas. 'Flowers of the Abyss.' *Songs of a Dead Dreamer* and *Grimscribe*. Penguin, 2015, pp. 309–18.

Ligotti, Thomas. 'In the Shadow of Another World.' *Songs of a Dead Dreamer* and *Grimscribe*, Penguin, 2015, pp. 366–79.

Ligotti, Thomas. 'Mrs. Rinaldi's Angel.' *The Nightmare Factory*. Carroll & Graf, 1996, pp. 399–408.

Ligotti, Thomas. 'The Mystics of Muelenburg.' *Songs of a Dead Dreamer* and *Grimscribe*. Penguin, 2015, pp. 45–59.

Ligotti, Thomas. 'The Sect of the Idiot.' *Songs of a Dead Dreamer* and *Grimscribe*, Penguin, 2015, pp. 200–10.

Ligotti, Thomas. *Songs of a Dead Dreamer* and *Grimscribe*. Penguin, 2015.

Lovecraft, Howard Phillips. 'The Call of Cthulhu.' *The Call of Cthulhu and Other Weird Stories*. Penguin, 1999, pp. 139–69.

Lovecraft, Howard Phillips. *Supernatural Horror in Literature*. Wermod & Wermod, 2013.

Mishra, Vijay. *The Gothic Sublime*. State University of New York Press, 1994.

Newell, Jonathan. *A Century of Weird Fiction, 1832–1937: Disgust, Metaphysics, and the Aesthetics of Cosmic Horror*. University of Wales Press, 2020.

Ralickas, Vivian. '"Cosmic Horror" and the Question of the Sublime in Lovecraft.' *Journal of the Fantastic in the Arts*, vol. 18, no. 3, 2003, pp. 364–98.

Ramsey, Shawn. 'A Graveside Chat: Interview with Thomas Ligotti.' *Deathrealm*, no. 8, 1989, pp. 21–3.

Royle, Nicholas. *The Uncanny*. Manchester University Press, 2003.

Schweitzer, Dahlia. *Haunted Houses*. Rutgers University Press, 2021.

Thacker, Andrew. *Moving Through Modernity: Space and Geography in Modernism*. Manchester University Press, 2003.

Thacker, Eugene. *In the Dust of This Planet*. Zero Books, 2011.

Van Eeden, Frederik. 'A Study of Dreams.' *Proceedings of the Society for Psychical Research*, vol. 26, 1913, pp. 431–61.

Vidler, Anthony. *The Architectural Uncanny: Essays in the Modern Unhomely*. MIT Press, 1992.

Virk, Rizwan. *The Simulation Hypothesis*. Bayview Books, 2019.

Weinstock, Jeffrey Andrew. 'The New Weird.' *New Directions in Popular Fiction: Genre, Distribution, Retribution*, edited by Ken Gelder. Palgrave Macmillan, 2016, pp. 177–200.

10

Night walking: the oneiric horror cinema

Murray Leeder

Is all that we see or seem
But a dream within a dream?

This quotation from Edgar Allan Poe's 1849 poem, 'A Dream Within a Dream', opens John Carpenter's film, *The Fog* (1980). Just a few years earlier, it figured prominently in Peter Weir's film version of *Picnic at Hanging Rock* (1975). In both cases, the invocation of Poe serves to help position the film as dreamlike or working according to dream logic. Do not expect ironclad sequential logic, it seems to be saying, or the tight chains of narrative causality for which classical Hollywood filmmaking is known. It signals to the audience: do not expect absolute closure. Expect an experience. This chapter will explore how cinema, and especially horror films, evoke and utilise dreams. It suggests that 'dream horror' is a distinct narrative and aesthetic subcategory that follows a lineage of the oneiric dating back to the origins of Gothic literature.

It is probably not possible or entirely useful to disentangle dreams from visions, hallucinations, and other alterities; certainly, the cinematic codes for each overlap extensively. Dream sequences in horror films are too numerous to reference and discuss in a single chapter, but just a few include the closing sequences of *Carrie* (1976), *Friday the 13th* (1980), and the hallucinatory rape scene in *Rosemary's Baby* (1968). There are other cases, as in *The Shining* (1980), where a film can contain no clearly marked dream sequences and yet still register as dreamlike, or nightmarish, experience. The nightmare functions for the horror genre much in the same way that the fairy tale does for the romantic comedy – as a kind of ur-signifier.[1] Andrew Tudor notes that the horror genre frequently, 'invokes psychoanalytic considerations, at times borrowing its imagery from the symbolic apparatus of dream interpretation as well as allowing fictional characters to advance pseudo-Freudian accounts of their own and others' motivations' (446). Horror films have borne names like *Deathdream* (1974), *Bad Dreams* (1988), *In Dreams* (1999), *Zombie Nightmare* (1986), *Nightmare in the Daytime* (1992), and, of course, *A Nightmare on Elm Street* (1984). Perhaps even more significant is the fact that documentaries about horror films have titles like *The American Nightmare* (2000), *Nightmares in Red, White and Blue* (2009),

Nightmare Factory (2011), and *Nightmare in Canada* (2004). Some of these documentaries share the names of academic books, including the seminal *The American Nightmare: Essays on the Horror Film* (1979).

Despite the sheer volume of dreams in horror, horror films are not the branch of cinema most studied for their oneiric qualities. That branch is, unarguably, art cinema, and though it is common for auteur-driven art films (Stanley Kubrick's *Eyes Wide Shut* (1999), David Lynch's *Mulholland Drive* (2001), or the aforementioned *Picnic at Hanging Rock*) to edge up against horror, they scarcely all do (e.g. Ingmar Bergman's *Wild Strawberries* (1957), Robert Altman's *3 Women* (1977), Martin Scorsese's *After Hours* (1985), or Richard Linklater's *Waking Life* (2001)). Even within mainstream films, dreams often provide spaces for the subversion of classical norms – albeit licensed subversion – allowing for baroque moments where the conventions of film form are often stretched and challenged, potentially into the realm of the avant-garde or the experimental. The most literal example of this is the Salvador Dalí-designed dream sequence in Alfred Hitchcock's *Spellbound* (1945). But one could equally point to Roger Corman's series of Edgar Allan Poe adaptations, starting with *The Fall of the House of Usher* (1960) and ending with *The Tomb of Ligeia* (1964). Almost all of them have a dream or vision sequence, wordless and often with alterations to film feed and garish colour filters, which breaks sharply and conspicuously from the films that contain them.

Dream sequences in films of all types often provide a temporary aesthetic break, sometimes aping the bold and non-naturalistic aesthetics of music videos. One thinks, for example, of comedies like *U.H.F.* (1989) or *The Big Lebowski* (1998). Sometimes dream sequences represent the intrusion of 'horrorish' or Gothic elements into films of other genres. The surreal, eerie imagery in the dream ballet in *Oklahoma!* comes to mind (1955). The famous dream sequence in Hitchcock's *Vertigo* (1958), full of such startling and vivid imagery, echoes numerous earlier horror films where the vexed psyche of a character is expressed through dream. Jacques Tourneur's *Cat People* (1942) presents another fine example where Irena Dubrovna (Simone Simon), convinced that she is one of the werewolf-like cat women of her native Serbia, experiences a vivid nightmare with animated cats (see Figure 10.1). As in *Vertigo*, this dream sequence conspicuously introduces animation into an otherwise live-action film, which is unusual for a classical Hollywood film.

This chapter will further suggest that horror films often represent dreams not simply because they are scary and disorienting, but also because they are revealing; they become a space for the demonstration of anxieties that are both individual and collective. Here again, the dream in *Cat People* provides a convenient example. Irena dreams about her therapist, Dr

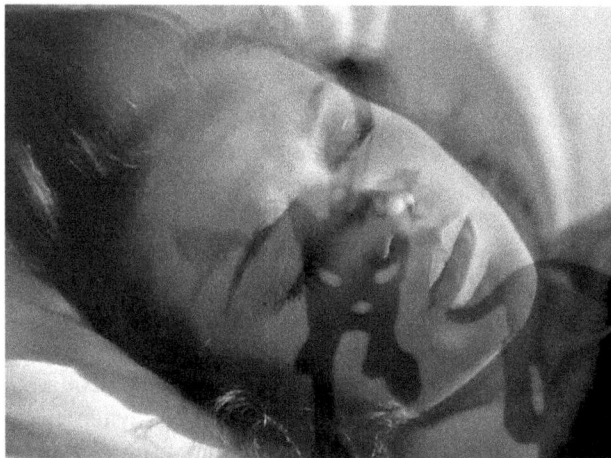

Figure 10.1 The collage-like nightmare sequence featuring animated black cats in *Cat People* (RKO Radio Pictures)

Louis Judd (Tom Conway), dressed in the armour of King John of Serbia, reputed in legend to have killed the original cat people; she looks to his psychoanalysis to liberate her from her supernatural curse. But this proves impossible, and Dr Judd turns out to be a manipulative predator himself. Irena's dream, ironically, signifies a liberation from patriarchy that can never actually happen.

Dream horror as cine-genre

Near the end of an article about classifications of film genres, Tom Gunning suggests that the cinematic horror genre derives its effectiveness not only from its ability to 'express semantic elements already present in other media' (59), as when it adapts or otherwise borrows stories or themes from novels or other media. Rather, Gunning advocates for attention to 'cine-genres', defined more by their aesthetics, the formal patterns of editing, mise-en-scène, cinematography, sound, etc., that tend to separate one group of films from another. Gunning offers an example of how horror can foreground an uncanny quality to the cinema that is as old as the medium but which has been buried by familiarity. To substantiate this claim, Gunning draws on dreams:

> If the ontology of the moving image no longer causes us anxiety, nonetheless specific genre narratives can reawaken such disturbing associations. I would claim that the greater genre interest that Wes Craven's *Nightmare* [1984–]

series of horror films shows over, say, the *Friday the Thirteenth* [1980–] Jason series lies primarily in their expression of the ontological confusion between reality and dreams through the ambiguous quality of the cinematic image, as the most recent entry *Wes Craven's New Nightmare* [1994] makes especially explicit. (59)

While some horror fans might dispute Gunning's prioritisation of one slasher franchise over another, the claim is an interesting one: that the central premise of the *Nightmare* franchise, about the ghostly maniac Freddy Krueger (Robert Englund) invading character's dreams, makes it fundamentally more cinematic. It permits a level of formal experimentation and display in its often elaborate and baroque dream sequences that cannot be matched by Jason Voorhees's machete work. Gunning might suggest that we can draw a distinction between a cine-genre of 'dream horror' and other kinds of horror.

Where might the Gothic sit in such a formulation? As Xavier Aldana Reyes notes – descriptively, not proscriptively – the cleavage between the Gothic and horror is often conceptualised in terms of the Gothic being subtle, suggestive, and moody, while horror is regarded as grisly, graphic, and embodied:

[Gothic is] highly psychological and preoccupied with hallucinations, vivid dreamscapes (often nightmares) and other provinces of the warped mind. Horror, by contrast, is seen as heavily graphic and explicit: it confronts viewers with terrifying images and cinematic 'numbers'. (8)

Interestingly, both of these descriptions seem to suit the *A Nightmare on Elm Street* films equally well, putting them in a slightly odd place. The franchise's rocky marriage of Gothic dream narrative and splatter film might be understood as 'elevating' it above *Friday the 13th* in Gunning's formulation. However, like Aldana Reyes, I would recommend caution in demarcating horror and the Gothic so neatly, and observe that this distinction tends to underpin categories of cultural taste as much as providing descriptive usefulness.

Analogies between films and dreams

Film theory has linked films and dreams in a variety of ways for more than a century, as part of various attempts to connect cinematic form to mental processes (Carroll 11–12; Rascaroli n.p.). Perhaps most famously, the German-American psychologist Hugo Münsterberg argued in 1916 that

[Film] can act as our imagination acts. It has the mobility of our ideas which are not controlled by the physical necessity of outer events but by the psychological laws for the association of ideas. In our mind past and future become intertwined with the present. [Film] obeys the laws of the mind rather than those of the outer world. (106)

Before going further, let us ask an elementary question: What do films have to do with dreams? Films can and often do depict dreams. When they do this, we identify with the dreaming character, except in those narratives where an external character penetrates an existing dream world, e.g. *Dreamscape* (1984), *The Cell* (2000), and *Inception* (2010), where we share the perspective of that outsider instead. Most narrative films encourage their audience to identify with their protagonist(s) and implicitly share their perspective, emotions, and even physical states, but dream sequences do this more directly, constructing psychological inner space as a landscape, if a protean one. In some cases, the revelation that we are watching a dream is preserved for a narrative surprise. *The Wizard of Oz* (1939) offers the most famous example. In some films – for example, the *It* duology (2017, 2019) and *Smile* (2022) – shifts between reality and dreamlike states occur so frequently that the audience is placed 'on guard', always expecting yet another such reversal.

Furthermore, even when films are not literally depicting dreams, at least not those of specific characters, they may be dreamlike or oneiric themselves. To call a film 'dreamlike' is slightly nebulous but tends to mean that it departs from both the conventions of realism, which deploys film form to suggest unmediated reality, and classicism, which depicts a coherent internal world with maximum clarity and comprehension. Instead, to say that a film is dreamlike is to affiliate it with formalism, which uses film form to create alternate, non-realistic impressions that may be suggestive of dreams. It is no surprise to find that some of the first theorists and filmmakers who advocated for a highly formal, non-realistic cinema, such as Jean Epstein and Riccotto Canudo, often pointed to dreams as a model for a truly poetic and provocative cinema. This strategy was put into practice most directly by early avant-garde filmmakers like Epstein, Jean Cocteau, and especially Luis Buñuel and Salvador Dalí, whose collaboration on *Un Chien Andalou* (1929) created one of the hallmarks of avant-garde cinema precisely because of strange, jarring imagery and dream logic-style construction. The Surrealists famously exalted dreams as spaces of freedom and used dream aesthetics as a guiding principle for their artworks. Yet *Un Chien Andalou* scarcely approximates a happy dream and has obvious affinities with horror, including the infamous slitting of an eyeball, which has been described as a 'figure for the rupture of the visual pleasure accompanying experiences of imagistic wholeness' (Jay 259) associated with classical Hollywood cinema.

It is worth noting that there is one significant non-parallel between horror films and nightmares. As Mathias Clasen writes:

> people do not normally experience their nightmares as a simulation, but as a reality. That is why it can be such a relief to wake up from a nightmare and realize that it was just a nasty simulation inflicted on you by your brain. You also cannot switch off or walk away from a nightmare. That element of control, along with the psychological distance provided by the knowledge that a horror film is not real, is lacking from a nightmare. That is why nightmares are no fun, in contrast to horror movies. (49–50)

Clasen goes on to note that the fact that horror films *can* produce recurring nightmares, the same as actual traumatic events, suggests that a common psychological mechanism may exist for both that fails to distinguish between deliberate and non-deliberate scare experiences (51). So while any film can, in principle, inspire dreams, horror films may do so most memorably. Several studies (see Cantor and Hoekstra et al.) have found that childhood exposure to horror films can include lasting effects, including recurring nightmares. *Poltergeist* (1982) is frequently mentioned in these studies, perhaps unsurprisingly, since it locates many of its supernatural events in children's bedrooms, as also occurs in *A Nightmare on Elm Street*. Certain horror films seem to have furnished society with collective nightmare experiences, both literal and metaphorical.

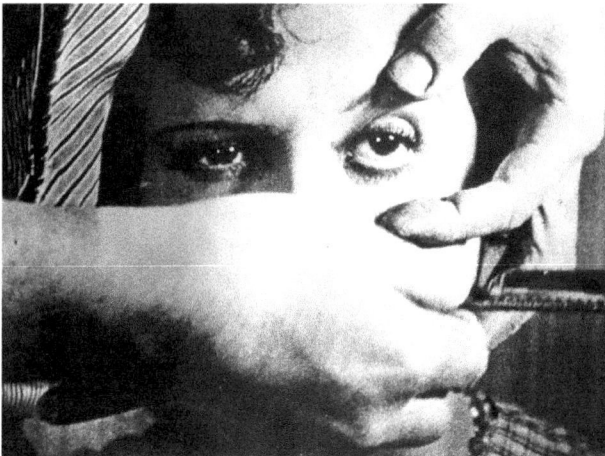

Figure 10.2 The infamous eye-slitting scene from *Un Chien Andalou* (Les Grands Films Classiques)

Cinema and dreams have also been linked in another way, with 'dreams' standing less for individual mental visions and more for an audience's collective hopes and desires, as in the phrase 'American Dream'. Some branches of film theory, notably the French apparatus theorists (see Baudry), have operated under the basic premise that cinema places its audience in a sleep-like, receptive position, uncritically and unknowingly receiving ideologically coded messages. When Hollywood is figured as a 'Dream Factory', as in the title of anthropologist Hortense Powdermarker's 1950 study, this is the operative metaphor: cinema provides escapist fantasies of wealth, power, glamour, beauty and prosperity, with a set of formal codes that naturalise its illusionism. From here, it takes only a simple rhetorical twist to position the horror film as the nightmare corollary that answers and undermines those rosy dreams.

This is precisely the approach taken in Robin Wood's 'An Introduction to the American Horror Film' (1979), which was published in the aforementioned chapbook, *The American Nightmare*. This essay would become the single most read, reprinted, and taught text in the field of Horror Studies. Working at the juncture of Marxism and Freudian psychoanalysis, Wood promoted the idea that horror films represent 'the return of the repressed', a violent, cathartic release of all that was suppressed by society. Wood sees tremendous potential subversive power in horror films since they narrativise the struggle with all those forces that society needs to repress in order to function. While detailing the idea of the return of the repressed, Wood gives a section to 'Dreams and Nightmares' where he proposes that Hollywood cinema has tended to create a sort of 'partial sleep of consciousness. For the filmmakers as well as for the audience, full awareness stops at the level of plot, action, and character, in which the most dangerous and subversive implications can disguise themselves and escape detection' (13). Wood proposes that horror films are 'our collective nightmare':

> The conditions under which a dream becomes a nightmare are (a) that the repressed wish is, from the point of view of consciousness, so terrible that it must be repudiated as loathsome, and (b) that it is so strong and powerful as to constitute a serious threat. The [genre's] disreputability ... the general agreement that horror films are not to be taken seriously – works clearly *for* the genre viewed from this position. The censor (in both the common *and* Freudian sense) is lulled into sleep and relaxed vigilance. (13; emphasis in original)

Wood seeks to awaken us to this collective nightmare and the subversive, revolutionary impulses it shelters. He identifies the Surrealists as one group of intellectuals who took American horror movies seriously, reporting that

The Beast with Five Fingers (1946) was a favourite film of Luis Buñuel. Wood notes, 'The association is highly significant, given the commitment of the Surrealists to Freud, the unconscious, dreams, and the overthrow of repression' (14). This point is demonstrated by a review of *King Kong* (1933) in the Surrealist journal *Minotaure* by Jean Ferry, who spends more than a page describing numerous absurdities in the film, including the fact that Kong 'perpetually changes size; one minute his hand is big enough to seize an underground train, the next it only goes round the torso of a woman we see waving her arms and legs about' (162). The review seems, at first, to be a pan. But then Ferry reverses course, stating, 'I think you begin to see what I'm getting at, and will not be surprised to find me on the beaten tracks of the dream, the dream in which, pursued by too pressing a danger, we create the elements of our salvation without being able to escape' (162). Ferry says that watching *King Kong*, he 'rediscovered bit by bit a striking detail from [his] personal nightmares and all the anguish and atrocious malaise that goes with it' (163). At the end of the review, he notes that the film's 'violent oneiric power' and 'monstrous eroticism' are among the values that combine into 'all that we mean by the adjective "poetic" and in which we had the temerity to hope the cinema would be its most fertile native soil' (164). Essentially, Ferry sees *King Kong* as a work of accidental Surrealism because of its dreamlike qualities, even though the film does not have a single actual dream sequence.[2] To evoke dreaming or the oneiric with reference to horror, for both Ferry and Wood, is to suggest that there is something more, something that a superficial descriptive account of a film cannot capture and that it is the responsibility of the critic to reveal.

'All just a dream': silent-era oneiric cinema

In a sense, the oneiric qualities of cinema can be traced back to before the invention of the medium itself, into the history of media involving projected light. According to Terry Castle's work on the eighteenth-century 'invention of the uncanny', the era of the Gothic novel's invention was also that of the internalisation of the supernatural into the mind, where once external forces metamorphosed into phantasmatic 'inner pictures' (7). The very term 'phantasmagoria', Castle notes, drifted from describing the external spectacle to referencing

> the phantasmic imagery of the mind. This metaphoric shift bespeaks ... a very significant transformation in the human consciousness over the past two centuries ... the spectralization or 'ghostifying' of mental space .... Thus in everyday conversation we affirm that our brains are filled with ghostly shapes and

images, that we 'see' figures and scenes in our minds, that we are 'haunted' by our thoughts. (142–3)

Once the mind is understood as a place, it becomes a representable place. Castle sees this new supernaturalisation of the unconscious as exemplified both by the emergence of Gothic fiction and by the phantasmagoria, the grim optical shows pioneered in France in the 1790s, which constitute a significant step on the road to cinema (see Heard). It is only a slight exaggeration to say that this modern reconfiguration of the mind as a place or environment underpins all cinematic representations of dreams.

For many decades, early cinema was described as being split between two founding styles: the slice-of-life realism of the Lumière brothers and the fantastical trick displays of Georges Méliès. It should not be surprising that the dream would be claimed by Méliès and other trick filmmakers, suiting as it does the display of substitutions, disappearances and appearances, superimpositions, and the like. An important early example is *The Astronomer's Dream* (1898) by Méliès. Here, Mephistopheles (played by the director) vexes an astronomer so that when he looks through his telescope, the moon appears as a gigantic, monstrous vision that devours everything in sight. Dreams are a common theme in Méliès's trick films, with other titles – now, largely lost – including *A Drunkard's Dream* (1896), *The Rajah's Dream* (1900), *Dream of the Ballet Master* (1903), and *The Dream of an Opium Fiend* (1908). In many of these, dream states are linked to mind-altering substances or to the creative process, linking dreams to other states of alterity that often share the same formal registers. Other trick filmmakers followed suit, notably Edwin S. Porter, who adapted Winsor McCay's print cartoons as the spectacular *Dream of a Rarebit Fiend* (1906).

Any discussion of silent-era dream films will inevitably turn to *The Cabinet of Dr. Caligari* (1920), a classic of German Expressionist cinema, featuring distorted, wildly artificial sets, and the famous twist that the whole film chronicles the recollections of a madman. *Caligari* is almost a fully oneiric film, a brilliantly conceived nightmare. It takes place in the town of Holstenwall and first tells the story of a young man named Francis (Friedrich Feher), whose life is disrupted by the travelling mountebank, Dr Caligari (Werner Krauss), and his somnambulist, Cesare (Conrad Veidt). After a series of murders and the attempted kidnapping of Francis's girlfriend Jane (Lil Dagover) by Cesare, Francis traces Cesare to a local insane asylum. Here it is revealed that Caligari is the director and has become obsessed with an eighteenth-century mystic named Caligari, to the point of re-enacting his crimes. Caligari is arrested and confined in his own asylum. The film then advances a strange twist where Francis is revealed to be the madman who has constructed a narrative around his fellow inmates at the asylum, casting the director as the villain in his paranoid fantasies. The film ends on a hopeful note: now that the director understands his delusions, Francis may be cured. To say that most audiences have found this ending disappointing is something of an understatement. The film's appeal, however, never lay in its plot but in its bizarre and fantastical sets and staging. Siegfried Kracauer famously interpreted it as a political allegory that anticipated the rise of Hitler (1947), although that interpretation has been heavily disputed. *Caligari*'s plot is arguably less significant than its formal elements – the drastically distorted mise-en-scène and wildly non-naturalistic performances.

The Gothic dream motif is also present in numerous other German Expressionist films, which clearly reflect the prominence of psychoanalysis in Weimar culture. The most literal is G. W. Pabst's *Secrets of a Soul* (1926), which was made in cooperation with Freud's associate Karl Abraham. It tells the story of a man who is haunted by a compulsion to murder his wife and who seeks help from a psychoanalyst who probes his dreams to unearth the motive. The film depicts elaborate and surreal dream sequences, but these ultimately serve a narrative that moves sharply towards closure: the dream images supply clues that help resolve the man's issues. In a sense, *Secrets of a Soul* anticipates such psychoanalytic detective stories as Hitchcock's *Spellbound*, which similarly balances the pure shocking imagery of dream sequences with the constraints of narrative integration. Another fascinating use of dreams occurs in the anthology film, *Waxworks* (1924), which features a writer (William Dieterle) who crafts text to accompany various wax museum figures. Its identification as horror rests on the final six minutes of its eighty-minute runtime, which captures the writer's nightmare, inspired by the demonic, superhuman figure from British folklore, Spring-Heeled Jack, who is conflated in the sequence with Jack the Ripper. The nightmare sequence features distorted carnival imagery similar to that in *Caligari* but with a new formal approach in the form of numerous layers of superimpositions. It is an extreme version of what I have elsewhere termed 'aesthetics of co-registration' (Leeder 2017), revealing the cinematic screen as a flat display surface upon which multiple layers of information are combined in a collage-like fashion. In *Waxworks*, the eerie effect of the superimpositions renders Jack as a protean, omnipresent figure who cannot be hidden from or fought. The sequence ends with the dreaming protagonist being stabbed by the killer, and as he is dying, a dissolve takes him back to reality for the film's rushed, happy ending.

Such dream films were not unique to Germany. There was an excellent example in Hollywood some years earlier in *The Avenging Conscience* (1914), made by D. W. Griffith immediately prior to *The Birth of a Nation* (1915).[3] *The Avenging Conscience* is a Poe adaptation of sorts, but rather than adapt an individual tale, it combines numerous motifs from Poe's stories, poems, and life into a sort of Poesque metatext, with lines from Poe's poems and stories appearing on intertitles. It tells the story of a nameless young man (Henry B. Walthall) whose attempts to marry the lovely Annabel (Blanche Sweet) are frustrated by his guardian, his eyepatch-bearing uncle (Spottiswoode Allen). The protagonist kills the uncle in a fit of rage and hides his body behind a wall, but his guilt overcomes him in a riff on 'The Tell-Tale Heart' (1843), during which episode he experiences hallucinations of demons and images of Christ. A very Griffith-style gunfight and standoff occur, and both lovers commit suicide. The end reveals that all was just a nightmare experienced by the nephew. Even the uncle's resistance to the marriage was fiction; he is actually friendly and welcoming. Years before *Caligari*, *The Avenging Conscience* grafts an unnaturally happy ending onto a dark, Gothic tale, seemingly to satisfy convention.

'All just a dream' has evolved into a shorthand for 'copout ending', a poor device that frantically undoes plot developments to secure a happy status quo. Time has not smiled on this device. Such endings, which were often studio imposed, are interesting because they generally fail to fully excise the dark materials they are frantically attempting to cancel out. Over time, 'just a dream' endings have been transformed into more ambiguous plays between reality and fantasy in films like *Jacob's Ladder* (1990), *Identity* (2003), and *Black Swan* (2010).

Comic nightmares

Critics and filmgoers would also do well to note that the Gothic and the comical are not strangers, and that horror and comedy frequently overlap. Sometimes the aesthetics are not that different: I once accidentally discovered in a classroom that, with the sound off, a sequence like Freddy Krueger getting hit by a sledgehammer and falling down a flight of stairs plays as slapstick comedy and not horror. Dream sequences can represent those points of contact, as in the silly 'daymare' sequence in Mel Brook's *Dracula: Dead and Loving It* (1995), where the Count (Leslie Nielsen) dreams of being human and then catches on fire while eating chicken at a picnic. Despite the tendency to think of horror parodies as a postmodern phenomenon, as early as 1932, only a year after the release of *Dracula* (1931) and *Frankenstein* (1931) inaugurating the cycle of sound-era horror films, Universal Pictures was already mocking its own nascent horror brand. The short film, *Boo!*, billed as 'A Universal Brevity', mixes genre parody and topical political comedy. The narration states, 'With times as tough as they are, we present a formula for cheap amusement: nightmares.' It shows a man (Morton Lowry) reading *Dracula* after eating lobster with milk, echoing *Dreams of a Rarebit Fiend*. The man passes out and the remainder of the film's nine minutes, silent except for the narration and comical sound effects, re-edits footage from *Nosferatu* (1922), *Frankenstein* (1931), and *The Cat Creeps* (1930), a lost sound remake of *The Cat and the Canary* (1927). The narration is irreverent and silly, often commenting on the film's technical aspects. For example, over a superimposition of the vampire in *Nosferatu*, the narration says, 'He thinks he's clever but we can see right through him.'

Boo! casually overturns all of the conventions of filmmaking, manipulating footage for comic effect. For example, it shows actor Gustav von Wangenheim in *Nosferatu* fleeing upstairs only to reverse the footage repeatedly as the narrator says, 'when he tries to go away, he meets himself coming back. It looks as though he's having his ups and downs. He acts like Congress and always ends up where he started.' Later footage of von Wangenheim moving his head back and forth gets replayed faster and faster while the narrator describes 'an attack of the pivot disease. It's like the hiccups – the more you do it, the more you have to. When you think you're over it, you're just beginning. The only way to stop is to do it faster and tire yourself out.' The footage dutifully increases in speed.

In addition to tampering with the film's mechanical substrate, *Boo!* provides commentary on the mixing of monsters, more than a decade before

Figure 10.3 The stuff of comic nightmares in *Boo!* (Universal Pictures)

Universal started melding the monsters in its horror series: 'Think of having Dracula and the monster from Frankenstein in the same dream', the narrator states. He also describes how 'A man tells Helen she has no business being in the same nightmare as Dracula', here referring to actress Helen Twelvetrees, the star of *The Cat Creeps*. Thus does he distinguish between different kinds of Gothic dramas – those built around monsters and 'old, dark house' mysteries – that should not be overlapping. *Boo!* only returns to the dreamer, 'our lobster and milk friend', at the very end of the short, finding him dangling from a chandelier. The narrator opines that 'It's a good thing he's waking up, or he might fall and break his chandelier.' The short ends with a nonsensical, parodic moral that 'you can milk a cow but a lobster is very ticklish'. All of *Boo!*'s silly comic reflexivity is underwritten by the fact that it depicts a dream and reminds us that a nightmare for one viewer can be amusement for another. This is the basic premise of horror comedies that feature comic actors playing fear for laughs, like Bob Hope in *The Ghost Breakers* (1940), Don Knotts in *The Ghost and Mr. Chicken* (1966), and Eddie Murphy in *The Haunted Mansion* (2003). *Boo!* is rife with multiple political jokes, including that about Dracula who 'decides to go back to his coffin and sleep for 100 years, until Congress decides to do something about the Depression'. Such topical comedy is licensed by the oneiric silliness.

An American dream sequence in London

We can turn to another horror comedy, John Landis's *An American Werewolf in London* (1981), to make a case study of a famously shocking dream sequence. It provides an example of 'it's all just a dream' in miniature, lasting only one sequence. The maggot birth sequence in *The Fly* (1986) is a comparable example. Werewolf attack victim David Kessler (David Naughton) convalesces in a London hospital, while his love interest, the nurse Alex Price (Jenny Agutter), watches over him. This section of the film features several dream sequences. We are first shown POV-coded camerawork of a figure rushing through a forest, as if hunting, and then see David, naked, killing and eating a deer. In a later sequence, we return to the first and see David as the prey, vulnerable in his hospital bed, still in the forest, multiple versions of David coexisting within this oneiric space. These sequences are clearly marked as dreams, although they come and go without clear setup or resolution.

The best-remembered sequence occurs after a flirtatious conversation between David and Alex, while he lies in his hospital bed. Alex reads aloud from Mark Twain's *A Connecticut Yankee in King Arthur's Court* (1899)

– itself inspired by a dream – and over his face, a scene transition is signalled by a dissolve. The transition is unobtrusive but also ambiguous; possibly it signals a flashback. A television screen shows a scene from *The Muppet Show* (1976–81), and the reverse shot shows an unremarkable American suburban family with a homey fireplace. Two children watch television while David does homework at the kitchen table. A knock is heard at the door and continues steadily. Menorahs sit on the mantle, indicating that this is a Jewish-American family home (David's Jewishness is only hinted at elsewhere in the film). The father walks to the door, opens it with a smile, and is promptly machine-gunned down by monsters on the other side – bipedal werewolves in Nazi uniforms. David reacts in terror to the events at the door as a werewolf assaults him from behind. What follows is a series of forceful cuts of the werewolves terrorising the family, smashing an image of Kermit the Frog on the television and spraying bullets across the family home. Cereal boxes, dishes, and vegetables are all obliterated. The parents and younger siblings are all killed. The werewolves take logs from the fireplace and make an inferno of the home. The film repeatedly includes short intercuts of a terrorised David, emphasising his eyes and a knife to his throat as he witnesses the carnage befalling his family. In the end, a werewolf slits his throat.

Then the film shows him waking in his hospital bed – it was 'all just a dream'. Pulling his wits together, he tells Alex, 'I've just had a nightmare.' She smiles and says, 'Don't worry, I've got just the thing', before opening the curtains. But when she draws them, there is a werewolf on the other side; it is a classic 'jump scare' achieved by the sudden and unexpected breaching of the frame. This werewolf is also armed, this time with a knife, which it drives into Alex's shoulder. The film cuts back to him yelling 'Alex!' as the werewolf repeatedly thrusts the knife into her body. In mere seconds, it is covered with blood. Although he awakens again after the nightmare has passed, he has yet to realise the darker truth – namely, that he is destined to become a werewolf as well.

The whole sequence is less than two minutes in length, and at first seems inexplicable, perhaps included to have at least one scare sequence in a relatively calm segment of the film. It also introduces the theme of uncertain boundaries between dreams and reality, which becomes important later in the film, as well as emphasising David's geographical isolation from his family and home as signalled in the film's title. The werewolves in this scene look and act quite differently than in the rest of the film. The dream seems to represent David's unconscious processing of recent events through, firstly, the conventions of Hollywood werewolf films, mentioned frequently throughout the film, and secondly, his fears as a Jewish-American male of the post-Holocaust generation (like the film's writer/director, John Landis).[4] Part of its utility as a dream sequence lies precisely in its ability to promote a subtext to a text.

Figure 10.4 David's throat is slit during the nightmare in *An American Werewolf in London* (PolyGram Pictures)

Comparisons are instructive to what is perhaps the other most famous scene in *An American Werewolf in London*, where the audience watches David's body painfully transform into his lupine form. That scene generates its effectiveness from relatively slow edits, which both show off the virtuosity of the special effects and makeup and let us fully experience David's transformation with horror and pity. In contrast, the Nazi werewolf dream sequence uses quick, jagged, disorienting cuts, abstracting the cinematic environment to convey the full intensity of the experience. In the dream sequence, David is forced to look; in the transformation scene, we look, helplessly, at him. Both are effective strategies for the creation of audience identification with the character, and the film is richer for employing them both. 'Dream horror' is a mode that a film might selectively and effectively employ only for specific sequences, and where effectiveness is gained by way of contrast.

Steady state: *Dead of Night*

Dreams can also complicate the conventions of Hollywood storytelling in another way: by denying closure. Perhaps *the* classic example is the 1945 British anthology film, *Dead of Night*, a film famous for its mix of cosiness and chilling horror. It is framed around the narrative of Welsh architect Walter Craig (Mervyn Johns) driving to a country cottage that he has been hired to renovate. He immediately tells the guests that he has seen them all before, in a recurring dream, which ends with tragedy. The bulk of the film features guest after guest telling their own stories of mysterious or paranormal events; one even involves another prophetic dream. However, one of the guests is the Dutch psychiatrist Dr van Straaten (Frederick Valk), who plays the role of sceptic for each story, though he dutifully provides a story himself: the story of a ventriloquist seemingly possessed by his dummy.

In the end, Craig is left alone with van Straaten and tells him that he is himself irresistibly compelled to kill. As Craig strangles van Straaten, the film moves through a surreal series of images connected to most of the earlier stories, ending with the terrifying image of Craig being strangled by a giant version of the ventriloquist dummy in a padded cell. The camera seems to pull back until the tableau of the strangulation is surrounded by blackness and becomes a fading luminous square at the back of the frame. It dissolves into the whiteness of a door in a sunlit room. It turns out that Walter Craig is just waking up. He tells his wife that he has had 'Another nightmare'. But the film raises the convention of 'all just a dream' only to provide yet another twist. The phone rings and he takes a call, which turns out to be from the owner of the cottage where the film took place. His wife opines that a weekend in the country 'Will help you get rid of those horrible nightmares'. The film flashes the words 'THE END' but replays its opening over its credits, creating the implication of a circular nightmare that never begins and never truly ends. Notably, the film inspired astronomer Fred Hoyle's steady-state model of the universe (Guerrier 874), which suggests an unchanging and fatalistically repetitive eternity.

Dead of Night uses the circular dream structure as a loophole to escape the narrative cinema's relentless drive towards closure, and winkingly employs the 'just a dream' reveal only to suggest, borrowing from Poe, that everything is a dream within a dream. Such a narrative seems deeply pessimistic, as it implies that patterns of ideology can never be broken.

Little slices of death: dream seriality and the Freddy franchise

The quote from Poe's 'A Dream Within a Dream' that opens this chapter is not the only place where we find an epigraph opening a dream horror film. Some of the *Nightmare on Elm Street* series opens this way too. *A Nightmare on Elm Street 3: Dream Warriors* (1987) opens with a Poe quote: 'Sleep. Those little slices of Death. How I loathe them.' At least this is attributed to Poe – where it actually comes from remains an open question.

A few scholars have written specifically about the role played by dreams in the *Nightmare* franchise. In his essay devoted to the *Nightmare* film franchise, for example, Steven Jones describes how it is 'more satisfying when viewed as a recurring nightmare, based around persistent motifs and patterns. As such, the series is dream-like (oneiric) rather than realistic' (81). Jones notes that the series is decidedly inconsistent in relation to the 'rules' of what Freddy can do in dreams as opposed to the waking world, and how and where humans can fight him, but argues that this 'looseness' is in fact the series' 'core strength' (84). Jones builds a fascinating case for the franchise's most derided elements – its inconsistency, and the volume of seemingly perfunctory sequels – as a secret strength, arguing that the central motif of dreaming 'naturalizes the kinds of discontinuity that are inherent to serial properties' (90).

For all of Hollywood's fondness for narrative composure and completion, it has also, since the silent era, shown an opposing tendency towards open-endedness, repetition, and serialisation (Singer 2001). Most film series embrace a sort of serial/closure hybridity; every entry draws most of its narrative lines to a close only to deliberately reopen them as a famed 'sequel hook'. This is as true for Marvel movies as it is for slasher films. In horror series, this often means that the monster is defeated, but this vanquishing is an illusion or only temporary. As Jones notes, the *Nightmare* films are uniquely equipped to suggest this because they borrow their structure from that of a recurring nightmare.

Drew Beard reads the *Nightmare* series through medieval dream visions, which serve 'to simultaneously destabilize cultural assumptions and contain dissent …, providing the reader with a wider range of extractable meanings while at the same time placing limits upon the discourse emerging from the text' (1). Beard even suggests that 'all horror films can be seen as evocative of the dream vision: the viewer witnesses the events, guided through the film not by the guide of the dream vision, but the apparatus of cinema itself' (3–4). He argues that the franchise is more ideological than is generally acknowledged, using its dream sequences to comment on a range of Reagan-era issues, including family and the 'War on Drugs'. He argues that Freddy functions as a version of the *oraculum*, a dream figure of authority, here presented as the darkest face of authority, 'committing violent acts that are felt outside the dream world' (11). In his nightmare spaces, Freddy represents the neoconservative nightmare of 1980s reality, simply with the mask dropped.

I would suggest that we can merge the perceptive readings and approaches of Jones and Beard. This dream vision of neoconservative America becomes even more terrifying in combination with the seriality and loose continuity that Jones identifies in the *Nightmare* series. What emerges is a nightmare that, although it might change, never truly goes away.

Night walking

Horror films evoke dreams and nightmares in a range of different ways that frequently serve aesthetically as subversions of the classical conventions of film form and narrative. I will offer a further note of caution that, for all of the ways nightmares are significant to horror films, the idea of 'horror film as nightmare' can be used too broadly and generally. We certainly can find special roles played by dreams in the horror genre, but I would not be inclined to say that horror films are inevitably nightmarish, except on the banal level that they contain frightening imagery. *Dawn of the Dead* (1978) is a horror film that gains its strength from its plausibility and logical consistency. It is not abstract or surreal in its style, but clear, grounded, and classical. The space of the mall, the film's principal setting, is clear and comprehensible, as might be the case in the war film; it contrasts sharply with the hotel in *The Shining*, the space of which is baffling, disorienting, and illogical. To return to the concept of cine-genres, it might be said that although both are horror films, *The Shining* falls into the broad category of 'dream horror', with *Dawn of the Dead* falling outside of it.

I will end with a lesser-known example that straddles the lines between horror, the Gothic, and the oneiric in fascinating ways – William Castle's *The Night Walker* (1964).[5] It is the melodramatic story of Irene Trent (Barbara Stanwyck), a bored middle-aged woman who is married to a cruel, rich, blind man. Irene has recurring dreams about a handsome young man, and her husband suspects her, wrongly, of infidelity. After her husband dies in an accident, she finds her dream seems to blur with reality. *The Night Walker* begins a set of jarring, surreal images, including numerous Daliesque eyes, accompanied by a ponderous narration: 'What are dreams? What do they mean? What do you know about the secret world you visit when you sleep? Strange eyes. Strange faces. Creatures that haunt our nightmares. Sometimes we watch them, and sometimes they watch us.' The narration lasts several minutes and ends with the statement, 'When you dream you wander into another world where everything is strange and terrifying. A world that exists only at night. When you dream, you become a night walker.' This narration is accompanied by the sound of a woman's scream. A hand then grasps an eyeball and thrusts it to the front of the screen, combining several images from *Un Chien Andalou*.

The eye/hand motif also appears on the poster for *The Night Walker*, directly over a design resembling Henri Fuseli's iconic painting *The Nightmare* (1781).[6] It shows a gargoyle-esque monster perched over a sleeping woman in a flowing nightgown who could not look less like Barbara Stanwyck's character in the film itself. Together, the combined Dalí and Fuseli motifs combine into the promise of a Gothic oneiric spectacle supreme. However, within the film, a putative dream sequence turns out not to be a dream at all, but an elaborately staged spectacle meant to exploit Irene's weaknesses for the all too quotidian motivation of separating her from her inheritance. This is perhaps the point: in the end, the 'creatures' are

Figure 10.5 Various dream motifs combine in the poster for *The Night Walker* (William Castle Productions)

revealed to be unscrupulous, greedy humans, and the film's nightmare space is actually American patriarchal capitalism. This idea maps neatly onto Robin Wood's formulation of horror films as a 'collective nightmare'. In dream horror, it often seems that dreams are not places of fundamental freedom and unbounded imagination, as the Surrealists held, but rather places where the horrors of the world are concentrated. They show us something that we need not wake up from but wake up to. It is just as Rosemary (Mia Farrow), crying out in *Rosemary's Baby*, articulates: 'This is no dream! This is really happening!'

Notes

1 In their more pleasant, escapist aspect, dreams play a parallel role in fantasy, for example, William Shakespeare's *A Midsummer Night's Dream* (1595–6) or Vincent Ward's *What Dreams May Come* (1998).
2 It is also striking that Ferry's specific descriptions of *King Kong* rhyme so well with *A Nightmare on Elm Street*, key recurring motifs of which include a body impossibly altering – our first full view of Freddy in the first film shows his arms stretching impossibly wide – and being chased by an implacable foe.
3 I read this film in more detail in Leeder (2022).
4 See Anderson (2018) for a reading of Jewishness in *An American Werewolf in London*.
5 See Petitti (2018) for a reading of *The Night Walker*.
6 Fuseli's painting is also cited directly in Ken Russell's film *Gothic* (1986), about the 'Haunted Summer' that inspired Mary Shelley (Natasha Richardson) to write *Frankenstein*. It served as the basis for the poster art for that film as well.

Works cited

Aldana Reyes, Xavier. *Gothic Cinema*. Routledge, 2020.
An American Werewolf in London. Dir. John Landis. PolyGram Pictures, 1981.
Anderson, Daniel. 'A Terrifyingly Fragile Border: Jewish Assimilation in *An American Werewolf in London*.' *Monsters of Film, Fiction and Fable: The Cultural Links Between the Human and the Inhuman*, edited by Lisa Wenger Bro, Crystal O'Leary-Davidson, and Mary Ann Gareis. Cambridge Scholars Publishing, 2018, pp. 363–77.
The Avenging Conscience. Dir. D. W. Griffith. Majestic Motion Picture Company, 1914.
Baudry, Jean-Louis. 'Ideological Effects of the Basic Cinematographic Apparatus.' *Narrative, Apparatus, Ideology*, edited by Philip Rosen. Columbia University Press, 1986, pp. 286–98.

Beard, Drew. 'Strange Bedfellows: The Chaucerian Dream Vision and the Neoconservative *Nightmare.*' *The Irish Journal of Gothic and Horror Studies*, vol. 8, 2010, pp. 2–16.

Boo! Dir. Albert Demond. Universal Pictures, 1932.

Botz-Bornstein, Thorsten. *Films and Dreams: Tarkovsky, Bergman, Skuroiv, Kubrick, and Wong Kar-Wai.* Lexington Books, 2008.

Britton, Andrew, Richard Lippe, Tony Williams, and Robin Wood, eds. *The American Nightmare: Essays on the Horror Film.* Festival of Festivals, 1979.

The Cabinet of Dr. Caligari. Dir. Robert Weine. Decla-Film, 1920.

Cantor, Joanne. '"I'll Never Have a Clown in My House Again" – Why Horror Movie Live On.' *Poetics Today*, vol. 25, no. 2, Summer 2004, pp. 283–304.

Canudo, Ricciotto. 'Reflections on the Seventh Art.' *French Film Theory and Criticism: A History/Anthology, 1907–1939*, vol. 1, edited by Richard Abel. Princeton University Press, 1988, pp. 291–303.

Carroll, Noël. *Mystifying Movies: Fads & Fallacies in Contemporary Film Theory.* Columbia University Press, 1988.

Castle, Terry. *The Female Thermometer: Eighteenth-Century Culture and the Invention of the Uncanny.* Oxford University Press, 1995.

Cat People. Dir. Jacques Tourneur. RKO Radio Pictures, 1942.

Un Chien Andalou. Dirs. Luis Buñuel and Salvador Dalí. Les Grands Films Classiques, 1929.

Clasen, Mathias. *A Very Nervous Person's Guide to Horror Movies.* Oxford University Press, 2021.

Dawn of the Dead. Dir. George A. Romero. Laurel Group, 1978.

Dead of Night. Dir. Robert Hamer et al. Ealing Studios, 1945.

Epstein, Jean. 'Visual Fabric.' *Jean Epstein: Critical Essays and New Translations*, edited by Sarah Keller and Jason N. Paul. Amsterdam University Press, 2012, pp. 252–6.

Ferry, Jean. 'Concerning *King Kong.*' *The Shadow and Its Shadow: Surrealist Writings on the Cinema*, 3rd edition, edited by Paul Hammond. City Lights Books, 2000, pp. 161–5.

The Fog. Dir. John Carpenter. Debra Hill Productions, 1980.

Guerrier, Simon. 'Those Horrible Nightmares Again and Again.' *Insight*, vol. 2, no. 10, 2015, pp. 873–5.

Gunning, Tom. '"Those Drawn with a Very Fine Camel's Hair Brush": The Origins of Film Genres.' *Iris*, vol. 19, 1995, pp. 49–61.

Heard, Mervyn. *Phantasmagoria: The Secret Life of the Magic Lantern.* The Projection Box, 2006.

Hoekstra, Steven J., Richard Jackson Harris, and Angela L. Helmick. 'Autobiographical Memories About the Experience of Seeing Frightening Movies in Childhood.' *Media Psychology*, vol. 1, 1999, pp. 117–40.

Jay, Martin. *Downcast Eyes: The Denigration of Vision in Twentieth-Century Century French Thought.* University of California Press, 1993.

Jones. Steven. 'If Nancy Doesn't Wake Up Screaming: The *Elm Street* Series as Recurring Nightmare.' *Horror Franchise Cinema*, edited by Mark McKenna and William Proctor. Routledge, 2022, pp. 81–93.

King Kong. Dir. Merian C. Cooper and Ernest B. Schoedsack. RKO Radio Pictures, 1933.

Kracauer, Siegfried. *From Caligari to Hitler: A Psychological History of the German Film*. Princeton University Press, 1947.

Leeder, Murray. 'The Birth of an Evil Thought: The Gothic in Silent-Era Cinema.' *Twentieth Century Gothic: An Edinburgh Companion*, edited by Bernice M. Murphy and Sorcha Ní Fhlainn. Edinburgh University Press, 2022, pp. 83–98.

Leeder, Murray. *The Modern Supernatural and the Beginnings of Cinema*. Palgrave Macmillan, 2017.

Münsterberg, Hugo. *The Photoplay: A Psychological Study*. D. Appleton and Company, 1916.

The Night Walker. Dir. William Castle. William Castle Productions, 1964.

A Nightmare on Elm Street 3: Dream Warriors. Dir. Chuck Russell. New Line Cinema, 1987.

Petitti, Michael. '"Where Did Our Love Go?": The Case of William Castle's *The Night Walker*.' *ReFocus: The Films of William Castle*, edited by Murray Leeder. Edinburgh University Press, 2018, pp. 189–205.

Powdermaker, Hortense. *Hollywood, the Dream Factory: An Anthropologist Looks at the Movie-Makers*. Secker & Warburg, 1950.

Rascaroli, Laura. 'Oneiric Metaphor in Film Theory.' *KINEMA*, 2002, n.p.

Secrets of a Soul. Dir. G. W. Pabst. UFA GmbH, 1926.

Singer, Ben. *Melodrama and Modernity: Early Sensational Cinema and Its Contexts*. Columbia University Press, 2001.

Tudor, Andrew. 'Why Horror? The Peculiar Pleasures of a Popular Genre.' *Cultural Studies*, vol. 11, no. 3, 1997, pp. 443–63.

Waxworks. Dir. Paul Leni, Leo Birinski. Nepture-Film A.G., 1924.

Wood, Robin. 'An Introduction to the American Horror Film.' *The American Nightmare*, edited by Andrew Britton, Richard Lippe, Tony Williams, and Robin Wood. Festival of Festivals, 1979, pp. 7–28.

11

Building the Gothic channel: dreams, spectral memories, and temporal disjunctions in *The Witcher*

Lorna Piatti-Farnell

While ostensibly presented as a fantasy series, *The Witcher* (Netflix, 2019) displays many elements that intersect heavily with the Gothic as a cultural form. Based on *The Witcher* books written by Polish author Andrzej Sapkowski, as well as its video game adaptations, the Netflix series capitalises on a number of genre-bending techniques and is filled with mutating monsters, dark magic, and frightening transformations. The horror hidden within the narrative often enters the scene through the flickering images and fragmented storylines of dreams. These commonly signal the discovery of buried secrets, whose unthinkable abject nature – from incest to murder and bodily torture – is moulded to the narrative in the form of layers of Gothic storytelling. In *The Witcher*, dreams assume many forms: at times, they morph into nightmares and act as a channel into a painful and torturous past, which re-surfaces to cast a dark shadow into the present; at other times, they are moulded into fever-induced daydreams, which question the very notion of reality and reside in the liminal space between the material and the immaterial. At other times still, dreams are presented as metaphorical notions, embodying that which one cannot have, while also, and often discordantly, engendering feelings of alienation and disturbance. Overall, dreams function in *The Witcher* as the ideal device for juxtaposing the concepts of humanity, Otherness, and complicated notions of evil, and engaging with questions relevant to this nexus of ideas.

Working as metaphorical channels, dreams in *The Witcher* help to bridge the gap between the Gothic and fantasy genres, constructing the much-needed, yet inevitably undependable, foundations for worlds and myth. Focusing primarily on Season 1 of the show, this chapter considers the presence of dreams in *The Witcher* as Gothic conduits, exploring how, through the notion of vision and representation, the narrative timelines of past, present, and future blend, mingle, and merge. Entangled as they are with the concept of magic, dreams mediate and subvert history, rendering it changeable and unreliable. Dreams uncover the very process of remembering as fraught, uncertain, and marked by spectrality. As such, they function as sites of the uncanny, challenging the seemingly 'normal' nature of the everyday and transforming it into a haunted, supernaturalised reality. Dreams, it is also suggested, reverberate across the multiple storylines of *The Witcher*, constructing layered interpretations of narrative that rely on the very process of dreaming as a Gothic storytelling device. In so doing, the dreams of *The Witcher* also provide veiled critiques of real-life cultural conventions, as 'magic' brings about nightmarish experiences of body modification. The boundaries between reality and illusion are challenged: time and space become channels for Gothic disjunctions, and the 'real' hauntings are shown not to be the ones we find in dreams, but the ones inhabiting our everyday.

The Witcher follows the story of Geralt of Rivia (Henry Cavill) as the titular character. Witchers are a guild of enhanced human beings who fight beasts and monsters for a living. A Witcher's abilities are said to be developed through magical rituals at a young age, in a process that is known to be physically and emotionally exhausting. Geralt's destiny becomes entangled with that of several characters and their socio-political schemes. The majority of the plot in Season 1 revolves around Geralt's eventual meeting with the young Princess Cirilla (Freya Allan) – or, Ciri – whose fate had been tied to the Witcher's. The linking happened long before Ciri's birth, through what is known as the Law of Surprise: this is a custom that is invoked when one person comes to another's aid, but the latter has nothing to give in return as a thank you. The Law of Surprise stipulates that the saved instead offers a form of treasure that they do not expect to have, or do not know they have yet. In the case of Geralt, at some point in the past, he provided aid to the knight Duny (Bart Edwards) and his bride Pavetta (Gaia Mondadori) – a princess of the city of Cintra – who will later be revealed to be Ciri's parents. Geralt reluctantly accepts the Law of Surprise as payment for his service; once it becomes clear that Pavetta was already unknowingly pregnant with Ciri at the time, the child becomes Geralt's 'surprise', and their destinies are so intertwined. Although Geralt does not express any desire to claim Ciri as his own child once she is born, he still swears to watch over and protect her as she grows up.

The storytelling structure in Season 1 of *The Witcher* is non-linear, creating a narrative flexibility that aptly opens the way for the exploration of many sub-plots, and only resolves its confusion in the eighth and final episode, while leaving events open for subsequent seasons. Dreams are omnipresent in *The Witcher*. Even though the label of 'dream' is questionable and unreliable, this term seems to best describe a number of the events that take place. Indeed, as is frequently the case in the narrative of the series, a certain layer of doubt is cast over the nature of the dreams themselves, and the viewers are often left wondering whether what they are seeing is a dream, vision, hallucination, or memory. The narrative snippets that are commonly associated with dreaming are presented in *The Witcher* in conjunction with episodes of sleeping, so their interpretation as dreams is possible – even if not fully confirmed – by the narrative itself. Dreams here become especially significant, precisely because of 'their very liminality' (Shulman and Stroumsa 6).

Overall, the frequent use of dreams as a narrative device, with the aim of manipulating timelines, is unsurprising. The existing scholarship on the meaning and characteristics of dreams, especially from a cultural perspective, underscores the relationship between dreams, dreaming, and our understanding of reality. Within this context, there has been particular emphasis on the part played by dreams in constructing our notions of time, space, and memory, and the relationship that these hold in relation to communication and identity. David Shulman and Guy Stroumsa, in particular, have enquired into whether dreams, as narrative and cognitive entities, either 'suppress or create time' (6). This question interrogates the place occupied by dreams in our construction of our pasts. Notably, while the process of dreaming happens in real time, so to speak, our experience of dreams is sited primarily in our retrospective remembering. And that recollection often sits in the liminal zone between sleep and wakefulness. This approach is made clear in *The Witcher*, as dreams inform the way in which the whole narrative plays with time. Because of this, one might be tempted to suggest that dreams in *The Witcher* construct their own narrative timeline, existing both in conjunction with our actual life and memories and as separate entities that maintain a firm hold on both past and present.

Blurry timelines

Although not fully relayed through the channel of dreams, the entire narrative of *The Witcher* maintains a dream-like quality throughout. The series often skips between disparate timelines, shifting its focus to different characters and plots, recurrently. For the most part, this has a confusing effect, and it is often difficult to discern the exact chronological placement of events, which are only brought together in the final episode of Season 1. This timeline skipping is not casual, as it aids the construction of multiple side narratives, and in so doing is able to provide more information. The strange narrative organisation also recalls, conceptually, the set-up of a fantasy game, which often provides offshoots from the main overarching storyline into side-quests for the characters. As Daniel Mackay suggests, the role-playing nature of the game narrative is 'less dependent upon a single character than a traditional story is' (166). The storytelling direction and characterisation of Netflix's *The Witcher* are perhaps unorthodox for a serialised television-style set-up, but fully in keeping with the world of fantasy gaming. Through this deviation, the narrative experimentation of *The Witcher* as a series openly recalls, both conceptually and aesthetically, *The Witcher* games on which it is based. This is especially true of its third instalment, *The Wild Hunt* (2011).

In addition to giving a nod to the game context, the narrative of *The Witcher* as a series is also ideally suited to channelling Gothic elements. Skipping around between timelines is not only evocative of the fragmented and selective nature of a dream, but it also helps to uncover distant, ungraspable, and otherwise disconnected events. It is precisely in this space that the narrative engages with Gothic storytelling, bringing into the foreground notions of the traumatic and the haunted via the exploitation of established Western cultural prohibitions. It should not be surprising to find the idea of monstrous realities entangled with alienating forms of storytelling, considering that, as David Punter suggests, a certain loss of self-integrity is to be found in 'the taboo quality of many of the themes to which the Gothic addresses itself – incest, rape, [and] various forms of transgression of the boundaries between the natural and the human' (16). Indeed, many of the events revealed by the untraditional sub-plot and dreamy set-up – which are seemingly narratively distant from the primary storyline of Geralt allegedly fulfilling 'his destiny' as the protector of Ciri – openly bring to the surface buried secrets and otherwise forgotten memories. Examples of this include Geralt's side-quest to eliminate the Striga, a monstrous creature who is revealed to be the cursed progeny of the incestuous affair between King Folstaf and his sister, Ada. Indeed, the majority of the narrative side-quests are focused on taboo occurrences, which, by being presented in a dream-like form of storytelling, become even more gothicised as part of the broader narrative. This representation is in keeping with the Gothic's general directional discourses, evoking a certain response – often characterised by fear and repulsion – 'through its relentless re-fashioning of archetypal taboos ... from incest to necrophilia' (Germanà 13).

The series, however, does more than simply evoke dream-like qualities in its storytelling. The focus also falls specifically on narratives taking place within actual dreams. The first instance of dreaming in *The Witcher* occurs in the opening episode, when we are introduced to Geralt himself, and his encounter with Renfri (Emma Appleton), the disgraced warrior princess whose death and memory will haunt the Witcher throughout the series. Although Geralt and Renfri do meet within the waking world, so to speak, their subsequent night encounter carries the qualities of both a dream and a vision. It is during this time that Renfri reveals a prophecy to Geralt, foreshadowing his destined entanglement with Princess Cirilla in later episodes. The memory of the dream will also cast a shadow over Geralt's romantic relationship with his later long-term lover, Yennefer (Anya

Chalotra). The cinematography and narrative structure of the night encounter between Geralt and Renfri is suggestive of a dream, as Geralt is later shown to be waking up in the morning. Nonetheless, the blurry atmosphere and muddled timelines of their encounter, not to mention its prophetic and distinctly magical nature, also place the narrative in the realm of a vision. As the episode shows Geralt and Renfri talking and making love during the night, there is also a possibility that what the viewers are shown is actually a memory that happened in real time. The dream-like narrative is filled with secrets and revelations, uncovering the most vulnerable side of Geralt, and presenting both his fears and desires in one seductively confusing package.

Indeed, it is precisely the blurred characteristics of the encounter between Geralt and Renfri, and the virtual impossibility of discerning its true nature, that make it significant. This is where the narrative of *The Witcher* exposes itself as unorthodox in its approach to storytelling and presents its propensity to play with timelines and history. The instance also foregrounds the abilities of dreams to mediate between timelines, narratives, and characters, proving to be the ideal and most obvious medium for expressing both uncertainty and revelation. Dreams in *The Witcher* are able to reveal both 'the present and the past' as well as 'the composition of the dreaming subject' (Shulman and Stroumsa 3), the latter being Geralt himself. The prophetic ability of dreams to reveal situations while also acting as a mediating channel between not only the past, the present, and the future, but also vision and reality, is also echoed in the very final episode of the series where Ciri is shown dreaming of her upcoming first meeting with Geralt, which had been prophesied by Renfri at the beginning of the story. This narrative dénouement between the first and final episodes places dreams at the centre of

Figure 11.1 Geralt's encounter with Renfri, Season 1, Episode 1, *The Witcher* (Netflix)

the narrative structure, positioning them as gothicised entities that reveal secrets and knowledge, and are able to build bridges between timelines and realities.

Through its play with storylines and employment of dreams as an often alienating narrative tool, *The Witcher* provides us with a highly gothicised version of time. As Isabella van Elferen suggests, 'Gothic time is always out of joint' (12). Its shadowy atmospheres testify to its interplay with haunted storylines, as the 'ghosts of various pasts' bring to the surface 'repressed fears and desires' (12). Dreams in *The Witcher* are spectral, but that spectrality does not necessarily rely on the presence of ghosts, which are actually conspicuously absent from the series. What is clearly present, however, are the metaphorical ghosts of the past, which resurface in dreams and, as a result, make the whole narrative ghostly. Spectrality, as Fredric Jameson has suggested, does not simply 'involve the conviction that ghosts exist or that the past (or maybe even the future they offer to prophecy) is still very much at work, within the living present' (39). Instead, as Jameson goes on to say, spectrality opens the way for seeing that 'the living present is scarcely as self-sufficient as it claims to be', and that 'we would do well not to count on its density and solidity', which might 'betray us' (39). This challenge to the present, as advanced through blurry timelines and the recurrent use of dreams in the narrative, is evident in *The Witcher*. Time in the series is not linear, and dreams contribute to its continuous sense of disaffection from the present by the addition of tangential timelines sited in memory, and prophetic moments belonging to an unidentified future.

Buried memories

While the narrative of *The Witcher* remains dreamy and evanescent, and the suggestion of dreams as prophetic channels is put forward on multiple occasions, the most significant dream incident in the series is found in the very final episode of Season 1, with another of Geralt's own dreams. The circumstances through which the dream comes about are especially noteworthy and expose the Gothic nature of the incident. While travelling at night, Geralt encounters a farming merchant who is clearing away the victims of a recent battle from the road. The atmosphere is already appropriately Gothic: the two men meet in the middle of a forest surrounded by a thick mist and darkness. Although he is unfazed by the bodies of the dead soldiers and civilians, Geralt is immediately alerted to a certain eeriness in the air and cautions the merchant to leave. The Witcher warns the merchant of something that may attack, whose bite would kill him immediately. Within seconds, the eerie atmosphere materialises into horror, as reanimated, zombified corpses emerge from the ground and attack Geralt. In spite of the Witcher's distinctly developed fighting abilities, one zombie is able to land a bite on Geralt's leg. As a result of his magically enhanced body, Geralt does not immediately die from the wound, but is instead taken by a fever and collapses shortly thereafter. The merchant then places Geralt on his cart to transport him to his farm where he can receive proper medical attention.

It is during this journey that the dream sequence occurs. Geralt is plunged into a feverish sleep, where he dreams of his childhood. Through this, the Witcher's deep-rooted anxieties and fears are brought to the surface for the viewer to witness. One can see here the role of dreams in connection to cultural notions of both anxiety and memory, as they serve to 'articulate issues and assumptions', implicitly or otherwise, about the nature of our 'public and private' selves (Shulman and Stroumsa 3). It is indeed significant that memories of the past should not only come forward through a dream – or, perhaps, a hallucination – but also be brought back into awareness by the bite of a zombie, a creature that belongs, appropriately, to the Gothic horror framework. The metaphorical use of the reanimated corpses emerging from the ground signals the presence of buried memories and, possibly, secrets coming back to the surface of knowledge. As the zombies resurface, so do Geralt's memories and the emotional challenges they bring. This set-up renders the dream a gothicised entity and builds a connection between dreaming, remembering, and a haunted notion of the past. The dream establishes a connection between what is known and what is unknown – or, to be more precise, what has been forgotten. In this, *The Witcher* joins a widespread cultural approach to dreams as able to offer a 'constant balance between the private world of latent images, fear, and hopes, and outside reality' (Shulman and Stroumsa 6). The images that emerge in Geralt's dream are somewhat hazy and unclear and, once again, do not fit the usual bounds of linear storytelling. At times, it is difficult to discern the nature of the occurrences that are being projected as Geralt's mind wanders in his feverish state.

The dream begins with memories of his childhood and the time he spent with his mother, who was gifted in the magical arts. It is significant that the memories that appear to be relayed in the dream actually show Geralt as a child. The focus on childhood particularly brings into the foreground the Gothic nature of the process, including the context of the dream itself. Indeed, it is particularly through the idea of the child as a metaphor that the dream comes into its own status as a Gothic channel. As Margarita Georgieva suggests, 'the obsession with memory' as connected to the child is 'characteristic of the Gothic' (109). Conceptually speaking, there is a connection between the child and the practice of remembering, as adults place

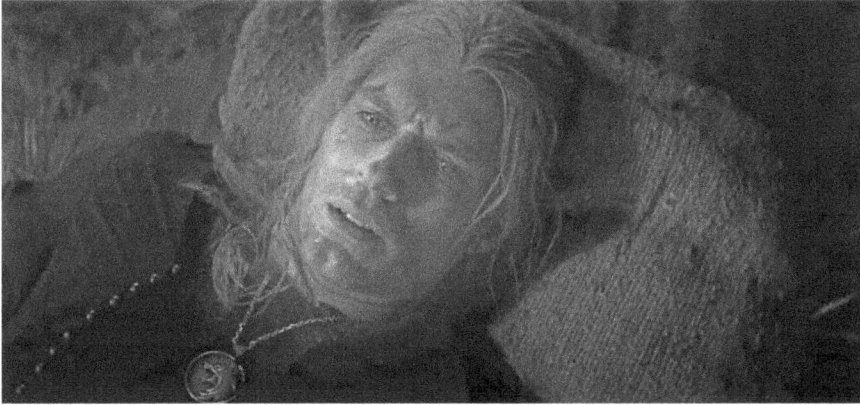

Figure 11.2 A feverish Geralt, Season 1, Episode 8, *The Witcher* (Netflix)

a particular emphasis on the events that happened in childhood. Traditional Freudian psychoanalysis has underscored the importance of the events belonging to childhood, but the connection goes well beyond the psychoanalytical sphere and extends into the cultural framework of the everyday.

Remembering childhood memories belongs to a process of self-identification that hinges on experiences of both happiness and unpleasantness, not to mention unavoidable issues of nostalgia. The latter is evident in Geralt's childhood memories of happy times with his mother, but it is also challenged by the fact that the narrative delves further into the traumatic recollection of abandonment. The dream here functions as the ideal conduit for bringing together the intersectional narratives of childhood, memory, and trauma. It is through this intersectionality that the dream emerges specifically as Gothic. The dream itself is, one might argue, a conceptual Gothic ruin, which is cast as a site of remembrance and unburied secrets. Through the slippery unreliability of memory, the dream transforms into a metaphysical location where remembering takes place, becoming akin to what Georgieva terms the 'Gothic edifice' (109). This particular physical location – often exemplified in a ruined building or ancestral home – is especially recognisable in early Gothic narratives, such as Horace Walpole's *The Castle of Otranto* (1764). Known to channel moments of remembrance, the Gothic edifice also acts as a 'receptacle of history' (Georgieva 109). By inhabiting the dream, buried memories re-enter consciousness, just as would occur if one were to physically enter an old building connected to one's past. As such, the memories of childhood in dreams become particularly compatible with the Gothic framework. Through this, the dream itself exists in *The Witcher* as a Gothic repository, continually carrying, as a gothicised physical location would, a 'substantial, material, albeit deteriorated message from the past' (109). As a channel, the dream not only houses memories but also maintains a transformative property in rendering identities for both the child and adult Geralt. The dream, therefore, exists as a paradoxically tangible and re-enactable conduit for past events, uncovering the significance of memory, and occurring not as that which has been lost, but as a reminder of that which remains.

The narrative circumstances of Geralt's illness flicker between the dream's memories of childhood – as a mixture of both nostalgia and trauma – and the mysterious presence of a healer who seems to appear at Geralt's side as he lies in his feverish state. The series plays with perception in this instance, not clarifying for some time whether the healer is actually there, a part of Geralt's dream, or a hallucination. The healer is ultimately revealed to be Visenna (Frida Gustavsson), Geralt's own mother. While not overtly communicated, the context of the narrative strongly suggests that Visenna may have simply and serendipitously come across the merchant and his travelling companion by the side of the road, stopping then to aid the ailing Geralt. However, this seemingly established narrative is rendered unreliable as Geralt appears to recognise a young Visenna as his mother, and begins to remember his pain and suffering after she abandoned him as a boy so that he could undergo the requisite training to become a Witcher. Memories of this painful time in Geralt's childhood flicker in and out of the narrative, making it impossible to know whether Geralt is dreaming or awake. As the conversation between Visenna and Geralt becomes heated, she refuses to continue speaking, instructing Geralt that it is 'time to sleep'. Simultaneously, however, Visenna also declares that she was 'just a dream', as Geralt unexpectedly wakes up from sleep. This revelation does very little to establish certainty in terms of the narrative trajectory. Trust is called into question, and one is left wondering about the reality of these episodes. By playing with the notions of dreaming and wakefulness, *The Witcher* challenges the reliability of storytelling, making it difficult to decipher what is true and what is imagined – or 'dreamt' – in relation to both narrative and character interactions. This in-between state engenders confusion and alienation, playing with repressed and uncertain memories and subverting the established flow of experience. In being disruptive, unreliable, and anxiety-inducing for both the characters and viewers, Geralt's experiences are also gothicised. By being declared a dream by Visenna, the exchange between Geralt and his mother, which was seemingly relayed as part of the wakeful narrative, is made undependable. The hybridised depiction of dream, memory, and reality that comprises the storytelling engenders a sublime reaction of horror and fear, capturing a 'disjunction between idea and representation' and the uncanny feeling that such a disjunction entails (Mishra 45). Through the introduction of possible dream interactions, which are never fully confirmed or denied within the narrative, *The Witcher* disrupts the historical flow of time and, in the process, denies the certainty of what is perceived as reality.

As far as the trajectory of *The Witcher* goes, dreams exist on the same narrative continuum as the parameters of wakeful storytelling. Not only do they occur in parallel, but they also advance the narrative by providing further information that shapes present events. As such, dreams are not additions, existing somewhere in a disconnected lateral status to the wakeful narratives. Instead, they are concomitant and complementary, and, at times, they even move the elements of storytelling in different directions by either providing more clarity or blurring the certainty of events as perceived by both the characters and the viewers. In light of this, it is possible to suggest that dreams in *The Witcher* exist in the same storytelling plane as events in the waking world. They are not limited to relaying remembered information and buried secrets, but to transforming these elements into an integral part of the overall narrative structure. By allowing an entry-point into the otherwise inaccessible 'dark passages' of the mind, dreams here make a virtue of the Gothic framework, allowing both writers and viewers to 'indulge in a taste for the uncanny' and 'to play with fantasies of impossible desire' (Samuel 381). This philosophical approach to dreams, which somewhat negates the long-standing psychoanalytical view that perceives them as additional entities, uncovers the practice of dreaming as intrinsically connected to the processes of meaning-making that exist in the wakeful world. As Jennifer M. Windt suggests, 'placing dreams on a continuum' with the 'spontaneous thoughts of wakefulness' helps to 'unlock the cognitive and mnemonic process' that happens during sleep (xx). That is to say, understanding dreams as part of the psychological processes of wakefulness uncovers how the gothicised practice of remembering buried secrets contributes to the process of awareness. Through this detailed and strategic treatment of dreams, *The Witcher* exposes the nature of both memories and identity creation as profoundly interconnected entities, where the experiences of alienation, marginalisation, and powerlessness – which seemingly characterise the status of non-wakefulness – exist as integral parts of each other within the logical processes of being and becoming.

Painful, elusive, and strangely real

Discussing the relationship between dreaming and wakefulness, Windt argues that dreams are 'strangely elusive' (xv). In their status as flickering images, dreams are inevitably ungraspable and often occupy a liminal space, somewhere between consciousness and unconsciousness. The elusiveness of dreaming is further reinforced by the fact that dreams rely on memories, both in terms of being conceived and generated, and in terms of being rec-ollected after sleep has ended. Dreaming, in this sense, involves 'profound alterations in conscious experience' and plays with forms of knowledge and behaviour (Windt xv). The liminal elusiveness of dreams is channelled in *The Witcher* as a way to build a bridge between past and present, and between memory and real-time experience. The narrative challenges the notion of consciousness by positioning Geralt's feverish recollections and exchanges somewhere between the states of dreaming and being awake. The continuous movement between narrative realities poses questions as to the validity of what is being experienced. Geralt's dreams remain elusive, and so does his grasp on memories. The latter is also a reflection on the intended viewers' experiences as no certainties are provided as to the direction of either wakefulness or dreaming. Indeed, the conditions of dreaming and being awake are presented as fully entangled, so it is very difficult to tell the two statuses apart, as *The Witcher* challenges the very notion of 'dreaming' as a separate activity.

It is important to remember that traditional psychoanalysis – Freudian and Jungian, in particular – has designated dreams as belonging to the uncon-scious; this approach has commonly also extended to repressed memories and desires (Windt xviii), putting both practices of dreaming and remem-bering within the sleeping realm as fully immaterial. This understanding of dreaming is certainly long-standing and continues to remain strong in both psychoanalytical discourses and the popular imagination. Nevertheless, the representation of dreams in *The Witcher* challenges the commonly under-stood status of dreams as belonging only to the unconscious. In its desire to blur the boundary between dreaming and wakefulness, past and present, and desire and fear, *The Witcher* tacitly suggests an understanding of dream-ing as a form of conscious experience. While this delineation of dreams as conscious entities may come across as somewhat oxymoronic at first, one needs to consider the delineation of dreams as having a form of experiential character in the series or, to put it simply, their ability to develop narrative trajectories in their own right. Geralt's dream about his apparent childhood experiences is strangely mixed with a subsequent dream about his mother in the present day, as the latter then merges with the wakeful storyline and makes direct references to the experiences of the Witcher as he lies feverishly on the ground. Although the events in 'the real world' seemingly progress without either Geralt's or the viewer's knowledge – with the Witcher being shown to have moved locations at some point, in an action that appears diegetically, but off-screen – a parallel progression of the narrative takes place in the bounds of his dream. The shift in location, from the back of a cart to the foot of a tree, appears in the dream as well, mirroring the events happening in the wakeful narrative. This move is pivotal in highlighting the 'conscious' nature of the dream itself as inseparable from reality. Indeed, the events taking place in Geralt's dream naturally deviate from the real world, but they also rely on their own internal logic. In this, the dream creates a fork in time and reality, providing a co-existing set of narratives and events. It is precisely through this temporal disjunction that it is possible to see Geralt's dream as being a form of conscious progress – a narrative projection that exists in real time, and also constructs its own parallel form of storytelling.

Further evidence of the dream's conscious status can be found in the experiences that it carries and the effects it has on Geralt's emotional state. Windt suggests that dreams can be 'intensely emotional and subjectively feel realistic' (xv). This is indeed the case for Geralt's dream of his present-day mother, as his exchange with her touches his own painful experiences of training as a Witcher – both physical and psychological – and uncovers the suffering of being abandoned to meet a potentially deadly fate. Geralt's dream is so realistic that it is difficult to distinguish it from simple memories and recollections, or, indeed, the events happening in the present. Although the exchange with Visenna could simply be the working of Geralt's imagination, its emotional effects tangibly continue after he awakens. Later, the memory of the dream of his mother will also influence how Geralt pursues his relationship with young Cirilla, who is placed in his care.

After witnessing the dream of Visenna, it becomes clear to the viewers why Geralt has a vested interest in looking after the young princess and would never consider abandoning her to a future of loneliness. The words uttered by Visenna to Geralt in the dream – 'People linked by destiny will always find each other. We have to cling to something'– drive his actions. As

Figure 11.3 Geralt and Ciri embrace, Season 1, Episode 8, *The Witcher* (Netflix)

a result, the dream of Visenna acts conjointly as a form of fortune-telling, a memory, and a cognitive instructor for Geralt's subsequent decisions. In blending emotions and timelines, Geralt's dream is provided with a conscious dimension in what has traditionally been regarded as an unconscious space. Geralt's dream of his mother is made tangible by the depth of his emotions and the pain of his previously buried memories, as well as the certainty of his future actions. The dream here becomes an unexpectedly conscious experience that brings forward tangible 'thoughts, images, and emotions during sleep' (Windt xviii).

Nevertheless, and in spite of the fact that dreaming can be seen to belong, ontologically, to the same continuum as the wakeful state, what persists is the distinct unreliability of information provided by the dreams themselves. It is true that dreams complement wakefulness by engaging with memories and, on occasion, providing grounds for the further scrutiny of wakeful knowledge. However, as Windt argues, it is also commonly recorded that dreams 'draw from waking memories in a highly selective fashion' (xx). This selectivity is what solidifies the status of dreams as fringe in *The Witcher* and forms the basis of the interaction between dreaming and wakefulness. Indeed, memories of childhood are presented to Geralt – and the viewers – only through dreaming. The time spent with his mother appears to be happy, but this projection is arbitrary. The trauma of abandonment experienced by Geralt – when he was, unexpectedly, left behind – is also well established, so his recollections of the time spent with his mother are, as a result, painted as a mixture of both resentment and longing. While the dream openly puts forward information that serves the narrative, there is no clear discerning of the difference between truth and wishful thinking. There is a sense in which Geralt's dreaming state may be altering his memories; no certainty is provided by the main narrative in this respect, one way or the other.

While Geralt has no control over the events of the past, his dream exchange with his mother brings to the surface hidden negotiations around his pain and suffering. As it uncovers the trauma of his abandonment, Geralt's dream takes on an uncanny quality and exposes the 'disorder' and 'alien-ness' in experience that the Gothic often seeks to address (Punter and Bronfen 8). *The Witcher* shows the dream as lying somewhere between the conscious and the unconscious, a liminal entity where emotions and experiences are transferred and re-modelled. The narrative employs elements of the Gothic imagination – often relying on repression and painful re-discovery – in order to channel, through the context of dreaming, the subversion of historical reality. Geralt's dream exchange with Visenna appears to be sited in his desire to discover the truth as to why she abandoned him and passed him on to become a Witcher. His questions drive the conversation, as does his desire for answers. As he recalls his experience, the attention falls on the physical pain that was involved in the process, which included magical enhancements and body transformations. Geralt was emotionally and physically scarred by both his mother's neglect and the pain he had to endure in order to become a Witcher against his will – 'Three out of ten boys survive the trial.' Geralt's sorrow and anger, spurred by the recollection of physical pain as well, construct the dream narrative.

This dream exchange also delineates the bounds of historical exchange, as buried memories intermingle with the events of the present. It is possible to suggest here that a further split is taking place: not only in the historical trajectory of the narrative but also in Geralt as a subject. His consciousness is divided between the trauma of his childhood and his current status as an adult Witcher. The dream channels a fragmentation of the self, as much as it allows a disruption of the spatio-temporal continuum. As Robert Miles argues, the Gothic represents the self 'in a condition of rupture, disjunction, fragmentation' (2). It is precisely in that disruption that the question of disorder ensues, alongside the challenge to both emotional and historical certainties. In *The Witcher*, Geralt's dream belongs to an openly fragmented space, where the logic of both past and present does not apply. The shifts in recollection and emotion clash with the reality of the exchange with Visenna, as the dream neither provides answers to Geralt's questions nor eases his past suffering. Indeed, Visenna instructs him 'to move on', leaving his painful memories behind – the latter being, of course, a rather arduous task. By providing a disjunction in time, the dream opens the way to questions regarding the veracity of experience. The truth, however, remains

Figure 11.4 An angry Geralt confronts his mother, Season 1, Episode 8, *The Witcher* (Netflix)

ungraspable and 'resists discovery' (Crimmins 39). The dream uncovers history itself as an evanescent entity, which is eventually lost to us.

The use of the dream framework to discuss ungraspable matters is not unexpected. In this, however, the dream also takes on a further metaphorical and representational value that goes beyond the narrative bounds of *The Witcher* itself and shows how the series engages with larger cultural preoccupations. Geralt's negotiations of the idea of body enhancement transform the presence of magic in the narrative into a technological conduit, allowing the dream to be interpreted as a critique of broader discourses over body augmentation and loneliness in the real world. As Shulman and Stroumsa suggest, the presence of dreams always signals an engagement with practices of 'decoding' that are 'expressive of culturally specific themes, patterns, tensions, and meanings' (3). It is possible to see Geralt's dream and its recollection of the process of physical enhancement as a veiled interpretation and negotiation of real-life practices of body augmentation – likely in the form of cosmetic surgery – which are often the cause of pain and extreme bodily and emotional suffering. At the heart of this lies the notion of a 'perfect body', a narrative of improvement we recognise all too well as part of contemporary discourses of beauty and image, especially as connected to the world of fitness and advertising on social media platforms. Although, naturally, *The Witcher* is not openly or directly engaging with these preoccupations, the channel of the dream allows its reach to extend beyond its own narrative structure and make a suggestive connection to contemporary cultural phenomena, especially as belonging to the Western context in which the series places itself. The fears and vulnerabilities that are exposed in Geralt by the dream of his mother are indicative of a cultural interpretation of the boundaries between private and public spheres, where the dream represents 'the means to re-establish the constantly shattered equilibrium between the two' (Shulman and Stroumsa 6).

Conclusion

Employed as a storytelling tool – especially in connection to both recollections of the past and divinations of the future – dreams in *The Witcher* rely on their own specific narrative structure: a system of recognition, reference, and, to some extent, cognitive and narrative subversion. The latter is made visible in *The Witcher* and relies precisely on the alienation and disruption that is proper to Gothic narratives, as dreams ostensibly carry messages and revelations that are often unclear to the characters, including Geralt. In the series, dreams become gothicised by bringing about memories that are constantly 'displaced' and 'undetermined' (Shulman and Stroumsa 7). The integrity of the images from the past and the sense of self associated with them become tortured and unreliable. As a result, the certainty of self-identity is ostensibly lost to the dreamer. While dreams in *The Witcher* carry meaning, that meaning is not necessarily made evident at the time of dreaming and is only revealed to both the characters and the viewers at a later moment in time. This interpretative confusion displaces the narrative, transforming it into a form of Gothic storytelling that, to borrow Ruth Bienstock Anolik's words, 'expresses the anxiety provoked' by 'moments of dispossession' (78).

Dreams have voices, but those voices are often difficult to hear in the cacophony of memory and symbolic interaction, as dreams mutate into evocative Gothic sites. Through this confusion, dreams transform into enigmatic representations that play with spatio-temporal coordinates and, in so doing, inevitably expose the fears, anxieties, and obsessions that haunt the dreamer in a multivocal process of cultural communication. The characters in *The Witcher* are often lost in the disrupted language of dreams and, as a result, so are the viewers. While the dreams channel a past that has apparently been suppressed, their moments of outward authenticity, to borrow Jürgen Habermas's words, 'interrupt' the 'continuum of history' and break away the structure of storytelling 'from a homogenous flow' (12). The dreams in *The Witcher* challenge the natural flow of time and, therefore, cast a shadow on the process of historical recollection. As a result, the memories put forward in the dream emerge as wavering, fragmented, and often unreliable.

By merging timelines, and flickering between the narrative structures of past and present, dreams in *The Witcher* act as a 'pivotal site of temporal experimentation' (Ross 3). The idea of time remains intangible. That intangibility, however, seems to be channelled in *The Witcher* in order to provide a process of meaning-making that is transformative in its approach to reality and authentication. Although the general approach to time is to perceive it as a somewhat linear entity, the dreams in *The Witcher* expose it, to borrow Christine Ross's words, as a seemingly 'dis-historicised' notion (3). The dream navigates around knowledge and over hurdles of remembrance, and is not stifled by temporal restrictions. By providing multiple narrative trajectories that eventually merge and blend to form a bewildering, yet internally logical path of storytelling, dreams in *The Witcher* solicit a gothicised understanding of experience and memory, projecting time as a negotiable structure rather than a cemented one.

Works cited

Anolik, Ruth Bienstock. *American Gothic Literature: A Thematic Study from Mary Rowlandson to Colson Whitehead*. McFarland, 2018.

Crimmins, Jonathan. *The Romantic Historicism to Come*. Bloomsbury, 2018.

Elferen, Isabella van. *Gothic Music: The Sounds of the Uncanny*. University of Wales Press, 2012.

Georgieva, Margarita. *The Gothic Child*. Palgrave, 2013.

Germanà, Monica. *Scottish Women's Gothic and Fantastic Writing: Fiction Since 1978*. Edinburgh University Press, 2010.

Habermas, Jürgen. *The Philosophical Discourse of Modernity*. Polity, 1985.

Jameson, Fredric. 'Marx's Purloined Letter.' *Ghostly Demarcations: A Symposium on Jacques Derrida's Spectres of Marx*, edited by Michael Sprinker. Verso, 2008, pp. 26–67.

Mackay, Daniel. *The Fantasy Role-Playing Game: A New Performing Art*. McFarland, 2017.

Miles, Robert. *Gothic Writing: 1750–1820*. Routledge, 1993.

Mishra, Vijay. *The Gothic Sublime*. State University of New York Press, 1994.

Punter, David. *The Literature of Terror: The Gothic Tradition*. University of Virginia Press, 1996.

Punter, David, and Elisabeth Bronfen. 'Gothic: Violence, Trauma, and the Ethical.' *The Gothic*, edited by Fred Botting, Brewer. 2001, pp. 7–21.

Ross, Christine. *The Past is the Present; It's the Future Too: The Temporal Turn in Contemporary Art*. Bloomsbury, 2012.

Samuel, Raphael. *Theatres of Memory: Past and Present in Contemporary Culture*. Verso, 1994.

Shulman, David, and Guy Stroumsa. 'Introduction.' *Dream Cultures: Explorations in the Comparative History of Dreaming*, edited by David Shulman and Guy Stroumsa. Oxford University Press, 1999, pp. 3–14.

Windt, Jennifer M. *Dreaming: A Conceptual Framework for Philosophy of Mind and Empirical Research*. MIT Press, 2015.

The Witcher, created by Lauren Schmidt Hissrich, Sean Daniel Company, Stillking Films, Platige Image, Cinesite, and Netflix, 2019.

'Lest the night carry on forever': the transcendent Gothic unconscious in *Bloodborne*

James Aaron Green

FromSoftware's 2015 video game *Bloodborne* foregrounds its Gothic status from the outset through a cinematic sequence that conjoins two topoi of the mode: blood and the unconscious. It opens *in media res* as the player character (PC), soon to be known as 'the Hunter', receives a response from a mysterious, blinded figure known as the Blood Minister; he affirms that 'Paleblood' is to be found in Yharnam, but that to unravel its mystery one must first sign a contract and undergo a transfusion. Pre-empting the horrors to come, he offers the oneiric as an interpretive frame by which to rationalise the proceeding action: 'don't you worry. Whatever happens … You may think it all a mere bad dream' (Miyazaki). Hypnagogia – the transitional state between sleep and wakefulness, characterised by hallucinations – does persuasively explain the imagery that follows the warning, in which a werewolf-like creature looms beside the Hunter's table before otherworldly entities clamber across them. Yet players might reasonably assume that the PC never wakens from the procedure, for Yharnam itself proves to be a nightmarish distortion of a historical European city, abounding in monsters. In resolving the city's mysteries, however, the nightmare and adjacent states of consciousness are found to possess more than merely figurative resonance, serving instead as a structuring principle for the ludon-arrative experience of FromSoftware's game.

These hypnagogic visions of a beast yielding to the otherworldly encapsulate a defining and acclaimed aspect of *Bloodborne* – its melding of Gothic and cosmic horror. Presenting initially as a meticulous pastiche of Victorian Gothic, the game becomes progressively interpolated by motifs, tensions, and narrative elements inspired by H. P. Lovecraft's work. This chapter builds upon the emergent scholarship on *Bloodborne* (Hoedt; Langmead; Stobbart) by examining the game's depiction of dreams, nightmares, and altered states of consciousness. Its dream-like opening and the Blood Minister's interpretive proposal are a cue for the primacy of the oneiric; I chart, following the game's own structure, how the oneiric serves, firstly, to site players within familiar Gothic territory, using intertextual readings to delineate the game's judicious homage to Gothic fiction and its deviation via aspects enabled by its digital medium. In the second section, I attend to the oft-cited Lovecraftian influences on *Bloodborne*'s oneiricism through comparative readings, before proposing that the playing experience itself can be understood as a form of nightmare affect.

Bloodborne is a 'spiritual successor' to FromSoftware's *Souls* series – *Demon's Souls* (2009), *Dark Souls* (2011), and the sequels to *Dark Souls* – and extends the series' ludic and narrative formula. It is an action role-playing game (action RPG) played from a third-person perspective, in which players control the Hunter and journey through Yharnam and its environs to resolve various loosely defined objectives. Enemies – monsters, antagonistic humanoids, and cosmic entities – must be overcome in combat and are the principal obstacles. New weaponry and items can be acquired from enemies and the environment to augment the Hunter's abilities, open shortcuts, and facilitate interaction with non-playable characters (NPCs). These mechanics are available to use at the 'Hunter's Dream', a location enabling transportation between areas previously explored, as well as management of the Hunter's inventory and upgrading of their attributes. 'Blood echoes', gained from fallen foes and the environment, can be exchanged for items and upgrades, whilst a rarer, secondary statistic, 'Insight', causes shifts in the game world that pertain to the cosmic backdrop.

Bloodborne's storytelling methods require clarifying, for as Keza MacDonald notes about *Dark Souls*' parallel methods, they are peculiar to the interactive digital medium and seldom met with even there (qtd. in Hoedt 3). Eschewing linear and compulsory forms of narration found in non-digital media, the bulk of *Bloodborne*'s story – though 'lore' or 'mythos' (Stobbart 36) may be more appropriate terms – is disclosed via sources that are fragmentary, fleeting, cryptic, and optional. These sources include environmental details, monologues delivered by NPCs, and item descriptions. Relatively little is guaranteed to be encountered in a single playthrough, however, and there is no internal indication of completeness. Exacerbating this potential fragmentariness is the fact that almost no subject is comprehensively narrated in a single place, while NPCs are liable to disappear, or not appear at all, under certain conditions. These aspects, as Madelon Hoedt suggests, decentre its auteur director Hidetaka Miyazaki in terms of the storytelling process (5–6): the story is shaped decisively by players assembling, contextualising, and interpreting diffuse sources to create meaning.

'Fear the old blood': Gothic horror

Despite *Bloodborne*'s affinities with the survival horror genre – its provision of a 'bounded experience of fear' through relentless challenge and abject visuals, to use I. C. Pinedo's definition (qtd. in Habel and

Kooyman 1) – the game's opening beguiles players with the comforts of the familiar. Due to the extensive similarities between the games, players of FromSoftware's *Souls* series are almost immediately conversant with *Bloodborne*'s mechanical aspects: its user interface (UI), control system, spatiality, and so on; yet even passing acquaintance with action RPGs gives some introduction to its kinaesthetic requirements. But, in addition, *Bloodborne*'s environmental storytelling prioritises 'evocative' or 'indexical' methods (Fernández-Vara). Central Yharnam, its initial yet oft-returned-to setting, is understood foremost by exploration of its dilapidated alleyways and soaring architecture, but, vitally, it is also primed by intertextual references: the game's meticulous invocation of a (neo-) Victorian Gothic aesthetic (see Figure 12.1). That is to say, players' appreciation for it as a location harbouring dangers and secrets is liable to be developed as much through their prior narrative experiences as by what happens in-game. Tanya Krzywinska's contention about the referentiality of the medium and the Gothic is ably proven by *Bloodborne*: 'videogame makers select elements from established game grammar to construct the particular vocabulary of that individual game. The same can be said of Gothic' (58). This last point recalls Eve Kosofsky Sedgwick's 1986 statement about the tradition's conventionality:

> Surely no other modern literary form as influential as the Gothic novel has also been as pervasively conventional. Once you know that a novel is of the Gothic kind (and you can tell from the title), you can predict its contents with an unnerving certainty. (9)

Figure 12.1 The player character (PC) confronting enemies in Yharnam (© Sony Interactive Entertainment)

Today this notion is less assured, especially when looking beyond the 'novel' to the Gothic's proliferation across new media (Wester and Reyes 4). Being a video game that melds cosmic and Gothic horror, *Bloodborne* exemplifies this ongoing trend towards greater self-reflexivity and genre experimentation. Yet, not least by its title, which indexes themes of disease and inheritance, the game purports to be a more conventional instance of Gothic – its packaging materials invite prospective players to 'hunt [their] nightmares' by enacting 'the Western' film archetype of the 'lone traveller' within the generically familiar setting of a 'cursed town'. Both by way of its advertised premise and the Gothic aspects it foregrounds, players are primed to discover that they have entered Yharnam on the night of 'The Hunt', an event aimed at curtailing the 'scourge of beasts' produced by the city's notorious Healing Church and its dabbling with blood ministration (Miyazaki). By all accounts, this Hunt has been ineffective – the streets remain populated by beasts, as well as by baying gangs of local denizens, themselves succumbing to the infection. Brief though it is, *Bloodborne*'s premise is nonetheless allusive of various Gothic themes: monstrosity and hybridity; humanity's atavistic nature; and suspicions of organised religion. Meanwhile, in hints regarding Byrgenwerth, an abandoned site of higher education, a misguided search for new knowledge looms as a potential explanation for the scourge's origin and a possible answer to the central mystery.

Dreams and nightmares are among the original and most enduring aspects of Gothic fiction, and so the oneiric's appearance serves most basically as a 'co-ordinate' (Krzywinska 59) by which *Bloodborne*'s players locate themselves generically. Yet, as the Blood Minister implies by suggesting 'you may think it all a mere bad dream', dreams are also a potential framework through which to interpret the narrative. This proposition is reinforced by the relative prominence of the sky within Central Yharnam's visual schema; it appears in the vibrant oranges of a sunset, establishing the setting temporally on the cusp of night. Defeating Father Gascoigne, Vicar Amelia, and Rom changes this visual backdrop to indicate discrete advances of time: from later evening to night proper, and finally a nightscape featuring a 'blood moon'. Such inexplicable, hybrid shifting of the temporal frame – neither entirely verisimilar nor static – makes it possible to interpret the action as a displaced journey through the stages of sleep, the Hunter functioning as a 'dream subject' uncertainly continuous with a dreamer (as in the identificatory dilemma outlined by J. J. Valberg [64–70]). The 'Sullied Bandage' item that players begin with can be examined to reinforce this possibility, while it complicates the distinction between wakeful and sleeping states. Its description reads 'worn upon awakening to the nightmare of blood and beasts. ... A faint memory recalls blood ministration, involving the transfusion of unknown blood. Not long after[,] the nightmare began'

(Miyazaki). Such details cultivate a decidedly Gothic uncertainty about whether some or all of *Bloodborne*'s action occurs in a dream or dream-like state, and I would argue that one of the first of the game's implicit objectives is to probe the 'level' of reality.

The ambiguous oneiricism of the game's initial action raises another question: If this is a dream, what is its meaning? The pathological contexts that surround the oneiric's first appearance – as anaesthesia induces unconsciousness in preparation for the transfusion, itself a way to access the corporeally inflected 'Paleblood' – gesture to a compelling possibility. As Ronald Thomas explains, the collocation of illness and the unconscious is a vital one in much Gothic fiction, where dreams become symptomatic of psychic disturbance:

> *Frankenstein, Confessions of an English Opium-Eater,* and *Wuthering Heights,* and the dreams in them present themselves through both story and discourse as neurotic symptoms, as attempts at 'recovery' centered in the conflict between supernatural and psychological explanations for the uncanny experience of dreaming. At stake … is the recognition of the powerful influence of irrational impulses on behavior and the need to take control over those impulses. (73)

These cases, for Thomas, express an essential characteristic of the Gothic: 'the narratives exist primarily as symptoms of an attempt to recover from a disordered state of mind which is most dramatically manifested in the narrator's dreams' (80). This dream-as-recovery interpretation initially seems persuasive in *Bloodborne*'s case, accounting as it does for the major themes of beastliness and transformation. It makes the dream a therapeutic canvas on which the 'impulses' being fought are those of an atavistic brutality that threatens to make hunters – those, like the PC, tasked with eradicating Yharnam's plague – akin to the beasts they hunt. One of the first anonymous messages left for the Hunter, 'to escape this dreadful Hunter's Dream, halt the source of the spreading scourge of beasts, lest the night carry on forever', is therefore understandable as a warning about the perils of letting the beasts remain versus becoming one in the process of eradicating them. Such a reading equally explicates the very first instruction: 'seek Paleblood to transcend the hunt' (Miyazaki), insofar as transcendence may imply an elevation beyond atavistic brutality and therefore, if the dream is curative, a restoration of the fractured psyche. By giving access to experiences and truths occluded from everyday life, the unconscious in *Bloodborne* therefore seems to mobilise 'the will to *transcend*' that David Punter deems a core motif within the Gothic tradition (17; emphasis added).

This 'scientific and biological' interpretation of the dream, seeing it as an expression of 'symptomatically disguised desires' held by the dreamer (Thomas 76), also resonates with the game's ludic form and the role-playing opportunities it affords. Although the role of 'Hunter' is pre-assigned and fixed, there is agency in how the role is enacted, not least in the choice of starting weapons: each enables the performance of distinct attitudes towards enemies. The severe blows of the 'Hunter Axe', for instance, evoke those meted out in archaic forms of capital punishment, its description ventriloquising the dehumanising viewpoint of its wielder: 'no matter their pasts, beasts are no more than beasts. Some choose this axe to play the part of executioner.' Contrarily, the 'Threaded Cane' is described as 'an attempt to demonstrate to oneself that the bloodlust of the hunt will never encroach upon the soul' (Miyazaki), and its move-set rewards precision over brute force. Even though progress without some combat is impossible in *Bloodborne*, agency over the extent and manner of violent encounters enables players to author a personalised story with respect to themes of atavism and redemption, thereby consolidating the possibility that the initial action is a form of psychic recovery, or relapse, pursued unconsciously.

But this interpretation of *Bloodborne* as a personal, psychological journey starts to falter, or at least to seem less than comprehensive, as more is discovered about the game world. Such a process begins in the 'Hunter's Dream'. Mechanically integral to the playing experience, and therefore traversed repeatedly, the location is equally vital in narrative terms as the home to two of the game's most enigmatic figures: Gehrman ('the first Hunter') and the Doll. Uncanny entities, each corroborates and is only comprehensible according to the logic of a dream. The Doll appears initially as her inanimate namesake, only enlivening upon acquiring Insight, in one of the first indications of this statistic's transformative effects. Gehrman seems to originate from the distant past and to lack presence in the 'waking world', existing purely as an oneiric entity; the Doll explains: 'he is obscure, unseen in the dreaming world. Still, he stays here, in this dream. Such is his purpose' (Miyazaki). This and other statements disclose a disquieting irony behind the location: it is not the 'Hunter's Dream' as of the Hunter (the PC) but as of Gehrman, 'the first Hunter'. This detail foreshadows the later realignment of dreams – from personal, psychological phenomena, as per the Gothic, to distinct physical realms, as per cosmic horror. The 'Hunter's Dream' is a complex and uncertain location, variably affirming and denying the conventional, bipartite idea that dreams reflect wakeful states. It affirms this idea via the inferences made to the 'waking world' by characters and dialogue options situated there, and by the existence, in the real world, of an uncanny double of the Workshop inside which Gehrman often sits. Yet it denies it via the transportation and 'respawn' mechanics contained there, which graft the atemporal and aspatial characteristics of oneiricism onto the supposedly real world of Yharnam; that is, since the Hunter suffers no lasting consequences from their violent excursions and erases distances by 'awakening', these supposedly wakeful activities co-opt the logic of lucid dreaming. The ludic aspects of the 'Hunter's Dream' therefore corroborate the location's narrative emphases to enact that classic Gothic unsettling of what 'reality' means in its relation to the oneiric.

This being so, and given the determinedly indexical storytelling methods that the game uses, it bears reading *Bloodborne*'s depiction of the unconscious intertextually with examples of Victorian Gothic fiction. Bram Stoker's *Dracula* (1897) is a logical starting point, being an admitted reference for *Bloodborne*'s environmental design (Cueto), while implicating two further propitious cases for comparison: Joseph Sheridan Le Fanu's novella 'Carmilla' (1872) and H. P. Lovecraft, who analyses *Dracula* in his 1927 essay 'Supernatural Horror in Literature'. 'Carmilla' merits notice not only for influencing *Bloodborne* indirectly through Stoker (Tracy xvii), but also for being an instance of Victorian Gothic that foregrounds the oneiric as phenomenally uncertain, as in the initial parts of FromSoftware's game. Equally, its moments of tension combine the unconscious with motifs of monstrosity and blood, a combination central in *Bloodborne*. Victor Sage remarks that 'the question of whose dream we are in (and whether life is "dream" or not) is a crux in ... "Carmilla"', equating it to the difficulty facing readers of *Wuthering Heights* when Cathy exclaims '"Let me in!" [during Lockwood's dream] – on what level is "reality" supposed to be?' (178). In Le Fanu's text, the dilemma originates with Laura's disbelief that a traumatic childhood experience is merely a dream. Upon meeting Carmilla, that young woman purports to have experienced the same vision from the perspective of its corresponding figure (260), so that, suggestively in respect of the 'Hunter's Dream', the oneiric experience is potentially *shared*. These questions are made urgent by a nocturnal episode that precipitates Laura's anaemia-like illness. Having spoken of the inescapability of dreams, she recounts, in terms redolent of confusion about the distinctions between dreaming and wakeful states:

> I had a dream that night that was the beginning of a very strange agony. I cannot call it a nightmare, for I was quite conscious of being asleep. But I was equally conscious of being in my room, and lying in bed, precisely as I actually was. (278)

Afterwards, a 'monstrous cat' appears and painfully extracts Laura's blood. As the scene reaches its nightmarish climax, yet as readers are mindful that her somatic response makes this potentially real, she declares that she 'waked with a scream'. Yet, and this is vital, the terror *persists upon waking*, as the spectral feline is replaced by a terrifyingly still 'female figure' (278). When General Spielsdorf recounts a parallel affair, Carmilla is not a feline but a 'large black object, very ill-defined' before becoming a 'great palpitating mass' savaging his daughter (311). Although the General and Laura's experiences are 'real', their variegated perceptions of Carmilla's form co-opt oneiric logic insofar as it seems to change according to the viewer's psyche. Crucially, however, dreams are not exclusively registered as dangerous; Carmilla's downfall is catalysed by Laura's late mother intruding on her daughter's sleep to warn against 'the assassin' (283). Drawing on prophetic conceptions of dreams, especially Macrobius's *oraculum* – a dream that contains advice from authority figures (Moore 3) – Le Fanu's text portrays the unconscious as equally a source of danger and discovery.

In *Dracula*, the nocturnality of the Count's predation is part and parcel of its threat, for sleep helps the protagonists to rationalise its horrific contents as those of a nightmare. Lucy Westenra recounts that 'as I remember no more, I suppose I must then have fallen asleep. More bad dreams. I wish I could remember them' (109). The inadequacy of this explanation is more striking when Mina later indulges it: 'I closed my eyes, but could still see through my eyelids. (It is wonderful what tricks our dreams play on us, and how conveniently we can imagine.)' (258–9). Ironically, and as in 'Carmilla', the existence of the monstrous Count blends the awful unreality of nightmare with the supposed mundanities of the waking world. Pertinently, Renfield speaks before his death of a 'terrible dream', only to renounce this as a palliative mistruth: 'I must not deceive myself; it was no dream, but all a grim reality' (278). *Dracula* and 'Carmilla' repeatedly highlight the importance of delving into the unconscious and its meaning, and admonish those that deem it unimportant or extricated from real-life. As Thomas observes, relatedly, dreams' therapeutic potential is only actionable in such stories if they 'are put into words and connected with the dreamer's waking life' (76). Whilst Laura realises this potential by heeding her mother's warning, Lucy's fatal failure to examine her dream experiences serves as an object-lesson for her friends to act conversely.

Bloodborne's atypical, undirected storytelling methods enable blissful ignorance about the aforementioned. It is eminently possible to play the game as a goal-oriented, hack-and-slash experience ('go there, kill this'), without any concern for the intersections of dream and reality. But such detachment is self-reflexively deprecated through Gehrman who, on first being addressed, extols an unquestioning and purely tactile engagement with the nightmarish obstacles: 'you're sure to be in a fine haze about now, *but don't think too hard about all of this.* Just go out and kill a few beasts. It's for your own good. You know, it's just what hunters do!' (Miyazaki;

emphasis added). Gehrman's suggestion invites scepticism on two fronts, however. First, it foists on the 'real world' the moral schema of a dream by invoking a longstanding thread of oneiric criticism: since dreams are involuntary and not 'really happening', moral judgments are inapplicable to them (Windt). Second, it contradicts the warnings given in Gothic fiction like 'Carmilla' and *Dracula*; Mina predicates Jonathan's future happiness and security upon resolving the epistemological uncertainties thrown up by the oneiric: '[it] may be ... the doubt which haunts him', she says, and once removed, 'no matter which – waking or dreaming – may prove the truth, he will be more satisfied and better able to bear the shock' (181). The wisdom and motivation behind Gehrman's assertion seem dubious, therefore, and *invite* scrutiny; as per reactance theory, the perception of constraints provokes a desire to breach them – here, by dissuading analysis of the game world, it motivates greater curiosity about the relationship between dream and reality. Ludic aspects intensify this idea, moreover; the purpose of 'Insight' is unknown when Gehrman says this, and it may be assumed to ludically chart and reward exploration of such threads – an instantiation of the oneiric's revelatory potential, as personified by Laura's mother's warning. In fact, as players progress and jarring (extra-Gothic) details accumulate, Insight is found to pertain to an occluded, cosmic narrative.

'The sky and the cosmos are one': Lovecraftian interpolations

Bloodborne's initial presentation as a meticulous pastiche of the Victorian Gothic is bound up with its depiction of dreams and nightmares. It aligns particularly with 'Carmilla' and *Dracula* in collocating illness and the unconscious, and in deploying monstrousness to signal a dissolution of boundaries between sleeping and wakeful states. The role-playing opportunities heighten the suggestion that the initial action may be an oneiric staging of competing impulses within the dreamer's mind, encompassing the themes of atavism and transformation. Such a reading is never certain, however, and as players progress, an ever-greater number of incongruous aspects conspire to posit alternatives. The 'Hunter's Dream' is one such, implying that the oneiric is not only a personal, psychological phenomenon, but also a shared physical space or experience. Similarly straining of Gothic expectations is the item known as 'Madman's Knowledge'. Encounterable on various corpses strewn about Yharnam and beyond, its description reads: 'skull of a madman touched by the wisdom of the Great Ones' (Miyazaki). Whilst its ludic function is unambiguous (it grants players Insight), the item's narrative purpose is unclear: for some considerable time, it has no obvious connection to the story either as told directly or as developed via those intertextual storytelling methods that establish Yharnam as a place of danger and secrecy in the mould of the Victorian Gothic city.

Such a detail points beyond Gothic horror to that of the cosmic, implicating specifically the work of H. P. Lovecraft. The imagery of a mind driven to madness by the acquisition of new knowledge posits *Bloodborne*'s setting in the aftermath of a trajectory recurrent in his fiction: the discovery of a 'strange suspension or violation' of mechanistic materialism and the invariably deadly dissolution of mental fortitude attendant on it (Joshi xv). Such a trajectory is never more succinctly expressed than in the opening to perhaps his best-known story, 'The Call of Cthulhu' (1928):

> [S]ome day the piecing together of disassociated knowledge will open up such terrifying vistas of reality, and of our frightful position therein, that we shall either go mad from the revelation or flee from the deadly light into the peace and safety of a new dark age. (139)

This correspondence is not coincidental. *Bloodborne*'s director, Miyazaki, professes, 'I was inspired by ... *The Call of Cthulhu*. Probably everyone who has played [the game] will know the considerable influence of Lovecraft on that work' (Scapin; translation mine). Criticism has recognised the game's indebtedness to that story (Stobbart 35–6), yet a crucial detail is overlooked: these influences are not evident from the outset, but only revealed by stages. In fact, the interpolation of the Gothic by cosmic horror unfolds in a manner that is itself Lovecraftian, insofar as seemingly disparate and incongruous aspects like 'Madman's Knowledge' – including unearthly monstrosities and cryptic messages about a 'lost master' (Miyazaki) – are gradually revealed to possess world-altering import; they culminate by inscribing Lovecraft's literary philosophy of cosmicism, or the insignificance of the human within an incomprehensibly larger and indifferent universe. Such details reveal that the Healing Church's blood experiments, and the 'scourge of beasts' they effected, were derived from Great Ones – cosmic entities unearthed by Byrgenwerth scholars. In the present of the game's action, the School of Mensis communes with an infant Great One, though this destroys them, pulling them into a 'Nightmare' world where the Hunter must follow. One ending to *Bloodborne* is achieved by slaying the infant's monstrous wet nurse, which ends the nightmare and prompts Gehrman to offer the Hunter a chance to re-awaken outside the dream (Miyazaki).

Bloodborne draws inspiration not only from 'Cthulhu', but from Lovecraft's broader oeuvre, in which dreams and nightmares are formative. Among other works, dreams are a major part of such stories as 'Beyond the Wall of Sleep' (1919), *The Dream-Quest of Unknown Kadath* (1928), and 'The Dreams in the Witch House' (1933). The oneiric perforates Lovecraft's creative vision more deeply, however, as the case of 'Dagon' (1919) illustrates. Chronicling sailors' traumatic encounters with the titular deity, the short story was at least partially inspired by a dream the author experienced. Such dream-as-source narratives are common in Gothic fiction, yet Lovecraft goes further by making the story comprehensible only according to oneiric logic. When critics decried the unbelievability of the protagonist's escape, the author used his 'In Defence of Dagon' (1921) essays to justify its truthful status. Yet he asserted its verisimilitude not with regard to real-life experience, but to his original dream: 'the hero-victim is half-sucked into the mire, yet he *does* crawl! … I know, for I dreamed that whole hideous crawl, and can yet feel the ooze sucking me down!' ('Cthulhu' 361; original emphasis). 'Dagon' precisely affirms Dina Khapaeva's contention that what Lovecraft sought, in contrast to writers concerned by the uncertain boundary of life and nightmare (like Le Fanu and Stoker), was the 'transformation of nightmare into reality, its materialization in prose and culture' (97). In 'Dagon', the terrors of nightmare are irrefutably a part of the reality the protagonists inhabit.

The story 'Witch House' is a closer model to *Bloodborne*, however, for it expresses how the Lovecraftian oneiric extends, rather than departs from, the Gothic's depiction of nightmares and dreams. Gilman, its protagonist, becomes 'psychically hypersensitive' (142) and prone to oneiric experiences as a result of overwork. Yet the story's inaugural line also rehearses the complex collocation of illness and the unconscious that Thomas identifies as a Gothic motif: 'whether the dreams brought on the fever or the fever brought on the dreams [he] did not know' (300). (*Bloodborne* begins, it should be recalled, with such an association between illness and dreams.) Gilman experiences increasingly troubling nightmares that, as in 'Carmilla' and *Dracula*, leave somatic impressions: 'puncture marks' and a burst eardrum, until his body is finally eaten away (318, 331). Whereas in those Victorian Gothic texts the unconscious belies the dangers of the waking world, the situation here is reversed; Gilman vainly ascribes his symptoms to rats before ignoring a physician's ominous query as to 'how such a sound [sufficient to cause deafness] could have been heard … without arousing' the entire neighbourhood (318). Initially approximating the Gothic, therefore, a quite distinctive idea of the oneiric emerges by the conclusion to 'Witch House'. Through his dreams, Gilman accesses dimensions as 'real' as that in which he exists, and the insight he obtains from them (of non-Euclidean geometry) is unaccountable in terms of psychic origin.

The trajectory of *Bloodborne* parallels that of 'Witch House': Gothic uncertainties about the level of 'reality' – the possibility that the action may be a therapeutic canvas on which the competing impulses of a sleeping subject are enacted – are increasingly cast aside and overwritten by a Lovecraftian sense of dreams as distinct physical spaces. Reaching the Lecture Building marks a turning point; formerly part of the college of Byrgenwerth, this ambiguous location gives access to the 'Nightmare Frontier' and then the 'Nightmare of Mensis', otherworldly landscapes akin to Gilman's 'twilight abysses' (310). Disparate in their environmental design, these areas further signal their difference by flouting the spatial coherency that means all other locations are traversable from Yharnam. Instead, as Hoedt observes, the supernatural means of accessing them (via portals in the Lecture Building) means that they register, like the Hunter's Dream, within and yet apart from the game world (130). These areas are familiar in one important sense, however: they *play* as other, 'non-Nightmare' areas do; that is, the mechanical requirements and kinaesthetic experiences between them are consistent. Such consistency establishes, in ludic terms, a phenomenal equivalence of the kind that Lovecraft proffers between dream and reality. Narratively, that same sense is reinforced by the character of Micolash, the 'Host of the Nightmare' of Mensis. Having willed the dream into existence to commune with a Great One, his case clearly echoes Lovecraft's 'Cthulhu'. Yet Micolash goes further by affording phenomenological priority to the dream he inhabits; he laments the prospect of awakening, doubting if the discoveries made in 'Mensis' are transferable to the real world: 'now I'm waking up, I'll forget everything' (Miyazaki). His case hence also invokes an admission by the narrator of Lovecraft's 'Beyond': 'sometimes I believe that this less material life [of dreams] is our truer life, and that our vain presence on the terraqueous globe is itself the secondary or merely virtual phenomenon' (n.p.). Further undercutting the 'real' here is the suggestion that the corpse used to gain supernatural access to the Lecture Building is none other than that of Micolash. This uncanny possibility posits the dream-self as something more than the projection of a sleeping subject, but rather as having transcended the corporeal altogether.

In what remains, I wish to consider how *Bloodborne* remediates another vital aspect of the Lovecraftian oneiric: its relation to curiosity. Such a focus gives a chance to reconvene on the game's atypical storytelling methods and the significance of the video game medium. Curiosity is what propels Lovecraft's protagonists towards revelation and ruin. 'Above all my bewilderment and sense of menace', explains the narrator of 'At the Mountains of Madness' (1936), 'there burned a dominant curiosity to fathom more of this age-old secret' (n.p.). This emotion is inextricable from the oneiric: either it directly prompts the exploration of dreams, as in 'Witch House' and 'Cthulhu', or else the feverish state that it produces is best expressed through the idea of nightmare. To this end, Khapaeva, expanding from Michel Houellebecq, describes as 'nightmare attraction' (91) the prevalent, irremediable curiosity that leads Lovecraftian protagonists to experience oneiric horrors – to indulge, often repeatedly, in a state of 'wonderment and fear' that she compares to the sublime (89–90). Significantly, and recalling the oneiric logic of 'Dagon', this affect is identifiable even in stories not explicitly featuring dreams. In 'From Beyond' (1934), for instance, a mechanical device detects and thereby manifests invisible monstrosities that circulate in the air. Set resolutely in the waking world, the story nonetheless exhibits 'nightmare attraction' and multiple affinities with 'Beyond the Wall of Sleep'. Crawford Tillinghast and the narrator experience something akin to sleep paralysis or hypnagogia as they witness the 'cosmic truth' (*Witch House* 28) in an enthralled state. Suggesting the hedonistic pull of the nightmare he has created, Tillinghast expires not from physical violence but physiological strain – killed by 'apoplexy' (*Witch House* 29).

The enigmatic, non-directed storytelling methods of *Bloodborne* lend extraordinary weight to curiosity, and the playing experience, I propose, is one structured by 'nightmare attraction'. The attempt to satisfy it is what leads players to first interrogate how dream and reality intersect, and then to question how the cosmic aspects fit within this. 'Interrogate' is the operative word here, for players are not passive recipients of the lore but instead determine it for themselves by 'piecing together … disassociated knowledge' as per Lovecraft's archetypal investigators. The same methods of close reading, retrieval, and inference – methods by which protagonists like Randolph Carter and Arthur Jermyn glimpse the cosmic truth – can be applied by players to myriad textual artefacts. Absent any internal indication as to the sum of possible knowledge, these investigative activities posit as many questions and new threads as they resolve. The result is the evocation, to a degree unusual in video games, of a sense of 'the unbounded': a feeling that 'the game system contains many more entities, mechanics and moving parts than the player's cosmic understanding of the game, at that point in her engagement with it, can account for' (Vella n.p.). That seemingly indefinite opportunity to satisfy curiosity propels players forward. One example must suffice: navigating Cathedral Ward, an area that emblematises the Gothic's ecclesiastical and burial imagery, players may be drawn to an item on a graveyard's edge. Lingering there causes a portal to materialise above them, attended by a 'whooshing' sound. Stopping any longer results in the PC being hoisted skywards by an unseen force before receiving fatal damage. Like 'Madman's Knowledge', this 'micronarrative' (Fernández-Vara n.p.) is inexplicable in terms of the environment's Gothic trappings and the story until that point. By iterative probing of the portal, further aspects can be uncovered, making it possible for curious players to pre-empt the portal's eventual discovery as a cosmically derived phenomenon.

To account for this micronarrative as simply New Weird generic hybridity is to belie the game's innovation. *Bloodborne*'s ludic form enables players to act out the injunctions given in weird fiction, as well as Victorian Gothic, to act upon curiosity about the unknown. Insight therefore comes into focus as a measure of the player's proximity to the cosmic truth, such that obtaining certain amounts of it unveils hidden aspects of the game world. Chief among these unveilings is that unseen force in Cathedral Ward discussed above, which proves to emanate from a cosmic entity known as 'Amygdala'. Named for a neural structure that processes fear and is associated with curiosity, this nomenclature indicates the centrality within the game of that two-fold emotional response contained within nightmare attraction: 'wonderment and fear'. That other examples of Amygdala guard one entrance to the ambiguous Lecture Building, and are present in both the real world of Yharnam *and* the Nightmare Frontier (see Figure 12.2), stamps the phenomenal equivalence of the oneiric and real, or, more precisely, the 'transformation of nightmare into reality' (Khapaeva 97) á la Lovecraft. The extent of that transformation is one uncovered by players themselves via their investigations; curiosity-driven discoveries made in nightmarish worlds eventually reveal a fluid 'reality' where monsters lurk outside ordinary perception. *Bloodborne* therefore extrapolates upon the disquieting conclusion of 'From Beyond' after Tillinghast's monster-revealing device is destroyed: 'it would help my shaky nerves if I could dismiss what I now have to think of the air and the sky about and above me' (*Witch House* 29). Those who perform repeat playthroughs of the game cannot help but sympathise as they view those vacant spaces in Yharnam where the otherworldly Amygdala wait to be revealed. A note found in Upper Cathedral Ward, a location powerfully

Figure 12.2 The Amygdala in the otherworldly Nightmare Frontier (© Sony Interactive Entertainment)

connected to such cosmic secrets, precludes all doubt: 'the sky and the cosmos are one' (Miyazaki).

But if, as I claim, the playing experience of *Bloodborne* is structured by nightmare attraction, is this not also the case for its spiritual predecessor *Dark Souls*, with which it shares so many similarities? Recall first that Khapaeva considers the aesthetic experience of the sublime to be resonant with nightmare attraction (90); Daniel Vella outlines *Dark Souls*' production of a 'ludic sublime' via precisely the sorts of elements outlined above in respect of *Bloodborne*: indistinct boundaries, unclear causes and effects, and undefined entities. Even more problematically for assertions of *Bloodborne*'s difference, Vella alerts us to how FromSoftware's earlier game simply 'foregrounds a sublime quality of mystery … integral to the formal structure of digital games'; that is, players' experiences within the medium are always riven by the 'phenomenally-given game object' – the experience of play – and the 'supersensible game object' – the sum of rules and procedures that generate that experience; engagement is forever partial, and a 'fundamental unknowability' surrounds the game object (Vella n.p.). If *Bloodborne* so closely follows its predecessor's formula, and even then only exacerbates a general quality of video games, how is it meaningfully distinct in its depiction of the oneiric?

Its distinctiveness lies, I contend, in the more meaningful relation between its ludic form and narrative. *Dark Souls* may cultivate sublimity through similar methods (while sharing mechanics and kinaesthetic requirements), yet that sublimity is only obliquely relevant to the genre of high fantasy to which it belongs. Contrarily, these aspects and emotions in *Bloodborne* consolidate the oneiricism of its Victorian Gothic and then cosmic horror trappings. 'Curiosity' propels players in both cases, but in *Bloodborne* it specifically evokes the Lovecraftian investigative model and the dangers and discoveries that that model discerns as existing within dream spaces. Combat is similar in *Dark Souls* and *Bloodborne*, yet that of the second is more frenetic, less encouraging of patience, and only there does it yoke horror and pleasurable excitement in a way that resonates with nightmare attraction. Moreover, liable to be repeated due to their difficulty, these combat encounters render the playing experience akin to the process by which, as Houellebecq writes, nightmare becomes ritual, instilling in its subject an irresistible desire to be 'seduced each time by a different repetition' (qtd. in Khapaeva 91). Fittingly, *Bloodborne*'s most emphatically oneiric locations – the Frontier, Mensis, and Hunter's Dream (revisited) – are among its last and, by the logic of escalating difficulty, those places in which this ritualistic repetition is liable to be most condensed and palpable. The unique message that appears upon defeating the Great One's wet nurse – 'Nightmare Slain' (Miyazaki) – hence signifies not only the expiry of the literal nightmare that the infant sustains, but also, since it can precipitate *Bloodborne*'s ending and the cessation of play, the termination of the nightmare attraction that has borne players along since the game's beginning.

Conclusion

Much more can be written about *Bloodborne*'s depiction of dreams and nightmares. For instance, this chapter has not considered how the game's oracular motifs are made metonymic for the limits of the human sensorium in relation to the cosmic truth – a refrain with clear bearings on the warning, common to both Victorian Gothic and Lovecraftian fiction, about being alert to the meaning of dreams and nightmares. It has also not broached how Gehrman's warning is readable as the typical (and invariably futile) command made in weird fiction to forego investigating the 'dark, dead corners and unplumbed depths' in which the nightmarish lies (Lovecraft, 'At the Mountains of Madness' n.p.). These and other topics require clarification.

This chapter aimed to delineate *Bloodborne*'s preoccupation with the oneiric and how its acclaimed generic hybridity is enacted through the shifting significations of dreams and nightmares. The coherency of this change – from the epistemological uncertainties of the Victorian Gothic to the awful truths of Lovecraftian fiction – attests to the game's meticulous invocation of both traditions and its effective prolongation of mystery. It also demarcates the proximity of Gothic and weird fiction via their depiction of dreams and nightmares, echoing Lovecraft's own short story 'Witch House'. Yet FromSoftware's game also broaches how the video game medium may extend these traditions' enduring fascination with the oneiric in chronological and phenomenological terms. Incorporating, whilst also exceeding, the self-reflexive strategies of the New Weird, *Bloodborne* shows how ludic forms may approximate the 'entrancement and horror' of the 'nightmare attraction', prompting players to probe and navigate dream-like spaces. Following Khapaeva's assertion that Lovecraft was formative to the 'creation of a consumer culture for the nightmare' (92), this chapter finds video games like *Bloodborne* poised to sustain that culture and perpetuate the oneiric as a culturally resonant force.

Works cited

Cueto, Gerard. 'GameStart 2014 – Bloodborne Interview With Masaaki Yamagiwa Talks Frame-Rate, Messengers and More.' *PlayStation Lifestyle*, 2014, www .playstationlifestyle.net/2014/10/29/gamestart-2014-bloodborne-interview-with

-masaaki-yamagiwa-talks-frame-rate-messengers-and-more/#/slide/1. Accessed 3 August 2023.

Fernández-Vara, Clara. 'Game Spaces Speak Volumes: Indexical Storytelling.' 2011 DiGRA International Conference: Think Design Play, Digital Games Research Association, 2011, hdl.handle.net/1721.1/100274. Accessed 3 August 2023.

Habel, Chad, and Ben Kooyman. 'Agency Mechanics: Gameplay Design in Survival Horror Video Games.' *Digital Creativity*, vol. 25, no. 1, 2014, pp. 1–14.

Hoedt, Madelon. *Narrative Design and Authorship in* Bloodborne: *An Analysis of the Horror Videogame*. McFarland & Co., 2019.

Joshi, S. T. 'Introduction.' *The Call of Cthulhu and Other Weird Stories*, by H. P. Lovecraft. Penguin, 2002, pp. vi–xx.

Khapaeva, Dina. *Nightmare: From Literary Experiments to Cultural Project*, translated by Rosie Tweddle. Brill, 2013.

Krzywinska, Tanya. 'The Gamification of Gothic Coordinates in Videogames.' *Revenant*, vol. 1, no. 1, 2015, pp. 54–78.

Langmead, Oliver. '"Grant Us Eyes, Grant Us Eyes! Plant Eyes on Our Brains, to Cleanse Our Beastly Idiocy!": FromSoftware's *Bloodborne*, and the New Frontier of the Gothic.' *Press Start*, vol. 4, no. 1, 2017, pp. 54–64.

Le Fanu, Joseph Sheridan. 'Carmilla.' *In a Glass Darkly*. Oxford University Press, 2008, pp. 243–319.

Lovecraft, H. P. 'At the Mountains of Madness.' *Astounding Stories*, 1936, Wikisource, en.wikisource.org/wiki/At_the_Mountains_of_Madness. Accessed 3 August 2023.

Lovecraft, H. P. 'Beyond the Wall of Sleep.' *Weird Tales*, vol. 31, no. 3, 1938, pp. 331–8, Wikisource, en.wikisource.org/wiki/Weird_Tales/Volume_31/Issue_3/Beyond_the_Wall_of_Sleep. Accessed 3 August 2023.

Lovecraft, H. P. 'The Call of Cthulhu.' *The Call of Cthulhu and Other Weird Stories*, edited by S. T. Joshi. Penguin, 2002.

Lovecraft, H. P. 'Dagon.' *The Call of Cthulhu and Other Weird Stories*, edited by S. T. Joshi. Penguin, 2002, pp. 1–6.

Lovecraft, H. P. 'The Dreams in the Witch House.' *The Dreams in the Witch House and Other Weird Stories*, edited by S. T. Joshi. Penguin, 2005, pp. 300–34.

Lovecraft, H. P. 'From Beyond.' *The Dreams in the Witch House and Other Weird Stories*, edited by S. T. Joshi. Penguin, 2005, pp. 23–9.

Lovecraft, H. P. 'Supernatural Horror in Literature.' *The Recluse*, 1927, Wikisource, en.wikisource.org/wiki/Supernatural_Horror_in_Literature. Accessed 3 August 2023.

Miyazaki, Hidetaka. *Bloodborne*. Sony Computer Entertainment.

Moore, Richard W. *Dreaming Change, Changing Dreams in the British Gothic Novel, 1765–1818*. Fordham University, 2018, PhD dissertation.

Punter, David. *Gothic Pathologies: The Text, the Body and the Law*. Palgrave Macmillan, 1998.

Sage, Victor. *Le Fanu's Gothic: The Rhetoric of Darkness*. Palgrave Macmillan, 2004.

Scapin, Pedro. 'BGS 2019: Hidetaka Miyazaki Diz o Que Mudaria Em Bloodborne.' *GameSpot Brazil*, 2019, web.archive.org/web/20191128023153/https://www

.gamespot.com.br/featured/bgs-2019-hidetaka-miyazaki/. Accessed 3 August 2023.

Sedgwick, Eve Kosofsky. *The Coherence of Gothic Conventions*. Methuen, 1986.

Stobbart, Dawn. *Video Games and Horror: From* Amnesia *to* Zombies, Run! University of Wales Press, 2019.

Stoker, Bram. *Dracula*. Oxford University Press, 2008.

Thomas, Ronald. *Dreams of Authority: Freud and the Fictions of the Unconscious*. Cornell University Press, 1990.

Tracy, Robert. 'Introduction.' *In a Glass Darkly*. Oxford University Press, 2008, pp. vii–xxvii.

Valberg, J. J. *Dream, Death, and the Self*. Princeton University Press, 2007.

Vella, Daniel. 'No Mastery Without Mystery: *Dark Souls* and the Ludic Sublime.' *Game Studies*, vol. 15, no. 1, 2005, gamestudies.org/1501/vella. Accessed 3 August 2023.

Wester, Maisha, and Xavier Aldana Reyes. 'Introduction: The Gothic in the Twenty-First Century.' *Twenty-First-Century Gothic: An Edinburgh Companion,* edited by Maisha Wester and Xavier Aldana Reyes. Edinburgh University Press, 2019, pp. 1–16.

Windt, Jennifer M. 'Dreams and Dreaming.' *The Stanford Encyclopedia of Philosophy*, edited by Edward N. Zalta. Metaphysics Research Lab, Philosophy Department, Stanford University, 2020.

Index

Note: 'n.' after a page number indicates the number of an endnote on that page. Works can be found under their authors' names. Page entries in *italics* refer to figures.

Milton Keynes UK
Ingram Content Group UK Ltd.
UKHW021823020624
443615UK00005B/12